PHILIP MELANCHTHON'S RHETORICAL CONSTRUAL OF BIBLICAL AUTHORITY

Oratio Sacra

John R. Schneider

Texts and Studies in Religion
Volume 51

The Edwin Mellen Press
Lewiston/Queenston/Lampeter

BR
335
.S44
1990

Library of Congress Cataloging in Publication Data

This volume has been registered with The Library of Congress.

This is volume 51 in the continuing series
Texts and Studies in Religion
Volume 51 ISBN 0-88946-794-3
TSR Series ISBN 0-88946-976-8

A CIP catalog record for this book
is available from the British Library.

The Edwin Mellen Press   The Edwin Mellen Press
Box 450   Box 67
Lewiston, N.Y.   Queenston, Ontario
USA 14092   CANADA L0S 1L0

Edwin Mellen Press, Ltd
Lampeter, Dyfed, Wales,
UNITED KINGDOM SA48 7DY

Printed in the United States of America

PHILIP MELANCHTHON'S RHETORICAL CONSTRUAL OF BIBLICAL AUTHORITY

Oratio Sacra

Table of Contents
(with subtopics in sequence)

Acknowledgments

Thirteen years ago, I began research for a doctoral thesis at the University of Cambridge on Philip Melanchthon. This book is a considerably more developed form of the work that I submitted for the Ph. D. in 1986. It is not difficult for me to single out the people who should be acknowledged publicly for their contributions to its completion. First, I must express my thanks to the late Reverend Professor E. Gordon Rupp, who supervised this project when it was on its first legs and who saw promise in me when I failed to see it in myself. I only regret that he did not live to see the work progress beyond its pedestrian dissertation stage into its present book form. I also regret that I cannot write with anything approaching the mastery of language and the humane disciplines which was his priceless gift and legacy to his colleagues and students. (I shall never forget his polite reaction to my first paper for him, when he noted gently the few "purple passages" and then, only after complimenting the piece for "showing promise," handed me a copy of Sir Arthur Quiller Couch's essay on avoiding jargon.) A debt of gratitude is also due Professor Heiko A. Oberman, now of the University of Arizona, who kindly gave me unlimited access to the library of the Institut für Spätmittelalter und Reformation in Tübingen, where he was then the director, during my stay in that city from 1978-80. Access to this superb library and his own personal example as a historical theologian were of inestimable help to me in finding an appropriate method for approaching the early Melanchthon and in setting a higher standard for myself than I had ever done. I must also thank my former teacher Geoffrey Bromiley, Professor Emeritus of Fuller Theological Seminary, for reading the entire dissertation before it was submitted. I hope that he will agree that at least some of his critical comments have now born fruit.

Others have helped the book along its course in ways both great and small. For his patient encouragement during very difficult circumstances, I should mention Dr. George (Bud) Blankenbaker, Academic Dean of Westmont College, where I taught from 1981-1986. For approval of funding the production of the manuscript, my sincere thanks go to Academic Dean Roger Griffioen and to the Department of Religion and Theology at Calvin College. For their professional assistance (and persistence) in the production of the final manuscript, special thanks are due to Robert Alderink and his publications staff at Calvin College, particularly Anne Dame, who did most of the keyboard work. For their invaluable help in preparing the bibliography and indices, I must thank Donna Quist and Esther Vander Tuig, who must surely be among the best departmental secretaries in academia. Finally, I must thank my wife, Winona, whose support turned from that of the quintessential spouse, at the very beginning, to that of the quintessential professional proofreader and editor, at the end. She supervised the editing of the entire manuscript with the eye of an eagle, spotting errors like small prey. No doubt some got away, nevertheless, but it is hard to imagine anyone doing a better job than she has done. And it is inconceivable that this book would ever have been written without her support through these years.

INTRODUCTION

The Unknown
Melanchthon

"It is not difficult to happen upon facts and connections which have remained unnoticed in the diversity of thought, and the unequalled many-sidedness of a Melanchthon. Anyone who works for decades with Melanchthon can put forward a great number of such things. Sometimes they are only small features; but when brought into the right connection they give forth a new kind of image. Many times it is merely a different interpretation of the evidence which fits clearer features into the whole picture." (R. Stupperich, *Der unbekannte Melanchthon*, p. 5.)

Context and Nature of the Study

Not long after his sixty-third birthday, and having just published a compilation of his own favorite writings, Melanchthon penned the last words that would ever be written in his elegant Latin script. They give us a rare, and moving, encounter with him in a deeply private moment. Now an old man, contemplating death, he wrote, "You will be redeemed from sin, and set free from the cares and fury of theologians."[1] Then turning his graceful hand to the right side of the page, and still burning with the Platonism of his youth, he pondered that he would soon come "to the light" and understand the "wonderful mysteries, which you could not comprehend in this life."[2]

Our interest in Philip Melanchthon was aroused more than a decade ago in our initial enthusiasm for the historical theology of Karl Barth and his critique of modern Christian thought since Schleiermacher. Barth believed that one detected already in Melanchthon the same anthropocentric mood that would eventually dominate the theology of Protestantism in the nineteenth century. That this professor of Greek, whom historians would name the Preceptor of Germany, had been an unwitting perpetrator of mediation between things properly distinct as human or divine was not a novel view. By the end of his life Melanchthon was worn out mainly by this sort of criticism from his contemporaries, and his reputation for dulling the dialectical edges of original Lutheranism has persisted through the centuries since his death.

The litany of complaints is a familiar one.[3] In 1522 he had given the "Zwickau Prophets"[4] a hearing, while others (including Luther) impatiently called for unequivocal condemnation. Not long afterwards, he again aroused suspicion, this time by making what in John Agricola's mind was a dangerously "Romanist" proposal, that Christian works might in carefully defined terms be called "good" without offending the God of grace.[5] Still later, fearing that all might otherwise be lost, he had capitulated to demands set forth in the Interims of Augsburg (1547) and Leipzig (1548).[6] It seemed that prowling political lions like Maurice and Carlowitz had intimidated him all too easily, and exposed his lack of theological conviction.[7] His very own former students, led by Matthew Vlacich (Flacius), now aimed an entire arsenal of "authentic Lutheran" gunfire at their former professor. In one year alone more than ninety pamphlets came out against Melanchthon from the new "chancellery of God" in Magdeburg.[8]

Approaching the end of his life, and despite having lately published one of the finest of all early Protestant writings, *The Saxon Confession*, Melanchthon found himself on the receiving end of still another assault, this time by Andreas Osiander, the new professor of theology at Königsberg, who became intensely devoted to exposing deficiencies in Philip's doctrine of justification as an external imputation of righteousness to humans.[9] And for many years there had been rumblings about a suspected "synergism" on the question of free will and election.[10] With such bitter memories running through his mind, it is little wonder that he wrote wistfully of death as release from the *rabies theologorum*. But here on earth the controversies persisted long after he was gone. For a time (1574-1760) his books were banned in Wittenberg, his supporters were denounced and sometimes imprisoned,[11] and in 1610 even his portrait was torn down and kicked to pieces.[12]

There was of course always some support for the Preceptor of Germany. His philosophical and educational texts had widespread influence in and outside of Germany,[13] and his use of the *loci*-method, if not his substantive theology, was paradigmatic in Lutheran dogmatics for generations to come.[14] Nevertheless, two centuries would pass before a broader, and less ideological, consensus about his reputation would begin to be reached. The atmosphere of the academic world in the Europe of 1777 was clearly very different from that of 1560. More temperate spirits, in more peaceful times, welcomed the commemorative edition of the biography which Melanchthon's closest friend, Joachim Camerarius, had completed nearly two centuries earlier. With this publication G. Th. Strobel[15] helped to inspire a school of interpretation in the German academic community that was largely sympathetic with Melanchthon.[16] In the mid-nineteenth century Heinrich Heppe[17] took a major step toward a more balanced assessment than was possible under earlier circumstances.[18] The emergence of the *Corpus Reformatorum*, an imperfect yet monumental achievement,[19] also helped lift Melanchthon to somewhat higher ground, as modern science and philosophy challenged orthodoxy in ways that made Melanchthon's various deviations pale by comparison. The reflective discipline of historical theology began to treat him as a figure of rank and as an essential link with the religious and social past of a Europe that was going through a crisis of identity in its present.

By the close of the nineteenth century, theologians of what H. Richard Niebuhr called the "culture Christianity" of modern Europe had become a powerful force in the German universities as elsewhere. Their metaphysical roots were in Kantianism, while their religious consciousness remained Lutheran, and they devoted themselves to the difficult art of holding both together in one piece. Melanchthon again figured prominently in attempts to mediate between Christianity and the larger philosophical culture. Albrecht Ritschl[20] and his followers Troeltsch,[21] Loofs,[22] Seeberg[23] and O. Ritschl,[24] among many others, reflected a generally unified assessment according to the standards of a modern philosophical Lutheranism. Their portrait of Melanchthon was to become normative for at least half a century, and it remains the dominant view in many places still, particularly the United States and Great Britain. The influential views of Barth clearly arose within the terms of this modern historiography, and one may venture to say that Melanchthon's popular image is mainly that of these nineteenth century modernist scholars. The main features of this historiographical tradition will be discussed in appropriate sections of our book, but a brief introductory summary will help the reader to begin with a clear view of the larger context in which we are working.

The scholarship of Lutheran modernism accomplished for Melanchthon at least one thing that he never achieved in his earthly life: it redeemed him from the meanness and violence of his own age. Gone were the dogmatic anathemas over alleged contradictions of "true Lutheranism." A brand new mood of gratefulness for Melanchthon's moderate character arrived. His stubborn defense of human dignity in varied forms, such as perceptive powers, moral integrity, freedom of will, responsibility and "natural theology," now received a nearly universal encomium of praise.[25] What had changed, it seems, was not so much the interpretation of Melanchthon as the hermeneutical standards and values by which one assessed him. Moral justification was now imputed, by virtue of historical shifts in metaphysics and society, to conciliatory souls such as Melanchthon, rather than to the unbending defenders of a dialectical world view. As Kierkegaard would say in another setting, the spirit of "both-and" had replaced in good measure that of "either-or."

But history not only freed Melanchthon from rabid theologians. One wonders if it did not in effect sentence him to the worst kind of condemnation, that which comes with faint praise. While ideologically less orthodox scholars valued Melanchthon for having been something of an ancestor to the irenic mind of modernity, he nonetheless emerged looking a rather weak and secondary figure, perhaps a "Luther's Boswell."[26] According to the generation that followed in Ritschl's steps, his systematic and confessional writings were miniature, mediating versions of what Luther had taught him, and his own independent efforts belied deep systemic conflict between his humanistic commitments and those of his Lutheran theology and biblicism. Worse still, Melanchthon seemed oblivious to his internal contradictions, a pathetic flaw in one whose entire philosophy was committed to self-knowledge. Consequently, under the impression that he was dutifully representing the cause, he pruned Luther's theological saplings into tidy, uninteresting clumps, bestowing upon later generations nothing more than a "theology of definitions"[27] and grist for the mills of seventeenth-century "Protestant scholasticism." Secondly, he mediated so strenuously between Scripture and the world, faith and reason, humanity and God, that the conceptual structure of his thought was at best inconsistent with Luther's, at worst simply incoherent and baffling, and was surely evidence itself of the need for a coherent plan along Ritschlian lines to push humanistic logic all the way through into the categories of orthodox religion, rather than living hopelessly in two incompatible worlds.[28]

The portrait of Melanchthon as an unwitting mediator between the Middle Ages and modernity has long been with us. For the Gnesio-Lutherans it exposed a contemptibly weak backbone and a lack of Christian sense. For the Kantian-Lutherans it depicted the virtue of tolerance, but metaphysically speaking showed that Melanchthon stood tallest perhaps in a land of dwarves. To those, like Barth, intent upon a reversal of modern metaphysical trends, it showed that he had not very great stature in the land of giants. A more irenic Gnesio-Lutheranism thus came to life in a dialectical theology of the Word and in its Promethean assault on humanistic inclinations of all sorts as being products of a titanic arrogance, "anthropocentrism" and, worst of all, "natural theology."[29]

When we began research for a dissertation on Melanchthon in 1976, it was to have served this larger Barthian theory of history and theology. However, during the third year of research into the seemingly endless corpus of Melanchthon's writings, our thinking about the nature and influence of Melanchthon's humanism began to change. The change grew from several sources. The year 1960, which marked the four hundredth anniversary of his death, generated the most textually inductive and painstakingly thorough scholarship in the history of Melanchthon studies. Men of rare ability, such as Wilhelm Maurer, Robert Stupperich, Ernst Bizer, Wilhelm Neuser, Peter Fraenkel and others, had made huge strides on every level of the subject. The fruits of their labors included showing that Melanchthon's humanism was much more idiosyncratic philosophically and linguistically than had been previously known, that it had a much deeper and more complex structure than it had been given credit for, that much of it (many debates are still to be untangled here) adapted more coherently to a Lutheran theology than was generally believed, and that Melanchthon must be judged by standards of some independence from traditional pictures of Luther and/or a deductive and unified concept of the Reformation and its "theology." Virtually all the various standards of evaluation have been subjected to criticism, so that it is difficult to know even how to begin assessing historical figures, while at the same time our improved knowledge of Melanchthon has brought forth new standards and a mixed but generally upward reappraisal of his works.[30]

The pattern of Melanchthon scholarship has been one of flash floods of writing on and around the anniversaries of his birth and death, followed by long dry spells with the occasional article or book appearing. It would seem that we are presently in one of those periods when publication slows to a trickle. Nevertheless, important books have come out to sharpen the picture that emerged mainly around 1960, and these studies have helped set the context for our present work.

The more recent movement in Melanchthon studies, and our own reading of Melanchthon's texts, have led us to the conclusion that during the years before he journeyed fatefully to Wittenberg he had developed, with considerable originality, his own peculiar slant on humanism (rather than simply adopting the program of Erasmus or Reuchlin), that at its core was a theoretical model of rhetoric which embodied the structures of a larger philosophical-linguistic system, that this system created a magnetic attraction to Luther's theology (and vice versa), that Melanchthon used it not merely to organize Luther's views but to refine, redefine and even prove them true in a public forum, and that his work is simply incomprehensible apart from this deeply complex structure and process. Several recent works point in these directions,[31] but consensus on the contours of Melanchthon's early development and the seam between it and his formative Lutheran theology (roughly 1509-1521) has only begun to emerge. The general aim of this book is to offer a hermeneutical point of view for *reading* Melanchthon that engages and advances the present state of the discipline.

As Luther once put it, Melanchthon was a man of both *res et verbum*. It was in the nature of his character and his humanism that for him truth and letters were quite simply inseparable from each other. This outlook and disposition made the Bible doubly important to his Christianity and theological method, and makes Melanchthon a prime example of what recent theologian David Kelsey has observed as true of all Christian theologians: their construal of Scripture (whether conscious or not) is a conceptual arena in which all the strands of a Christian world view form an "intra-textual world."[32] This intra-textual vision becomes for a theologian something like a map which he uses to interpret the world outside. The configuration of the "map" arises in part from a theologian's initial, basic construal of the text. Perhaps Kelsey's most original contribution was to have noticed how diverse these construals are among theologians, and thus to have amplified the problem of judging theologies simply "by the text." As Gordon Rupp put it, a pure biblical theology was no more possible in Luther's age than it is now, and philosophical-linguistic scaffolding was quickly built around the new edifice of Lutheran theology.[33] Melanchthon was clearly a central figure in the early development of not only Protestant dogmatic theology but of a hermeneutical system to support it. He consciously erected this structure from the elements of his humanistic literary theory of truth. Students of the history of method will find already in the young Melanchthon an interpreter of the text whose hermeneutical practice was logically contingent upon first-order concerns about the nature of truth, truth and literature, literature and Scripture, and Scripture and fundamental human realities. The larger thesis of this book is that Melanchthon construed Scripture literally as sacred rhetoric, *oratio sacra*, and that detailed tracing of how this construal governed his hermeneutical processes and systematic formation of doctrine is indispensable both to understanding and to assessing him and the prevailing historiography.

Peter Fraenkel was correct when he wrote more than twenty years ago[34] that deeper examination was needed still of Melanchthon's work as an exegete. Since then a good deal of progress has been made,[35] but there is as yet no systematic treatment of Melanchthon's conception of the text in the context of a general *doctrine* of Scripture. Much has been written on Melanchthon's compromising view of *sola scriptura*, with respect to philosophy, but there is as yet no satisfactory treatment of his concepts of *sola* or *scriptura*, much less of how exactly he conjoined them. The tendency has been to use this catch phrase as if only one standard meaning were possible. Much has also been written on how Melanchthon took the Bible to be a book of doctrinal propositions, but we have merely begun to clarify the meaning of terms such as *doctrina pura* in the linguistic stock which he understood himself (as apparently others did as well) to be using, and to show how he worked with these formal and material concepts to hammer out others, such as that of biblical primacy, unity, inspiration, canonicity, perspicuity, efficacy, diversity and truthfulness. All were essential properties of biblical authority for Melanchthon (and enduring categories for later Lutheran and Reformed dogmatics), and all were powerfully shaped by his peculiar rhetorical philosophy. Our hope is that by centering on his rhetorical construal of the Bible fresh light will be cast on many familiar subjects, particularly the intricate relationship between faith and reason in Melanchthon, which, as Neuser rightly observed, is a kind of bellweather for his theology as a whole.[36]

It is difficult to imagine anything entirely new coming forth about the Preceptor, who is so well known to us. On the other hand, as Stupperich's ironic title, *The Unknown Melanchthon*, suggests, there is a sense in which this familiar figure remains "unknown" and is a stranger even unto his own. This book aims at being the kind of work which Stupperich, in the citation with which this introduction began, invited the next generation of Melanchthon scholars to write: happening upon unnoticed facts and connections, bringing them into new interpretive form, and in those ways giving forth a "new kind of image." The learned reader must judge the quality of the image here put forth.

A more distant hope in writing this study of the sixteenth-century reformer is that it will be of interest to modern hermeneutical theologians as a study in the history of interpretation, and that it might contribute to the currently widespread discussions about theological language and its referents. One perspective on Melanchthon and his method makes it disturbingly obvious how fragile were (and are) the epistemic foundations of orthodox Protestant theology (not merely with respect to their truth claims, but also to their claim to being obviously "biblical"). Another perspective, however, reminds us of how frightfully bleak the theological landscape becomes when our Christian language is drained of semantic correspondence with reality, its truth nothing more or less than *itself* and its users. If there is a responsible way back to a theology of both *verbum et res*, then perhaps Melanchthon can teach us something, if not directly by example, then indirectly by urging us honestly toward that end.

Method, Organization and Sources

Method is seldom arbitrary. It is nearly always the product of underlying assumptions about one's subject. Inappropriate assumptions can generate methods which are not proper to the materials at hand. For some time the prejudgment that Melanchthon's theology *began* to take shape only under the influence of Luther led to questionable practices in evaluating him as a theologian. The systematic editions of the *Loci communes* were often made the center of focus, and were handled in a manner that one would expect, given the assumption that they contained little more than a "theology of definitions." Until about the time of his four hundredth *Todestag*, it was rare to find a general treatment of his theology that maintained contact with literary and historical-social contexts, particularly those related to the pre-Lutheran time. With the exception of a few biographical works, the majority have been highly systematic and dogmatic in nature.[37] The great work of Wilhelm Maurer has shown beyond question how dubious a procedure it is to examine Melanchthon's theology in abstraction from as detailed a chronological picture of his experiential circumstances as the sources permit. The fact that Maurer's meticulous work, spanning three decades, brought him only to the time of the Augsburg Confession is itself a commentary on the status of systematic styles that aim at comprehending the whole of Melanchthon's thought in one volume. It is simply inconceivable that such a method, at this stage in the development of the field, not lead to overlooking important matters. Thanks to Maurer, and to the extraordinary labors of Heiko Oberman,[38] the sources permit a great deal more access than in any previous time to social and intellectual contexts in South Germany on the monumental bridge between the fifteenth and sixteenth centuries; they are giving forth a new image of how the Reformation emerged from late medieval traditions, and how humanistic impulses entered into the developing movement. There is a sense in which Melanchthon was a microcosm of this fascinatingly complex time.

In this book, we have built gratefully upon the research of Maurer and Oberman, choosing to use a historical-chronological method rather than a systematic theological one. In the early chapters the focus is upon the pre-Lutheran Melanchthon, during his formative years as a student at Pforzheim, Heidelberg and Tübingen. The conceptual aim of these chapters has been to define as clearly as possible the nature of his linguistic system and pre-Lutheran religious outlook that he brought with him to Wittenberg in 1518. The focus of the middle chapters is upon the deeply interesting manner in which he adopted Luther's theology, not merely how this theology called for powerful revisions of his life and thought (a theme which has been all too prevalent in the literature), but particularly how he constructively used his pre-Lutheran stock of language to give a peculiar shape and authoritative power to Luther's message. An essential element of this procedure was in constructing a Lutheran construal of Scripture and its authority as *oratio sacra*. We have treated the *Loci communes* of 1521 as the consummation of these important developments, rather than as the beginning of his noteworthy theological production, and have interpreted them in this light. In the final chapter the discussion has been devoted to Melanchthon's historiographical status, mainly with respect to three levels of "faith and reason" in his overall system of thought. The controversial issues of "anthropocentrism," "intellectualism" and "natural theology" have been treated in view of the preceding discussion of Melanchthon's rhetorical conception of biblical authority. As one might expect, recommendations have been made for considerable revision, on each level and all together, of standard methods and their ensuing portraits of the man.

It must also be stressed that, although we have attempted to consider the historical influences upon Melanchthon, and to portray him as part of a much larger historical setting, the main focus of the book is upon Melanchthon himself. In reference to his fellow classicists, however, we have attempted, mainly through secondary authorities such as Maurer, Oberman, Hartfelder and others, to illumine the context in which he carried out his linguistic work. In reference to the elusive subject of Melanchthon's theological sources and influence the aim has also been more indicative than exhaustive. Nevertheless, we have ventured several proposals on the relationship between Melanchthon and Luther which should be of interest to those who are attempting to determine degrees of continuity and discontinuity from the late Middle Ages to German humanism and the Lutheran Reformation. We have also offered tentative proposals on Melanchthon's relation to later, seventeenth-century Lutheran dogmatics. During the course of our studies it has become clear that, although he may have been their forefather on the level of formal method, his entire approach to Scripture and theology was both conceptually and spiritually different from theirs in his acute attentiveness to the human dimension of the text.

Before beginning our discussion we should include brief remarks about the text of Melanchthon's writings which we have used. As P. Fraenkel has noted,[39] the study of the young Melanchthon has suffered from a plague of textual difficulties. First among them is that the main critical edition of Melanchthon's works, the *Corpus Reformatorum*, has an unsettling frequency of error, particularly in the dating of letters. This weakness has been pointed out and is being painstakingly corrected by H. Scheible, who is director of the Heidelberg Academy.[40] In attempting to use the most reliable texts, we have normally not used the *Corpus Reformatorum* unless it was possible to check it against comparable sources, mainly Scheible's *Regestenbände*, in which he has re-dated all the correspondence and prefatory materials used by us. We have mainly relied upon modern editions, such as the *Supplementa Melanchthoniana* [41] and the more recent *Melanchthons Werke*.[42] In other instances we have had access to rare imprints of Melanchthon's writings that were available through the University Library of Cambridge, the

Universitätsbibliothek of Tübingen, and the *Institut für Spätmittelalter und Reformation*, which was then under the able guidance of Professor Oberman. It should finally be indicated that we have attempted to use a textual apparatus which well represents Melanchthon's thought up to the end of 1521. The few writings which have been omitted from detailed discussion would have created unprofitable repetition. Such omissions have been noted in the text and briefly explained in endnotes. All citations from the Latin have been translated with literal clarity as a somewhat greater aim than eloquence of style. It must also be noted that, in those instances where we have not given full Latin citations in the endnotes, we have done our best to insert important terms and phrases into our translations in brackets.

Notes to the Introduction

1. R. Stupperich, *Melanchthon*, (tr.) Robert Fischer, Philadelphia 1965, p. 148.
2. *Ibid.*
3. For a helpful review of Melanchthon's many controversies, *ibid.*, pp. 100-150.
4. *Ibid.*, p. 56.
5. *Ibid.*, pp. 68ff.
6. *Ibid.*, pp. 123f.
7. *Ibid.*, p. 126.
8. *Ibid.*, p. 134.
9. *Ibid.*
10. C. Manschreck, *Melanchthon: The Quiet Reformer*, New York/ Nashville 1958, p. 298.
11. *Ibid.*, p. 15.
12. *Ibid.*, pp. 15f.
13. *Ibid.*, pp. 13ff.
14. R. Stupperich, *op. cit.*, pp. 151f.
15. *Ibid.*, p. 152; J. Camerarius, *De vita Philippi Melanchthonis narratio*, Recensuit, notas, documenta, bibliothecam librorum Melanchthonis aliaque addidit. Ge. Theodor. Strobelius, Praefatus est Iohannes Auc. Noessell, Halle 1777.
16. Stupperich, *op. cit.*, p. 153.
17. H. Heppe, *Die konfessionelle Entwicklung der altprotestantischen Union und die gegenwärtige konfessionelle Lage und Aufgabe des deutschen Protestantismus*, Marburg 1854. Neuser has aptly called this work the first instance of modern critical research into Melanchthon. W. H. Neuser, *Der Ansatz der Theologie Philipp Melanchthons*, Neukirchen 1957, p. 2, "Die wenigen Bearbeiter Melanchthons vor Heppes Veröffentlichungen sind unkritisch eingestellt."
18. W. H. Neuser, *op. cit.*, pp. 5f.
19. G. C. Brettschneider, H. E. Bindseil (eds.), *Corpus Reformatorum: Philippi Melanchthonis Opera, quae supersunt omnia*, 28 vols., Halis Saxonum 1834-1860.
20. A. Ritschl, "Die Entstehung der lutherischen Kirche," in *Gesammelte Aufsätze*, Freiburg/Leipzig 1893, pp. 170-217. Also the English work, *The Christian Doctrine of Justification and Reconciliation*, Edinburgh 1902.
21. E. Troeltsch, *Vernunft und Offenbarung bei Johann Gerhard und Melanchthon*, Göttingen 1891.
22. F. Loofs, *Leitfaden zum Studien der Dogmengeschichte*, Halle 1906.
23. R. Seeberg, *Lehrbuch der Dogmengeschichte*, Bd. IV/2, Basel/Stuttgart (1920) 1960.
24. O. Ritschl, *Dogmengeschichte des Protestantismus*, Bd. I, II, Leipzig 1908, 1912.
25. W. H. Neuser, *op. cit.*, pp. 7ff.
26. E. G. Rupp, "Philip Melanchthon and Martin Bucer," in *A History of Christian Doctrine*, (ed.) H. Cunliffe-Jones with Benjamin Drewery, Philadelphia (1980) 1984, pp. 371ff. This essay is as fine a brief evaluation of Melanchthon as one can hope to find in print.
27. Troeltsch coined this description of Melanchthon's theology, *op. cit.*, p. 59.
28. For detailed annotation see chapter 11, pp. 234ff.
29. Cf. chapter 11, pp. 237ff.
30. For a critically annotated bibliography of this period, see P. Fraenkel, "Fünfzehn Jahre Melanchthonforschung: Versuch eines Literaturberichtes," in *Philipp*

Melanchthon: Forschungsbeiträge zur vierhundertsten Wiederkehr seines Todestages dargeboten in Wittenberg 1960, (hrsg.) W. Elliger, Göttingen 1960, pp. 11-55.

31. Very important ones include W. Maurer, *Der junge Melanchthon*, Bd. 1, 2, Göttingen 1967, 1969, particularly Bd. 1, "Der Humanist," on the pre-Lutheran Melanchthon; P. Fraenkel, *Testimonia Patrum: The Function of the Patristic Argument in the Theology of Philipp Melanchthon*, Geneva 1961; E. Bizer, *Theologie der Verheissung: Studien zur theologischen Entwicklung des jungen Melanchthons 1519-1524*, Neukirchen 1964; H.-G. Geyer, *Von der Geburt des wahren Menschen*, Neukirchen 1965; K. Haendler, *Wort und Glaube bei Melanchthon: Eine Untersuchung über die Voraussetzungen und Grundlagen des Melanchthonischen Kirchenbegriffes*, Gütersloh 1968; and S. Wiedenhofer, *Formalstrukturen humanistischer und reformatorischer Theologie bei Philipp Melanchthon*, Bd. I, II, Bern/Frankfurt/München 1976. This last work most nearly resembles our own in technique and topical focus, though there are huge differences between us, partly due to the vast comprehensiveness of Wiedenhofer's work, comprising the "form-structures" of Melanchthon's entire theology. Specific matters of interpretive differences will be brought forward in our text.

32. D. Kelsey, *The Uses of Scripture in Recent Theology*, Philadelphia 1975; the actual expression "intra-textuality" derives, we believe, from the provocative works of G. Lindbeck, cf., *The Nature of Doctrine*, Philadelphia 1984.

33. E. G. Rupp, *op. cit.*, p. 374.

34. P. Fraenkel, "Fünfzehn Jahre Melanchthonforschung," p. 49.

35. The most recent works which touch upon aspects of Melanchthon and the doctrine of Scripture are P. Fraenkel, *Testimonia Patrum*, pp. 208ff. and 321ff. on Scripture and Melanchthon's concepts of *doctrina pura* and "perspicuity," 70ff. on the relationship between the Old Testament and the New, 338ff. on Scripture and the logic of *primum et verum*; also H. Sick, *Melanchthon als Ausleger des Alten Testaments*, Tübingen 1959, has written a solid piece of work on Melanchthon's use of rhetoric and dialectic to handle biblical texts; K. Haendler's massive book, *op. cit.*, is interspersed with comments about Scripture, e.g., pp. 35ff. on biblical unity, 56ff. on inspiration and inerrancy, 186ff. on literal versus allegorical interpretation, 62ff. on connections between Melanchthon's rhetoric and "law and gospel" as the core of Scripture; H.-G. Geyer, *op. cit.*, included useful discussion of how Melanchthon's rhetorical classifications helped to shape his literary understanding of the Bible, pp. 24ff., 52ff., 125ff., 189ff., as elsewhere in passing; Wiedenhofer's work, *op. cit.*, also contains sections of interesting commentary on Melanchthon, Scripture and method. References to these works will be given as they are engaged in our discussions.

36. W. H. Neuser, *op. cit.*, p. 17, "Melanchthon's attitude toward philosophy proves itself throughout his entire life a precise standard of measurement for his theological orientation." See also E. G. Rupp, *op. cit.*, on the need for going more deeply into all these subjects connected with faith and reason.

37. See R. Stupperich, *op. cit.*, "A Word about Melanchthon Research," pp. 151ff.

38. We are deeply indebted to the many writings of Professor Oberman which are cited below in context, particularly with respect to South German nominalism in its manifold expressions.

39. P. Fraenkel, *Testimonia Patrum*, p. 8.

40. H. Scheible (hrsg.), *Melanchthons Briefwechsel*, (Kritische und kommentierte Gesamtausgabe), Bd. 1-3, Stuttgart/Bad Cannstatt 1978ff., cf. Bd. 1, pp. 22ff., on difficulties with the *CR*.

41. O. Clemen (hrsg.), *Supplementa Melanchthoniana, Werke Philipp Melanchthons, die im Corpus Reformatorum vermisst werden*, Bd. 1-5, Leipzig 1910ff.; repr. Frankfurt 1968.

42. R. Stupperich (hrsg.), *Melanchthons Werke in Auswahl: Studienausgabe*, Bd. I-VII/2, Gütersloh 1951ff.

CHAPTER 1

The Years as a Student at Pforzheim and Heidelberg

"Everything is the sum of its past," wrote the theologian Chardin. Melanchthon will be a mystery to us so long as his earliest years as a student at Pforzheim and the universities of Heidelberg and Tübingen remain in the shadows of confessional predisposition to concentrate mainly on his Lutheran years. A more ecumenical time, and the profoundly important works of Oberman and others in bringing to light the roots of Protestantism in the fourteenth and fifteenth centuries, have made it possible now to attend with some confidence to the specialized study of Melanchthon before the Reformation. The main contribution of the present chapter (and the next, too) is to deepen our knowledge of his earliest development and, thereby, to suggest a portrait which attributes to him a good deal more intellectual integrity and originality than is typically done. A sharply focused picture of these pre-Lutheran years will then serve as an interpretive framework for assessing his theoretical construal of Scripture and manner of handling Christian doctrine.

Childhood and Pforzheim

On a winter evening after *invocavit*, the sixteenth of February in 1497, a first son was born to George and Barbara Schwarzerd of Bretten.[1] They named him Philip after the Prince of Baden, in whose service George had managed to win something of a reputation for himself as a skillful maker of arms.[2] The bountiful hills and sun-bathed forests which surrounded and blessed this little family in South Germany were, like Eliot's April, the "cruelest" of beauties. In

1504 when Philip was but seven his father drank from a poisoned well and never quite recovered.[3] In years to come a haggard Melanchthon would confess to having a melancholy nature, but would blame this partly on the powerful impression that his young father's death in 1508 made upon him.[4] When the widowed Barbara took her five children to live at her parents' home in Pforzheim, she could not know that her eldest was being spirited by larger forces to his destiny as one of the great scholars of his century.

Barbara Reuter's mother was a sister of the great Hebraist John Reuchlin, who made certain that the fatherless boys (a brother, George, had been born in 1501) received a solid education. He and John Ungar, who worked as their private tutor in Latin and Greek, became like fathers to the boys. Melanchthon would one day write with great warmth for Ungar: "He made me a grammarian ..., he was the best of men; he loved me as a son, and I him as a father."[5] As Maurer has poignantly written, the school became Philip's family, his teachers his fathers, the study of classical languages the center of his world.[6]

After a year in the home of his grandmother, Philip enrolled in the Pforzheim school of grammar which, according to Camerarius, was widely esteemed for its excellence.[7] One of the strong personalities at the school was its rector, George Simler, whose intellectual direction was typical of those who had a lasting influence on Philip. Simler was inflamed by love for the Platonism which he had learned by reading Florentine masters, such as Ficino and Pico della Mirandola.[8] The German historian Irenicus wrote of Simler that he was "a born teacher."[9] He must have been delighted to have, among an already superb class, this "born student" who was eager to ascend above the rudiments of grammar to more advanced levels. Melanchthon later wrote of Simler that "he first interpreted for me the Latin and Greek poets, and led [me] to a purer philosophy, often comparing the text of Aristotle, which we had then, with the Greek sources."[10] Alongside this very early introduction to textual criticism in handling the Greek poets and Aristotle (incorporated into the Platonized curriculum rather than excluded from it) was the Ciceronian vision of the scholar as public orator and man of action.[11] This oratorical conception of one's calling was the underlying premise of Reuchlin's *Ars Praedicandi* [12] and, in a broad sense, of the entire philosophy of learning at the school.[13] Everything we know about Melanchthon's education at Pforzheim indicates that the revolutionary new methods of literary and textual criticism that were beginning to gain currency in pockets of South Germany were more assimilated by him than learned, so that they became more a way of life than a methodology.

Reuchlin once wrote, "St. Jerome I revere as an angel, I esteem Nicholas de Lyra as a great master, but truth I worship as a god."[14] The famous essays of Paul Joachimsen have shown brilliantly that Italian scholarship, when it crossed the Alps into South German lands, inspired something of much greater complexity than a reformation in philosophy and method in the liberal arts.[15] The religious *sensus* which inspired the scholarly mission of Reuchlin and others is well illustrated by a widely known anecdote. It was Reuchlin's custom to visit the Pforzheim school on occasion to inspect the boys' progress.[16] On one occasion Simler[17] directed the students in a performance of Reuchlin's school comedy, *Henno*.[18] The author was so pleased by his grandnephew's part in the presentation that he re-christened him "Melanchthon," the name which he would bear for the remainder of his life. The story itself is well known, but Maurer has shown its deeper meaning by comparing it with the initiatory rites of medieval monasticism.[19] Bestowing Greek names upon those who excelled in the new forms of learning was comparable to the rituals practiced by German religious orders, for the new name signified nothing less than entry into a new life. "In both instances it has to do with the birth of a new man. He enters into a new realm of life, becomes the member of an order, and is thereby lifted above the course of ordinary men."[20] If the path of Martin Luther was through the religious moralism of the Augustinian canons, Melanchthon's was through the moralistic religion of hellenized Christian scholarship. Both came to Wittenberg seeking "justification," but each from somewhat different sources, and with different casts of mind. It is quite remarkable how two men so very different from each other could fit together, the one a complement to the other, in attending "the deathbed of a world and...the birth of a new age."[21]

Heidelberg

Camerarius introduced the second phase of Melanchthon's academic life with these words:

> ...and he was sent to Heidelberg..., where there was a famous university. Now a young man, flourishing among the multitude of learned men, Philip created the opinion that he himself would be fit to teach others.[22]

On the 14th of October 1509, he entered the University of Heidelberg.[23] Although he pursued the baccalaureate degree in the liberal arts, Philip, no doubt by arrangement through Reuchlin, boarded at the home of Pallas Spangel who was a professor of theology.[24] Spangel was, in Hartfelder's estimation, "one of the most influential personalities at the University of Heidelberg at the turn of the fifteenth century."[25] By the time Melanchthon entered the university he was well up in years, an accomplished member of the faculty for nearly half a century who had been elected as rector no fewer than four times.[26] Spangel embodied the very spirit of that university, which had preserved something of what had been (before the Bavarian War) a South German "renaissance" that for a while made Prince Philip's court "the seat of the Muses."[27] It was customary for these dedicated scholars, having performed their required lectures, to invite the most promising students to private seminars on freshly uncovered finds in the classical arts, and to put before them the growing challenge of using these discoveries in the context of orthodox Christian tradition.[28] Then, as now, an integrated world view was the pressing concern of the day in the Christian schools. In an essay on nominalist theologian Stephen Hoest's method of preaching, Spangel's star pupil, and now the ranking classicist at Heidelberg, Jacob Wimpfeling (often ignored as a profound influence upon the younger Melanchthon), referred to Spangel as exemplary in achieving the desired synthesis of eloquence and wisdom.[29] Spangel himself published very rarely, and we have been unable to locate any primary sources of his work; nevertheless there is a useful summary in Hartfelder's biography.[30] His description of Spangel's outlook is worth citing at length:

> ...he is typical of the relationship between humanism and the university [of Heidelberg] at this time. Closely befriended by and in allegiance with humanists, who in part highly honor him as their teacher, he stands entirely in the world view of the old church. He is a devoted scholastic and professes the system of the Thomists. The "new arts" are for him merely an educational expedient, and the better Latin, which he learned from [Rudolf] Agricola, is for him only a tool for making the doctrines of the church...more pertinent to the higher demands of the present.[31]

What of Spangel's influence on the young Melanchthon? In 1539, upon publication of Agricola's *Lucubrationes*, an older Melanchthon rated Spangel next to Reuchlin for his pure, disciplined Latin and for his weighty theological judgment.[32] Especially important to Melanchthon was Spangel's fruitful use of Agricola's writings.[33] It was Spangel to whom he owed his introduction to the works of Agricola:[34] "Rudolf Agricola will meet us often in Melanchthon's educational history; the Friesian did not shape him, but spurred him on constantly to intellectual reform."[35] Melanchthon applauded Agricola as one of the great heroes of German history, as one of the first Germans to write in good Latin and as the very first to establish needed reform in the discipline of dialectic and in a general method of instruction in the universities.[36]

The importance of Agricola's dialectic to Melanchthon will be a recurring point of reference throughout our treatment of Melanchthon's pre-Lutheran training. This element of his linguistic system had its official beginnings under Spangel, in whom he found a professor devoted deeply to conserving the theological traditions of the Christian past, but also keenly aware that the Greco-Roman masters, through their precision and elegance (and also their actual metaphysics),[37] were of great value to theological and ecclesiastical ministries. He thus put their works to use, particularly as filtered through the doctrines of Agricola as a model for German students.

Similar values appeared in the writings of Jacob Wimpfeling, Melanchthon's professor of rhetoric and "the first representative [in Germany] of a pedagogical humanism."[38] In Maurer's words (the implications of which have too often been neglected), "no one took over his ideas, indeed under entirely different religious and political presuppositions, and put them into practice so completely as Melanchthon."[39] In contrast to Spangel, Wimpfeling left an expansive legacy of published writings.[40] Perhaps one can think of Wimpfeling as the mirrored reflection of his master. If Spangel led his students of theology into the new arts to help them understand and conserve their Christian heritage, Wimpfeling led his students of the arts to Christian theology that they might better understand the utility of pagan wisdom.

Wimpfeling belonged to the circle of "Upper Rhineland humanism," was (as the adult Melanchthon would become) a "conservative man" interested less in new Italian ideas than in whatever might help reform the church, and was somewhat "prudish," to use Maurer's term, in his selection of pagan sources, as in his preference for the "Christian" Vergil and for the moral poetry of the humanist Baptista Mantuanus.[41]

The writings of Wimpfeling display a strong belief in the proposition that theoretical reforms within the foundational disciplines of grammar, dialectic and rhetoric were essential to change in the larger culture. In an essay entitled *Epistola Jacobi Wimpfelingi de inepta et superflua verborum resolucione in cancellis*, he railed against the grammatical ineptness of South German preachers and presented himself as part of a front, with Spangel and John Geyler of Kaisersberg, which stood firmly against the common linguistic abuses of the day.[42] In his textbook on rhetoric entitled *Rhetorica Jacobi Wimpfelingi pueris utilissima*, published in 1509 (the year Melanchthon entered the university), Wimpfeling defended the place of rhetoric as essential to the liberal arts.[43] Working self-consciously out of the philosophical traditions of Aristotle, Cicero and Quintilian[44] (and thus implicitly through Spangel and Agricola), he defined the essential purpose of *genus demonstrativum*, against the common view of this class of rhetoric as mere flourish and emotive manipulation; he described it rather as "to incite others to virtuous living."[45] It is important to notice how Wimpfeling the rhetorician adopted the theoretical proposal that *dialectical* argumentation was essential to this overall purpose. "Moreover, rhetoric has arguments [*enthymemata*] fitting to itself, just as dialectic has syllogisms."[46] The suggestion of analogy between the structures of rhetorical and dialectical persuasion was (initially through Agricola) a pervasive idea at Melanchthon's Heidelberg, and would always be at the core of his own theoretical linguistics, giving them a peculiar sort of Aristotelian logical rigor that will become important to our later discussion.

There is a common belief that the young Melanchthon was a disciple of Erasmus. We shall discuss this relationship in greater depth in the next chapter, but it ought to be kept in view that the formative influences upon him through Reuchlin, the faculties at Pforzheim and Heidelberg and his independent studies were greatly complex and are most difficult to separate analytically. If he was an "Erasmian" before he became a "Lutheran" (and every German humanist was in some sense dependent upon the Dutchman), he had also acquired a philosophy of the liberal arts and Christianity that had an identity of its own. Maurer is surely correct in his judgment that this tradition, particularly with respect to its nominalistic philosophy of method, which included an Aristotelian theory of dialectic and rhetoric and a high view of scholastic, systematic theology, was a "humanism" which complemented but was of a significantly different order from that of Erasmus and was thus not simply derived from it.[47] The peculiarities of Melanchthon's linguistic system begin to emerge from examination of Wimpfeling and his influence upon the brilliant student.

It is true (and a bit odd) that Melanchthon never once, in any known source, wrote of his indebtedness to Wimpfeling. Maurer has perhaps best explained this silence with the judgment that "Melanchthon made the ideas from Wimpfeling so completely his own that later on he was no longer conscious of the outside origin."[48] However that may be, the influence of Wimpfeling upon the young Melanchthon is firmly documented by the student's first known publications, which appeared as poems of dedication to each of two writings by the master. The first, more suggestive of a student rising to defend the position of his professor than being politely honored by him, was a polemical essay against the poet Jacob Locher, *Contra turpem libellum Philomusi defensio theologiae scholasticae et neotericorum.*[49] In the essay Wimpfeling defended the presence of scholastic theology in the curriculum of the universities[50] and made the argument that a rigorous use of philosophical methods in the arts, especially the ones which his contemporaries at Heidelberg from the camp of the *via moderna* (such as Stephen Hoest) promoted, was in the best interest of doctrinal purity and reform.[51]

In the context of this argument by Wimpfeling, Maurer has called attention to what seems a subtle but very important basis for a distinction between the humanism of pre-Reformation Heidelberg and Wimpfeling, on the one hand, and that of Erasmus on the other: "In no way did Wimpfeling wish that the scholastic philosophy be opposed; he much rather attributed to it a certain value for sharpening the intellect and for fighting against heresy."[52] In addition to this affirmative approach to scholastic rigor, Wimpfeling's ideal of church reform was built mainly upon an appeal to the fathers of church doctrine and to the works of Gerson.[53] Moreover, Oberman's independent research into the intellectual history of Germany on the eve of the Reformation has shown with unprecedented force of textual evidence that Heidelberg (in Melanchthon's time) was deeply enmeshed in the intricacies of linguistic philosophy, and that the *via moderna*, there, had managed successfully to construct a systematic theory for its curriculum which had lacked categories that were adequate to containing the flood of fresh learning. The essential tool was "disciplined, puritanical use of words, whereby concepts [*Begriffe*] could be aligned only with clearly appointed content, demonstrated in each individual context [*proprietas dicendi*]."[54] This they managed to combine with a fresh feeling for practical wisdom in theology instead of hair-splitting and abstraction. In spite of his many criticisms of scholastic theologians, Melanchthon had obviously absorbed and benefited greatly from the analytical methods and discipline of the schoolmen. Even more masterfully than Wimpfeling, he was able to combine this devotion to logic and a proper use of terms as essential to truth with the more Socratic side of his nature, which pinned everything on seeking the right, truly human truths.

Hermann Hesse's character Narcissus defined scholarship as "the making of distinctions." It is reasonable and illuminating to think of Melanchthon's life-long infatuation with semantical and logical precision, and his positive passion for Aristotle's systems of classification, as having been cultivated at a very formative level while he was a student with Spangel and Wimpfeling. His dedicatory poem exhibited approval of his master's side of the controversy with Locher and, notably, the rigorousness of classification by which he made clear the distinction between Christianity and pagan wisdom which elevated the one clearly to a position of superiority above the other, but without disparaging Apollo, the Muse or the "stars."

> Yield, Pierides, let learned Apollo yield!
> Yield, Phoebus, whom the chorus celebrates!
> Yield now Greeks, yield pagan Muse!
> Here is the glory of wisdom, sweet-tasting dogma!
> The One who made the stars, who made the constellations of
>   bright heaven,
> And the deep, which things are the powerful will of God,
> Whatever worship there is in the world of the divine name,
> Whatever piety lives from human art,
> Completed wisdom will show you, candid reader,
> Read carefully that your name might be illustrious in the
>   world.[55]

The poem, while no great masterpiece, at very least shows the budding of an early loyalty, on Melanchthon's part, to the methods of Wimpfeling and the *via moderna* at Heidelberg, in their manner of handling profound philosophical (and thus curricular) crises on the level of faith and reason.

The dedicatory poem which Philip wrote for Wimpfeling's biography of Geyler of Kaisersberg (composed on the occasion of his death)[56] complements the other, showing that Philip's linguistics were framed already by a theory of sacred history and a sense of Germany's own historical position within the larger plan of things.

> What saints once proclaimed with a great voice,
> What the sacred throng of Christ's prophets announced,
> In whom the highest law of Christ teaches all
> Mortals in the sacred religion of faith,
> One German example alone, Kaisersberg,
> Proclaimed these things well to Christian people.[57]

Of Melanchthon's other teachers and studies we know little; the most complete summing up occurs in Hartfelder.[58] The student attended Peter Gunther's lectures on rhetoric, learned astronomy from Conrad Helvetius and continued to study Greek texts on his own. One source testifies to Melanchthon's prodigious abilities in Greek. A professor was frustrated by a problem with his text and cried out in the middle of a lecture, "Where shall I find a Greek?" The class responded in unison, "Melanchthon! Melanchthon!"[59]

In order to take the exams required for the baccalaureate degree within the *via antiqua* (in which Philip was still formally matriculated), all students swore an oath that they had studied thoroughly Alexander's textbook on Latin grammar, several writings of Aristotle, such as *Liber de anima*, and the logic of Peter Hispanus; so Philip must have performed these duties, too.[60] On the 18th of June in 1511 he passed the exams and thus earned his first academic degree.[61] The official records are of the mundane sort that one expects from administrative documents,[62] but a more extravagant description of Melanchthon's prowess appeared in Viet Winsheim's graveside address. The former classmate recollected that his friend had been a marvel at solving logical problems: modal propositions, the reality of universals, problems as complicated as a "Gordian knot," all these the student Melanchthon "unraveled...and [he] removed these rivalries to the great admiration of all."[63] Was Winsheim's recollection merely an apocryphal form of funereal eloquence, as Wiedenhofer believed it was?[64] Perhaps. Nevertheless, the image fits with what the other evidence suggests: Philip had begun to find himself, in spite of initial entry into the older philosophy, within the methodological techniques of South German nominalism. In the next chapter we shall show how this philosophical-linguistic process continued at Tübingen under exposure to a great variety of influences there, and how it prepared the way for his encounter with the theology of Martin Luther.

Notes to Chapter 1

1. For useful accounts of Melanchthon's early childhood, J. Camerarius, *De vita Philippi Melanchthonis narratio*, Recensuit, notas, documenta, bibliothecam librorum Melanchthonis aliaque addidit. Ge. Theodor. Strobelius, Praefatus est Iohannes Auc. Noessell, Halle 1777, pp. 1ff.; K. Hartfelder, *Philipp Melanchthon als Praeceptor Germaniae*, Berlin 1889, pp. 1ff.; C. Manschreck, *Melanchthon: The Quiet Reformer*, New York/Nashville 1958, pp. 27ff.; W. Maurer, *Der junge Melanchthon*, Bd. 1, Göttingen 1967, pp. 14ff.

2. C. Manschreck, *op. cit.*, pp. 29f.

3. *Ibid.*

4. W. Maurer, *op. cit.*, pp. 15f. and references.

5. *CR* XXVII, p. 2.

6. W. Maurer, *op. cit.*, p. 8.

7. J. Camerarius, *op. cit.*, p. 8, "Illis temporibus literarum ludus Phorcensis celebrari prae ceteris." See J. Pflüger, *Geschichte der Stadt Pforzheim*, Pforzheim 1862, pp. 193ff., for a similar judgment.

8. J. Haller, *Die Anfänge der Universität Tübingen, 1477-1537*, Stuttgart 1927, Bd. I, p. 263; Bd. II, pp. 99, 108; and W. Maurer, *op. cit.*, p. 20.

9. K. Hartfelder, *op. cit.*, p. 7.

10. J. Camerarius, *op. cit.*, p. 8.

11. W. Maurer, *op. cit.*, p. 20.

12. *Ibid.*

13. *Ibid.*, p. 202; Also P. Meinhold, *Philipp Melanchthon: Der Lehrer der Kirche*, Berlin 1960, pp. 9ff., on the curriculum.

14. L. Spitz, "Reuchlin's Philosophy: Pythagoras and Cabala for Christ," in *Archiv für Reformationsgeschichte*, 47, 1956, p. 9.

15. P. Joachimsen, "Der Humanismus und die Entwicklung des deutschen Geistes," *Gesammelte Aufsätze*, (hrsg.) N. Hammerstein, Aalen 1970, pp. 325ff.; also H. Oberman, *Werden und Wertung der Reformation*, Tübingen 1977, pp. 56ff., on the *devotio moderna* in Germany.

16. J. Camerarius, *op. cit.*, p. 9.

17. The story that Philip himself directed the play is apocryphal. So W. Maurer, *op. cit.*, p. 20.

18. H. Holstein, *Johann Reuchlins Komödien*, Halle 1888, pp. 11ff.

19. W. Maurer, *op. cit.*, pp. 20f.

20. *Ibid.*

21. E. G. Rupp, *Luther's Progress to the Diet of Worms*, (London 1951), New York/Evanston 1964, p. 25.

22. J. Camerarius, *op. cit.*, pp. 11f.

23. W. Maurer, *op. cit.*, pp. 23ff.; cf. G. Töpke, *Die Matrikel der Universität Heidelberg*, Heidelberg 1884, p. 18.

24. W. Maurer, *op. cit.*, p. 23; K. Hartfelder, *op. cit.*, pp. 18ff., contains the most useful account of Spangel and Melanchthon that we have been able to find.

25. K. Hartfelder, *op. cit.*, p. 18.

26. *Ibid.*

27. W. Maurer, *op. cit.*, p. 23.

28. *Ibid.*; and K. Hartfelder, *op. cit.*, pp. 19ff.

29. K. Hartfelder, *op. cit.*, p. 4 in ref. to *Modus praedicandi subtili et compendiosus Stephani Hoest theologi viae modernae heidelbergensis*, 1513.

30. *Ibid.*, pp. 15ff.
31. *Ibid.*
32. CR III, p. 673.
33. *Ibid.*
34. *Ibid.*
35. W. Maurer, *op. cit.*, p. 24.
36. CR XI, p. 439; and K. Hartfelder, *op. cit.*, pp. 15ff.
37. Hartfelder placed Spangel in the *via antiqua* in the tradition of Thomas Aquinas, *ibid.*
38. W. Maurer, *op. cit.*, p. 24.
39. *Ibid.*
40. On Wimpfeling, G. Knod, "Wimpfeling und die Universität Heidelberg," *Zeitschrift für die Geschichte des Oberrheins*, 40, 1886, pp. 331ff.; G. Ritter, *Die Heidelberger Universität*, Bd. I, (1306-1509), Heidelberg 1939, pp. 483ff.; and O. Herding (ed.), *Jakob Wimpfelings Adolescentia*, Munich 1965; W. Maurer, *op. cit.*, p. 24f., was the first, and remains the most penetrating analysis of Wimpfeling's influence on the thinking of Melanchthon.
41. W. Maurer, *op. cit.*, pp. 24f.
42. We found a rare edition of this work in the University Library of Tübingen, published in Basel, 1503. In his introductory remarks Wimpfeling wrote in unflattering terms of the state of linguistic usage in theology and preaching in Swabian pulpits: "...audivi ego quosdam doctissimos et profundissimos theologos nobiscum consentire, qui et ipsi abhorrent et fastidiunt hanc rusticissimam resolucionem et supervacuam rusticitatem. Saepe et multum id detestatus est Pallas [Spangel] et Jo. Kaisersbergus uterque et praestantissimus theologus et concionator, et observandissimus mihi praeceptores quorum sententiae plus tribuo quam illis ineptis insulsi depravatoribus latinae et graecae linguae."
43. J. Wimpfeling, *Rhetorica Jacobi Wimpfelingi pueris utilissima*, Pforzheim 1509, E8, "Indignum est eum, qui se magno sumptu et acri labore septem disciplinarum (quas liberales vocant) tandem gradum aliquem attigisse profitetur, ne rhetoricae quidem tenuissima rudimenta degustavisse."
44. *Ibid.*, "Ex Aristotele, Cicerone et Quintiliano comportasse...possitis."
45. *Ibid.*, F, "...finis huius generis demonstrativi est, non solum benedicare, sed etiam ad honeste vivendum alios incitare."
46. *Ibid.*
47. This proposal seems not yet to have established deep roots in the secondary literature, but is essential to Maurer's overall thesis. In the course of our studies we have come gradually to believe that Maurer was exactly correct in his judgment that, with respect to his philosophy of language, Erasmus was a secondary rather than primary influence upon Melanchthon. This point and references to Maurer will emerge and unfold variously in the following chapter.
48. W. Maurer, *op. cit.*, p. 24.
49. O. Herding, *op. cit.*, pp. 16, 22, 60 for discussion of its contents; also K. Hartfelder, *op. cit.*, pp. 31ff.; and W. Maurer, *op. cit.*, pp. 25f.
50. W. Maurer, *op. cit.*, p. 25.
51. *Ibid.*
52. *Ibid.*
53. *Ibid.*
54. H. Oberman, *op. cit.*, p. 46.
55. Text in *SM* I, p. 1; also K. Hartfelder, *op. cit.*, p. 31, and his comments on its style.
56. W. Maurer, *op. cit.*, p. 26.

57. *SM* I, pp. 2f.; K. Hartfelder, *op. cit.*, p. 31, text, p. 32, commentary; also *CR* X, p. 669.
58. K. Hartfelder, *op. cit.*, pp. 24ff.
59. *Ibid.*, p. 26.
60. *Ibid.*, pp. 27f.
61. *Ibid.*, p. 28 and n. 2.
62. *Ibid.*, "Philippus Schwarzerdt bretanus defecit in duabus ordinariis responsionibus et una extraordinaria, pro quibus casu, quo promotus fuerit, bis disputabit."
63. *Ibid.*, p. 74, n. 9.
64. S. Wiedenhofer, *Formalstrukturen humanistischer und reformatorischer Theologie bei Philipp Melanchthon*, Bd. II, Bern/Frankfurt/München 1976, p. 74, n. 9.

CHAPTER 2

The Years as Student and Teacher at Tübingen

"In that time the fame of the University of Tübingen...was becoming greater...every day...." (J. Camerarius, *De vita Philippi Melanchthonis narratio*, Halle 1777, p. 13.)

"...so great was his power of mind, and ardor for learning, that he believed there was nothing he should not undertake and understand." (*Ibid.*, p. 15.)

Tübingen and Its Intellectual Climate

In this chapter we shall examine Melanchthon's passage from the rank of beginner into that of mature classicist and teacher of the liberal arts. The discussion will be centered first upon the academic environment in which Melanchthon pursued his studies at Tübingen; secondly, upon the several scholarly works which he produced while teaching there as *Magister Artium* from 1514-1517. Among the main influences upon him were the works of Reuchlin and John Stöffler (both of whom were fascinated by Pythagorean idealism and astrology), the rhetorical methods of Heinrich Bebel (it seems more a negative influence than a constructive one) and professors of theology Wendelin Steinbach, an academic grandson, through Gabriel Biel, of the great Occam, and Jacob Lemp, who represented the *via antiqua* at Tübingen and had been Reuchlin's teacher.

As a teacher, writer and co-worker with Thomas Anselm in his publishing house, Melanchthon was touched by other currents of thought as well, including the writings of Agricola and Erasmus and a fresh interpretation of Aristotle that he developed in the context of lectures on dialectic under Franz Stadian. In the discussion of Melanchthon's own texts it will become clear how these diverse influences became the materials from which a gifted young classicist fashioned his linguistic system. We shall see how this system emerged from within a larger epistemic, metaphysical and moral framework, and how Philip had begun to shape (and be shaped by) an intricate concept of "literary authority" which would powerfully affect his construal and use of Scripture.

Upon passing his examination for the baccalaureate degree at Heidelberg, Melanchthon applied for permission to study for the master's degree.[1] The authorities were reluctant to admit him because, according to one account, "er so jung und kindisches Ansehens war."[2] Maurer has argued rather convincingly that this reason must have been a pretext to disguise deeper reservations. Comparative accounts show that he would not have been unusually young for pursuit of advanced studies.[3] Whatever the truth of the matter, an offended Melanchthon did not wait long to shake the dust off his feet and go to the next town.

While intrigue may have been brewing behind the scenes at Heidelberg, there were good independent reasons for going to Tübingen, anyway. The reputation of this relatively young university was on the upswing.[4] Furthermore, it must have held out some attraction for Philip that Reuchlin himself was actively involved as a frequent visitor there,[5] and that two of his former teachers from Pforzheim, Latinist John Hildebrandt and old friend George Simler, had joined the faculty.[6] According to the official documents, Melanchthon entered the university as candidate for the degree of *Magister Artium* on the 17th of September 1512.

It seems that Melanchthon, as he had begun to do at Heidelberg, preferred to place himself methodologically within the fraternity of nominalism. In spite of considerable contention over the subject in this century, the evidence seems to us clearly to warrant no other conclusion. Primary textual evidence is the detailed testimony of Camerarius which until recently was never put in doubt. The reader must here permit us a lengthy citation from this most interesting text.

> At the time the study of philosophy, by which theology was enveloped, was divided chiefly into two parties. One of these defended the Platonic opinion on ideas or forms, [i.e.,] as abstract and separate from those things, whose physical mass is subject to the senses.... These were named realists [*Reales isti sunt nominati*]. The other party, more following Aristotle, was teaching that the species [or idea] is inferred from the whole group of things, which have their own nature, and that this notion, existing as   drawn from individual instances, is

conceived by the understanding. [They taught] that these natures preceded neither the individuals nor the thing, but consisted in name only: They were called nominalists and modernists [*Nominales appellati fuere et moderni*].[7]

Each side, wrote Camerarius, had its own "leaders and authors," and sometimes gentlemanly debate fermented into fisticuffs: "And so there were not only debates and quarrels between the dissenting parties, but also combats and fights were engaged upon."[8] Where did Melanchthon stand amid the tumult? Camerarius wrote believably of his friend's mediating disposition that he "did not love . . . the disputations,"[9] but that he did align himself with a preference for the methods of Aristotle. "Philip approved a sure method of teaching and arguing, and he perceived that Aristotle held the first rank in matters of this sort."[10] Moreover, although he asserted his own beliefs, and had little trouble defending them against criticism, the young Preceptor did what he could to bring about reconciliation between the two parties, so that in spite of differences of opinion a "union of wills" might obtain among the scholars.[11]

Camerarius's portrayal leaves the same impression as Vinsheim's graveside speech: Melanchthon was absorbed in the theoretical problems of his day, but was as conciliatory as he was brilliant in solving them. He seems to have taken a strong position and to have placed himself within the general framework of nominalism, but also to have drawn lines of mediation between the camps in order to avoid extremism and unnecessary bitterness. It is not difficult to imagine Melanchthon in this role. His instinctive response to conflict was always to look for common ground and eventual consensus between factions. One might say that for Melanchthon the existence of factions was simply against the natural system of things. We shall see that he rejected any attempt to polarize the ontologies of Aristotle and Plato. Nevertheless, his model of language was more directly indebted to the works of Aristotle. The irenic commitment of Melanchthon's later thought and practice as a rhetorician would have been the natural evolution of his approach as pictured by Camerarius. For these reasons and others most have taken it for granted that Melanchthon was officially enrolled in the faculty of the *moderni*, and that this is of some importance to viewing him in the larger sense of his development.[12] In what ways this context is important remains to be seen.

However, at the beginning of this century the writings of Müller, Clemen and Hermelink set off a controversy on the subject, and several recent scholars have followed them in the view that Melanchthon was after all a member of the rival party.[13] The most recent and forceful assembly of evidence in support of the revised view is that of Wiedenhofer. The main ground for doubting the initial assumption is a letter that Clemen and Müller found as they were editing the *Supplementa Melanchthoniana*. To their wonderment Melanchthon had, on the 20th of August in 1516, written to the abbot of the cloister in nearby Alpirsbach and commended the realists at Tübingen for their true Christian zeal.[14] They drew the conclusion that Melanchthon must thus have been an official member of the older way.[15] A second argument derives from the historical premise set forth by Haller that Camerarius's depiction of the *Wegestreite* as actually coming to violence greatly overstated the matter of students' philosophical intensity at the time and served mainly to make Melanchthon out (in the bitter climate later on in the century) to be a grand peacemaker.[16] Wiedenhofer has offered two further arguments of his own: Melanchthon would not have had time both to switch faculties and finish his M.A. within two years as he did, and Camerarius did not make the explicit claim that Melanchthon *belonged* to the modernist faculty, but only that he preferred the didactic methods of Aristotle.[17] Taken in the light of the previous points, these add support to the conclusion that Melanchthon studied with the realists.

None of these arguments seems either valid or sound, however. That Melanchthon wrote on behalf of the realists no more implies his membership than his commendatory prefaces to Wimpfeling's writings implied that he belonged to his teacher's fraternity of scholars. Maurer quite sensibly interpreted the letter rather as support for the claim that Philip took every opportunity to create good will between the warring camps. "Is it not possible that he performed this service for a friend without belonging to his fraternity? Indeed, Camerarius viewed things correctly: he counts Melanchthon among the . . . modernists (which he believed had a better reading of Aristotle) but stresses his peaceable manner."[18] Secondly, Haller's proposal that philosophical differences could not have run so deep as to cause riots seems, in view of Oberman's recent (and more textually thorough) research, more gratuitous than solidly grounded in evidence. In Oberman's judgment, it is precisely this description of "bellicose rivalries" that best comports with recent evidence and enhances the stature of Camerarius as a reliable source.[19] Thirdly, it is precarious to say with finality that Melanchthon could not have completed his program within a span of two years. He was brilliant, and he had already read widely outside the curriculum in which he had done his examinations at Heidelberg. We have all known fast workers, who have managed to complete in two years what would normally take three or even four to accomplish. Finally, it seems very difficult to avoid the conclusion that, by associating Melanchthon with Aristotle (whom he had just identified as the metaphysical flag-bearer of nominalism), Camerarius clearly meant to connect his friend with the fraternity most devoted to this philosopher.

The weight of the evidence favors the view that Melanchthon studied with the faculty of the modernists, whose linguistic methods and values he found useful and right. We shall see that this view is further supported by his apparent preference for Wendelin Steinbach's theological methods over those of the realist Jacob Lemp and also by indirect evidence from later writings which suggest an initial devotion to the school of Occam.[20] This is not to say that his philosophy was categorically nominalistic; his stress on innate structures (to be discussed momentarily) provided an epistemological balance and stability, one might even suggest naiveté,[21] that would forever be his trademark as a thinker.[22] Nevertheless, the point we wish to make is that he developed his great skills as a theoretical and practicing linguist, dialectician and rhetorician within the school of nominalism that existed in Tübingen at the beginning of the century. Knowing this is useful in working out the several sides to his distinctive identity as a Christian humanist in the pre-Lutheran years[23] and in getting at the very slippery issue of similarities and differences between him and Luther.[24] It will also help us define the larger metaphysical context of his later work as a theologian and hermeneuticist on many levels, particularly when we come to the controversial questions about faith and reason in his early Lutheranism.[25]

Melanchthon completed his studies for the degree in January of 1514.[26] During these two years the work which he had begun in Pforzheim and Heidelberg ripened into mature form. He polished his already considerable skills in the study of Greek under the direct supervision of Reuchlin.[27] His study of rhetoric included hearing the lectures of Heinrich Bebel, described by one author as "Tübingen's greatest humanist."[28] Recent studies have been less generous, however,[29] and the sources make it doubtful that Bebel had a deep or lasting influence on Melanchthon as a rhetorician. Reuchlin once lamented the "puerile" level of Bebel's Latin and Greek,[30] and an older Melanchthon, referring to his Tübingen experience, would recall, "insigniter ibi deliravit Bebelius."[31]

A brighter light on the horizon was Melanchthon's study of dialectic, which became deeply important to his progress in developing a theoretical basis for the trivium.[32] He began attending the lectures of Franz Stadian in the winter of 1514.[33] Only a year and a half separated them in age, and they quickly became friends.[34] Stadian was a passionate devotee of Aristotle, whose works he had devoured and learned "magna cum laude," as Melanchthon put it.[35] In the course of Stadian's lectures on the *Second Analytics*, Philip introduced his teacher to a work from the fourth century by Themistios.[36] This Latin translation by Hermolaos in Venice of a Greek paraphrase of the *Second Analytics*[37] contained what Melanchthon and Stadian believed was a revolutionary new thesis about the scope of Aristotle's philosophy. Together they began to explore an idea that would become fundamental to Melanchthon's world view. Their dream of publishing an entirely new text of Aristotle never materialized,[38] but Melanchthon emerged from their discoveries having pioneered what Maurer has reckoned among the "most original work in the history of philosophy in the sixteenth century."[39] The hermeneutical framework for this contribution was a fresh interpretation of Aristotle's work as a whole. Professional scholars treated it as a speculative system of metaphysics in its essential nature and purpose. In contrast, the writing of Themistios convinced Melanchthon and Stadian that Aristotle had been motivated by much more practical concerns than those of scholastic metaphysicians. The direction of his thought was in fact not at all toward otherworldly truth, but rather toward this world. The true essence of Aristotle's system, they believed, was its *scope* and *teleological* function as rhetoric. Exactly what Melanchthon meant by "rhetoric," how he understood it to be used philosophically by Aristotle to bring coherence and practical power to the entire *orbis artium* and how he, Melanchthon, would develop these thoughts in linguistic directions of his own, will require intricate and extensive discussion through the next two chapters. Nevertheless, it must be noted, here, that

Melanchthon's work on Aristotle's dialectic was a development of the philosophical view of literature which he had begun to learn from Spangel (through Agricola) and Wimpfeling. A positive relationship between rhetorical and logical methods was essential to the success of human studies in the schools and larger society. We also agree with Maurer that this vision of a "purified" interpretation (not simply or even through, in this instance, a purified original text) of Aristotle went well beyond the horizon of Reuchlin's humanism and its somewhat uncritical reception of Florentine Platonism.[40] Melanchthon's humanism, for all its varied elements, was from the beginning inseparable from the semantical and logical contours of Aristotelian thought, and in that sense was never lacking in the medieval scholastic concern for precision of structure in language and the essential relation between truth and rational coherence of terms and propositions. No doubt Maier was correct in disparaging Melanchthon's use of Aristotle as "flattened,"[41] although perhaps not as correct as he thought he was.[42] The point here is that, while Melanchthon shared the common concerns of humanists like Reuchlin and Erasmus, his program was from very early on secured (more so than were theirs)[43] by a theory of knowledge that gave fundamental importance to the logical operations of the intellect, even as he viewed the mind as the essential link between people and their external world of moral action.

In Melanchthon's study of the mathematical and natural sciences the professor who seems to have made the greatest impression on him was John Stöffler.[44] Stöffler, a friend of Reuchlin (who helped him with Hebrew in exchange for explanations of astral phenomena),[45] was a firm believer in astrological prediction, and in his lectures he included the ancient works of Pythagoras, Zoroaster and Plato; as well as more recent texts, such as Gregor Reisch's *Margarita Philosophica*, a compendium of the physical sciences in which great stress is placed upon the practical value of such studies, because of the essential connection between the human and natural orders.[46] Melanchthon's enduring belief in the doctrines of innate knowledge and the orderly design of the physical universe gained, here, a highly articulated and compelling form.[47] What Maurer has called Melanchthon's "natural piety" (*Naturfrömmigkeit*), the basis of his "natural theology,"[48] was developed during these studious beginnings. His debt to Stöffler will become clearer in our discussion of the declamation *De artibus liberalibus*, written in 1517 and dedicated to this teacher. It is apparent that, if the philosophical context of his linguistic theory was that of a disciplined nominalism that was rooted methodologically in Aristotle, Melanchthon's epistemological and ontological framework was that of the Italian Platonism and Pythagoreanism that he had begun to learn from his teachers at Pforzheim. It is not true that these initially disparate traditions created irreconcilable, countervailing forces within his world view.[49] Rather, we shall observe once again his inclination to synthesize competing theories into coherent form.

After completing his examinations to become Master of Arts in January of 1514, Melanchthon remained at Tübingen as a *Konventor*, or instructor of courses for new students.[50] The statutes of the university required that beginning instructors do advanced studies in one of the three higher faculties: medicine, law or theology.[51] The evidence favors the view of Heyd and Wiedenhofer that Melanchthon spent these two years with the theological faculty.[52] This judgment is supported by the testimony of Camerarius who wrote of his friend's great interest in theology: "His desire was especially inclined towards the study of theology, for he was aflame with love for religious piety."[53] As Wiedenhofer has correctly pointed out, the unusually brief time that it took Melanchthon to complete the baccalaureate degree at Wittenberg suggests almost certainly that earlier studies had been transferred and credited to his required work.[54] Maurer has observed, moreover, that with the exception of Stöffler, "it was almost only theologians whom Melanchthon later considered his authoritative teachers at Tübingen."[55] When one considers that Melanchthon went to Wittenberg with more than a neophyte's grasp of the subject, his ready comprehension of Luther's theology and its significance in the contemporary theological setting and his headlong plunge into the sea of public theological polemics seem somewhat less astonishing than otherwise.

So unlike Faust, who "leider auch" studied theology, Philip elected to pursue the "queen of the sciences" with a native interest in the subject matter. His professors of theology were Jacob Lemp, who represented the faculty of the *via antiqua*,[56] and Wendelin Steinbach, the student of Gabriel Biel (who was a student of Occam) who represented the modernists.[57] We are persuaded by the sources that Maurer's assessment of Melanchthon's pre-Lutheran theological preferences is correct,[58] and that the views of Wiedenhofer on this subject are vulnerable to criticism.[59] In Maurer's judgment, Melanchthon found much to admire in the work of Steinbach, but held Lemp in very low esteem. In September of 1521, Melanchthon wrote of Lemp to fellow classicist Willibald Pirckheimer: "And there reigned in that place [Tübingen] certain unlearned ones, unless one might wish to count the theologian Lemp among the learned, that first among *ton matailogon*."[60] There is some question about the meaning of the term used by Melanchthon to describe Lemp. Both Wiedenhofer and the editors of *Melanchthons Werke* have suspected an allusion to typically Erasmian expressions which would suggest an almost jargon-like satirical synonym for "scholastic," that is, someone really not up to an acceptable level of erudition.[61] A more literal translation would be something like "chatterbox," or "babbler." Neither sense of the term is complimentary. Nevertheless, Wiedenhofer, persisting in the assertion that Melanchthon's framework was "Erasmian" and thus in accord theoretically with the realism of Lemp (and Reuchlin), has taken this expression to mean something like respectful indulgence: "He was a 'scholastic,' but, as 'scholastics' go, he wasn't such a bad sort."[62] While this rendering is perhaps possible on purely grammatical and literary grounds, it seems to us most difficult to sustain by weight of evidence, and simply improbable on other considerations.

Wiedenhofer's two arguments can be dealt with briefly. The first is that Melanchthon belonged to the *via antiqua*, and that, therefore, his sympathies would have been with the style of Lemp.[63] Secondly, a fictional letter, written in the style of the famed *Letter to Obscure Men* by one "John Kraft," satirically professed amazement that Melanchthon would attack the theological faculty of the Sorbonne in Paris (which he had done in the year 1521).[64] The letter concluded, however, that there may be a certain logic to it after all, since Melanchthon always did so dearly love Scotistic theology, the chief rival of the Parisian party.[65] Even if Melanchthon had belonged to the *via antiqua*, which it seems clear that he did not, the inference begs questions that are pressed forward by the evidence that he was unimpressed by Lemp himself. (Of course, if he did not belong to the *via antiqua*, then there is no argument to be made from this premise at all.) Secondly, "John Kraft's" claim that Philip had always loved Duns Scotus is so outrageous, as is the entire letter, that those who knew Philip must have laughed till they cried.[66] As we shall see, Melanchthon's critical judgment of the Sorbonne grew from attachment to the substance of Luther's theology, not from a prior disposition against the school of nominalism; in fact, earlier loyalties may have intensified his disappointment and his willingness to engage precisely this party in debate.

Moreover, in the only other clear reference to Lemp in Melanchthon's later writings, his verdict was unequivocally negative toward his brand of scholasticism.

> I remember that once in Tübingen Lemp portrayed transubstantiation on the chalkboard. I was amazed at the tastelessness of the man; neither then nor now do I wish to foster abuses of the sacrament by citing counterfeit opinions....[67]

There is thus good reason to agree with Maurer[68] that Melanchthon recalled his own sentiments accurately and that these words signified more than a minor "qualification," to use Wiedenhofer's term.[69] There is some reason, though, for surprise at the forcefulness of Melanchthon's critique, for Reuchlin had once praised Lemp as the theologian from whom he had learned his entire theology,[70] and there was polite respect between Lemp and Melanchthon's revered teacher Wimpfeling.[71] It would be interesting to explore Maurer's suggestion that these things revealed an ominous rift already between Reuchlin and his grandnephew that was rooted in deeper differences between them on truth and method.[72] Flights of speculative imagination, whether those of an aging scholastic writing on the chalkboard or a Christian Platonist delving into the numerology of Cabala, all were distasteful to him. It was neither in his nature nor in his theory of truth and language to grant to such pursuits an authoritative or even a positive status. They violated his canons of *proprietas dicendi* (in ways that astrology apparently did not). We believe that there is important truth in Maurer's words about this scene in Lemp's lecture hall toward the end of Melanchthon's time in Tübingen: "it is a symptom of the inner change, which had already begun in him at that time, and would soon lead him away out of Reuchlin's fatherly care."[73]

The main theological authority for Melanchthon at Tübingen seems to have been the Occamist Steinbach, of whom years later he wrote respectfully, "Steinbach, along with Gabriel Biel, Steinbach's predecessor, and Konrad Summenhart, could be reckoned among those earlier theologians who were holy and of worth."[74] He explained that "...Wendelin, since he was an assiduous reader of Augustine and of the sacred books, saw that there were many errors in the writings of Thomas and Scotus."[75] The older Melanchthon's account is quite revealing, particularly in the light of Oberman's research into connections between the theology of Steinbach and that of his Occamist master, Gabriel Biel.[76] Steinbach's essay on the mystery of the Eucharist[77] exemplifies his theological style, which he modeled largely on the Frenchman Gerson.[78] Steinbach's was a method that must have been attractive to the young Melanchthon: its main traits were stress on the limits and boundaries of human language before its sacred subject,[79] a propriety of topical selection favoring matters which were suitable to human capacities and could be put into coherent language,[80] and placing the focus upon the experiential meaning and realities made present thereby. As Oberman put it (and one ponders the contrast to Lemp), "a piety of the Lord's Supper [*Abendmahlsfrömmigkeit*] must accomplish everything that a theology of the Lord's Supper [*Abendmahlstheologie*] might have offered."[81] It was Steinbach's theologically "pious rhetoric"[82] which formed a theoretical and spiritual bond between the *via moderna* at Tübingen and a South German humanism that was deeply motivated by the concerns of a "new" rhetoric.[83] And again Oberman must be cited: "Its strength was from the beginning onward in the realm of dialectic and in the clear definition of concepts and terms...."[84]

Maurer has rightly understood the significance of Steinbach for the young Melanchthon: "the path to Luther clearly was made easier for him working from these [Steinbach's] assumptions."[85] The "common dependency upon Biel is helpful for understanding the theology of the Reformation."[86] And the remarkable intersection of fifteenth and sixteenth century philosophical and theological patterns in the larger arena of European history was also true of Melanchthon; indeed, the one cannot be fully understood without the other. The essential elements of this intersection are strikingly familiar to anyone who has read the later Melanchthon: an economy (*Sparsamkeit*) of words, and "the attempt to reduce all theological assertions to the religious essentials."[87]

In his contact with Biel (through Steinbach), Melanchthon began to cultivate a theological method which comported with the basic values of his linguistic philosophy. The systematic development of a concept or "construal" of Scripture and the hermeneutical formation of a Lutheran theology were partly continuous with these philosophical commitments which Melanchthon had made already under the guidance of his professors and colleagues at Tübingen. While the influence of Luther upon him would be very great, one must also remark upon the nature and extent of such developments in his pre-Lutheran time.

Besides Melanchthon's professors, there were others who, mainly through their writings, made an indelible impression upon him. It is well documented that he spent a good share of his time helping out in Thomas Anselm's publishing house.[88] This small printing business was a source of stimulation, for it was "an academy in miniature, stood entirely under Reuchlin's influence and, as the publisher of Reuchlin's writings in the struggle against Cologne, was in the center of public interest."[89] Although he mainly helped with proofreading and preparing texts for publication, the grandnephew of Reuchlin found himself warmly included in elite company. The press was an outlet from the somewhat parochial context of the university into the exciting world of international movements in letters and learning among the avant-garde. His elders awarded him the honor of writing the preface to the *Letters of Illustrious Men*, and he thus was thrust (quite willingly) into public prominence.[90] It was during this period that John Oecolampadius, Reuchlin's good friend (fifteen years older than Melanchthon and former disciple of Wimpfeling at Heidelberg), now in Basel with Erasmus, sent Philip a copy of Agricola's *De inventione dialectica*.[91] A new edition had just come out, and Oecolampadius gave this fine gift to Melanchthon at the behest of the great Erasmus himself.[92] The book proved more an affirmation of his present thinking than it was a profound influence.[93] Nevertheless it must have been a catalyst in the process of gaining a fresh vision of dialectic in service of rhetoric and thus public life.[94] And it had to have been a great source of encouragement to be in good stead with Erasmus.[95]

Perhaps we are in a position now to make some preliminary comments about Erasmus and the extent of his influence upon the young Melanchthon. The Preceptor frequently fell victim in his lifetime to those who cast his views in terms which he felt were simply unfair in their rigidity. The same thing has also occurred in modern historiography. There has been a widespread tendency to think of him in his pre-Lutheran days as an "Erasmian," and in his post-Erasmian days as a "Lutheran" (at least until 1522!). Such categorical treatment leaves the impression that Melanchthon was a sort of human lexicon for reference into minds that were much greater than his own. The element of truth is that he was not a "great man" in the sense that Luther was, nor did he have anything like the breadth and literary powers of Erasmus; and he was greatly dependent upon both of them. It is quite true, as Gordon Rupp has said, that Philip was not "one of the original thinkers of mankind, but one who belonged...to that great band of under-rated and under-estimated men who have had an immeasurable influence for good."[96] Nevertheless, we are certain to underestimate him if we fail carefully to explore and make needed qualifications of these dependencies upon those greater than he.

The subject of Melanchthon's indebtedness to Erasmus requires a subtlety of analysis and comprehensive treatment that we cannot undertake here. However, in the light of our discussion to this point, we can begin to evaluate the thesis that Melanchthon was an "Erasmian." Finer nuances of the relationship between them can be brought out in later sections. Wiedenhofer has given the most recent defense of the thesis that Melanchthon's overall world view was adopted from Erasmus. He has defined "Erasmian humanism" as a propositional system that comprised six doctrines. Firstly, the concept of Christian revelation is "imprinted by a dialectic between revelation and historical reason."[97] Secondly, what separates Christian doctrine from "all human doctrines of salvation" is its heavenly origin.[98] Thirdly, Christ is the *verbum et sermo dei*, the center and moral example of basic Christianity.[99] Fourthly, Holy Scripture is "the deposit of sacred doctrine, the divine books the wellsprings *[fontes]* of theology."[100] Fifthly, Scripture is also "immediately present" to the reader.[101] Finally, there is an ordered union of revelation and reason through Platonic ethics.[102] Wiedenhofer has detected just this framework in the early theology of Melanchthon and has thus labeled him an "Erasmian."[103]

The label "Erasmian" is not altogether inappropriate. Melanchthon did in fact affirm each and every one of the propositions which Wiedenhofer has set forth (experts on Erasmus will have to judge their accuracy) as essential to "Erasmian Christian humanism," and sometimes he used the very same vocabulary, much of which was common parlance among those who looked to Erasmus as head of their literary movement. Transferring methods of textual criticism (seeking the purest sources of truth) to the study of theology owed more to the Dutchman than anyone else. And terms like *ad fontes* and particularly the controversial view of Christ as the *sermo dei* are to be attributed to him.[104] Furthermore, the young Melanchthon's consciousness of Erasmus (and vice versa) is evident from the older man's reference to the younger (in the preface to his *Thessalonians*) as "a promising youngster," who, while still nearly a boy, was a master of languages.[105] In return, Melanchthon wrote two poems in Greek praising Erasmus as a godlike figure in letters and erudition.[106] In a letter from 1514 to his friend Ambrose Blaurer he referred to Erasmus's Latin as the standard: "Latina est. Erasmica est. . ." was the best rating that he could give Blaurer's progress.[107] In another letter, this one to Reuchlin in January of 1518, upon having read Erasmus's *Paraphrases* on Romans, he burst with enthusiasm, "'Oh Zeus!' you will exclaim, 'Oh Brontes!'"[108] Finally, as we shall later see, his textbook on rhetoric, *De rhetorica libri tres*, in which he put forth mainly his philosophy of language and the arts, is sprinkled with references to Erasmus's linguistic writings, *De duplici copia verborum et rerum*,[109] *De ratione studii*[110] and the *Adagiorum collectanea*.[111]

Nevertheless, to put the label "Erasmian Christian humanist" on the young Melanchthon seems a too reductionistic maneuver. On closer analysis, Maurer has adeptly shown that there were many important differences between Melanchthon and Erasmus. "What the young Melanchthon became, as philosopher, historian and as teacher of the natural sciences, he became without Erasmus, indeed, at times in opposition to him."[112] There existed differences between them in their approaches to philosophy,[113] history,[114] the natural order,[115] geography, medicine and astrology.[116] But perhaps most relevant to our own themes is the complex matter of how Melanchthon's rhetorical system ought to be viewed in relation to that of Erasmus. Similarities and dependencies are as obvious as they are numerous, and they will be pointed out in our treatment of his rhetoric in greater detail than is possible here. On the other hand, Melanchthon's independence from Erasmus's system, while not so obvious, is also in evidence and is clearly important to understanding the man as an individual in his own right. Maurer[117] has penetrated more deeply into this subject than anyone else, and our own reading of Melanchthon persuades us that he was essentially right in his main judgments. The independence and originality of Melanchthon's rhetorical theory consisted of diverse but interrelated elements, not just one homogeneous stream of tradition. The pedagogical tradition of which Erasmus was a recent representative was one which the young Melanchthon joined partly through his teachers at Pforzheim, Heidelberg and Tübingen and partly by his own hard work. His world view did not simply come to him as "Erasmian humanism," but rather, as we have seen, in a much more diffuse and particularistic way than most studies would suggest. That is why Maurer has written of Erasmus's influence that "it did not make the young Melanchthon a formally dependent student of Erasmus, but taught him to view the witnesses and masters of ancient rhetoric with his own eyes, and to judge them independently."[118] Furthermore, we would add that this was not merely a difference in context and *Geistesentwicklung*, but was also the manifestation of very different outlooks, including significantly dissimilar dispositions toward dialectic and Aristotle in the context of truth theory.[119] Melanchthon's intent to bring out a fully re-edited text of Aristotle is something that Erasmus no doubt would not have disapproved of, but neither would it have occurred to him to publish such a work.[120] We shall often return to discussion of dialectic and logic in Melanchthon's rhetorical system and later hermeneutical formation of doctrine; along the way we shall occasionally note this same kind of distinction between his methods and those of the great Erasmus. Meanwhile, the many and diverse sources which we have discussed in this part of the present chapter must be kept in view as we now begin to examine Melanchthon's own writings and publications that came gushing forth in an impressive flood from about 1517 onward, and as we seek to give preliminary shape to the central themes of this book.

Melanchthon's Published Works at Tübingen

During his last years at the University of Tübingen, Melanchthon began to merit a reputation as a promising and productive young classicist. While teaching required courses, he also published a steady stream of texts, mainly for use in the classroom. A much needed Greek grammar was perhaps the most notable and influential product among them, but his edition of Terence's comedies, referred to by Baldwin as "the great pedagogical edition of the century,"[121] was used all over Europe and in Britain (where it probably was known to Shakespeare).[122] And there were many other projects, large and small, including the rudiments of his textbooks on rhetoric and dialectic which would come out in Wittenberg in 1519 and 1520. In this second part of the chapter our aim is not merely to chronicle his progress as an author, but as a theoretician and philosopher of the liberal arts. Philip did not operate by the modern principle of "publish or perish"; his written products were born of a clear-headed philosophy of learning and a strong motivation to serve. And it is this philosophy, with its underlying theory of truth, that would eventually give conceptual form to his theology.

Melanchthon's first independent publication was a new edition in 1514 of a Latin grammar entitled *Dialogus mythologicus*. This textbook by Bartholomaus Zehender (or Coloniensis), which had probably been used both at Pforzheim and Tübingen,[123] had already seen four earlier printings and was particularly prized in the Dutch schools, where the influence of the *devotio moderna* could be felt.[124] Melanchthon wrote a new preface, in which he praised its pedagogical virtues.[125] This grammar was a model of its own mission to use language that was "commended by fittingness and purity."[126] Using the metaphor of mythology to state a philosophical premise, Melanchthon stressed that from a proper and right use of words we may know the "minds of the gods..., by the word of power."[127] Zehender had also related his lessons in Latin to the great moral issues of life, and thus accomplished much more than merely teaching grammar: "it prescribes rules of life as much as of speech."[128]

Similar ideas can be found in Melanchthon's preface to the *Letters of Illustrious Men* that came from Anselm's presses in the same year.[129] It seems somewhat surprising that Philip wrote not a word about the bitter controversy itself, and as always his work was without a trace of satire. The preface is a cheerfully unencumbered commendation of Reuchlin's literary style as exemplary for all the *optimi adolescentes*:

> So then, you excellent young men, you have [here] letters composed in pure and perfect style [*sermone puro*] which sheds light on things, what Cicero calls the Latin style; the style is familiar, lucid and concise [*familiari, dilucido ac brevi*]..., and, finally, it is appropriate [*proprio*], so that the matter seems to be expressed as plainly as possible.[130]

In 1516 Melanchthon published his widely acclaimed edition of Terence's comedies which "made his name known in the literary world."[131] In what was by his standards a lengthy preface (to Paul Geraeander)[132] he included a theory of how the Roman comedies had developed from seeds that had been planted by the Greek philosophers and poets. With remarkable maturity of vision,[133] he ventured the proposal that there was an inner unity to all of Greek culture. Its essence was in a reflective moral disposition toward things. All the great Greek authors, Aesop, the oracles, Socrates and Diogenes, aimed at forming models for right living.[134] They did not waste time with trifling matters (*nugatoria*), but instead devoted their lives to what was most useful in shaping the good morals of people and society.[135] Melanchthon traced this tradition all the way back to the most ancient poets and writers such as Homer and Hesiod.[136] Once the Greek *polis* had been created, great poets arose whose purpose in writing public dramas was to summon all their powers of expression to display before the people a "model of living [*vivendi formam*]:... they attempted both to bring profit to good minds [*prodesse bonis mentibus*], and to allure and to influence the people with the theme of virtue [*delectare afficereque virtutis argumento populum*]."[137] First the tragedies were born, under the patronage of Pisistratus.[138] Then followed the comedies, a lighter method of accomplishing the same goal. Melanchthon thus came to his main philosophical point: "And so these are the beginnings of comedy; this is also the goal, that we might use it as a looking glass for directing life [*ceu regundae vitae speculo utamur*]."[139]

The Romans mainly imitated the Greeks, and thus were born the Latin comedies, the very best of which were those of Terence.[140] Melanchthon selected the comedies of Terence, whom both the ancients, such as the great

Quintilian, and giants of the present, such as Erasmus, judged "the best and greatest figure in letters."[141] The greatness of Terence, as with all great writers, was his powerful manner of combining style with morality. "There are many things in this poet which tend to the cultivation of life and character, and of elegance of speech."[142] The ancient playwright was "a master of both oration and life."[143]

The same philosophical humanism was behind Philip's textbook of Greek grammar, *Institutiones Graecae Grammaticae*, which came out in May of 1518.[144] Melanchthon aimed this highly successful book (it would live through eighteen printings in the first half of the century) at the more advanced students,[145] and his preface (to his close friend Bernhard Maurer)[146] reveals its philosophical direction: "The Greek grammar reached well beyond mere pedagogy."[147] Sounding all too familiar to our modern ears, he blamed the troubles of the German nation on poor skills in language. "The [Latin] method of speaking [*dicendi ratio*], and so the very thing which shapes both minds with judgment and morals with refinement, is neglected."[148] The outlook which a proper *ratio dicendi* makes possible is one of clarity of mind and purity of heart. It was on these fundamental levels of our humanity that this textbook on grammar was to have made its contribution. "This alone is the genius of the work, that it might be profitable [*ut prosit*]."[149]

The spirit of these first publications is clearly that of a South German humanism which was infected with an almost religious faith in language and an almost linguistic philosophy of religion. By using the metaphor "minds of the gods" (and here we observe a very qualified nominalism), Melanchthon gave expression to his belief that words, when rightly used, would open the way to eternal truths, and to our being truly human. In putting out the Greek grammar, the edition of Terence and several lesser works, he sought to become more than a schoolmasterly technician; his aim was nothing less than helping professors and their students throughout Germany and Europe make the vivifying and redeeming connection between disciplined speech and the deepest truths of moral life, *oratio et vita*.

One of the fullest presentations of Melanchthon's pre-Lutheran philosophy is the declamation *De artibus liberalibus oratio Philippo Melanchthone Tubingae anno 1517*.[150] As its title states, the oration was about the liberal arts. Melanchthon counted them in the traditional way as grammar, dialectic, rhetoric (the *trivium*), arithmetic, geometry, music and astronomy (the *quadrivium*),[151] to which he added history and poetry.[152] The occasion for this writing is somewhat mysterious. It appears to have been an edited version of a declamation that Philip gave while still at Heidelberg, perhaps for his examinations.[153] He had evidently rewritten it on an unspecified occasion at Tübingen. The style is unusually complex and cumbersome for someone who publicly professed the "plain" Latin style of Cicero and Reuchlin, and it suffers from an abundance of obscure literary allusions which serve more to intimidate the reader than to illumine the subject. Parts of it are nearly impossible even for experts in Latin to follow easily, and this was probably true for the original audience.[154] It is difficult to avoid thinking that he wrote it that way on purpose. He was given to condescending moods toward the end of his stay at the university; he lamented in letters to Reuchlin that Tübingen was to him a "workhouse" in which he was being tormented, a place worse even than the cave of Heraclitus, and that he was regressing to become again a "boy among boys."[155] In any event, the style certainly matched the tone of his opening remarks, in which he scolded those whom he anticipated might lack the powers of concentration necessary to comprehend his meaning. Such lackluster hearers might just as well get up from their chairs and leave![156] And the opening anecdote of Socrates visiting a philosophy class where the students were lost, reminds one of that all too familiar scene: a brilliant young graduate, full of himself and his grand ideas, faced by the stares of freshmen who have not yet caught fire. No doubt Melanchthon meant it when he said, "wisdom, that most holy thing, does not belong to all."[157] And perhaps he believed it when he assured them that his message would be clear to those in possession of "good minds," who were accustomed to listening for substance and did not need to be entertained.[158]

The declamation is not merely about the liberal arts, but about the philosophical foundations beneath them. "The arts," he wrote, were "ministers of philosophy [*administras philosophiae*]."[159] Using the imagery of the Socratic demon, he wrote of the transcendent status of philosophy, its "head" hidden behind heavenly clouds, breathing forth something greater than merely human wisdom; it was the "voice of the demon [*Ea est vox daemonii*]." His point was that, because the arts themselves originated from this transcendent "voice," they were valid for men everywhere. Perhaps one can detect something of his declining enthusiasm for an extreme realism in his recollection that the earlier version had overstated this point. "This was my aim at that time, since I wished to derive the arts from their original sources [*suis fontibus*]: to show that their first principles are inherent in the nature of the mind [*animi naturae...insita earumi nitia*]."[160] The assertion was about the ontological structure of this world and of the human mind; the cosmic order was, he had argued, the same everywhere: "For just as the nature of the good and the just is the same for all races, under every sky (the sources of justice are the same), so is knowledge of nature everywhere the same (when effort is also equal), and to put it comprehensively, King Jupiter is the same to all."[161] Here is clear indication of Melanchthon's greater interest in logical *fontes* than in those that one considers in textual criticism.

In this second version it seems that Melanchthon adopted a modified stance, making it clear that his concern was with innate structures, and not with ideas that could be abstracted from language. No passage in the earliest texts communicates his sense of carved epistemological design better than this one does.

> My present concern is with the knowledge of nature, not with the voice of the demon; and I believe [this knowledge], appropriate to our natures, comes by the use of reason [*putoque nostris ingeniis propria, rationis usu contingit*]. It lies partly in language, partly in things. [*Ea est in oratione partim, partim in*

rebus.] The knowledge of things comes first, but we shall speak in the common manner. Those things which pertain to language are considered the first principles of training young minds. [*Quae ad sermonem spectant, ingeniorum puerilium exercendi habentur initia.*] [162]

As Maurer has also observed, this passage sheds light on the problem of how Melanchthon held together the main epistemological elements of his linguistic theory. By connecting nature with the voice of the demon, "...Melanchthon established the bond between the 'modern' epistemology and Platonism."[163] As Camerarius has shown, this was a metaphysic of mediation between the extremes of an "otherworldly" realism and a "too-worldly" nominalism. Melanchthon was a philosophical realist, and would always remain one, in the sense that he believed knowledge corresponded to and derived from the essential nature of things; he was a nominalist in the sense that he believed language was an essential condition for truth—the better the language, the clearer the truth, which was thus "partim in oratione, partim in rebus." What he meant by the concepts of language (*oratio*) and truth, and how these would eventually shape his literary theories, and they his doctrine of Scripture, will become clear in the chapters ahead.

Just how deeply into the substance of things Melanchthon believed human reason to be capable of going is a most difficult subject.[164] It would seem that there was some ambiguity in his epistemological dislike for what he regarded as scholastic flights of fanciful metaphysical speculation, on the one hand, and his realism, which extended logically to his theology, on the other. We shall later explore the view that this very philosophical tension manifested itself in several ways during Melanchthon's career as a theologian, particularly in developing a doctrine of God.[165] On another level, it helps to clarify the unusual make-up of a man who was as famous for his diffidence and humility as he was for his stubbornness and intellectual self-esteem.

In any event, one must notice the theoretical view of the *trivium* which Melanchthon advanced in this declamation. The basic linguistic disciplines of grammar, dialectic and rhetoric together made possible disciplined language. Again using mythological images, he expressed their inner unity by comparing them with "three strings in the harmony of the Lyre, the playing of the three Muses."[166] Everyone acknowledged the fundamental position of grammar, and so this required no defense.[167] For Melanchthon, the deepest issue was not language as grammar, but rather as dialectic, and of course by that he did not mean simply the logic of propositions, but the semantic ordering of thought in pursuit of knowledge. The focus of the speech (and of the next years of his classical labors) was upon the nature and purpose of dialectic in the whole scheme of education through the *orbis artium*.

The art of dialectic was "a subtle method of discourse [*subtilis disserendi ratio*]," but more than this: "if it may be put somewhat more boldly, it alone, in my view, can be considered the mother of all the arts [*sola mihi omnium mater artium*]."[168] Without dialectic all attempts to become learned will be in vain.[169] The first example was notably Aristotle, a wise man (*vir animi sagax*), whose dialectic was more skillful and erudite than anyone else's[170] and who could "pierce through to the very depths of everyone's thoughts, as with a Delphic sword."[171] Aristotle "performs *inventio, dispositio,* is bound to dialectic; for how clearly and by what beautifully distinct lines of thought he signifies *what* a certain thing itself *is,* what *coheres* with each."[172] Next in line was the "Platonist" Augustine (even his examples reflected a synthetic, irenic nature), who provided an example of how useful Plato's methods could be: "If it is permitted to bring the Platonists to the discussion, how greatly among them does Augustine stand out, using dialectic like the wings of Mercury (so lofty a place do the Platonists assign to the power of the mind). He surpasses human limits and comes nearest to the divine."[173] The Christian Augustine had ridden on the wings of Platonic philosophy (dialectic) to divine realities.

Melanchthon thus exhorted students to submit themselves to this discipline of learning to form *enthymemata,* syllogisms, theses, definition and division, that they might also learn "to speak with discrimination, certainly, soundly."[174] In conclusion, he reminded them of the story of Bias, one of the seven sages of Athens who, when once asked what should be among the foremost delights to anyone, answered, "quid proprium."[175] "Moreover, reasoning [*ratiocinatio*], dialectic, the diligent contemplation of each thing, is greatly appropriate to mankind [*maxime proprie humani*]."[176] Just as the poets imagined Proteus in countless forms, the human mind lacked stability without the shaping powers of this art, which alone could teach one to "discern the species of things"[177] and enabled one to acquire "a universal and unshakable knowledge of the truth."[178] The dialectical tones all but drowned out those of rhetoric, the "third string" in the Orphean harmony. "...Cynthius...urged that rhetoric was above [the other arts]. What is that in truth? A part of dialectic [*pars dialecticae*], teaching in a popular manner certain *loci* of arguments."[179]

The words of the declamation are spare, but they also reveal that the main elements of a coherent and mature linguistic philosophy were in place. One ought particularly to notice the commanding position of dialectic, the paradigmatic role of Aristotle (without excluding the Platonists), the dialectical use of what were usually rhetorical terms (*inventio* and *dispositio*), the combination of exact discrimination between species and the use of syllogism and *enthymemata,* all in pursuit of the higher truths. The fusion of dialectic and rhetoric had begun to take shape on all these levels. Many ancient and more recent voices spoke through the young teacher, but he was beginning to speak with a mind and spirit that was distinctively his own.

Melanchthon devoted what remained of his declamation to offering a theory of the *quadrivium.* In this second main section he put forward his enduring belief in the existence of innate rational forms or, as he put it, *prima notitio,*[180] which men "could use either to discern principles of universal theories [*vel ad universalium contemplationum principia agnoscenda*] according to a prolepsis, as the learned man Epicurus calls it, or to investigate the parts of particulars [*vel vestigandas singularium partes*]."[181] This primal intuition or proleptic knowledge comprised the structural "rules of order, the rules of number."[182] Melanchthon's term was *regulae,* or rules, which once again illustrates his modified assent to neo-Platonistic mediation between Plato and Aristotle and a deep commitment to epistemic realism (and eventually theological realism) if not to the general methods of the *via antiqua* in his environment. In systems of numbers Melanchthon believed, with Plato, Pythagoras and others, that we behold the cohesive rational power of the universe in action. The numerical arts were thus a foundation for rational metaphysics, as was apprehended by Pythagoras, "who placed numbers as the *principia* of philosophy,"[183] and Plato, who once wrote, "to do arithmetic was to philosophize, and to do geometry to know God."[184] Melanchthon's words were ripe with what Maurer called a "piety of nature," but did they also imply a "natural theology"? There is a soaring quality to his language about the rational coherence of the creation: "what sweetness, what nectar is poured out upon the one contemplating! Nay, what light discloses itself from that chaos of things. . .; it draws and leads the mind, which clings to sensible objects, to an intelligible and eternal nature."[185] This sense of an eternal cosmos underlying the sensible "chaos of things" was certainly not the product of an extreme nominalism, but neither was it a simple realism or logical system of religious truth. He made no attempt at proving God's existence, but only the assertion of logical structure to the world and to the mind. And yet it was quite evidently God's world, and there was no logical reason why one might not explore this assumption as also being an inference from nature. We shall observe a similar ambivalence in the writings of later years and shall argue that his general development of a "natural theology" was mainly consistent with both his philosophical and Lutheran principles.

Melanchthon included only very brief passages on the remaining arts of music and astronomy. He promised that, in a future oration, he would do greater justice to the wondrous harmonies of music,[186] which in many ways was superior to the other arts in immediate power: "the others lift our minds to heavenly realms, this alone brings the gods down from heaven to the world of men."[187] Finally, music "contributes to morals, since nothing is more fitting for making tranquil the affections of living things."[188] Once again we observe the structured moral-metaphysical dimension in the realism of the young Melanchthon. Music was not an entity that was good in itself (*bonum in se*), but rather to the extent that it unleashed the powers of nature for good upon our moral affections; it was good in the sense of being a *bonum pro nobis*. This view of music and harmony would play a small but important role in his later hermeneutical model for interpreting the Psalms.

At the conclusion of his speech, Melanchthon made a brief appeal on behalf of history and poetry. "Writings of every kind use history and poetry; nor are the other ancient authors read with more fruit or value than are the historians and poets."[189] He encouraged the scholars to pursue these arts as useful to leading lives of nobility and virtue: "let nothing be more desired and contended for by you than noble literature, that you might know virtue."[190] Wisdom that one acquired through these arts would make one immune to the arrows of Cupid, like great Athena, whom Cupid feared more than Mars, god of war.[191]

In this speech one has a view of how Melanchthon, using resources that had been given to him, sharpened his theories of the mind and nature, and of the techniques with which he would acquire and apply truth. As we shall see in the next two chapters, the young Melanchthon was already hard at work to develop these ideas in programmatic detail, particularly in his important textbook on rhetoric, but also in his use of Scripture and approach to academic theology.

As Melanchthon wrote his declamation on the liberal arts and worried about his deteriorating circumstances "among boys," the name of Martin Luther as yet had no existential import for him, and the northern city of Wittenberg would have occurred to him only as a place far from the sun and forests of his beloved Swabia. His hopes and dreams were probably those of a chair at a more prestigious university, Leipzig perhaps, or even Paris. But very soon he would be on his way to Saxony. There, to use Bornkamm's words, he would meet not so much a colleague as a destiny.

Notes to Chapter 2

1. K. Hartfelder, *Philipp Melanchthon als Praeceptor Germaniae*, Berlin 1889, p. 29; W. Maurer, *Der junge Melanchthon*, Bd. 1, Göttingen 1967, pp. 28ff.; and J. Camerarius, *De vita Philippi Melanchthonis narratio*, Halle 1777, pp. 15f., whose account is taken as factual by both of the above scholars.

2. K. Hartfelder, *op. cit.*, p. 29, n. 1.

3. W. Maurer, *op. cit.*, Bd. 1, pp. 28f.

4. J. Camerarius, *op. cit.*, p. 13, citation here above; H. Oberman's supporting remarks, *Werden und Wertung der Reformation*, Tübingen 1977, pp. 17ff.; for a general history of the university, cf. J. Haller, *Die Anfänge der Universität Tübingen, 1477-1537*, Bd. I, Stuttgart 1927, (in the light of Oberman's revisions).

5. W. Maurer, *op. cit.*, Bd. 1, p. 30.

6. *Ibid.*

7. J. Camerarius, *op. cit.*, p. 22; cf. appendix in H. Oberman, *op. cit.*, pp. 424ff., and the fascinating discussion of this text in the light of his own research.

8. J. Camerarius, *op. cit.*, p. 22, "Habet utrumque quasi agmen suos ductore et autores, quorum sectam sequi placuerat. Atque non solum contentiones et iurgia inter dissentientes sed dimicationes etiam ac pugnae commissae fuerunt, interdum concertationibus non tantum pertinacibus verborum, sed quoque manuum violentis."

9. *Ibid.*

10. *Ibid.*, "Philippus, qui certam docendi disserendique rationem probaret, et Aristotelica in hoc genere primas tenere intelligeret...."

11. *Ibid.*, "Quamvis autem in verborum contentionibus suam sententiam ita assereret, ut adversantes facile refelleret; id tamen eximia humanitate et parata omnibus, qui uti vellent, opera perfecit, ut sua autoritate inter sectas illas odia restinguerentur, et quamvis studia disereparent, voluntatum tamen maneret coniunctio."

12. L. Heyd, *Melanchthon und Tübingen 1512-1518*, Tübingen 1839, p. 29; K. Hartfelder, *op. cit.*, p. 42; G. Ellinger, *Philipp Melanchthon: Ein Lebensbild*, Berlin 1902; H. Maier, *An der Grenze der Philosophie*, Tübingen 1909, pp. 29ff.; B. Sartorius von Waltershausen, "Melanchthon und das spekulative Denken," in *Deutsche Vierteljahresschrift für Literatur und Geistesgeschichte*, 5, 1927, pp. 644ff.; W. Maurer, *op. cit.*, Bd. 1, pp. 218, n. 1.

13. O. Clemen, *SM* VI/1, pp. 18-20; H. Hermelink, *Die theologische Fakultät in Tübingen vor der Reformation, 1477-1534*, Tübingen 1906, pp. 133ff.; R. Rau, "Philipp Melanchthons Tübinger Jahre," in *Tübinger Blätter*, 47, 1960, pp. 16ff.; W. Rosin, "In Response to Bengt Hägglund: The Importance of Epistemology for Luther's and Melanchthon's Theology," in *Concordia Theological Quarterly*, 44, 2-3, July 1980, pp. 134ff.; S. Wiedenhofer, *Formalstrukturen humanistischer und reformatorischer Theologie bei Philipp Melanchthon*, Bd. I, Bern/Frankfurt/München 1976, pp. 104ff.

14. *SM* VI/1, pp. 18ff.

15. *Ibid.*

16. S. Wiedenhofer, *op. cit.*, Bd. I, pp. 102ff., building on Haller.

17. *Ibid.*

18. W. Maurer, *op. cit.*, Bd. 1, p. 219, n. 1.

19. H. Oberman, *op. cit.*, pp. 35ff.

20. S. Wiedenhofer, *op. cit.*, Bd. II, p. 79, n. 31, who wondered why Melanchthon would later write of Occam as "once his beloved." Cf. also the marginal note in his dialectics of 1521, "nihil reale est in universalibus," in W. Maurer, *op. cit.*, Bd. 1, p. 44 and references. Cf. Wiedenhofer's note, "In der Tat ist seine Universalienlehre nominalistisch," *op. cit.*, Bd. I, p. 416.

21. Cf. S. Wiedenhofer, *op. cit.*, Bd. I, p. 420, who rightly noted that Melanchthon's epistemology resembled a "naive realism." Also W. Rosin, *op. cit.*, *passim*.

22. It is not entirely wrong to say that Melanchthon was a "modified realist," W. Rosin, *op. cit.*, pp. 135ff., as long as one recognizes the complexity of his early philosophical and linguistic background, and that in other respects his was a "modified nominalism."

23. E.g., knowing this side of Melanchthon's earliest linguistic training and development weighs against categorizing his pre-Lutheran humanism as simply "Erasmian humanism," as in Wiedenhofer's entire framework of discussion. This seems an important oversimplification in an otherwise very penetrating study.

24. This of course has been one of the burning questions in the history of Lutheranism. Cf. W. Rosin, *op. cit.*, p. 1; and the many references to recent discussion in P. Fraenkel and M. Greschat, *Zwanzig Jahre Melanchthonstudium*, Geneva 1967, pp. 48ff.

25. Chapter 11.

26. K. Hartfelder, *op. cit.*, pp. 40ff.; W. Maurer, *op. cit.*, Bd. 1, pp. 30f.

27. W. Maurer, *op. cit.*, Bd. 1, p. 33.

28. R. Rau, *op. cit.*, p. 17.

29. H. Oberman, *op. cit.*, pp. 20ff.; W. Maurer, *op. cit.*, Bd. 1, pp. 35ff.

30. H. Oberman, *ibid.*

31. *CR* I, p. 928; see H. Oberman, *op. cit.*, pp. 17ff., on the state of humanism at Tübingen; and P. Meinhold's statement, "Ein grosser Kreis junger Humanisten umgibt ihn in Tübingen," in the light of Maurer's detailed study and somewhat modified picture, *op. cit.*, Bd. 1, pp. 45ff.; and also Maurer's opinion that Melanchthon's learning was already greater than Bebel's, p. 35.

32. Cf. J. Camerarius, *op. cit.*, p. 15; R. Rau, *op. cit.*, p. 17; esp. W. Maurer, *op. cit.*, Bd. 1, pp. 74ff.

33. W. Maurer, *op. cit.*, Bd. 1, pp. 74f., on Stadian and these lectures. For Melanchthon's account, see *MW* III, *De corrigendis adolescentiae studiis*, his inaugural speech at Wittenberg, pp. 36f. and below, pp. 56ff.

34. Cf. W. Maurer, *op. cit.*, Bd. 1, pp. 74ff.; also *MW* III, pp. 35.23ff., "Amicus mihi quispiam est non vulgaris, sub quo primum puer praeceptore in Suevis Tubingae, dialecticis merui annum unum aut alterum, hactenus ut fratre semper familiarissime usus, Franciscus Stadianus...."

35. W. Maurer, *op. cit.*, Bd. 2, p. 75.

36. *MW* III, p. 36, n. 6, on Themistios.

37. *Ibid.*, p. 36.5ff., n. 7.

38. Cf. *ibid.*, p. 36.1ff., on Melanchthon's bold plan, in consort with Reuchlin, Stadian and others, to publish a new Aristotle along with this new theory of interpretation; also his postscript to the grammar, April/May 1518 (so Scheible, *MB* 1, p. 48), *CR* I, p. 15, *et al.*

39. W. Maurer, *op. cit.*, Bd. 1, p. 75.

40. *Ibid.*

41. H. Maier, *op. cit.*, pp. 67f. "Die grossen, spekulativ-metaphysischen Gedanken werden überall ins Rhetorisch-dialektische umgedeutet, verflacht oder verflüchtigt...."

42. Cf. recent interpretations of Aristotle in the context of rhetorical theory, E. Grassi, *Rhetoric as Philosophy: The Humanist Tradition*, University Park/London 1980, pp. 26ff. Also, the brilliant work of P. O. Kristeller, *Renaissance Thought and Its Sources*, pp. 218ff., has indicated that, while Aristotle subordinated the art of rhetoric to that of other disciplines, he did link it in important ways with logic and dialectic and with an aim at influencing public ethics and polity. It was this moral-mindedness and purpose of metaphysics and analytics that caught Melanchthon's interest.

46 • *Oratio Sacra*

43. It is unthinkable that Melanchthon would have written anything like Reuchlin's *De arte cabalistica,* cf. L. Spitz, "Reuchlin's Philosophy: Pythagoras and Cabala for Christ," in *Archiv für Reformationsgeschichte,* 47, 1956, pp. 5ff. On Melanchthon's disparaging reaction to it, see p. 16. And we shall see that his critique of allegorical exegesis was more tightly controlled by logical and semantic concerns than was true of Erasmus. The comment of H. Maier is appropriate, *op. cit.,* p. 1, "Von der geistigen Gährung, von dem Faustischen Dränge, der durch die Zeit geht, ist bei ihm nichts zu spüren. Auch die Mystik, die Luther so tief ergriffen hatte, bleibt ihm innerlich fremd." We generally agree with this assessment, although Maier understated the extent to which Melanchthon linked knowledge with the passions.
44. W. Maurer, *op. cit.,* Bd. 1, pp. 129ff.
45. *Ibid.,* p. 131.
46. *Ibid.*
47. *Ibid.*
48. Cf. below, chapter 11.
49. So H. Maier, *op. cit.,* p. 35.
50. K. Hartfelder, *op. cit.,* p. 42; W. Maurer, *op. cit.,* Bd. 1, p. 30.
51. S. Wiedenhofer, *op. cit.,* Bd. I, p. 99.
52. *Ibid.*
53. J. Camerarius, *op. cit.,* p. 16.
54. S. Wiedenhofer, *op. cit.,* Bd. I, pp. 100ff.
55. W. Maurer, *op. cit.,* Bd. 1, p. 36.
56. J. Haller, *op. cit.,* pp. 195ff., 258ff.; H. Oberman, *op. cit.,* p. 38.
57. H. Oberman, *op. cit.,* pp. 54ff., 118ff. and 499ff.; *eodem,* "Via moderna–devotio moderna: Tendenzen im Tübinger Geistesleben 1477-1516," in *Theologen und Theologie an der Universität Tübingen,* (hrsg.) M. Brecht, Tübingen 1977, pp. 1ff.; W. Maurer, *op. cit.,* Bd. 1, pp. 36ff., on Melanchthon and Steinbach.
58. W. Maurer, *op. cit.,* Bd. 1, pp. 36ff.
59. S. Wiedenhofer, *op. cit.,* Bd. I, pp. 101ff.
60. *MW* VII/1, p. 138.13ff.
61. *Ibid.,* n. 6; S. Wiedenhofer, *op. cit.,* Bd. I, p. 101.
62. S. Wiedenhofer, *ibid.*
63. *Ibid.*
64. *Ibid.,* p. 102.
65. *Ibid.*
66. *MW I,* p. 86.20, "...Scotus, vir hoc nomine longe dignissimus." Cf. Melanchthon's wordplay on the terms Scotus and the Greek *scotos,* meaning darkness.
67. *CR* IV, p. 718.
68. W. Maurer, *op. cit.,* Bd. 1, p. 41, n. 44.
69. S. Wiedenhofer, *op. cit.,* Bd. I, p. 101.
70. W. Maurer, *op. cit.,* Bd. 1, p. 41.
71. *Ibid.*
72. *Ibid.*
73. *Ibid.*
74. *CR* XVI, p. 1026.
75. *Ibid.*
76. H. Oberman, *Werden und Wertung,* p. 55.
77. *Ibid.,* full text pp. 419ff.
78. W. Maurer, *op. cit.,* Bd. 1, pp. 37f.
79. H. Oberman, *Werden und Wertung,* p. 55.
80. *Ibid.*

81. *Ibid.*
82. *Ibid.*, "In ehrfurchtsvoller Scheu werden aus der reichen mittelalterlichen Tradition die unterschiedlichsten Elemente, die in 16. Jahrhundert von verschiedenen Parteien von Luther über Trent bis zu den Sakramentalisten jeweils einzeln zur einzig richtigen Deutung erhoben werden, übernommen und in einer Kette frömmer Rhetorik miteinander verbunden."
83. *Ibid.*
84. *Ibid.*
85. W. Maurer, *op. cit.*, Bd. 1, p. 37.
86. *Ibid.*
87. *Ibid.*
88. *Ibid.*, pp. 30f.
89. *Ibid.*
90. *Ibid.*
91. *Ibid.*, pp. 59ff., 65ff.; also K. Hartfelder, *op. cit.*, p. 44.
92. W. Maurer, *op. cit.*, Bd. 1, p. 67.
93. *Ibid.*, p. 59, "...die Dialektik Agricolas...verhilft ihm keineswegs, wie man gemeint hat, zu einer neuen Wissenschaftslehre...."
94. *Ibid.*, p. 113.
95. *Ibid.*, p. 68, "Oecolampad steht allein zwischen Melanchthon und Erasmus."
96. E. G. Rupp, "Philip Melanchthon and Martin Bucer," in *A History of Christian Doctrine*, (ed.) H. Cunliffe-Jones, Philadelphia (1980) 1984, p. 378.
97. S. Wiedenhofer, *op. cit.*, Bd. I, p. 31.
98. *Ibid.*, p. 32.
99. *Ibid.*, p. 34.
100. *Ibid.*, p. 37.
101. *Ibid.*
102. *Ibid.*, p. 41.
103. *Ibid.*, esp. pp. 112ff.
104. See below, p. 58, on Erasmus and this expression in Melanchthon.
105. W. Maurer, *op. cit.*, Bd. 1, p. 179.
106. *CR* X, p. 670; *SM* I, p. 16; also K. Hartfelder, *op. cit.*, p. 109, tr. into German; the second (1516) in *SM* I, p. 20, with tr. into Latin by J. B. Kan, p. 21.
107. *SM* I, p. 10; and *MB* I, p. 44; cf. W. Maurer, *op. cit.*, Bd. 1, p. 179.
108. *MW* VI/1, p. 31.13.
109. W. Maurer, *op. cit.*, Bd. 1, p. 185, n. 28 on Melanchthon's use of this work.
110. *Ibid.*, n. 27.
111. *Ibid.*, n. 26.
112. *Ibid.*, p. 171, and discussion, pp. 171ff.
113. *Ibid.*, p. 171, on Erasmus's disinterested attitude toward the Pythagorean tradition.
114. *Ibid.*, pp. 172f., on Erasmus's general lack of a sense of historical continuity, in contrast to Melanchthon.
115. *Ibid.*, p. 174.
116. *Ibid.*, pp. 174ff.
117. *Ibid.*, pp. 182ff.
118. *Ibid.*, p. 187.
119. *Ibid.*, e.g., pp. 206ff. in support of this proposition.
120. *Ibid.*, p. 206, the first full paragraph.
121. Cf. ref. in C. Manschreck (tr. and ed.), *Melanchthon on Christian Doctrine*, (repr. Oxford 1965), Grand Rapids 1982, preface, p. xxi.

122. *Ibid.*
123. W. Maurer, *op. cit.*, Bd. 1, p. 46.
124. *Ibid.*
125. *CR* I, p. 14; *SM* VI/1, p. 8 for text and editorial discussion.
126. *Ibid.* both references, "Nam dialego, quod sermonum genus est familiaritate et puritate commendatum."
127. *Ibid.*, citing from Cornutus.
128. *Ibid.*, "...tam vitae, quam orationis regula praescribatur."
129. *CR* I, p. 5; *SM* VI/1, p. 6; *MB* I, p. 43; see W. Maurer, *op. cit.*, Bd. 1, pp. 179ff. for discussion.
130. *CR* V, p. 6.
131. W. Maurer, *op. cit.*, Bd. 1, p. 50; text *CR* XIX, pp. 655ff.; preface, *CR* I, pp. 9ff.; *SM* VI/1, pp. 17ff.; *MB* I, est. date as "vor März" in 1516.
132. Cf. *SM* VI/1, p. 17.
133. Cf. W. Maurer, *op. cit.*, Bd. 1, p. 50.
134. *CR* I, p. 9.
135. *Ibid.*
136. *Ibid.*, p. 10.
137. *Ibid.*
138. *Ibid.*
139. *Ibid.*
140. *Ibid.*, p. 11.
141. *Ibid.*, p. 12; also W. Maurer, *op. cit.*, Bd. 1, p. 52.
142. *CR* I, p. 12.
143. *Ibid.*, p. 13.
144. W. Maurer, *op. cit.*, Bd. 1, pp. 47ff.; preface in *CR* I, pp. 24ff.; *SM* VI/1, p. 30ff.; ref. in *MB* I, pp. 47ff.
145. W. Maurer, *op. cit.*, Bd. 1, p. 47.
146. *Ibid.*, p. 78 on Bernhard Maurer.
147. *Ibid.*, p. 47.
148. *Ibid.*, p. 25.
149. *Ibid.*
150. Text in *MW* III, pp. 17ff., which seems mainly a reproduction of the text in K. Hartfelder, *Philippus Melanchthon: Declamationes* (lateinische Literaturdenkmäler des XV. und XVI. Jahrhunderts), 4, Berlin 1891, pp. if.; the best discussion of its contents is W. Maurer, *op. cit.*, Bd. 1, pp. 53ff.; also S. Wiedenhofer, *op. cit.*, Bd. I, pp. 348ff.; preface in *CR* I, pp. 15f.; *SM* VI/1, pp. 24f.; *MB* I, p. 48 dates preface and publication "vor Juli 1518," and not 1517 as in *CR, ibid.*
151. On Melanchthon in relation to the history of classifying the liberal arts, see S. Wiedenhofer, *op. cit.*, Bd. I, pp. 348ff., and W. Maurer, *op. cit.*, Bd. 1, pp. 103ff., esp. 110ff. on pioneering contributions to German educational theory, particularly in the field of history.
152. *Ibid.*, both references.
153. *MW* III, pp. 18.36ff., n. 36.
154. So W. Maurer, *op. cit.*, Bd. 1, p. 53, who blames it on the "...Schwülst eines noch nicht abgeklärten Stils...." This explanation seems weak, though, when one compares the text with everything else that Melanchthon wrote before, during and just after the time of this oration.
155. *MW* VII/1, to Reuchlin, July 12, 1518, pp. 32.3-10.
156. *MW* III, p. 18.20ff.
157. *Ibid.*, p. 18.18f.

158. *Ibid.*, p. 18.27ff.
159. *Ibid.*, p. 18.31.
160. *Ibid.*, pp. 18.36-19.1ff.
161. *Ibid.*, p. 19.6ff., "Nam ut eadem gentibus omnibus, atque adeo omni caelo aequi bonique ratio, iidem iusti fontes, sic eadem ubique naturae scientia, modo par studium accedat, et ut in summa dicam, rex Juppiter omnibus idem."
162. *Ibid.*, p. 20.27ff.
163. W. Maurer, *op. cit.*, Bd. 1, p. 54.
164. Cf. esp. B. S. v. Waltershausen, *op. cit.*, pp. 644ff.
165. We think that v. Waltershausen, *ibid.*, overstated the consistency of Melanchthon's nominalism, i.e., with respect to the relationship between thought and its object. Q. Breen, "The Two-fold Truth Theory in Melanchthon," in *Review of Religion*, 1945, pp. 115ff., esp., 132ff., seemed also to brush too quickly past the question of "realism" in Melanchthon's general epistemology. W. Rosin has made some good, if undeveloped suggestions about pursuing the "moderate realism" of both Melanchthon and Luther, *op. cit.*, pp. 134ff. With respect to Melanchthon's actual fraternal affiliation, however, "moderate nominalism" is a more suitable description. We also agree with S. Wiedenhofer's criticisms, *op. cit.*, Bd. I, p. 349 and Bd. II, p. 288, n. 186, of W. Maurer, *op. cit.*, Bd. 1, pp. 103ff. on *De artibus liberalibus*. Wiedenhofer rightly judged that the *vox daemonii* was a metaphor and that Melanchthon's development there was away from, rather than toward, a Platonistic metaphysic. (One may wonder why Wiedenhofer did not incorporate this interpretation into his reckoning of Melanchthon's allegiance to the *via antiqua*.)
166. *MW* III, p. 22.27ff.
167. *Ibid.*, p. 20.33ff.
168. *Ibid.*, pp. 20.37-21.1ff.
169. *Ibid.*, p. 21.3ff.
170. *Ibid.*, p. 21.11ff.
171. *Ibid.*, p. 21.14f.
172. *Ibid.*, p. 21.16ff.
173. *Ibid.*, p. 21.18ff.
174. *Ibid.*, p. 21.27ff.
175. *Ibid.*, p. 22.10ff.
176. *Ibid.*, p. 22.12ff.
177. *Ibid.*, p. 22.15f.
178. *Ibid.*, p. 22.18, ". . . perpetua et inconcussa veri scientia."
179. *Ibid.*, p. 22.24ff. We do not believe that Maurer has correctly evaluated this section of the speech. He detected a very different view of rhetoric, less than six months later, in Melanchthon's classical works. He attributed this shift to the fresh reading of Aristotle with Stadian. But Melanchthon's oration on the arts was published almost at the same time as his inaugural speech at Wittenberg (in which these differences allegedly are evident) and, as we shall seek to show, there is no conceptual inconsistency between his view of rhetoric here as *pars dialecticae*, and that of his works from the following year. W. Maurer, *op. cit.*, Bd. 1, pp. 193ff. On this same subject we must also disagree with the general framework of assessment used by Q. Breen in his article, "The Subordination of Philosophy to Rhetoric in Melanchthon," in *Archiv für Reformationsgeschichte*, 1952.
180. *MW* III, p. 22.35.
181. *Ibid.*, p. 22.36ff.
182. *Ibid.*, p. 23.1ff., "...quaeso quae est alia, quam ordinis, quam numeri regula...."
183. *Ibid.*, p. 23.15f.

184. *Ibid.*, p. 24.8ff., "Sic Plato *arithmein* philosophari, et *theon aei geometrein* commodum afficta notatione dixit, id est, semper aeternam veri naturam intelligendo versari."

185. *Ibid.*, p. 24.4ff.

186. *Ibid.*, p. 24.12ff.

187. *Ibid.*, p. 24.18f., "Erigunt aliae [artes] ad caelestia mentes nostras, haec una caelo superos ad humana deducit...."

188. *Ibid.*, p. 24.21f.

189. *Ibid.*, p. 26.3f.

190. *Ibid.*, p. 27.6f.

191. *Ibid.*, p. 27.15ff.

CHAPTER 3

Melanchthon's Inaugural
Speech at Wittenberg

"Capnio [Reuchlin] sent me as a boy into Saxony, not knowing the burden, and no more fit for such a thing than, as they say, an ass is fit for gold." (Melanchthon, letter to J. Baumgartner, in J. Camerarius, *De vita Philippi Melanchthonis narratio*, p. 25.)

In 1518 Melanchthon complained to his granduncle about troubles he was having at Tübingen. Many years hence a worn and haggard Melanchthon would look back on the days of youthful innocence when he was led to Saxony to bear a golden burden that would often prove too much for him. In any event, to the younger man things could only get worse in this "workhouse" with its tedium. Thomas Anselm had left the city in 1516,[1] and Philip clearly was ripe for a new setting, where he could do advanced work as a professor and author in his own right. That the faculty of Tübingen had no appointment for him was probably more a matter of finances than of his being slighted.[2]

Camerarius remembered times in the early sixteenth century when men sensed themselves to be carried beyond their control by higher powers to an appointed end.[3] The call of the young Melanchthon to Wittenberg evokes something of that sense of destiny. It is well known that Frederick the Wise of Saxony was looking to procure reputable scholars for his newly endowed university.[4] The Elector first invited the estimable Reuchlin to come as professor of biblical languages, but age and the storms of controversy over his writings had drained his spirits. He viewed the appointment at Wittenberg as better suited to a younger man and urged that Frederick consider "my dear nephew."[5] This recommendation from Reuchlin was enough for Frederick to select Philip over the established linguist Peter Mosellanus, who was the preferred choice among the faculty, Luther included.[6] After the post was secured Reuchlin wrote the more extravagant words of confidence in his protégé: "Among the Germans I know of no one who surpasses him except Erasmus, who is Dutch, and he surpasses us all."[7] To Philip he wrote the words of God to Abraham, "Go forth from your land, and from the house of your father, and go into a land which I will show you, and I will make your name great and you will be blessed."[8] He must have felt a bit like Abraham, leaving his home country in South Germany for the colder and less salubrious climate of the north, with its peculiar dialect, foods and ways that were strange to him. It was August of 1518 when he rode off on a horse that was borrowed from the Elector and hitched to a wagon filled with books.[9] On the journey of seven days he met briefly with Frederick in Augsburg,[10] had an amicable meeting with Mosellanus in Leipzig (from whom he perhaps received his first knowledge of Luther)[11] and polished off the oration which he was to give as his inaugural address.[12]

The title of this address was *De corrigendis adolescentiae studiis*.[13] We have chosen to discuss it before examining Melanchthon's rhetorical textbook, *De rhetorica libri tres* (which was mainly written in Tübingen), because the themes of the speech follow naturally from that of the previous section on *De artibus liberalibus*. Also, the book on rhetoric came out after the first semester early in 1519 and had thus accumulated features which made it somewhat less ambiguously a pre-Lutheran document, although it was essentially that. In the inaugural speech Philip presented his views on the liberal arts in more detail than in the earlier declamation on this subject and (making vital contact with the theologians) spoke eloquently on the substance of a learned theology. The speech is thus of inestimable worth to us in seeing Melanchthon's Christian humanism, or humanistic Christianity, as it was before he adopted a distinctively Lutheran world view.

Philip found the faculty and students mainly receptive to his theories on reforming the curriculum.[14] Besides the electrifying developments in theology that radiated from the works of Luther and Andreas Karlstadt, and the uncertain prospect of interviews with the papal legate Cajetan forthcoming in Augsburg, there was also a great deal of movement on the matter of how rightly to constitute the curriculum. The older faculty evidently felt the direction of the winds and stepped aside to give the younger generation of scholars power to do it their way.[15] Melanchthon came with a mandate from the Elector himself (who had a genuine taste for the humanities) to establish the study of Hebrew and Greek in the university[16] and throughout his career was given an almost completely free hand to shape the academic program.

Philip entered the lecture hall, thinly built, looking more like a boy than a grown man. When he began to speak with the halting, deliberate diction that made him sound like he was stuttering slightly,[17] the skeptics in the crowd must have stiffened, fearing that sentiment for Reuchlin had clouded the Elector's better judgment. In less than an hour, however, when he spoke the final words (in what is to our modern ears the tedious repetition of flattering vows that is typical of the declamations of that kind), he looked up from his manuscript to see the audience giving him a tremendous ovation.[18] Philip had transcended his physical limitations as a speaker; besides the fittingness of his proposals on the arts, he had spoken boldly against religious traditionalism, perhaps without fully knowing the extent to which this subject had begun to define the emerging Wittenberg theology.[19]

The body of the speech can be divided into three connected parts. The first was an artful condemnation of what had been, in his view, many centuries of decline in the schools throughout Europe,[20] the second, a long discourse on the liberal arts and the essential place of dialectic.[21] The final section was on sacred theology and its relationship with classical studies.[22]

According to Melanchthon the process of decline was set in motion by the barbarian invasions and devastation of Rome. "Eight hundred years ago, I think, when nearly the whole world was shaken by the Goths, Italy was devastated by the Lombards; Roman literature went to ruin together with the Roman Empire."[23] During these warlike times only Gregory, "whom they call 'the Great' and I [call] the protector and torchbearer of a perishing theology,...ruled the Roman church and upheld an unhappy age from falling as best he could, through teaching and writing."[24] From that age nothing else of great worth, in literature, was left to posterity.[25]

In Ireland and Scotland, it was true, a long and enduring peace had nourished the cultivation of the arts, and in England the most notable example was the Venerable Bede, "in both Greek and Latin by no means commonly learned, so erudite was he in philosophy, mathematics and divinity that he may also be compared with the ancients."[26] But in the meantime Italy and France were "frigid," and "Germany as usual was better equipped with arms than letters."[27] Into this sorry state of affairs the great Charlemagne was born, who "when he had pacified the borders of the Roman Empire, set his mind to the establishment of letters."[28] The Parisians produced several shining lights: Alcuin, Hugo and Richard of St. Victor.[29]

In time, however, "certain men fell in...with Aristotle."[30] Obscure enough in Greek, their text of Aristotle was "maimed and mutilated..., rendered into Latin in such a way that it would have tested even the augury of a raving Sibyl."[31] Greek learning was gradually lost, and such confusion followed that "instead of the noble arts, those which are ignoble began to be taught."[32] And from this confusion proceeded the several academic factions, "Thomists, Scotists . . . and the rest of their offspring more numerous than the offspring of Cadmea."[33] In these times men not only despised good learning but destroyed and banished it whenever it occurred.[34]

Melanchthon concluded this first section of his speech with a point which he would elaborate in the last section. The demise of learning in the arts, he asserted, coincided with the ruination of sacred studies. "When Greek mathematics was abandoned, sacred culture was neglected even more,"[35] as evil a plague as there can be.[36] Before Greek learning was vanquished by barbarism, "all philosophy was Greek."[37] And besides the writings of Cyprian, Hilary, Ambrose, Jerome and Augustine, nothing of great worth was written by Latin theologians.[38] Moreover, the theologians of the East depended so much upon the Greek language that it was impossible for the one to be unaffected by the collapse of the other.[39]

Melanchthon's theory of historical development was typical of humanism in its widespread forms, although in Maurer's view, he was exceptional in the quality of his historical mind. "He understood antiquity as history; and in the sense that he lived *in* it spiritually, he was one of the first Europeans consciously to live *historically*."[40] His deep awareness of historical tradition, as we shall see, would affect his conception not only of the history of theology, but of Scripture itself. Moreover, the underlying power behind the development of any tradition was in its philosophical values and methods. When these values were properly cultivated, the movement within a culture would be toward consensus in truth; when not, the movement was inevitably degenerative and toward the incoherence of factionalism and (thus) falsehood.[41] The true Christian tradition was clearly dependent upon properly honed thought and language, and these upon the technical methods that had flourished in antiquity and were flourishing once again. We shall later see how the mutual interdependency between Christianity and classical culture was reflected in his doctrine of Scripture and biblical authority.

The second main part of the speech was devoted to the arts, and mainly to the fundamental role of dialectic within the larger arena of learning. "Logic treats all the power and the distinctions of language, and since the way into the higher arts is through this one, it is the first rudiment of education...."[42] Dialectic taught one to be literate; "...by rules it tightens propriety of speech [*proprietatem sermonis*], or by connecting the literary figures of authors, it indicates what you should pay attention to."[43] Advanced students, too, should use dialectic to cultivate proper methods of critical thinking, or *iudicium*.[44] The methods of dialectic enabled one to describe the limits, origin and boundaries of things (*quo metas rerum, ortus, fines*), so that "whatever topic must be handled precisely, you may have everything in ready money [*in numerato habeas*], as it were, which pertains to your purpose, and...you may so capture the sentiments of the hearers [*sensus auditorum capias*] that they will not be able thoughtlessly to disagree."[45]

Melanchthon thus amplified the position which he had put forth in Tübingen. Working within his Aristotelian-Ciceronian (nominalistic) logical framework, he used dialectic in a very broad sense to comprise a variety of rational functions; sharpening and "tightening" one's speech through proper definition and the making of right distinctions, and bettering one's critical judgment promised more than mere intellectual exercise. The final aim was to unleash all the power of language to persuade of truth.

In our century, Wittgenstein and others have made it almost a modern dogma that philosophy does nothing more than indicate the logical structure of propositions. The Preceptor detected something of a preoccupation with logical structure at the expense of learning universal truths in the scholastic circles of his own time. They thus bore the brunt of his many criticisms. The conceptual mainstay of this criticism was his attempt at fusing together dialectic with rhetoric, as we have observed in several brief summations. This part of his inaugural speech helps one to penetrate somewhat further than we have yet into this idea that would be fundamental to his theory of language, truth and method, to the core of his pre-Lutheran world view and to his later understanding as a Lutheran theologian of the authoritative sense of Scripture. What he had just described as the functions of dialectic, Melanchthon wrote, might also be called rhetoric. "These are the functions of that which I call dialectic, others rhetoric, for authors vary in names, while the art is the same."[46] This comment helps illuminate the enigmatic and abrupt proposal that he had made about rhetoric in *De artibus liberalibus*, that its status was that of a *pars dialecticae*, and nothing more than this. We shall see that his point was not to downgrade rhetoric (although he probably meant to be critical of the way that Bebel handled the subject at Tübingen, independently of philosophy), but rather to re-connect both it and the dialectical arts with an existentially (not just morally) powerful metaphysics.

In contrast were the counter-examples of the widely used dialectics of the Scotist Peter Tartaretus, Thomas Bricot, John Versor, John Eck(!) and the Bursa Montis of Cologne.[47] During his six years of teaching this subject, and using their texts, he knew firsthand that what these "unlettered masters of ignorance" taught was not properly called dialectic.[48] True dialectic, "a certain compendious method . . . by which the order and discernment of each thing to be treated is manifest, so that we may see in a thing what it is, how great, what sort, why, in what manner, if it is simple, if it is complex, if it is true or false," thus brings us into the light.[49] How unlike this conception of the art (which Melanchthon believed to be the ancient, Aristotelian and normative one) were the techniques of the present *magistri inscitiae*, who forced fine notions "through places thick with rust, and profound darkness."[50]

Melanchthon's view of their failings and his own positive theory are illuminated further still by his comments on the use of Aristotle. Philip's disposition toward the great Aristotle has long been a matter of debate among scholars.[51] Ambiguities abound because this disposition was a complex one. In one moment (as here, above), he could condemn those who "fell in with Aristotle" as though they had dealt with Lucifer himself; but in the next (as here, below), he could propose a restoration of Aristotle's philosophy as essential to the recovery of Christian civilization. Now he announced before the assembled multitude at Wittenberg his vision of a renewed text and a revolutionary new way of reading and using Aristotle.

What exactly was wrong with these modern *magistri*, and what was it that made them masters of "ignorance" instead of true philosophy? For one thing, in teaching fundamental methods (on "simple themes"), they neglected to use Aristotle's book of *Categories*, from which "every skill of *inventio* flows, as from a wellspring, and the *Categories* are nothing if not a certain method of simple themes."[52] Instead of giving them sound training in the art of dialectical *inventio*, Melanchthon charged, scholars led their students into endless metaphysical speculation about the reality or non-reality of individual assertions: "and here they argue whether a single *genus* 'really universally' (as they say) discriminates, and about this the Scotists still do not agree among themselves...."[53] Moreover, they abused Aristotle's *Second Analytics*, for, "while [it is] a series of *dispositio* and, as Simplicius the Peripatetic has written, a canon and measuring rod of artful disputation, our men render it among the metaphysics...."[54] In brief, they took something "not entirely difficult, and wondrously useful to the noble handling of studies, and rendered it both difficult and useless [*et difficilem et inutilem*]."[55]

Thus, we have the context for Melanchthon's dream (alas, never to be realized) to collaborate with his teacher and friend Stadian, among others, to produce an edition of Aristotle's text with this revised interpretive system.[56] The Latin commentary by Themistios had persuaded Philip, first, that Aristotle's final purpose in the *Analytics* and *Categories* was to use them as a foundation upon which to erect a system of rhetoric, and not (as was typically believed) for ever-new metaphysical speculation. "Above all I urged that *rhetoric* was taught by Aristotle in that place."[57] Stadian, convinced that his student had made a monumentally important discovery, proposed the idea of putting out the new edition, thereby liberating European studies from the barbarism that now prevailed everywhere.[58] The idea was to wipe the slate clean and to start over from scratch, or rather from the newly won assumptions of the ancients.[59]

As the words rolled from Melanchthon's lips and filled the lecture hall, the audience must have wondered at what they heard. If Maurer is right in his judgment that not even Erasmus had come up with so bold a vision of Aristotle's contemporary value to lectern, chancel and marketplace, these were unfamiliar and challenging ideas. Luther was all too familiar with Aristotle, and it is well known how tired he had become of Aristotle's philosophy. Others on the faculty, particularly the older theologians,[60] used Aristotle in the conventional ways; an eyebrow or two must have been raised. What they were hearing was that Aristotle was in essence a rhetorician, that his *Categories* was not intended to serve speculative metaphysics, but instead was a work of "inventive" theory that served proper rhetorical purposes. And the *Second Analytics* was essentially a paradigm of rhetorical disposition. For anyone who had not read very carefully both Agricola's dialectic and Erasmus's rhetoric, these were challenging notions indeed. We shall see in due course how Melanchthon, although he abandoned the textual project, vigorously pursued the concepts behind it in his rhetorical writing, which was already far along, and then in his theological doctrine, which of course was not yet in view.

Behind all these literary projects was an underlying epistemic theory that was distinct from the norm (in his and others' analyses of the situation) in the schools in much the way that Common Sense philosophy of Scotland differed from metaphysical philosophy on the continent, or that weak foundationalism in modern philosophy is distinct from the evidential or classical foundationalism in the traditions of Descartes and Locke. The essential distinction is between the view that allows for "properly basic" beliefs and rational consensus on basic norms apart from rational demonstration or the use of evidence, and that which says that only those views can be held as basic which are self-evident to the senses and/or are analytical truths which one simply cannot deny coherently.[61] In Melanchthon's view, Aristotle taught a foundationalism of the weaker sort and thus left many questions, now being debated to death by philosophers and theologians, as simply irreducible and epistemically archaic. The vision was thus directed to the world of knowable objects, and instinctively, in the tradition of Socrates, to the goal of building a morally coherent social polity from the ruins of factionalism that inevitably followed from the desperate attempt to secure *everything* by argument. Without a broad foundation of *archai,* or *loci communes,* as "seats of the arguments,"[62] civilization would disintegrate from sheer deontological division and exhaustion. On this view, Melanchthon departed not so much from the general truth theory of coherence and correspondence that pervaded certain scholastic methods, but from a preoccupation with proofs and demonstrations of peculiar themes that, in his judgment, betrayed a lack of common sense and destroyed the foundations of both church and polity.[63]

There was yet another element to this second part of the oration that should be included in brief summary. Melanchthon urged that not only did Aristotle's metaphysics have a final purpose to serve the arts, but that the arts themselves of grammar, dialectic and rhetoric also aimed at serving something greater than themselves. When connected together and practiced by competent scholars, the arts of grammar, dialectic and rhetoric prepared students for successful study of the higher faculties, and more importantly, they assisted them in reaching the greatest goal of all: "first to knowledge of nature, then to forming morals...."[64] The Greeks were essential for this second purpose. Melanchthon recommended the use of Aristotle's *Ethics,* Plato's *Laws* and the poets Homer (*Graecis fons omnium disciplinarum*), Vergil and Horace.[65] He also strongly recommended reading the histories, the benefits of which were comparable to those of the entire *orbis artium,* teaching memorable lessons about every part of life.[66] "In the consensus of our forefathers it was proclaimed that the Muses were born from memory; by that, unless I am mistaken, they signified that every class of the arts flowed from history [*ex historia omne artium genus manare*]."[67]

As he finished this section on the arts, Melanchthon captured what he believed was the core of all Greek erudition in the double intuition of his own linguistic theory. "By the name philosophy I embrace, therefore, knowledge of nature, the rules and examples of morals."[68] A dialectically rigorous understanding of reality (*natura*) within the encompassing horizon of a moral universe was the idea that he promised to develop fully in his forthcoming book on rhetoric.[69]

The third and final section of the speech would by itself be of inestimable value as a source of information about Melanchthon's earliest handling of biblical themes. We have heard Camerarius's testimony that from very early on (much before his rendezvous with Martin Luther) his friend's insatiable thirst for knowledge included an affection for sacred theology. Camerarius also told the story (and we see no compelling reason to take it as apocryphal) of how Reuchlin had given Melanchthon a Latin Bible, which he sat reading during chapel services at Tübingen and was seen always to have with him.[70] The last part of his inaugural address left no doubt that he had given serious thought to the matter of how the liberal arts, newly recovered and revised, might profitably be related to sacred studies and how a new brand of theology might come to prevail against the older one. His remarks, which sounded forth his debt to both Reuchlin and Erasmus, had mainly to deal with using original languages to get back to a pure rendering of the sacred text, on the assumption that there *was* in fact a purity, and thus a particular kind of authority to Scripture that set it above the mass of merely human traditions. This authority was not for him primarily grounded in the principle of *ad fontes* in the sense of historical-critical purity (the more ancient, the purer the text), but essentially in that of the native power of language as the source of semantic, logical and existential truth. The power of reality was unleashed quite directly through *terms* properly designated and logically developed. There was great emphasis in his philosophy of language upon the logical functions of terms in bringing forth the existential and affective energies of people and societies. For Melanchthon the slogan *ad fontes* was much more a testimony to the holistic power of reality and the essential function of logic as the fountainhead of human truth, than it was a philological principle or a matter of textual criticism. His greatest passion was for the interpretation of texts through his distinctive system of rhetorical structures that will be the subject of discussion in our next chapter.

Melanchthon proposed the analogy that the linguistic arts were to theology what foreign brass was to the Temple of Solomon.[71] "And so, since theology is partly the study of Hebrew and partly Greek (for we Latins imbibe their waters), the foreign languages must be learned...."[72] Mastery of the languages made possible understanding the true sense of Scripture: "the splendor and propriety of words appears and the true and genuine sense of the letter shows forth as under the noonday sun."[73] Moreover, "As soon as we perceive the letter, we follow the essential theme of matters."[74] The reward for so interpreting by the pure letter, instead of relying on the standard "glosses" and "concordances" (and "discordances"), was a great one, indeed: "we begin to know Christ, His commandment becomes lucid to us, and we are bathed by that blessed nectar of divine wisdom."[75] Coming to "know Christ" evoked in him images from the Old Testament as well as the New; by divine wisdom we are "inserted into the members" of the Lord, and "we live, we breathe, are enlivened, contemplating Zion, and in silence...adoring Salem. This is the fruit of heavenly wisdom."[76] Therefore, he concluded, "let us cultivate it [divine wisdom] as purely as possible, not corrupted by our cleverness."[77]

Both dimensions of Melanchthon's earliest concept of truth and authority are evident in this summary of hermeneutical theory. It might be true for Melanchthon that pepper was sold both in Paris and Rome,[78] but no great poet or *autor* would bother to write about it. Authoritative truth was always embodied in literature that conveyed deeply human truths with a pristine *proprietas sermonis*, and these *words* of truth possessed an authoritative power to help human beings become more human. In the instance of biblical letters, Scripture made a person one with Jesus Christ. The authoritative power of words was less in their historical verity (not that he denied that they were historically true) than in their reference to the moral and spiritual cosmos. And their mode of reference to these realities was unfailingly a matter of strict logical and semantic connection. In our modern terms, his literary epistemology was closer to that of certain contemporary versions of narrative hermeneutics than to historical-critical forms of interpretation. His later biblical works are almost devoid of a philological mentality and are taken up with the logical-rhetorical structures of themes.[79]

The concluding segment of the speech was obviously a signal to Luther and his colleagues that he would be an ally of their cause. He elected to use the Apostle Paul (the patron saint of the university, and very much at the center of the recent discussions) as the example *par excellence* of right doctrinal discrimination between the things of God and the things of men.

> That is what Paul oftentimes impresses [upon us], particularly in his epistle to Titus where he sedulously requires uncorrupted integrity [*adiaphthorian integritatem*] from the doctrine of a Christian man.... Furthermore, [he requires] a holy purity [*semnoteta mundiciem*], lest we improperly contaminate sacred teachings with alien letters. I believe he knew the future; if profane teachings were intermingled with sacred ones [*si sacris prophana miscerentur*], it would happen that profane affections, hatred, love of factions, schisms, feuds would closely follow at the same time.[80]

No doubt Luther was not alone in listening very intently to this young scholar allude to the issue of "good works" as connected with that of biblical primacy.

> After we began to be pleased by the commentaries of men and overcome by love of our own works, we consumed Baal Peor instead of manna, we began to be men, not Christians. I wish to appear to say things as I think. And I think nothing other than that decrees of the church ought to be tested by evangelical truth....[81]

He promised that his forthcoming lectures on the Greek text of Titus[82] would prove his claims about Paul true. In this little epistle, "you will be able to observe how much a propriety of language may bring to the understanding of sacred mysteries...."[83] With that the new professor committed himself to the Saxons, to their university and to his students. Together they would do their part to bring about a new age of wisdom and virtue.[84]

The text of this speech shows that Philip came to Wittenberg already in possession of intuitions that would lead him naturally to agreement with essential themes of Luther's theology. The razor that he used to discriminate between ontologically distinct classes of things, particularly between the divine and the human, Scripture and tradition, moral legalism and evangelical Christianity, was an essential epistemic instrument in carving out his pre-Lutheran world view. We have observed that these distinctions were modified by a metaphysical and epistemic realism that made possible a synthetic view of the world, but that integration of elements presupposed an antecedent discrimination between them. His initial point was that the contemporary mind lacked the propriety of thought necessary to making the basic distinctions that were essential to the life of society as an integrated whole. The lack of proper distinctions had led to conceptual and thus moral adultery in all areas of Christian doctrine and practice. Melanchthon discriminated with the larger purpose of integrating the various elements of reality and life into a coherent world view, not with the aim of creating a logical abyss between Christ and culture. In our judgment, this value never changed and must be kept in view when interpreting his early critique of metaphysical speculation in theology and Christology.

In the next chapter we shall see how Melanchthon developed his truth theory in the context of formal rhetoric and how his rhetorical theory had begun to shape his idea of biblical truth and authority. Only after following this complex conceptual process through to his emergence as a distinctively Lutheran theologian will we be in a position to begin assessing the quality of his commitment to biblical authority with respect to catchwords like "sola scriptura" and "sola gratia."

Notes to Chapter 3

1. Cf. H. Oberman, *Werden und Wertung der Reformation*, Tübingen 1977, p. 23.
2. W. Maurer, *Der junge Melanchthon*, Bd. 2, Göttingen 1969, p. 10.
3. J. Camerarius, *De vita Philippi Melanchthonis narratio*, (ed.) G. Th. Strobel, Halle 1777, p. 20, "Haec tempora intuenti et negotia consideranti vis mihi quaedam invicta fatorum ob oculos versata est."
4. M. Grossman, *Humanism in Wittenberg, 1485-1517*, Nieuwkoop 1975; J. Camerarius, *op. cit.*, p. 24; W. Maurer, *op. cit.*, Bd. 2, p. 9.
5. *CR* I, pp. 29ff.
6. Cf. W. Maurer, *op. cit.*, Bd. 2, pp. 9ff.
7. *CR* I, p. 34.
8. *Ibid.*, p. 32.
9. W. Maurer, *op. cit.*, Bd. 2, pp. 10ff.
10. *Ibid.*, p. 10.
11. *Ibid.*, p. 11.
12. *Ibid.*, pp. 13ff.
13. Text in *MW* III, pp. 29ff.; *CR* XI, pp. 15ff.; K. Hartfelder, *Philippus Melanchthon: Declamationes*, Lateinische Literaturdenkmäler des XV. und XVI. Jahrhunderts, 4, Berlin 1891, pp. 64ff.; for the best discussions, cf. *eodem, Philipp Melanchthon als Praeceptor Germaniae*, Berlin 1889, pp. 64ff.; W. Maurer, *op. cit.*, Bd. 2, pp. 13ff.; H. -A. Stempel, *Melanchthons pädagogisches Wirken*, Bielefeld 1979, pp. 26ff.; S. Wiedenhofer, *Formalstrukturen humanistischer und reformatorischer Theologie bei Philipp Melanchthon*, Bd. I, Bern/Frankfurt/München 1976, pp. 116ff.
14. W. Maurer, *op. cit.*, Bd. 2, pp. 14ff.
15. *Ibid.*
16. *Ibid.*
17. J. Camerarius, *op. cit.*, p. 8.
18. On Luther's well-known reaction, cf. WABr I, no. 88.
19. W. Maurer, *op. cit.*, Bd. 2, p. 14.
20. *MW* III, pp. 31-33.
21. *Ibid.*, pp. 34-39.
22. *Ibid.*, pp. 40f.
23. *Ibid.*, p. 31.18ff.
24. *Ibid.*, p. 31.26ff.
25. *Ibid.*, p. 31.31.
26. *Ibid.*, p. 31.35f.
27. *Ibid.*, pp. 31.38-32.1.
28. *Ibid.*, p. 32.3ff.
29. *Ibid.*, p. 32.11ff.
30. *Ibid.*, p. 32.19ff.
31. *Ibid.*, p. 32.21ff.
32. *Ibid.*, p. 32.25.
33. *Ibid.*, p. 32.25ff.
34. *Ibid.*, p. 32.27ff.
35. *Ibid.*, p. 33.7ff.
36. *Ibid.*, p. 33.10f.
37. *Ibid.*, p. 33.11f., "Nam cum ad eam usque aetatem, et philosophia tota Graeca fuisset...."

38. *Ibid.*, p. 33.13ff., "...et sacrorum Latinae litterae, praeter Cyprianum, Hilarium, Ambrosium, Hieronymum, Augustinum nullae insignes extarent...."
39. *Ibid.*, p. 33.15ff.
40. W. Maurer, *op. cit.*, Bd. 1, pp. 110f., on Melanchthon's distinctive role in historical studies; ref. to citation in our text, p. 111.
41. For a penetrating and full account of Melanchthon's conception of history and its "rules" or "laws" of advance and decline, see P. Fraenkel, *Testimonia Patrum: The Function of the Patristic Argument in the Theology of Philipp Melanchthon*, Geneva 1961, esp. pp. 52-109.
42. *MW* III, p. 34.3ff., "Logicum vim omnem ac discrimina sermonis tractat, et cum per ipsum in illa superiora sit iter, primum formandae pueritiae rudimentum est...."
43. *Ibid.*, p. 34.5ff.
44. *Ibid.*, p. 34.8f.
45. *Ibid.*, p. 34.8ff.
46. *Ibid.*, p. 34.13ff., "Hae partes illius sunt, quam nos dialecticam, alii rhetoricam vocant: Nominibus enim variant auctores, cum ars eadem est."
47. *Ibid.*, p. 34.19ff., "...de dialecticis videamus quae adhuc ex Tartaretis, Bricot, Perversore [Versor!], Eckiis, Copulatis Bursae Montis...et aliis huius farinae petimus. Licet hac parte mihi liberius agere, nam iisdem ego annos sex perpetuos paene detritus sum." Cf. n. 20 on these dialectics.
48. *Ibid.*, pp. 34.24-35.1ff., "...non esse *dialektika*, quae isti amussi, inscitiae magistri profitentur."
49. *Ibid.*, p. 35.4ff., "Primum dialectica, ut dixi, methodus quaedam est omnium quaestionum compendaria...: qua constat ordo et iudicium cuiusque rei tractandae, ut in quoque videamus, quid, quantum, quale, cur, quomodo, si simplex sit, sin complex, verum ne an falsum."
50. *Ibid.*, p. 35.9ff., "Simplicium discrimina, notionesque isti per loca senta situ, noctemque profundam."
51. P. Peterson, *Geschichte der aristotelischen Philosophie im protestantischen Deutschland*, Leipzig 1921.
52. *MW* III, p. 35.14ff., "Librum *kategorion* aiunt dialecticae tabulis non censeri, cum inde omne artificium inveniendi, ceu e fonte fluat, et *kategoriai* non sint nisi *methodos* quaedam simplicium."
53. *Ibid.*, p. 35.17ff., "...et hic argutantur: num singula genera generalissime realiter (ur vocant) discrepant, atque de eo nondum inter Scotistos ipsos convenit...."
54. *Ibid.*, p. 35.21ff., "Analytica posteriora, cum sint disponendi series, ac ut Simplicius Peripateticus ait, canon ac amussis artificiosae disputationis inter metaphysica nostri rettulerunt."
55. *Ibid.*, p. 35.24ff.
56. *Ibid.*, p. 36.1ff.
57. *Ibid.*, p. 36.9ff.
58. *Ibid.*, p. 36.16f., "Ad haec male precatus nugis, obnixe a me contendit, Aristoteli purgando socias manus adicerem: conaturum omnia sese pro viribus, uti artium elementa vindicta barbarorum liberarentur."
59. *Ibid.*, p. 36.14f., "...scholae simplicitur ac candide summam rei *to alpha kai omega* traditurus."
60. W. Maurer, *op. cit.*, Bd. 2, pp. 14f.
61. Cf. a detailed discussion in A. Plantinga and N. Wolterstorff (eds.), *Faith and Rationality: Reason and Belief in God*, Notre Dame/London 1983; also E. Grassi, *Rhetoric as Philosophy*, University Park/London 1980, esp. pp. 25f., in which he interprets the *Second Analytics* in much the way that Melanchthon did.

62. Cf. chapter 4 on the concept of *loci communes*.
63. Cf. E. Grassi, *op. cit.*, on the distinction between "inventive" and "rational" philosophy in the sense of Descartes and modern rationalism, pp. 35ff.
64. *MW* III, p. 39.5f.
65. *Ibid.*, p. 39.9ff.
66. *Ibid.*, p. 39.22ff.
67. *Ibid.*, p. 39.23f.
68. *Ibid.*, p. 39.25ff.
69. *Ibid.*, "...atque haec in rhetoricis nostris longius." Cf. chapter 4, our discussion of this work.
70. J. Camerarius, *op. cit.*, p. 16.
71. *MW* III, p. 40.9f.
72. *Ibid.*, p. 40.11f., parentheses ours.
73. *Ibid.*, p. 40.14ff., "Ibi se splendor verborum ac proprietas aperiet et patescet velut intra meridiana cubilia verus ille ac genuinus litterae sensus."
74. *Ibid.*, p. 40.16f., "Proxime cum litteram percepimus, sequemur elenchum rerum."
75. *Ibid.*, p. 40.19ff., "Atque cum animos ad fontes contulerimus, Christum sapere incipiemus, mandatum eius lucidum nobis fiet, et nectare illo beato divinae sapientiae perfundemur."
76. *Ibid.*, p. 40.26ff. Maurer views these remarks as showing Melanchthon's dependence on Reuchlin rather than Erasmus, because the play on Old Testament images and the "mystical" pictures that he drew from them did not comport with Erasmus's general lack of interest in the Old Testament. In support of this impression of Erasmus and the Old Testament, cf. J. Aldridge, *The Hermeneutic of Erasmus*, Richmond/Zurich 1966, pp. 46ff., in ref. to his retreat from the Reuchlin controversy.
77. *MW* III, p. 40.28f., "Eam igitur quam purissime non interpollatam nostris argutiis."
78. Cf. *ibid.*, p. 35.13f., his example of how ridiculous the "nugatoria" of the classroom had become.
79. A comparison with Erasmus is beyond the scope of our writing, but even a cursory reading would show this to be an important difference between them, not that it was clearly a point of contention or disagreement.
80. *Ibid.*, p. 40.30ff.
81. *Ibid.*, p. 41.6ff., "Postquam hominum commenta placere coeperunt, et amore operum nostrorum victi, pro manna Beelphegor gustavimus, homines non *Christoi* esse coepimus. Haec velim ita dicere videar, ut sentio. Sentio autem omnino aliud nihil, quam quod evangelicae veritati ecclesiae decretis probatur...."
82. On these lectures, esp. W. Maurer, *op. cit.*, Bd. 2, p. 16, n. 10; also here below, chapter 4.
83. *MW* III, pp. 41.36-42.1ff.
84. *Ibid.*, p. 42.5ff.

CHAPTER 4

Melanchthon's Rhetoric of 1519

"The Lord to whom the oracle at Delphi belongs says nothing and conceals nothing—he indicates, he shows." (Heraclitus, cited in E. Grassi, *Rhetoric as Philosophy*, p. 21.)

"For the gods must clearly be supposed to call things by their right and natural names." (Plato, cited in M. O'Rourke Boyle, *Erasmus on Language and Method in Theology*, p. vii.)

Melanchthon's inaugural speech was an impressive performance. Luther had been skeptical, but now wrote to Court Secretary George Spalatin to report that Philip had dispelled all doubt and to express his gratitude to Prince Frederick for having made such a wise decision. "On the fourth day after his arrival Melanchthon held a speech so learned and so excellent, which found such approval and amazement, that you need not recommend him to us anymore. We have given up the earlier opinion, in spite of his external appearance, and we give thanks both to you and the illustrious Elector."[1] Luther only hoped that enough would be done to help Melanchthon resist the tempting offers being made by Leipzig.[2] In the first weeks Luther was particularly impressed by Melanchthon's learning: "...he makes all the theologians, high and low, his students in Greek."[3] And from the start Philip found in Luther the irresistible force of a genuine German hero. In Greek verse he described him as "a man of love, a messenger of divinely inspired wisdom and righteousness, inbreathed by the eternal word."[4] Luther would now join Reuchlin and Erasmus to form a learned triumvirate of models.[5] The two men were as dissimilar as night and day in disposition, temperament and style.

Luther was still very much the medieval "Doctor" and out of that methodological tradition,[6] and he was volatile, as capable of extreme rage as of the tenderest of sentiments, as aesthetically gifted as he was honed of mind. Philip, by way of contrast, was the classical pedagogue, a schoolmaster, as properly ordered as the world which he viewed through his humanism. They were an unlikely pair. Yet, as Rupp has said, through the many years they would complement each other to an astonishing extent, so that Lutheranism is unthinkable apart from either of them.[7] And they remained friends for life, despite some differences between them, until Luther's death left Philip to soldier on by himself, his flanks exposed to attack, not only from Rome, but also from his own ranks.[8] For the moment, though, Philip proved himself an academic marvel of industry and output. These first months at Wittenberg were perhaps the happiest and most promising of his life.

In a letter to Spalatin on the 12th of October he gave an account of his various labors. He lectured to a full auditorium[9] and worked on textbooks for use in the classroom.[10] "Now the epistle to Titus[11] is being hammered out. You know how elegant it is and how apt for correcting morals. The rest [of my time] I am giving to a lexicon...."[12] The largest project, however, and by far the most important to our discussion, was his textbook on the art of rhetoric: "The rhetoric is coming along."[13]

Indeed, Melanchthon's *De rhetorica libri tres* was ready for the Grünenberg presses by the end of the first semester. But infuriating troubles with their printer delayed publication until March or April of 1519. The manuscript itself had been finished since January, when he wrote the dedication to his dear friend Bernhard Maurer.[14] It must be strongly stressed that *De rhetorica* was not merely a manual on techniques of composition. Wilhelm Maurer's observation (which has not figured prominently in the secondary literature) is absolutely essential to interpreting the early Melanchthon on the most fundamental levels of his thought and practice: "This first great scholarly work of the young Melanchthon . . . brought together the harvest of his activities as an instructor at Tübingen."[15] Further, the textbook on rhetoric was more deeply a philosophy of composition than simply a repetition of classical paradigms. The young Preceptor rigorously applied the principles of his general truth theory to the writing and interpretation of texts within the formal framework of the classical systems of rhetoric. It was thus a synthetic statement of his philosophy of truth as embodied in texts, and it was this philosophy of texts and textual *auctoritas* that would operate as a *preunderstanding* of the world and text (more than as the product of self-conscious, interpretive *action*, on his part) in grasping, weighing, adopting, formulating and eventually defending the theology which he was even now learning from Luther. It was this theoretical view of textual authority that shaped his early Lutheran construal and handling of the biblical text as authoritative. We thus judge that a thorough knowledge of his rhetorical foundations is essential to understanding and assessing the shape of doctrine and biblical authority in the young Melanchthon, and we have devoted an entire chapter to discussion of the relevant texts.[16]

The Purpose and Plan of Melanchthon's De Rhetorica

In the preface to Bernhard Maurer, Melanchthon clearly stated what his philosophical purpose was in writing *De rhetorica*. Introducing his rhetoric with themes which recall the contents of both *De artibus* and his inaugural speech, he wrote lamentingly of the "impure and unlearned letters..., which in this time are alone called philosophical."[17] He exhorted his former student to consider a different method of study from the present one which was both "degenerate" and "diluted."[18] "For believe me, the method of letters, by which you may instruct the mind, teach morals, teach understanding of universal things is something different."[19] In ages past, young men who had learned the rudiments of grammar would advance to study under the rhetoricians.[20] Rhetoric would connect them with every sort of human study, which was of much good to them in cultivating both the arts of speaking and making intelligent judgments.[21] But today the rhetoricians have been succeeded by those "who imbue the youth, as I speak modestly, with that artless dialectic...."[22] Their failing was not that they taught and stressed logical discipline, "For I also love dialectic, and so it seems to me...that no one is able to be rightly educated who has not learned it."[23] It was rather a dialectic which Melanchthon called "the nonsense of these times"[24] which prompted his criticisms, a dialectic which had been a thorough disaster: "...by which [nonsense] it has been accomplished that, instead of apostolic letters, we have sophistic ones; instead of those of Augustine and Nazianzus [we have] those of Lyra, Carrucanus and six thousand Sentences."[25]

As he had done briefly in the inaugural oration, he now, in greater breadth and detail, blamed these recent methods for lamentable confusion between the sacred and the profane, and for the banishment of a Christianity that comported with "that evangelical spirit."[26] The precious and noble ones who now bravely put up a defense of the pure Christian faith, men such as Erasmus, Reuchlin and Luther, received too little honor from the schools and carried on their work at great peril to their lives.[27]

> From this herd [*grege*] there are those who still look disapprovingly upon the great Erasmus, who first...called theology back to its sources [*ad fontes revocavit*]; that faction does not suffer Reuchlin, who protects excellent libraries from the flames.... They cannot bear Martin Luther, because he warns what is right [*quod recta moneat*].[28]

What was to be done? One of Philip's strengths in his younger years was that he believed so deeply in the truth of his proposals that he radiated confidence in the prospect of wholesale reform in Germany. Unlike in later years when one sometimes found him discouraged and fighting off depression, the Melanchthon of 1519 was energized by an uncomplicated optimism. In this spirit he dedicated the rest of the preface (and the text) to development of the idea upon which all else in his philosophical system converged. The central idea was that the disastrous divorce between dialectic and rhetoric must end and that they must be remarried and resume their proper function as partners in holding the world on course. He now explained this proposal at some length and in *De rhetorica* would work it out in great technical detail within the framework of the classical models.

As in *De artibus* and the inaugural speech, the catalyst for the whole program was dialectic. "And unless my judgment fails me, all things which are the elements of studies depend on dialectic...."[29] We have seen how this idea grew during Melanchthon's years at Heidelberg and Tübingen into a fundamental philosophical belief. The "mother of all the arts" was herself the voice of a rational universe, our only hope for making sense of life amid various forces of chaos and darkness. But here Melanchthon went another step in explaining this proposal. "Letters once prospered when it [dialectic] also was sound, that is, when they were instructing the youth in both dialectic *and* rhetoric in equal parts."[30] He defined the "degeneration" which he had, in other writings, decried as grievous and widespread: "Now that rhetoric has been expelled from the schools, behold how paltry, how maimed, how useless dialectic is...."[31] As in the inaugural speech, he asserted that the union of dialectic with rhetoric might have endured had scholars understood the purpose and usefulness of Aristotle's *Second Analytics*.[32] But because now so few people were learned in letters of this kind, Melanchthon wrote, he must take it upon himself to devote his main work to defining "what the use of dialectic and rhetoric is...."[33] Under present concepts of these arts, dialectic was taught merely because it was a traditional part of the curriculum,[34] and rhetoric had been dwarfed, by comparison with its former stature, and had become the menial technique of composing letters (epistles) or writing "false praises of princes...."[35]

Before a reunion between these two arts would be possible, conventional misconceptions about them must be demolished and fresh new theories must replace them. Once again Melanchthon proposed that dialectic and rhetoric were two elements of the same substantive procedure, rather than discrete disciplines, and that differences between them were strategic and secondary.

> That you might know the nature of the studies about which I am speaking: the argument is the same for both the rhetorician and the dialectician; the one [dialectic] navigates between the limits of a proposed theme with sails somewhat more tightly drawn; the other wanders more freely. The language of the one [dialectic] is accommodated to teaching, the other to inspiring....[36]

What exactly did these proposals mean? The main purpose of the preface was to state the larger philosophical framework for fusing the two disciplines. The two main elements of this philosophy of rhetoric were, first, the concept of *inventio* which one best learned from Aristotle,[37] Cicero[38] and Plato,[39] and, second, the immensely important concept of *loci communes*, the best explanation and use of which was in Erasmus.[40] Philip gave a condensed view of how dialectic and rhetoric became one "speech action," to use a modern expression. The voices of his masters, from Reuchlin to Spangel, Agricola,

Wimpfeling, Erasmus and others, spoke together in his pronouncement that the aim of his book was to redefine the procedure of rhetorical persuasion (in the *genus demonstrativum*) as being essentially related to the structures of logical demonstration as conceived in the Aristotelian (and Ciceronian) tradition. With that he would illustrate how "Dialectic supplies...the 'wood' of an oration...."[41] In the conceptual structure of human oration, logic (dialectic) was at the core, "primum inter pares," its *loci inventionis* essential to the composition as a whole. Secondly, he would cultivate the Erasmian technique of relating everything to *communae causae*, or *loci communes*. Thus he combined an analytical foundationalism with what one, for lack of a better term, may call an existential one. "Therefore dialectic must first be taught, in which...the art and the objects of its method—the *loci inventionis*, forms of argument, the nature of arranging—are more readily understood."[42] Then,

> ...if the use of dialectic has established a foundation, I believe that the young man should be led entirely to *communas causas*; in these *loci communes* of virtues, fortune, death, wealth, letters and the like, let him practice. The result will be that he will bring an instructed mind to the noblest disciplines, he will make suitable judgments of others' writings, and he will be able to produce new things [*commentari nova possit*].[43]

Before we begin looking at the elaborated structure of Melanchthon's rhetorical theory, it will be useful to keep in view an outline of its plan as a whole. *De rhetorica* consists of three books, each devoted to its special themes. In Book One, Melanchthon restated his main purpose: to redefine the appropriate methods of rhetoric, which "holds first place among the noble arts."[44] Melanchthon wrote his work primarily "that the youth might understand what dialectic and rhetoric have in common, and what they do not."[45] In the first book he would give systematic treatments of the three standard *genera causarum*: (1) the *genus demonstrativum*, which is suitable for "teaching, narrating history, praising or condemning,"[46] (2) the *genus deliberativum*, "which pertains to counsel, e.g., ought we take a wife or not?"[47] and (3) the *genus iudicale*, "of legal disputes, e.g., did Milo slay Clodius legally?"[48] In this formal outline of topics Melanchthon of course followed the structural conventions of classical rhetoric.[49]

The essential purpose of Book One (which comprised all but about twenty pages of the entire writing and contained the theoretical substance of his method)[50] was to apply his fresh ideas about logical form and existential substance to the traditional *oratoris officia*: (1) *inventio*, or using *loci inventionis*, and (2) *dispositio*, or the "artful arrangement of the 'invented' topic."[51] So the main body of the work was about the most fundamental elements of selecting, structuring and expressing thought in right words. Its scope was not simply to apply the right methods of selection and organization of language, but to identify the right values behind the formation of ideas into *oratio*. Books Two and Three were thus scarcely more than appendices on *dispositio* and then *elocutio*, "the adornment or outward appearance of the oration."[52] Melanchthon explained that his stress on *inventio* and *dispositio* was necessary because they had been most neglected by rhetoricians in recent times and were simply crucial to getting the whole thing right.[53]

A main element of the rhetoric would thus be a fresh approach to the system of rules governing *dispositio*, or the "parts of the oration," *partes orationis*: (1) an *exordium*, or introduction, (2) *narratio*, "which is the exposition of one's theme," (3) *contentio* (or *confirmatio*), "by which we confirm our view and defend it against opposing ones," and (4) *peroratio*, "which is the end of the oration."[54] As we shall see, his greatest concern by far was with the third function, which constituted the main force of one's speech in relation to objective and essential human truth.

A complete structural, theoretical and comparative study of this mass of diverse rhetorical concepts is clearly not within the scope of our present work. Our discussion of the main themes of *De rhetorica* will thus be centered upon his methods of *inventio* and *dispositio*, and stress will fall upon the features of these methods which were to have a shaping influence on his idea of Scripture and its authoritative power. It seems that his philosophy of rhetoric expressed a confluence of intuitions that made him a kind of "scholastic humanist." There was that side of him which was puritanically rigorous in a disciplined use of terms, logical syllogism and inference to build upon one's basic foundations of natural truth, and was driven to seek perfect logical coherence for the whole of one's *oratio*. There was also the more typically humanistic side of his nature that was allergic to what he would call the *nugatoria*, the abstract logical gaming that went on in the schools, and gave him his passion for relating everything to the universally human structures of our existence, to the *caussae communes* that ordered our experience as human beings. That Philip was incapable of separating these intuitions has been and remains the source of many peculiarities (when compared, say, with Luther and Erasmus) that have made him so difficult to figure out as a person and theologian. Understanding the nature of the complexity will help us to assess the extent to which he successfully integrated the different traditions that intersected in his theological mind.

The Main Ideas and Concepts of Melanchthon's Rhetoric

Inventio

In the book *De inventione dialectica*, Rudolf Agricola had lamented the fact that *dialectical* "invention" was now a lost art: "...the orators have written more precepts on *inventio*, which we attribute to dialectic, than have any of the dialecticians."[55] Indeed, *inventio* was considered the principal duty of rhetoric—"finding" one's topic and the proper structural forms in which to present it.[56] In his textbook on rhetoric Melanchthon chastised the rhetoricians of his day, not for having abandoned the practice of *inventio*, but for a wrongheaded construal of the concept itself and what it was all about.[57] Here we have the fully developed form of his proposition that return to the original theories of the great Aristotle, and their systematic evolution in the writings of Cicero and Quintilian, was of the essence for rhetoricians. Thus, if Agricola had set his sights on using these sources to rejuvenate the dialectical discipline, Philip aimed at using them to bring off a general reformation in the field of rhetoric.[58] He wished to accomplish something very like what Grassi has observed in the writings of Plato, a union of knowledge and passion.[59]

Perhaps the most important section of *De rhetorica* was the treatment of the *genus demonstrativum* at the head of Book One. In this section Melanchthon assumed the conventional notion of rhetorical "invention" as "finding" the correct, or most suitable, structure (*genus*) for one's theme. But it was a deeper, more ancient idea of rhetoric, long forgotten by Europeans, that Philip now invited his students to ponder. This deeper rhetoric required of its practitioners the intuitive wisdom of a Socrates and the surgical precision of an Aristotle. It presupposed a concept of *inventio* that was born of a profound philosophical sense of the world.

Writing on the *genus demonstrativum*, he pointed out that this traditional form of rhetorical composition was typically the one that would be enlisted in constructing an oration either for straightforward teaching or for the purpose of praising, or perhaps condemning, the actions of someone.[60] Rhetoricians had written a good deal about the second of these functions,[61] but seemed to have lost sight of the plain, didactic forms of writing and speaking.[62] That was because contemporary rhetoricians stressed those things "common in the forum and in councils,"[63] but the disciplined and artful rigor of pure *dialectical invention*, "from which the other [forms of rhetoric] draw their waters, they left to the schools."[64] Thus, by beginning with the *genus demonstrativum* in its *didactic* form (applying the Aristotelian values of Cicero and Quintilian), Melanchthon would reconnect his preferred methods of dialectic with rhetorical composition and help fellow humanists rebuild the foundations of contemporary rhetoric.

As far as we have been able to determine, making the *genus demonstrativum* the formal link between dialectic and rhetoric and, thus, the foundation of one's entire rhetorical system was original with Melanchthon.[65] In later editions he would create a separate classification, the *genus didascalicum*, which did the same job of comprising the dialectical *loci inventionis*. In 1521 the same systematic proposal emerged.

> Moreover, there is a dialectical form of speech [*dialecticum genus*], a particular certain and plain method by which the natures, causes, parts and functions of things are inquired into by certain fixed laws, so that there is nothing that can be known exactly and properly [*ut exacte et proprie nihil cognosci queat*], unless circumscribed by dialectical instruments [*nisi dialecticis organis astrictum*].[66]

This quotation shows that for Melanchthon dialectical methods not merely served rhetoric, but were essential to proper epistemic procedure and to exact and proper knowledge of anything. How deeply this epistemic belief and its underlying theory of truth would permeate his construal of Holy Scripture and his concept of Christian doctrine and how they became features of his unique personality as a theologian (next to others like Erasmus and Luther) will continue to emerge in the course of our study.

But what exactly was the nature of this method of *rhetorical* invention that Aristotle once called the "head and ruler" of dialectic, without which it had no "use and power"?[67] Building upon the "questions" of Aristotle's *Second Analytics*, Melanchthon proposed a list of nine *inveniendi organa*, which would enable students to know "whatever can be known about any subject...."[68] This Aristotelian instrument consisted of a series of formal questions, or *loci inventionis: An sit? Quid sit? Quibus caussis partibus ne constet? Unum an multa? Quae partes? Quae comparatio partium? Quae officia? Quae affinia? Quae contraria?* In these *loci inventionis* the rhetorician had all that he needed from the volumes of dialectic.[69]

This is where the *loci inventionis* of dialectic operated as the principal rules of rhetorical practice. The most basic rhetorical action rested on an Aristotelian metaphysic which claimed that all things had categorically universal natures and were thus open to rational definition of their "predicates" or properties (and that these "natures" were dialectically related to our thoughts or terms for them). The initial use of dialectical questions presumed the applicability of these "common notions..., categories, as Aristotle called them."[70] Whether one labeled them "classes [*ordines*]," "categories," "predicates" (as in more recent theory)[71] or "modes of knowing" (as insightfully done in Arabian logic),[72] the important thing to remember was that these *rerum capita* existed and that they worked when put to epistemic use. Of all methods of knowing, "the most certain of all [*modo omnium certissimo*] is definition."[73] When Melanchthon spoke of going to the "sources," he had in mind the a priori seats of truth in the universe. "Our purpose is to derive what is taught from the *sources*, from the 'starting line,' as they say...."[74] The basic categories or predicates (such as "substance," "quantity," "quality" or, to use another framework, "essence," "movement," "status") must be memorized and practiced by the rhetorician so that "whatever must be treated artfully, you should first seek these classes of things, from whence definition of the theme must be taken."[75] The second step toward final demonstration (*divisio*) would be then to derive (as we shall see, through methods of inference) "axioms, hypotheses, syllogisms."[76] The best examples of this kind of procedure were to be found in the logic of Boethius and the *Second Analytics* of Aristotle.[77]

We take this first important section on rhetorical "invention" to be the product mainly of Melanchthon's contact with that brand of South German nominalism which men like Jacob Wimpfeling, Wendelin Steinbach and Franz Kircher defended as essential to a life of devotion and action. Metaphysically and epistemically moderate on the question of universals (but clearly not "skeptical" or "relativistic" on the knowledge of reality), they staked everything on the semantic propriety of language in the systems of Aristotle, filtered (in individually diverse ways) through Cicero, Quintilian, Boethius, Cassiador and others. Melanchthon grafted this semantic tradition directly into the foundation of rhetoric on the basic level of *inventio*. On this level there was simply no difference between dialectical and rhetorical "demonstration." More than a separate *genus rhetoricae*, this method of persuasion became for Melanchthon, as he had said, the way into all the other *genera*, the heart of rhetoric itself. This would eventually become true for his idea of biblical truth as well.

But there was yet a second phase to "finding" the proper logical and semantic categories of rhetorical discourse, and here one detects the clearest evidence of Philip's membership within the contemporary movement of Erasmian humanism.

> Students must be diligently admonished about the *end* to which these things pertain; they should be taught examples; definitions should be brought from the orators, poets, theologians..., especially of the *loci communes*, so that they might be imbued with civil judgment and a common sense of things.[78]

To our knowledge, this was the first occurrence of the now-famous expression *loci communes* in his work. These were "universals" of a very special kind. When one was aware of them and used them properly, one's speech ascended above merely logical, semantic and elocutionary perfection, to realms of great cosmic power.

> It will be entirely useful for the youth, from the beginning of great studies, immediately...to study the *loci communes* with this method, by which they might observe the *nature and pure, deep power* of these subjects. ...*loci communes* are virtues, vices, fortune, life, death..., finally, all things which generally occur in common affairs.[79]

This concept that would become of great prominence in Melanchthon's later theological vocabulary is one of the standard topics in any review of his works. Nevertheless, it has been only in the last two decades that anything like a consensus has been reached on exactly how Melanchthon *himself* understood and used it.[80] There is still need for clarification. Part of the difficulty, as Wiedenhofer has rightly said, is in the fiendishly complicated history of the term since classical times.[81] And to make matters worse, as Sperl has indicated, Melanchthon himself used it in a bewildering variety of senses.[82] It is very important to have as clear a view as possible of how Philip stitched these various meanings together into a complex but coherent whole, as we believe that he mainly did.

The research of E. Grassi and others has shown that the term *loci* was first used rhetorically by Cicero to translate Aristotle's *topoi* into Latin.[83] Both Aristotle and Cicero distinguished between "inventive" and "critical" (typically Stoic) philosophy. The most basic philosophical act was for them not deduction but "invention" or "finding" the right kinds of arguments that are needed for demonstration. What some modern analytic philosophers call "properly basic beliefs" seems a close analogy to this broad sense of the term *loci communis*.

These *loci* are not derived by inference or logical process, but are themselves irreducibly underived truths. They are, as Cicero put it in his widely used definition, the "seats of the arguments" (*sedes argumentorum*).[84] The metaphor indicates that they are foundational truths. But there is something still more basic about them than the term "truth" elicits. Aristotle referred to them as "the first inherent parts of which a thing is constructed and which cannot be analyzed formally into a different form...."[85] Ontologically they were *archai*, or "first things," the stuff of reality that made truth possible in the epistemic sense, and were simply implicit *in* knowing and believing.[86] Logically and rhetorically they therefore could operate as premises for various kinds of definition and argument, but they also stood for an ontology that generated a profound sense of epistemic and didactic optimism.[87] The power of arguments was not only logical (though it was *rational*), but was finally dependent upon the natural force of these "topics" or *loci*.

It is quite obvious that Melanchthon was deeply a part of this philosophical tradition in rhetoric. Without referring to the master, he could quote Cicero's definition of the *loci inveniendi* as the "seats of the arguments" as if it were his own.[88] We have seen how, in his review of demonstrative speech, he worked within the methodological paradigms of Aristotle, Cicero and Agricola to infuse his rhetorical system with the hardwood quality of logic. The term *loci* for Melanchthon included the meaning of basic structures and principles which made human discourse (and formal logic) both possible and valid.[89] *Loci communes* for him included this ontological view of basic realities that generated rational truths malleable to the operations of logic, and these operations were essential to knowledge of the truths inherent in these "seats of the arguments." That was the essence of his connection, as a rhetorician and reformer, with Aristotelian metaphysics and logic.

But there was yet another meaning for *loci communes*—a meaning which is illustrative of Melanchthon's debt to Erasmus (and Oecolampadius's Agricola). In fact, when he used the term *loci communes* (rather than *loci inventionis*), most of the time he was referring to one of two classes of things (or sometimes ambiguously to both). The one was simply "topics" in the primary sense of the English word, but with respect to those topics which disclosed the categorical, universal threads running through human history and experience. One might say that the purely logical sense of the *loci communes* as archaic, or first, things and as basic beliefs, was here writ large onto the canvas of world history and human nature. Geyer was absolutely right in seeing that this sense of the term was very near to that of Heidegger's concept of "existentials,"[90] or *formal* universals that demand engagement and toward which no reflective human is indifferent. Belonging best to the *genus demonstrativum* (in its didactic sense), topics such as "virtue," "life" and "death" were handled "inventively" through the organs of definition, and great orations were born of reflection on great themes.

Toward the finish of his lengthy section on the *genus demonstrativum*, Melanchthon inserted a distinct subsection entitled *De locibus communibus*, in which he summed up his views on their nature and utility. In this subsection (as in the introduction), he defined the term *loci communes* as "forms of things which commonly fall in the experience of human affairs and letters, such as fortune, wealth, honor, life, death, virtue, prudence, justice...."[91] Students must concentrate their energies on such *loci communes*, which are "partly from classes and offices of virtues and vices, partly from the other things, which...are of chief importance to the affairs of mortals...."[92] They should then do rigorous exercises with them, using inventive methods by which to "discover" the nature and power of such topics.

> The counsel, which I have given above, that students should perform exercises with the inventive method in *loci communes*, is useful for this purpose: that they might appropriately perceive the nature and power of each [*singulorum naturam vimque proprie perspicerant*].[93]

By performing exercises of this kind, students come into contact with the deepest seats of nature itself and thus begin to gain new wisdom in life. The expanded ontological notion of the *loci* retained its link with the structures of reality. "Do not suppose that these have been thought up by chance; dug out of the deepest seats of nature, they are the forms or rules of all things."[94] Melanchthon advised (and here one sees the deeper senses of his later use of the term as topics appropriate to a discipline) that each discipline, be it law, theology or any other, should have as its topics *loci communes* which are appropriate to it: "as, in theology, faith, ceremonies, sin; in law, equity, servitude, punishment...."[95] The more basic philosophical point, though, was that each discipline and the whole curriculum must be grounded properly in existentially universal realities, their ideas and concepts growing therefrom.

It should be evident by now, and must be duly noted for future reference, that Philip's concept of the *loci*, while deeply engaged in Aristotelian metaphysics, epistemology and linguistics, was no simply cognitive matter. It was Plato who wrote of the blessed union in great discourse of knowledge and passion. This union was taken for granted in the norms of Aristotle, Cicero and Quintilian in antiquity, and by Agricola and Erasmus on the contemporary scene. Melanchthon inherited this humanistic nose for the core of things, for what really mattered (and thus ought to matter). Rhetorical action began with the categories of logic, but was not completed until the journey through one's topic had reached its destination in the heart. In a final section entitled *De affectibus*, in the context of demonstrative rhetoric of the most didactic kind, Melanchthon proposed that rhetoric must appeal to the "affections," as well as to the mind. He appealed to Aristotle's theory that moving the soul of the hearer must be in view, "For he will persuade perfectly, who will best affect the soul of the hearer."[96] Pointing at the examples of Quintilian, Cicero and Demosthenes, he stressed the utility of "propriety and splendor of words" for bringing power (*vis*) to bear upon the affections.[97] By "propriety and splendor" Melanchthon obviously did not mean to say that one should be manipulative, but rather, on a solid rational basis, should use the power and splendor of language to bring out the "force" (*energia*) of the circumstances: "an affection is the power of circumstance."[98] These "circumstances," or conditions set up by one's appropriately "invented" subject, would through proper speech unleash a power of their own.

But the concept of *loci communes* in this more "existential" sense was broader still. Maurer, Sperl and Geyer were quite correct in pointing out that Melanchthon used it not only in reference to the universal forms of human existence, but also (going beyond the scope of its usage in Erasmus and Agricola, and reviving the original Ciceronian view) to material propositions or rules that govern it.[99] Once again we are made aware of the ambiguity in viewing the *loci* as basic structures, on the one hand, and as cognitive truths that are part of the ontological order, on the other. Ambiguity ought not be assumed to be vagueness, however, for Melanchthon's usage seems initially a coherent expression of his modified nominalism. He developed this idea in the context of his remarks on the *genus deliberativum* and the *genus iudicale*.

> So there are in both persuasive and judicial speeches *loci communes*, certain universal rules of living [*regulae quaedam vivendi generales*], established for men by nature [*natura hominibus persuasae*], which not for nothing I shall have called laws of nature, i.e., certain propositions that are clearly necessary [*sententias quasdam adeo necessarias*], so that commonly conceived they sound forth nothing that the hearer might be able to deny.[100]

His examples were ethical: "kindness should be repaid with kindness," "parents ought to be honored," "violence ought to be done to no one...."[101] The author of good rhetoric in this context must use such universal wisdom as a kind of *ius gentium* or hermeneutical moral core of truths for the construction of clinching arguments. As we shall see, the dialectical mechanism for this *divisio* and *confirmatio* was sometimes the classical syllogism deployed as a literary structure.

In Melanchthon's concept of the *loci communes*, an earlier pattern of thought was in evidence. The complexity and breadth of this concept is testimony to the great range and systematic gifts of the young Melanchthon. Although he may have oversimplified the variety of influences upon the young Preceptor, Sperl was among the first to notice that "...Melanchthon adopted the particular elements from R. Agricola, Erasmus and Cicero out of which he then independently formed a system of his own," and, in spite of dependencies on greater minds than his own, "so is this kind of work thoroughly original, and it betrays an independent thinker of great systematic power."[102] It seems that, at this very young age, Philip had fused the distinct (but not separate) linguistic traditions of South German nominalism and its vigorous affirmation of "scholastic" perfection in logic and semantics with those of Northern European (Erasmian) humanism and its equally vigorous affirmation of real life and the pursuit of virtue. His own creative skill enabled him to use Aristotle to mediate coherently between them and to emerge with his distinctive brand of thought. His theory of rhetorical "invention" represented a genuine synthesis of dialectic and rhetoric (rather than the subordination of the one to the other) and gave systematic linguistic expression to a deeper view of the ontological *status* of thought and language. A properly sharpened and focused linguistic method captured the power of the created universe. This power was as fully a matter of the mind as it was of the heart, as much a matter of right thinking as of right moral action. Finally, his strong consciousness of the existence of this ontological order enabled him to move freely into the world of pagan literature and life. How (and how successfully) he managed to carry all of these linguistic elements into his *Lutheran* reconception of Christianity and how these two systems engaged each other in his later writings are large-scale questions that are still ahead of us.

Before finishing our discussion of Melanchthon on the *loci communes*, we should perhaps include a brief summary of his views on the art and use of history, for this subject is very near to the other.[103] We have seen that he thought "historically." In *De rhetorica* he unveiled his idea of history and historical truth in the context of his rhetorical theory. He considered the past a collective memory in which there stood out peculiar, exemplary or "paradigmatic events." The term "history," in fact, had two senses in his vocabulary. One meaning pertained to *res gestae*, the recorded actions performed by people of great character and stature. The other was the more interpretive notion that authors (*auctores*) used these narratives to make exemplary points from the reserve of *loci communes* which emerged from them. The first kind of history was rhetoricized and used in the second. Writing history was, therefore, of immense service to one's world. "Two things are necessary for historical narration," he wrote, "circumstances and *loci communes*."[104] In his section on demonstrative rhetoric (in the sense of praise or vituperation), he explained that writing history demanded more than merely relating facts or events; facts and events must be related to *loci communes* which lie buried inside them.[105] Melanchthon referred to this method as *usus historiarum*, that is, the use of events of the past, yielding a harvest of *loci communes*, to assess events of the present and to inspire men to higher things. Through the *loci communes*, comparisons became possible between the past and the present. The close connection between historical examples and the literary notions of type and allegory emerged. "As if one were to compare the theologians of our age with the generation of Pharisees...."[106] Thus, as in his inaugural speech, he asserted (sharing the judgment of Erasmus) "that no one will effect anything at all noble who has not put great labor into history. Moreover, an oration is powerless [*inefficax est*] if it is lacking in history."[107]

Maurer and Wiedenhofer have both observed that there was in the young (and older) Melanchthon, amid his commitments to the universality of concepts, also a sense of *history* running its course, a "linear" passage with "waves" of decline and rebirth.[108] The historical consciousness which Melanchthon inherited from a complex of sources, filtered through Augustine and the Italian Renaissance,[109] gave him a sense of human culture as a unified whole since the creation of the world.[110] This sense was of course strengthened by an epistemic hold on the real presence of an *ius gentium* that manifested itself, some times more intensely than at others, through the ages. History was typology. Where human nobility broke the chains of evil, there were *exempla*, living "examples" for all of us. Where human evil choked what was good and true, there were also *exempla*, warnings of what may happen.[111] We shall see that Melanchthon quite characteristically divided between typology and allegory, affirming the one and mainly putting the other at arm's length. The more logically and semantically structured notion of typology (which he would relate to the scholastic concept of tropology) would at once limit his access into the imaginative world of allegorical exegesis (in significant contrast to Erasmus and Luther) and open the way to shaping a concept of biblical *unity* and coherence that comported with his underlying theory of truth.

Dispositio *and the* Partes Orationis

In Book Two of *De rhetorica* Melanchthon developed his theory of rhetorical *dispositio*. He adopted the classical and conventional framework by which to arrange one's composition in several connected parts. First was an *exordium*, or introduction; then one's *narratio*, in which the main point was asserted; next a *confirmatio*, in which it was defended, and finally a *confutatio* of possible objections and a *peroratio* or concluding summary of things.[112] What is interesting, and directly of pertinence to our thesis, is how Melanchthon unfolded this theory in the larger linguistic context of fusing dialectic and rhetoric. We judge that the essential elements of this fusion appeared in his concept of the *status caussae*, or *scopus dicendi*, and in the theory of *confirmatio* that he proposed. The first had mainly to deal with the semantic purity and general coherence of one's entire composition, the second with the power of its arguments in the sense of logical deduction. Both concepts would be of great importance to his construal of biblical authority.

The concept of the *status caussae* was closely connected in ancient rhetoric with the art of *inventio*.[113] It seems to have originated in the Greek legal system and became essential to the rules governing composition of orations in the several *genera* of rhetoric.[114] Melanchthon's understanding and use of this concept was very important to the structure of his rhetorical system, particularly in his manner of combining dialectical methods with those of rhetoric as commonly taught.[115] He discussed the nature and use of the *status* in his sections on the *genus deliberativum* and on the *genus iudicale*. In both sections he defined it as

> ...the principal and chief theme of which the controversy consists, and as the *one* single thread of argument [*argumentum*] to which all the varied arguments [*argumenta*] of the oration must be referred. And indeed one looks for the *status* at the beginning of the oration, that it might be known whence the arguments must be referred.[116]

The *status* established the basis of coherence and kept one from intermingling contradictory themes.[117] And, as the citation makes clear, Melanchthon pictured the coherence of a writing as that of a logical "referral."

There were several kinds of *status*, but whichever kind one finally decided upon,[118] its "entire composition...was born from the methodological or dialectical questions...."[119] The *status* and unifying element of an oration was thus a proposition which had a logically derived sense and truth-value. The method by which one derived and proposed one's *status* depended to an extent on what the nature of the *status* was. Without going into unnecessary technical detail, it can be said that the process ranged from simple definition from the properties of terms to the more complex syllogistic operations. As we shall see, the logic of the *status* would then determine the argumentative strategy or disposition of the oration as a whole.[120] For Melanchthon the *status* was the logical equivalent of the widely used term *scopus*. "Knowledge of the *status* is necessary in disputations, so that one might comprehend concisely and briefly what an author means."[121] Whether reading or writing a text, then, for Melanchthon the *status caussae* was a condensed statement of the literal sense or meaning of the whole, and this *sense* of texts, as parts related to the whole, was a matter of semantic propriety and logical progression to a final conclusion. An essential condition for the *authority* (not merely truth) of a text, then, was logical progression from known truths to demonstrated conclusions. His notion of the *scopus* of texts presupposed something stronger than mere formal consistency between propositions. The model was one of positive logical flow from premises to conclusions; the *status* was indeed the conclusion drawn from a rhetorical syllogism that structured one's oration.[122] As will become clearer, his was a kind of hermeneutical foundationalism that would play an essential, if not unproblematic, role in the development of early Lutheranism.

As Melanchthon progressed from each stage of his rhetorical theory to the next, it became evident that his norms or rules for what had *authority* in literature traded in the currency of literal propositions more than in allegorical or tropological figures (not that he judged them utterly invalid). The ascendency of a literal sense of texts over these other senses and of *texts* literally composed over those of other less straightforward sorts was put forth in bold, uncompromising terms by Melanchthon. We shall see that he was not very patient with mystical or symbolic construals of biblical texts, as Luther and Erasmus sometimes were.[123] His entire approach to the unity, clarity, efficacy and uniqueness of Scripture was very much in line with a hermeneutical tradition that went back to what Karl Froehlich has called the "Antiochene Antithesis" to the Alexandrian methods.[124]

Melanchthon's theory of *confirmatio* was closely connected with that of the *scopus* or *status caussae*.[125] *Confirmatio* was the required proof of one's *status* or main proposition.[126] The kinds of *confirmatio* differed from one rhetorical structure to another, but all used inventive definition of terms and syllogistic or inferential reasoning.[127] In the *genus demonstrativum*, for example, one must construct arguments from definitions (in this instance arising with the *locus, quid sit?*).[128] In the *genus deliberativum*, however, one's basic *loci (an honestum, an utile, an facile sit?*) would typically produce assertions that called for the more inductive invocation of *loci communes* (in the sense of human laws) and the construction of a single, comprehensive syllogism to confirm the truth of one's claim. For instance (to use Melanchthon's timely illustration), one might wish to prove that taking part in the Turkish wars was a moral obligation. The *locus communis* that "men are morally obligated to do what is just" is uncontested among rightly thinking people.[129] One must next construct an argument showing that this war represented a just cause. An inductive syllogism could now be formed, using the *locus communis* as the major premise and the proposition that fighting against the Turks is just as the minor one.[130] The logical conclusion from these premises (the truth of the one inherent in nature, that of the other derived from induction) was one's thesis or *status*: "what one offered as the *status* followed from these; it is proved by the two superior propositions."[131] The unifying structure and force of the entire composition was, therefore, that of a logical syllogism whose premises were either incorrigibly and basically true, or the outcome of evidence and arguments, or a combination of the two kinds of truth. The authority of such rhetoric was not merely in its unity and personal relevance, but finally in both together shaped by inescapably powerful logic. The idea of *oratio* in Melanchthon is incomplete without all these dimensions operating at once. Rhetoric for Melanchthon had the "priestly" function of mediating between the realm of eternal truth and that of mortal human beings at the points where contact between them was most crucial. Properly crafted rhetoric made language something like Jacob's ladder, with the angels ascending and descending from heaven to earth and back again. The archaic, powerful contacts were made through the structure and contents of the essential *loci communes*, ascent and descent made possible by the natural power of disciplined logical functions. We are not saying that authority for Melanchthon was limited to these logical functions, for it most certainly was not, but that textual authority for him was incomprehensible without them. On the other hand, the many things that have been written in the past century and a half about his "intellectualism" will have to be qualified to account for larger senses of truth and authority in his writings. Already we have observed in his theories of *inventio* and *dispositio* that he affirmed the existence of realities that transcended simple distinctions between reason and affection. Reason was itself a passion, and one's passion was always reasonable. In his view the deepest seats of nature opened the salient powers of God's creation to human beings and human beings to lives of action born of truth.

Biblical Writings as Rhetoric

In the foregoing discussion we examined the doctrines of Melanchthon's rhetoric which were to have the greatest power over his theological grammar, syntax and even semantics. In this final section on *De rhetorica* we shall see that his conceptual transference from philosophy to theology was already in an advanced stage of development by the time he came to Wittenberg and that he had also begun to absorb the new Lutheran theology. *De rhetorica* mainly reflected his synthetic achievements while studying and teaching at Tübingen, but it was also a transitional work. Abundant illustrations from theology and sacred Scripture reflected the intellectual interests of Philip's new surroundings, although the linguistic methods that he used for analysis of Christian doctrines or concepts were much older and more familiar to him than were the proposals about Paul's teachings on justification by faith.[132] Whatever his theological stance at the time of this writing, he made it very clear that biblical doctrines were themselves the products of a kind of *sacred* rhetoric, for the biblical authors had composed their letters by classical standards. And, for Melanchthon, the idea of "classical" had all the elements and the distinctive shape as a whole that we have observed. In this section our purpose is to discuss the places in *De rhetorica* where he used biblical writings as examples of good rhetoric and to see how he had come to picture the text of the Bible itself as *oratio sacra*.

In the main, Melanchthon's comments on biblical literature occurred in Book One under the subheading *enarratio*, or the rules for interpretive rhetoric. On this subject, he made detailed references to Paul's epistle to Titus,[133] the epistle to the Hebrews,[134] the epistle to the Romans,[135] the Psalms[136] and Genesis.[137] He made the general literary assumption that any rightly constructed text would qualify as one of four kinds of writing: didactic, historical, persuasive or allegorical.[138] A most effective method of interpreting persuasive discourse was employed by Erasmus in his *Paraphrases* on Romans.[139] The main idea in paraphrase was this: "that you render the meaning of an author as appropriately and purely as possible [*proprissime ac purissime*], meanwhile adding polish and confirmation."[140] Melanchthon wrote that he had used such a method to expound Paul's epistle to Titus.[141] This epistle was well suited to paraphrase, "both because it contains many *loci communes* and because they [the students] could interpret the things which Paul has comprehended most concisely by added reasons [*subjectis rationibus*], arguments, confirmations, examples and the like."[142] For example, Paul wrote that a bishop ought not be quick-tempered. "It was not fortuitous [*non ociosum est*] that Paul admonished this at the beginning, for what a pestilent vice stubbornness is in those who administer public affairs may be declared, indeed, by examples...."[143] The essential point was getting at the power of the words themselves as transparently as possible. The interpreter must explain Paul's meaning by methods "which relate the nature of the words and the power of the oration, not adulterated, but truly and appropriately."[144]

From Melanchthon's comments on the method of paraphrase, one can begin to form some ideas about his distinctive textual construal, although thus far the picture is generally Erasmian in nature. In the one instance, rhetorical paraphrase was an effective means of interpretation, because the epistle to Titus was itself a source of *loci communes* (here it would seem in the sense of actual assertions about how men ought to live) and was therefore a fountain of practical wisdom. Moreover, Titus was arranged according to a design, the power of which was in its orderly (*non ociosum*), literal expression of moral commonplaces in the context of Christian teaching on life within the church. There is nothing in the discussion to identify the precise kind or rhetorical structure (*genus*) of the writing, nor did Melanchthon comment on the literary methods by which Paul "most concisely comprehended" the many *loci communes*. He did, however, view the epistle as a very useful work, suited to methods of rhetorical *enarratio*, exemplifying the universal patterns of great literature.

Melanchthon's specific image of biblical texts as rhetorical literature emerged more clearly in his section on methods of "exegesis": "The other is the method of *exegesis*...,when we explain authors in whole commentaries."[145] The epistle to the Hebrews (which, unlike Erasmus,[146] he took to be from Paul) was a model of historical interpretation, in which one related events or *circumstantiae* to *loci communes*.

> I think that this method of interpreting history should be most
> effectively observed in sacred studies. For example, Paul, in the
> epistle to the Hebrews, weighs many histories against faith, as a
> *locus communis*, meanwhile illustrating certain things most
> excellently with the circumstances.[147]

His construal of Hebrews was connected with a generalization about biblical literature as a rule. Sacred writing was usually historical, was categorically distinct from allegorical literature and must thus be interpreted by methods that matched the historical manner of writing.[148] His critique of imaginative uses of allegorical interpretation took shape. "Perhaps it will be preferable so to interpret sacred literature that its greatness becomes manifest in the history [*dignitas historiae constet*] which in general has been written that it might teach the truth, rightly instructing the good mind [*vera doceat, recte erudiat bonam mentem*]."[149] His sensitivity to the Lutheran theme of human depravity also began to guide him in apprehending the sense of certain historical texts in doctrinal terms that he believed were inherent in the stories themselves, taken just as they stood. It was mistaken, he wrote, to allegorize events which seemed distasteful or immoral to us. "I ask, what good is it to excuse the perfidy of certain men with imagined allegories, when they have been written for this purpose, that we might be warned of our lot [*nostrae sortis admoneamur*], that man is a lie and a vanity [*mendacium ac vanitatem hominem esse*] and that God is truth?"[150] Instead of fabricating allegories which paint moral whitewash over the stained surface of human behavior, one must look honestly for the *loci communes* arising to meet us in the events themselves, releasing their "native power."[151] For example, the history of Abraham, who was commanded by God to kill his only son, "is not ignoble."[152] Melanchthon apparently believed that the point of the story was generally missed by the experts. Through the obedience of the old man *we* learn the *locus communis*, "burial of the flesh, cleansing the affections of the flesh."[153] In an immensely interesting passage, Melanchthon indicated that the intent of spiritual application had degenerated into practices far removed from the sources and that tightening the rules of interpretation was essential to recovering contact with the native power of God's Word. One begins to see how Philip's concepts of "God's Word" and its "native power" were thoroughly grounded in his linguistics of *sermo proprius* and that he scarcely sensed that there was anything constitutive or interpretive about his own exegetical practice. In a context of rightly formed language and method, the *dignitas* and majesty of the Word *itself* would come forth. The pure mind was an essential condition for the pure Word, and Melanchthon seemed fully confident that there was nothing circular or problematic about attaining such a noetic structure through right methods.

> In this manner the ancients were accustomed to interpret the sacred histories, with the Spirit as their guide; today they are led by allegories too far from the sources for them to retain their native power. Truly, the Word of God is powerful, it lives and burns when, in its own majesty, it is poured out upon good and pure minds; but when it has been diluted by our cleverness, I do not know how much power it may have.[154]

The living, burning majesty of God's Word was in its historical expression of universal truths about the life of faith.

In a later passage Melanchthon conceded that allegorical exegesis might be valid, but only on the condition that learned interpreters had found the *loci communes* which arose from within the stories. The plain letter of the histories controlled one's exegesis at all levels in a mainly logical, didactic manner of progressing, by "comparison," from story to meaning. For example, he objected to what he called absurd efforts to find the seven liberal arts or seven sacraments lying hidden hermeneutically within the history that described the seven columns of Solomon's Temple.[155] This loosely imaginative interpretation was for him unwarranted and destructive, because it was without any logical or conceptual connection with the natural meaning or *scopos* of the *particular* text (even though one might argue for a connection with the *larger* sense of Scripture and Christianity).[156] The outlines of what one may call a hermeneutical foundationalism was apparent, wherein the relationship between text and doctrine was clearly that of logical consistency, if not always direct inference.

> In the histories, allegory is very perilous. But nevertheless, in my view, one must consider the nature of that which is handled by allegory. For by all means, if the natures of the things compared are in disagreement with each other [*si discrepent eorum inter se naturae*], then the allegory is absurd [*absurda est allegoria*].Thereafter, we should use the forms of the *loci communes* [*locorum communium formis utamur*].[157]

It would seem that Melanchthon meant to say more than that one's allegorical interpretation must *comport* logically with the natural sense of one's text (although, still sounding rather like Erasmus, he did permit rendering the brambled bush as the scribes and Pharisees who entangled Christ the ram).[158]

He elaborated his rules more thoroughly in reference to the story of Cain and Abel. "Two things, therefore, must be observed in allegories. The nature of the histories [consists of] both the character of the person who is written about and the *loci communes*."[159] Thus when reading of Cain's atrocity, one was reminded by the character of Cain, in the text itself, of a *locus communis* or commonplace about *sin*. The interpretive process was that of conceptual comparison, or *comparatio*. "For Cain cannot be compared with a just man. From that comparison [*comparatio*] of Cain with a sinner, the *locus communis* of sin is born, the power and cruel tyranny of which must be handled with amplifications."[160] In this instance, the "character" of an individual player in the plot of sacred history reflected the universal human experience of being fallen. The conceptual *locus* of "sin" was found through the logical process of "comparison" or *comparatio*, and Cain's history became authoritative for our own.[161] Note, too, the holistic nature of that authority as exemplified by the concept of a *locus communis*. This was no mere teaching or proposition, but rather a powerful knowledge of oneself that would lead to right affections and actions.

Melanchthon did allow that students should practice relating certain biblical details mechanically to other standardized *loci communes*: the Nazarites signified the priesthood of Christ; the horns of Joshua, the preaching of God's Word; manna, the Word of God, and so forth.[162] This procedure was that of classical "amplification," or going from an assertion or level of meaning of relatively small significance to larger and larger ones. However, it is evident that he believed it necessary that the persons, events and details of the text must give a basis for conceptual comparison to justify such folding of meaning upon meaning from one passage. It is equally evident that Melanchthon, like Erasmus (and now Luther), thought of Scripture as teaching a coherent system of doctrines, so that individual parts of the canon never stood entirely on their own, but always in relation to a center of meaning that arose from elsewhere, a *scopus* of central interpretive significance and power. How individual parts might be related exactly to this *scopus* and just what the nature of the *scopus* was are questions to be treated in their turn. Nevertheless, it should be noticed that Melanchthon would himself practice this *allegorical* style of amplification only very rarely, and the preferred construal of biblical texts was as logically structured orations that combined inductively to form the theological whole or literal sense of the canon. The *scopus* of Scripture was thus itself founded by the logic of the text. His later *annotationes* on Genesis 1-3, for example, show that he could be sensitive to literary symbolism (such as the two trees in the garden), but that he operated with a larger sense of this text as a didactic historical composition.[163]

Melanchthon's section on the rules of interpretation for persuasive oration, *suasoria oratio*, are extremely illuminating in the context of our study.[164] This kind of rhetoric was commonly composed according to the *loci* of the *genus deliberativum*.[165] Proper interpretation required careful attention to three main features: (1) its *status caussae*, (2) its arguments and (3) the affections to which it appealed.[166] "He who has marked these three things in persuasive orations...will easily follow the author."[167] Most important among one's duties, though, was to observe the *status*, apart from which "it is impossible to do justice to the theme."[168]

The first example given by Melanchthon of classically composed persuasive rhetoric is evidence of his growing familiarity with, and perhaps deepening interest in, the theological currents that were beginning to swell like huge waves originating from Wittenberg. Paul's epistle to the Romans had itself been written to defend a clear *status*, which the competent interpreter must grasp, define and explain to his readers. Here we have the first positive proof of his contact with Luther's distinctive theology.

> For example, in Paul's epistle to the Romans, when this is the *status*: the law does not justify, grace justifies; the letter kills, the spirit gives life, one will do one's duty as interpreter by the method of teaching, if he writes what the letter *is*, what the spirit *is*.[169]

Next, one must turn to the argument "that there is no one who is not a slave to sin"[170] and notice, "These are everywhere adorned with affections and rhetorical figures."[171] In sum, Romans exemplified the classical execution of right rhetorical *inventio, dispositio* and *elocutio*. In other references, Melanchthon placed Paul's argument in Romans alongside Plato's proof of the soul's immortality as noble examples of how to develop a "complex theme" in the *genus demonstrativum*.[172] This fact would suggest that Melanchthon classified Romans as *demonstrative* rhetoric, but also as very similar to forms of deliberation or judicial argument, whose characteristic center was a *status caussae*.[173]

In Book Three of *De rhetorica*, Melanchthon used both Romans and Galatians as examples of rhetorical excellence.

> ...both have a *scopos* and many of the same arguments. Nevertheless, in the epistle to the Romans, [the author] soars with many figures of words and sayings, with various allegories of the new and old Adam, of letter and spirit; everywhere he inserts examples taken from the histories. Here he is an orator, if one can describe him in human words [*hic est orator ille, si fas est eum verbis humanis praedicare*]....[174]

Paul may be compared favorably with great Pericles himself.[175] Melanchthon had discovered in Paul the "Pericles of Israel." The great extent to which he carried this idea in future writings cannot be overstated. Paul would become for him the saint of rhetoricians, apostle of the word and, as such, the paradigm for Lutheran theology. In Melanchthon, Luther's Christological and Pauline focus would become inseparably fused with the epistemic-literary norms of *oratio*.

In this same section on persuasive rhetoric, Melanchthon wrote that the Psalms, or at least many of them, contained a *status* and were written with a purposeful structure or arrangement in mind.

> Many of the Psalms pertain to the genus of persuasive oration; in these one must observe with great diligence the *status*, or summary of the argument, *what* is stated...and *why* it is said in *these* words and in *this* order.[176]

One must also notice his approval of Erasmus, the most excellent master of interpretation of this sort,[177] indicating once again that there was important continuity, if not an identity, between their methods of exegesis.

Melanchthon's use of Scripture in *De rhetorica* shows how he had begun to combine his proven resources, drawn from the linguistic traditions of both South German nominalism and Erasmus's hermeneutical writings, with new influences arising in Wittenberg. The (still developing) result was not an exact copy of any of these three interrelated traditions, but had its own distinctive cast of mind. Perhaps most striking was Philip's compulsion to have every biblical writing catalogued according to the norms of classical rhetoric. He did not merely *use* rhetoric to interpret Scripture philologically and morally (as was often the case with Erasmus, and nearly always with Luther).[178] He believed that Scripture *was* rhetoric all the way through, from parts and (as will become clear) to the whole. And his sense of Scripture and Christ together forming an *oratio* or *sermo* from God was much less metaphorical than was Erasmus's famed translation in similar terms.[179] For the Preceptor, the unity of the canon was that of a contained school of thought developed rhetorically in the manner of "antiquity," taken as a normative idea of a unified era. His developing concepts of biblical perspicuity, efficacy and unity would all absorb an idiosyncratic content from this theoretical framework of rhetorical invention, disposition and elocution.

A second matter of some note is the topical and doctrinal focus upon Romans and the Psalms and the rapid movement that the young Melanchthon was able to make between these complex and controversial new issues and his existing categories. Eventually the dialectically conceived concept of the *scopus* would be broadened to comprise not merely Paul's rhetorical structure and message, but that of God Himself throughout all of sacred history and in all the sacred writings taken together as a whole. The movement here within his various traditions—the more parochial ones from Heidelberg and Tübingen and the great, internationally known ones from Erasmus and Luther—would take shape to form the first Protestant dogmatics. And this dogmatics would be erected quite systematically upon a construal of Scripture as *oratio sacra*, where the term "oratio" reflected the distinctive linguistic system that he had constructed before going to his destiny in Wittenberg. The sense of the term "sacra" would obviously be that which he would adopt from the great Luther, but the conjunction of these terms was in the essence of Melanchthon's identity as a theologian.

Notes to Chapter 4

1. WABr I, no. 88.
2. *Ibid.*
3. *Ibid.*
4. *MW* VII/1, pp. 46.7-47.8ff.
5. Cf. E. G. Rupp, *Luther's Progress to the Diet of Worms*, New York/Evanston 1964, p. 373, following Maurer.
6. *Ibid.*, p. 374.
7. *Ibid.*, p. 375.
8. See R. Stupperich, "Der junge Melanchthon als Sachverwalter Luthers," in *Jahrbuch des Vereins für Westphälische Kirchengeschichte*, 1949, pp. 47ff.; also P. Fraenkel, "Fünfzehn Jahre Melanchthonforschung: Versuch eines Literaturberichtes," in *Philipp Melanchthon: Forschungsbeiträge zur vierhundertsten Wiederkehr seines Todestages dargeboten in Wittenberg, 1960*, (hrsg.) W. Elliger, Göttingen 1960, pp. 40ff.
9. *MW* VII/1, p. 50.21, "audior enim frequenti schola." *Ibid.*, n. 7: four hundred students attended his lectures on Greek; also, *ibid.*, p. 54.22, n. 4.
10. *Ibid.*, p. 50.20, "Doceo, in chalctypis laboro, ut habeat iuventus...,ubi sese exerceat."
11. These lectures, published in Wittenberg in 1518 as *Epistola Pauli ad Titum qua compendio vere christiani hominis vitam et mores format*, have evidently been lost. Cf. *MW* VII/1, p. 50, n. 8; W. Maurer, *Der junge Melanchthon*, Bd. 2, Göttingen 1969, p. 31, and n. 32. Melanchthon's interpretation can be derived in part from allusions to the text in *De rhetorica*.
12. *MW* VII/1, p. 50.23 and n. 9. The reference here is to a Greek lexicon that was never published.
13. *Ibid.*, p. 50.25f., and n. 12.
14. *Ibid.*, p. 67.20f., letter to John Lang in Erfurt, April 3, 1519, "Rhetorica mea mitto..., pleraque deprivata sunt nostri *chalkotypou* socordia." Cf. n. 9 on Luther's similar complaints. On date of publication, *ibid.*, p. 50, n. 12; on the letter and preface to Maurer, *MB* I, p. 55; *CR* I, pp. 62ff.; *SM* I, pp. 56ff., and discussion in W. Maurer, *op. cit.*, Bd. 1, p. 187.
15. W. Maurer, *ibid.*
16. Perhaps one reason this writing has been neglected is that it has never been published in modern critical form. It exists only in rare printings and is rather difficult to find. We have used a photocopy of the original Wittenberg edition, alongside a printing (perhaps pirated?) that came out in Cologne in 1523. The Wittenberg edition (Witt.) was made available to us by Heiko Oberman, then director of the Institut für Spätmittelalter und Reformation in Tübingen. The Cologne edition (Col.) was made available to us by the library of Trinity College, Cambridge, through E. Gordon Rupp. For a complete list of imprints, see R. Keen, *A Checklist of Melanchthon Imprints*, Sixteenth Century Biography 27, St. Louis 1988, pp. 50f.
17. Witt., A1r; Col., A1r.
18. Both *ibid.*, "...bonorum studiorum degenerem quandam et dilutam philosophiam praescribant."
19. Both *ibid.*, "...nam crede mihi, alia est literarum ratio, qua ingenium, qua mores, qua rerum communium sensum erudias."
20. Witt., *ibid.*; Col., A2vf.
21. Both, *ibid.*, "...quibus autoribus, omni genere humanorum studiorum alebantur. Sic universa tractari solebat, ut eorum esset usus aliquis dicendo, iudicando."

22. Both, *ibid.*, "Rhetoribus successerunt, qui iuventutem dialecticiis iliis inconditis, ut modeste dicam, imbuunt...."

23. Both, *ibid.*, "Nam et dialectica amo, et sic mihi...videtur, neminem recte erudiri posse, qui non et illa discat."

24. *Ibid.*

25. Witt., A2r; Col., A2v.

26. Both, *ibid.*, "Dolet animo eas iacere literas, quibus devictis, sacra omnia et prophana conspurcari coeperunt...." (Col., A2v, end Witt. A2r), "...ausim dicere, parum admodum in iis esse, quod cum spiritu illo Evangelico recte conveniat."

27. Witt., A1r; Col., A2r.

28. Both, *ibid.*

29. Witt., A2v; Col., A2r, "Ac nisi me fallit opinio mea, ex dialectica pendent omnia, [comma Witt.] quae... sunt initia studiorum...."

30. Both, *ibid.*, "Vigebant literae quondam, quum et illa esset salva, hoc est cum paribus officiis dialectica et rhetorica iuventutem erudirent."

31. Both, *ibid.*, "Iam explosa e scholis rhetorica, vide quam sit exigua, quam sit manca, quam sit inutilis dialectica...."

32. Both, *ibid.*

33. Witt., A2v; Col., A3v, "Perpauci enim sunt, qui hoc ipsum genus studiorum intelligant.... Quare visum est mihi paucis, idque obiter tantum notare, qui dialectorum qui rhetorum usus sit...."

34. Both, *ibid.*, "Primum omnium, ut dialectica non ulla ratione alia discuntur, quam ut horum temporum moribus satissiat...."

35. Both, *ibid.*, "...ita sunt qui rhetoricam arbitrantur, modum epistolarum scribendarum, aut falsa principum laudes." Cf. below on the use of the *genus demonstrativum* in Italian courts, n. 61.

36. Both, *ibid.*, "Nam scias, quae sit ratio studiorum de quibus dico, commune argumentum est rhetori et dialectico, hic intra fines propositi negocii velis contractioribus navigat, ille evagatur liberius, huius ad docendum, illius ad movendum est accommodata oratio...." Col. has "ad monendum" rather than the earlier "ad movendum."

37. Witt., A2r; Col., *ibid.*

38. Both, *ibid.*

39. Both, *ibid.*

40. Both, *ibid.*

41. Both, *ibid.*, "Organon dialectica ministrabit, ut si qua inciderunt forte, habeat ceu sylviam orationis et artificium, quo argumenta recte dispensit." See W. Maurer, *op. cit.*, Bd. 1, pp. 195ff., on the sources of this element of Melanchthon's rhetoric extending back through Vives, Cassiodor, Boethius and Cicero to Aristotle. Maurer is critical of H. Maier and the standard view that Melanchthon's interpretation of Aristotle as a rhetorician was shallow and inaccurate, pp. 198, and nn. 55-56.

42. Witt., A2v-A2r; Col., A3v-A3r. On the concept of *loci communes*, see below.

43. Both, *ibid.*

44. Witt., A3v; Col., A4r.

45. Witt., *ibid.*; Col., A5v.

46. Both, *ibid.*

47. Both, *ibid.*

48. Both, *ibid.*

49. Cf. U. Schnell, *Die homiletische Theorie Philipp Melanchthons*, Berlin/Hamburg 1968, pp. 10ff.

50. In our view, W. H. Neuser, in *Der Ansatz der Theologie Philipp Melanchthons*, Neukirchen 1957, pp. 10ff., was incorrect in his proposal that the later *Institutiones*

rhetoricae (1521), which centered upon *elocutio*, expressed a "Formalizierung" of rhetoric under Luther's theological influence. There is nothing in the document to suggest that Melanchthon changed his essential theory of rhetoric (although he obviously changed his doctrine of human nature) from the epistemically dialectical model of 1519 to a merely elocutionary one in 1521. In our view, it is more accurate to see the second work as filling gaps left by the first one. This interpretation is supported by U. Schnell's comparisons between statements from the many editions of the rhetoric. Cf. *op. cit.*, pp. 10-45.

51. Witt., A4v; Col., A5r.
52. Witt., A3r; Col., A5r.
53. Both, *ibid.*, "Ego in hoc potissimum scribo, ut locos inventionis, iudicii, et dispositionis aliquanto facilius assequare, quam vulgo traduntur. Nam hi fere . . . negliguntur, cum ea sit sola dialectorum facultas." Cf. U. Schnell, *op. cit.*, in support of Melanchthon's judgment, pp. 13ff.
54. Witt., A3r; Col., A5r.
55. R. Agricola, *De inventione dialectica*, (ed.) W. Risse, Hildesheim/New York (repr.) 1976, p. 291.
56. Cf. U. Schnell, *op. cit.*, pp. 10ff., and ref. n. 3 to W. Kroll et al. on the history of ancient rhetoric.
57. *Ibid.*, pp. 13f.
58. See, E. Grassi, *Rhetoric as Philosophy: The Humanist Tradition*, University Park/London 1980, pp. 43ff., on the use of Aristotle in the rhetorical systems of Cicero and Quintilian, particularly in their concept of *inventio*.
59. *Ibid.*, pp. 27ff.
60. Witt., A3r; Col., A6v, "Versatur enim genus demonstrativum primum in docendo, deinde in laude et vituperatio."
61. In this context, see J. W. O'Malley, "Grammar and Rhetoric in the Pietas of Erasmus," *Journal of Medieval and Renaissance Studies*, 18, Spr. 1988, pp. 81ff., particularly on the orators of the papal court and their use of this *genus*, esp. p. 94.
62. Witt., A3r; Col., A6v, "De posteriore multa satis rhetores. Prior species parcius colitur...."
63. Both, *ibid.*
64. Both, *ibid.*, "...ex quo alia rivos ducunt, scholis reliquerunt."
65. See U. Schnell, *op. cit.*, pp. 41ff., "De rhetorica stellt den ersten Versuch Melanchthons dar, der Dialektik den ihr gebuhrenden Platz innerhalb der Rhetorik zu sichern. Die antiken Rhetoren hatten kein spezielles Lehrgenus ausgebildet; allerdings stellten sie gelegentlich die Frage, ob nicht für den Lehrvortrag ein besonders Genus aufzustellen sei. Diese hatte jedoch zu keinen praktischen Konsequenzen geführt."
    Of his contemporaries, Erasmus was perhaps nearest to him in using logic for the (here subordinate) purpose of serving piety, cf. W. Maurer, *op. cit.*, Bd. 1, pp. 190ff., but as Maurer has stated, and as the penetrating studies of O'Malley, *op. cit.*, and O'Rourke Boyle, *Erasmus on Language and Method in Theology*, Toronto/Buffalo 1977, esp., pp. 123ff., have shown, the Dutchman was moved much more by a love for moral piety than by passion for semantics and syllogistic method. In Erasmus, dialectic tended to be absorbed by his Christian philosophy; in Melanchthon, Christian truth depended upon logical coherence.
66. *Philippi Melanchthonis institutiones rhetoricae*, (1521) Basel 1522, A2v-A2r; cf. also U. Schnell, *op. cit.*, pp. 41ff. This statement would seem to confirm that Melanchthon had not effectively changed the substantive philosophy of his rhetoric since 1519.
67. Witt., A4v; Col., A6r.

68. Both, *ibid.*, "...per locos suos impromptu habeat statim quicquid de unaquaque re dici potest...."

69. Witt., A4r; Col., A7r; also W. Maurer, *op. cit.*, Bd. 1, pp. 193ff., esp. 206 on Melanchthon's independence from Erasmus on this level of his concept of *loci*. Maurer's point is that this was more a dialectical term for Melanchthon than it evidently was for Erasmus.

70. Witt., B1v; Col., A8r, "Iam communes rerum notiones, certo quodam ordine comprehendere oportet, ut quicquid propositum fuerit, definias, quum in quem ordinem referendum sit, intellexeris. Hi rerum ordines *kategoriai* Graecis vocantur."

71. Both, *ibid.*

72. Both, *ibid.*, "Sunt ex Arabum scholis, qui praedicamenta recte cognoscendi modos appellant."

73. Witt., A4r; Col., A8v.

74. Witt., B1v; Col., A8v, "Nostrum institutum est, ex fontibus atque aiunt, *apo grammes* quod docetur, derivare...."

75. Witt., B1v; Col., A8r, "...modo intelligas eum esse usum, ut quicquid inciderit tractandum artificiose: primum requiras hos rerum ordines, unde finitio thematis colligenda est...."

76. Witt., B1r; Col., B1v.

77. Both, *ibid.*

78. Witt., B1r; Col., B1v-B1r.

79. Witt., B4r; Col., B6v, "Fueritque admodum utile, adolescentem a primis statim pràeludiis magnorum studiorum locos communes hoc artificio tractare, videlicet, quo naturam, vimque illorum integram, ac penitam introspiciat.... Loci communes virtutes, vitia fortuna, vita, mors..., denique omnia quae generaliter in communes causas incidunt."

80. The writings of P. Joachimsen were of inestimable value in showing that the concept of the *loci communes* in Melanchthon was part of a much larger vocabulary stock throughout European humanism. P. Joachimsen, "Loci communes: Eine Untersuchung zur Geistesgeschichte des Humanismus und der Reformation," in *Gesammelte Aufsätze: Beiträge zu Renaissance, Humanismus und Reformation; zur Historiographie und zum deutschen Staatsgedanken,* (Ausgewählt und eingeleitet von N. Hammerstein), Aalen 1970, pp. 387ff.; also, W. Risse, preface to Agricola's *De inventione dialectica, op. cit.,* pp. 5ff.; the most important recent works on Melanchthon and the *loci communes* are: A. Sperl, *Melanchthon zwischen Humanismus und Reformation: Eine Untersuchung über den Wandel des Traditionsverständnisses bei Melanchthon und die damit zusammenhängenden Grundfragen seiner Theologie,* (Forschung zur Geschichte und Lehre des Protestantismus, 10, XV), München 1959, pp. 34ff.; Q. Breen, "The Terms Locus and Loci Communes in Melanchthon," in *Christianity and Humanism: Studies in the History of Ideas,* (ed.) N. P. Ross, Grand Rapids 1968, pp. 93ff.; W. Maurer, *op. cit.,* Bd. 1, pp. 199ff.; S. Wiedenhofer, *Formalstrukturen humanistischer und reformatorischer Theologie bei Philipp Melanchthon,* Bd. I, Bern/Frankfurt/München 1976, pp. 373ff.; and H.-G. Geyer, *Von der Geburt des wahren Menschen,* Neukirchen 1965, pp. 49ff. Of them all we have found Geyer's analysis of this concept in Melanchthon to be the most penetrating.

81. S. Wiedenhofer, *op. cit.,* Bd. I, p. 373, "Einfach...ist diese Frage nicht, weil die Wörter *topos, locus, locus communis*...bereits seit der Antike eine mehrfache Bedeutung besitzen." Cf. references to E. Mertner et al., in Wiedenhofer, *op. cit.,* Bd. II, p. 305, n. 286; for penetrating inquiries into the subject of *loci communes* and antiquity, cf. J. Brake, *Classical Conceptions of "Places": Study in Invention,* (diss.) Michigan State University 1965; and D. Ochs, *The Tradition of the Classical Doctrines of Rhetorical Topoi,* (diss.) University of Iowa 1966.

82. A. Sperl, *op. cit.*, p. 34, "Es ist...darauf zu achten, dass er diesen Ausdruck nicht immer in genau der gleichen Bedeutung gebraucht, sondern ihn auf verschiedene Erscheinungen anwendet, die sich nicht völlig unter einen Begriff subsumieren lassen...."

83. E. Grassi, *op. cit.*, pp. 42ff., ref. to Cicero's *De oratore*, and following discussion of the relationship between logic and rhetoric in Aristotle, Cicero and Boethius.

84. On properly basic beliefs, cf. A. Plantinga, "Reason and Belief in God," in *Faith and Rationality: Reason and Belief in God*, (eds.) A. Plantinga and N. Wolterstorff, Notre Dame/London 1983, pp. 16ff.; on Cicero, E. Grassi, *op. cit.*, p. 42.

85. D. Ochs, *op. cit.*, p. 168, from Aristotle's *Metaphysics*.

86. E. Grassi, *op. cit.*, pp. 24ff., pp. 42ff.

87. *Ibid.*

88. Witt., D1v; Col. C6v, "Illi enim sunt argumentorum sedes."

89. Cf. S. Wiedenhofer, *op. cit.*, Bd. I, p. 374; but also W. Maurer, *op. cit.*, Bd. 1, p. 206, who, in making the same observation, stressed that the concept of *loci communes* was for Melanchthon more deeply interwoven with logic than it was for Erasmus (whose influence, here, Wiedenhofer viewed as co-equal with Agricola's). "Stärker als Erasmus, aber die humanistischen Bemühungen um die Eloquenz bewusst festhaltend, hebt Melanchthon die Verwurzelung der Loci-Lehre in der *Dialektik* hervor, halt er die Verbindung mit dem Aristotelismus aufrecht." This qualification fails generally in the literature on Melanchthon's humanism.

90. H.-G. Geyer, *op. cit.*, p. 52, n. 162.

91. Witt., E3r; Col., E2r.

92. Both, *ibid.*

93. Witt., E3r; Col., E3v.

94. Witt., E4v; Col., E3r, "Neque vero putes eos timere confingi, ex intimis naturae sedibus eruti, formae sunt seu regulae omnium rerum."

95. Witt., E3v; Col., E2v.

96. Witt., E4v; Col., E3v, "Aristoteles in rhetoricis suis rationem affectuum prudenter tractavit."

97. Witt., E3r; Col., E4v, "Plurimum valet in affectibus vis proprietasque et splendor verborum."

98. Both, *ibid.*

99. A. Sperl, *op. cit.*, pp. 35f., "Es ist oben schon angedeutet, dass die ethischen Normen aber auch für sich genommen als 'loci communes' bezeichnet werden können." Sperl noted Joachimsen's failure to observe this difference between Melanchthon, on the one hand, and Erasmus and Agricola, on the other; cf., p. 40; also W. Maurer, *op. cit.*, Bd. 1, p. 207, "Das ist etwas Neues; weder Agricola noch Erasmus haben jene Gleichsetzung vollzogen."

100. Witt., F4r; Col., F4v.

101. Both, *ibid.*

102. A. Sperl, *op. cit.*, p. 41.

103. On Melanchthon's view of history, see esp. P. Fraenkel, *Testimonia Patrum: The Function of the Patristic Argument in the Theology of Philipp Melanchthon*, Geneva 1961, pp. 52ff.; also W. Maurer, *op. cit.*, Bd. 1, pp. 99ff.; discussions on the *loci communes* and history in Melanchthon occur also in S. Wiedenhofer and H.-G. Geyer, *op. cit.*, same references as above to discussions of Melanchthon on the *loci communes* generally.

104. Witt., C1r; Col., B8v, "Duo igitur sunt ad historicam enarrationem necessaria, circumstantiae, et loci communes."

105. Witt., D1r-D2v; Col., C8r-D1r.

106. Witt., D3v; Col., D2r.

107. Witt., E2r; Col., E1v-E1r; and citing Erasmus's *Copia*, "...videantur mihi non posse reflorescere studia, nisi ad historias quoque redeamus." Witt., E2r-E3v; Col., E1r.

108. S. Wiedenhofer, *op. cit.*, Bd. I, pp. 472ff.; W. Maurer, *op. cit.*, Bd. 1, pp. 99f.

109. So Maurer, *op. cit.*, Bd. 1, pp. 100ff.

110. *Ibid.*

111. S. Wiedenhofer, *op. cit.*, Bd. I, p. 473.

112. Cf. above ref. to sources on classical rhetorical theory, n. 56.

113. U. Schnell, *op. cit.*, pp. 11-12.

114. *Ibid.*

115. U. Schnell, *op. cit.*, pp. 13ff., has argued that post-classical forms of rhetoric centered mainly on using the decorative methods of "figures," such as metaphor, tropological language and allegory (which they also applied to the biblical text to discern meaning), rather than on the straightforward literal sense.

116. Witt., E4r; Col., E5r.

117. Both, *ibid.*

118. There were three kinds of *status*, "definitive" or *finitivus*, "conjectural" or *conjecturalis* and "qualitative" or *qualitatis*, each corresponding to the categories or questions that one happened to be using. Cf., both *ibid.*

119. Both, *ibid.*

120. Both, *ibid.*

121. Witt., F1v; Col., E6r on the equivalence between the terms: "ille sit status et scopus totius orationis...." Melanchthon's use of this term *scopus* in his theological hermeneutics will emerge in the course of later discussion. For now note the distinction, as well as similarities between his usage and that of Erasmus, cf. below n. 123.

122. Both, *ibid.*, "Id autem status est, hoc est id plane quod ad summum intendit auctor. Et (si mihi *dialectice* loqui permittitur) cum omne negocium in syllogismum colligi possit, conjuncta se probatione cum negotio, eius quidem syllogismi...conclusio, status est."

123. U. Schnell, *op. cit.*, in agreement with W. Maurer, "Melanchthons Loci communes von 1521 als wissenschaftliche Programmschrift," in *Luther-Jahrbuch* 27, 1960, p. 34; H. Sick, *Melanchthon als Ausleger des Alten Testaments*, Tübingen 1959, pp. 44ff.; K. Hartfelder, *Philipp Melanchthon als Praeceptor Germaniae*, Berlin 1889, pp. 331ff.; Schnell has located the recovery of ancient *inventio* in the realm of exact *Wortsinn* in the works of Melanchthon more than in Erasmus, who strongly supported the moral and allegorical use of texts to promote Christian piety. The work of M. O'Rourke Boyle has shown that the relation of parts to the whole in Erasmus's *Philosophia Christiana* was not generally "a progressive mathematics of meaning, as in dialectic." See *op. cit.*, pp. 123ff. She has also shown that Erasmus systematically used the concept of the rhetorical *scopos* more in the sense of "sighting" than in that of dialectical and logical *status caussae*, pp. 76ff.

124. K. Froehlich, *Biblical Interpretation in the Early Church*, Philadelphia 1984, pp. 19ff. By "Antiochene" the author meant a hermeneutical theory that presupposed Aristotelian theories of truth very like those that we detect in Melanchthon. Froehlich also traced such theories among one school of ancient rabbinic biblical exegesis that existed alongside other less logically rigorous ones.

125. Melanchthon discussed methods of *confirmatio* mainly in Book One, in his segments on the *genus deliberativum*, Witt., F2v-F2r; Col., E7r-E8r, and the *genus iudicale*, Witt., G3v-G4v; Col., F8r-G3v, and in Book Two as the main office of *dispositio*, Witt., H2r-H3r; Col., G6r-G8r.

126. Witt., F2v-G3v; Col., E7r, F8r.

127. Cf. *MW V*, p. 381, "In der *confirmatio* wird die *propositio* bewiesen. Dabei leiten die *loci* dazu an, die nötige *materia argumentorum* zu finden. Die Dialektik liefert das formale Gerüst (Syllogismen) und wacht über die logische Stichhaltigkeit...."
128. Witt., F2v; Col., E7r.
129. Witt., F4v-F4r; Col., F3r-F4, "Haec igitur perpetua erit regula: Incepturus probationem artificialem a communi aliqua sententia ordire..., declarat enim vim ipsam negocii ac naturam.... Nam ea est ratio locorum communium, ut cum persuasi vulgo sint, qui illis nititur, facile quoque persuasurus videatur."
130. Witt., F4r; Col., F4r, "Secunda pars probationis coniungit consilii tui summam ceu finem cum caussa, quam in priore parte confirmationis posuisti."
131. Witt., *ibid.*, Col., F3r. On this syllogistic structure, Witt., H2r-H3v; Col., G7-G7r.
132. L. C. Green, "Formgeschichtliche und inhaltliche Probleme in den Werken des jungen Melanchthon," *Zeitschrift für Kirchengeschichte*, 1973, pp. 30ff., seems to have assumed that Melanchthon's early references to justification in *De rhetorica* implied an equally penetrating grasp of this doctrine, or even conversion to it, in a Protestant sense by 1518. Maurer's critique seems to us valid, cf., *op. cit.*, Bd. 2, p. 32, in which he concluded that such illustrations in the rhetoric were "ein Christentum zweiter Hand." Nevertheless, it is a difficult thing to judge the depth and intensity of a man's textbook illustrations. It is virtually certain that his interest in the doctrine of justification was by then more than simply a matter of abstract homework lessons and pedagogy. Cf., below, chapter 5, on how Melanchthon assisted Luther with his volumes on Galatians and the Psalms. See also L. C. Green, *How Melanchthon Helped Luther Discover the Gospel*, Fallbrook 1980, for some interesting, if not always convincing, proposals on this elusive subject.
133. Witt., B4r; Col., B6r.
134. Witt., C1r; Col., B8v.
135. Witt., C2v; Col., C1v.
136. Witt., C2v; Col., C1r.
137. Witt., C3v; Col., C3v.
138. Col., B7v, "Omnis oratio est, aut ad docendum composita, aut historica, aut suasoria, aut allegorica."
139. Witt., B4r; Col., B6r, "Habes exempla, Erasmicam in Pauli epistolam paraphrasin...." The reference is to *In universas epistolas apostolorum...paraphrasis.*
140. Witt., B4r; Col., B6r.
141. Both, *ibid.*, "In hunc modum, cum sacram illam ad Titum epistolam praelegissem, hortabar scholam, ut si qui studiosi essent, hoc genere exponendi se exercerent...."
142. Both, *ibid.*
143. Witt., B4r; Col., B7v.
144. Witt., C1v; Col., B7v, "...quae naturam verborum vimque orationis non adulteratam, sed vere ac proprie referant."
145. Both, *ibid.*, "Alia est *exegeseos* ratio..., cum integris commentariis autores explicamus."
146. See, J. W. Aldridge, *The Hermeneutic of Erasmus*, Richmond 1966, p. 64. Erasmus's reason for not taking Hebrews as Pauline was, interestingly, because it was written according to rhetorical, rather than "apostolic," norms. "Siquidem quae fertur ad Hebraeas, praeterquam quod multis argumentis coniici potest non esse Pauli, cum stilo rhetorico verius quam Apostolico sit scripta." The citation is from his preface to the *Paraphrase on the Epistle to James*, cf. references in n. 19, H. M. Allen, *Opus Epistolarum Erasmi*, Oxford 1906-47, no. 1171.1.
147. Witt., C1r; Col., B8v-B8r.

148. K. Haendler, *Wort und Glaube bei Melanchthon*, Gütersloh 1968, pp. 192ff.; H. Sick, *op. cit.*, pp. 21, 66ff., for discussions of Melanchthon's mainly negative view of allegorical exegesis.

149. Witt., C1r; Col., B8r.

150. Both, *ibid.*

151. Both, *ibid.*

152. Both, *ibid.*, "Non ignobilis est Abrahamae historia...."

153. Both, *ibid.*, "Locis communis, carnis interitus, affectuum carnis purgatio."

154. Both, *ibid.*, "In hunc solebant veteres modum sanctas historias tractare, spiritu magistro; hodie allegoriis longius a fontibus ducuntur, quam ut nativam vim retineant. Vere est efficax, vivitque et ardet verbum domini, cum maiestate sua bonis purisque mentibus illabitur. Sed nostris argutiis dilutum, ne scio quantum virium habeat."

155. Witt., C3v; Col., C3v.

156. It would seem that Melanchthon and Erasmus agreed on the matter of attaining the plain sense of texts, but differed as to how particular parts were related to the *scopus* or sense of Scripture as a whole canon. As O'Rourke Boyle has shown, Erasmus viewed this as less a logical-conceptual coherence than as something that an interpreter *did* by relating particulars to the *scopus*, construed in the terms of his *philosophia Christiana*, *op. cit.*, pp. 123ff.

157. Witt., C3v; Col., C3v.

158. Both, *ibid.* On Erasmus's use of Christ as the *scopus* of allegory, cf. esp. O'Rourke Boyle, *op. cit.*, pp. 123ff., and O'Malley, *op. cit.*, pp. 90ff.

159. Witt., C3r; Col., C3r.

160. Both, *ibid.*, "Nec enim comparari cum iusto poterit Cain. Ex illa comparatione Cain cum peccatore, nascetur locus communis, peccatum, cuius vis et crudele imperium amplificationibus tractandum est."

161. On Melanchthon's dialectical conception of *collatio*, cf. *M W* V, glossary of rhetorical terms, p. 381.

162. Witt., C3r; Col., C3r.

163. *In obscuriora aliquot captia Geneseas P.M. annotationes.* (*In caput Exod. xx. scholia. Discrimen legis et evangelii*), Tubingae 1523; cf. W. Maurer, *op. cit.*, Bd. 2, pp. 139ff.; our edition in the University of Cambridge Library. One ought also to notice that Melanchthon classified the Gospels, or "historiae Evangelicae," as belonging to the *genus demonstrativum, laudis ut vituperii*. Witt., D3v; Col. D2v, "Quanquam omnium maxime velim erudiri teneras mentes statim a pueris historiis Evangelicis, quarum cognitio non potest non saluberrima esse." Melanchthon's method of founding the *scopus* of Scripture in the text will be handled at length in following chapters.

164. Witt., C2v; Col., C1v.

165. Both, *ibid.*

166. Both, *ibid.*, "Et in his potissimum spectabitur, ac primo loco status causae; deinde quae ille poscat argumenta; demum, quos admittat affectus."

167. Both, *ibid.*

168. Both, *ibid.*

169. Witt., C2v; Col., C1v-C1r, "Ut in Pauli episto. ad Rhomanas cum hic status sit, legem non justificare, gratiam justificare; literam occidere, spiritum vivificare; suo fungetur munere *ho exegetes*, si quid litera, quid spiritus sit, pro docentis artificio tractet."

170. Witt., C2v; Col., C1r, "Accedit argumentum, neminem esse, qui non peccato sit obnoxius."

171. Both, *ibid.*, "Haec passim affectibus et pulcherrimis rhetorum figurae ornantur."

172. Witt., D1r; Col., C7v.

173. On Melanchthon's later classification of Romans as belonging to the *genus iudicale*, below chapter 8.

174. Witt., H4r; Col., H1r; on Melanchthon's view of Galatians, cf., also below, chapter 5.

175. Both, *ibid*.

176. Witt., C2v; Col., C1r, "Ad suasorium genus plerique psalmorum pertinent, in quibus non mediocri diligentia status, seu summa argumenti, quidne...statuatur, et quorsum pertineat, quod sic his verbis, hoc ordine dicitur contuendum est."

177. Both, *ibid*.

178. We have already cited J. W. Aldridge, *op. cit.*, p. 64, on Erasmus's view of Hebrews and the non-rhetorical, "apostolic style" of Paul. Thus it would seem that Melanchthon viewed the relationship between Paul and rhetoric and, to that extent, the sense of Scripture and rhetoric, to have been much closer to that of a literary identity than did the Dutchman. For concurring analyses, W. Maurer, *op. cit.*, Bd. 2, p. 105, on Melanchthon and Erasmus.

179. M. O'Rourke Boyle, *op. cit.*, pp. 41ff., on Erasmus and the translation of the *logos* as *sermo*.

CHAPTER 5

The Prefaces to Luther's Psalms and Galatians

"It would be saying too much to speak of Melanchthon's 'conversion.' Men of his kind do not experience a sudden conversion. The way which Melanchthon trod was very different from that of a Luther or a Calvin." (R. Stupperich, *Der unbekannte Melanchthon*, p. 14.)

During Melanchthon's first semester of teaching at Wittenberg, he grew to admire Martin Luther for his many gifts.[1] Most of the older studies of Melanchthon portray him as a rank beginner in theology, utterly impressionable, and as almost passively falling under the powerful spell of his senior colleague.[2] There is some truth in the tradition, but its underlying premises about Melanchthon's maturity and strength of mind (or general lack thereof), as well as Luther's nearly superhuman qualities, have to be revised. Our research into his pre-Lutheran development helps to confirm the judgment of Stupperich that Melanchthon's evolution into a "Lutheran" theologian was much more gradual, and less one-sided, than the older historiography made it out to be. To be sure, Luther's new ideas, and the force of his personality now beheld at close range, moved the younger man to what was for him a new theological foundation and a deeply changed personal life. However, one must not forget the complex of values that Melanchthon had been cultivating for more than ten years. These turned out to be points of genuine contact with Luther and, as we shall see, were not only adapted to this new theological vision, but also began to modify and shape it. Stupperich's reticence to call it a "conversion" and Herrlinger's judgment that

"...Melanchthon entered into Luther's actual intentions only very deliberately"[3] seem needful corrections. There is no evidence of a shining moment or "tower experience" to explain the transition. His personal letters and writings from the period provide no warrant for presuming the occurrence of a shattering event in the course of the year. On the contrary, he seems to have occupied himself quite happily with impressing the public (and his new employers) by working night and day, mostly on classical projects and curriculum.[4]

And yet, amid the tedious reports to Spalatin of his seemingly endless activities,[5] one senses an aroused interest, not merely in applying linguistic values to Christian tradition, but in the *elements* of the tradition itself. The collaboration with Luther on Galatians and the Psalms was more than a mere interdisciplinary arrangement; there was a spiritual displacement of some sort behind Melanchthon's work on these projects.[6] Melanchthon kept his personal struggles mostly to himself, but the sources eventually revealed that his fresh studies with Luther and his independent work with Pauline letters were no mere academic progressions. He promised his friend John Lang, "Several fuller *scholia* on the epistles of Paul and James will come out, inscribed to you."[7] His later writings would connect these studies with his personal quest for self-knowledge and moral rectitude and testify to the jolt which he received from the letters of Paul (as viewed through Luther's commentaries).

There was a kind of natural growth into this new outlook (just as recent historians have shown that there was a continuous evolution from the Late Middle Ages into the Reformation), but there was also, in the quiet course of it all, a momentous change of mind. Before knowing Luther, Melanchthon had indeed held theology in high esteem, but its status (in the form of original Catholic confessions and basic formulations) had been a matter of simply finding, and returning to, the purer and better *consensus* which the "Cadmean offspring" of medieval theology had obfuscated beneath their tower of Babel. On the condition that a propriety of method obtained, he presumed both the existence and binding authority of a purified Catholicism. His passion was thus for the liberal arts reformed in the image of an eternal *sermo* that would *uncover* the consensus (in the manner, say, of Geilor or Gerson), not *discover* hidden biblical truths that put parts of that consensus in question (in the manner of Luther). One might say that theology became a much more fundamental and dangerous affair than he ever imagined it could be before knowing Luther. And it is a testimony to his intellectual courage that he took this step from reform through application of his given tradition, a method of "correlation," to use Tillich's term, into the kind of revolutionary setting that inevitably arises when parts of the foundation itself are shaken and the deadly struggle for power over authoritative norms begins.

Philip had intended to go to Wittenberg to make a name for himself as a professor of Greek. In Luther, as Bornkamm put it, he met not so much a colleague as a destiny. It was not his part to enjoy a life of full devotion to the Greek literature that he loved so dearly, although he never ceased to labor tirelessly with these texts. His destiny was to give himself to the demands of warfare. Luther's answer to the question of authority set off explosions in Rome, and in the imperial courts of Europe. Considering the anti-philosophical element of Luther's theology, its uncompromising demands of loyalty to the Word of God and its terrible decrees about human nature, it is a wonder that Melanchthon did not retreat in some more or less polite fashion to the posture of an Erasmus or a Mosellanus. His collaboration with Luther on Galatians and the Psalms in 1519 was the quiet beginning of a long siege for him on the battlefield of theologians.

In the early part of the year 1519, as it happened, Luther wrote and published two exegetical works: *Operationes in Psalmos* [8] and *Martinus Luther, in epistolam Pauli ad Galatas commentarius*,[9] to which Melanchthon wrote prefaces.[10] In contrast to *De rhetorica*, in which we began to view the formal linguistic structures that he applied to Scripture as an authoritative text, these prefatory documents enable us to penetrate into the theological progression which was to be its substance. In addition, they help us to begin the secondary, synthetic job of showing how this formal (although not purely so) rhetorical system was not only engaged critically by the Lutheran theology, and in one sense was forced to adopt a lesser role in relation to it, but at the same time wielded a powerful shaping influence over it and thus generated the endlessly intriguing problem of assessing Melanchthon's views on biblical authority with respect to philosophical reason. The process was rather like what Kierkegaard called "repetition," where one dies to one's older self and is reborn into a new identity. However, the paradox of "repetition" is that one's new identity is a creative repetition of the old one. The older self is not destroyed after all, but revivified within the new existential context that comes about by faith. To gain a sense of oneself as an integrated, whole human being thus becomes the struggle to become one's true self. Melanchthon would find this quest for self-knowledge and identity no easier than would those who sought to understand him in after years.

Theologiae Studiosis Philippus Melanchthon Salutem

Luther's *Operationes* grew from lectures on the Psalms during the fall and winter of 1518-19.[11] At the same time, Melanchthon, a replacement for the Hebraist John Boschenstein,[12] perhaps not coincidentally, lectured on the Hebrew text of the Psalter.[13] The extent of Melanchthon's linguistic influence on Luther must be determined by the keen eye of an expert on the older scholar's skills in Hebrew and Greek.[14] Nevertheless, the heavily linguistic use of the biblical text, Luther's generous professions of general amazement at the younger man's knowledge and the simple fact that Melanchthon wrote the preface to this work all suggest a high degree of team spirit. It would be very strange to think that the only beneficiary of the relationship was Melanchthon. It should also be mentioned, as Ebeling pointed out, that Luther's hermeneutical progress from use of a somewhat unregulated allegorical method to that of a more consistently tropological-Christological literalism had taken him years, since 1513. Is it a mere coincidence that the *Operationes in Psalmos* was something of a final breakthrough and triumph for that "new hermeneutic" and thus for the origin of Protestantism?[15] Luther was himself aware of his own place in the history of interpreting the Psalms, and one cannot but feel the stir of something eventful in his words to Prince Frederick, in the introduction, "For everything that Augustine, Jerome, Athanasius, Hilary, Cassiodor and others have brought to bear upon the Psalms is most true, but from the sense of the *letter* they are sometime most distant."[16] Luther's emergence into a kind of conceptual clearing, then, coincided with Melanchthon's arrival and six months of collaboration with him in Wittenberg (including Melanchthon's lectures on the Hebrew text of the Psalter). The evidence strongly suggests that, just as Melanchthon found in Luther astonishingly new ways of seeing the theological sense of Scripture, Luther found in Melanchthon exactly the right linguistic discipline (not merely in grammar and languages, but in linguistic theory) for a final push into a systematic control over its literal sense. While this connection cannot be pursued here, it appears that Melanchthon's part in the entire history of Protestant hermeneutics is still a subject in need of comparative investigation in the context of Erasmus and Luther. As for points of Luther's influence on Melanchthon, the fresh theories of biblical interpretation introduced in the preface show that Melanchthon had now begun to read and construe Scripture, as a whole, in Luther's theological sense of things, particularly in respect to his theory on how *canonical* meaning emerges through Romans and other texts which constitute a "canon within the canon."[17]

Melanchthon began the preface optimistically, asserting that by God's grace an enslaved age was at last being redeemed by "those who are calling genuine and pure theology [*synceram ac nativam Theologiam*] back into the light of day."[18] Everywhere, he wrote, books were being written, "by which good minds can be called back to evangelical studies [*ad Evangelica studia*]."[19] There were philological and textual praises for Erasmus of Rotterdam, to whom was owed "the study of both the Greek and the Latin languages..., an illustrious text of the New Testament and of Jerome."[20] Reuchlin, Wolfgang Capito and Oecolampadius had variously made contributions to a revived knowledge of Hebrew, Greek and Latin; and, on the theological front, "...Andreas Karlstadt has confuted several frigid sentences of the schools, equally, with faith and solicitude."[21]

Without mentioning Luther, but in obvious deference to him, Melanchthon turned to the matter of biblical interpretation and its crucial importance. "Those who are versed in interpreting the divine scriptures effect much."[22] Philip's brief comments on the Psalms show that, to an extent that seems remarkable, he now moved within the hermeneutical and theological world of Luther, but in a manner that was distinctively his own. The main elements of what would become his Lutheran idea of biblical authority emerged here in embryonic form. That there was a secret "canon within the canon" and that Romans was the key to discovering it were the dominant themes. But perhaps still more fascinating is the manner in which he stated them in the terms and thought-structures of his rhetorical philosophy. His own distinctive concepts of biblical unity, clarity and affective power thus emerged in identifiable form.

Melanchthon began, writing that it was essential to understand those books of Scripture "which are most necessary, least understood."[23] Some books were thus more necessary than others; but he was quick to qualify this statement by adding (in conformity with the intuitions of his truth theory) that books of Scripture were equal in rank, if not in weight.

> I am not saying this: that not all the sacred and canonical books are to me of the same rank; but that certain ones are generally read more frequently, and such is their composition that they are able to act as interpreters [of] or commentaries on the rest.[24]

The underlying intuition was that if all the books were from God, then they also had the properties of revealed truth. In that sense they were all of the same rank. But not all biblical books had the same properties of composition; there was diversity in the kinds of literature within the canon. Finally, this diversity of literary forms was explained in terms of a purposeful intra-canonical engagement of some writings by others. Some books not only *functioned* theologically to interpret the others, but their *composition* was such that they themselves served as commentaries on the rest.

Philip next identified the epistle to the Romans as one of those interpretive sacred writings that was essential to the sense of the others as a whole. In doing this he obviously chimed in with Luther and other Wittenberg theologians. But one must also notice the language and thought-forms that he used to give shape to this profoundly important and problematic hermeneutical ploy.

> For example, among the Pauline epistles, the one written to the Romans is a *scopus*, or Attic Mercury, which indicates the way into the rest; just so, either public usefulness or the series of arguments makes some books preferable to others.[25]

We shall see that, for Melanchthon, the point was not that Romans operated somewhat like a *scopus*, to use this term in a metaphorical or analogical sense. The idea was that Paul, in Romans, actually constructed and defended the *scopus* of the entire biblical canon, and that he did so by the rules of Melanchthon's kind of rhetorical theory. Melanchthon *identified* the main thesis and arguments of Romans as the *scopus* of the biblical tradition. Having made this point, however, he returned to the qualification that, meanwhile, all the divine books have the same *authority*: "authoritas eadem omnibus est."[26]

Just as in *De rhetorica* Melanchthon compared the literary forms of Romans and the Psalms, so now their manner of service within Scripture.

> In this manner the Psalms come before almost [all] the remaining books of Scripture, not only because of their public use in the church, but also because they everywhere narrate nearly the entire sacred history [*quod universam prope sacram historiam...perstringunt*].[27]

He elaborated his concept of narration in the Psalms, again illustrating to us his extravagant use of rhetorical structures of thought and also suggesting a deepened spiritual involvement with the text. They contained "prophecies about Christ the savior, the calling of the Gentiles, the church of Christ...."[28] In these things "...David comes before the rest of the prophets."[29] Finally, "just as from historical letters of *res gestae* and knowledge of *laws*, the power and force of the history [*vis et energia historiae*] is taken from David...."[30] This "power and force" is so great that "it excites our souls, through the harmony of the Psalms, and carries them, aroused, toward heavenly realms."[31] The Psalms "have this 'genuineness' [*gnesion*], as it were, for they join together examples of sacred history with making all our affections tranquil."[32] This *gnesion* was the deep meaning of the "sacred histories," the redemptive senses in which the sacred past was related to human beings, and the literature of the Psalms conveyed such meaning to us with great effect. That effect was born of what one may call a right sense of properly human *inventio*, or proper focus upon the existentially essential relationships between sacred events and human beings. The intuition was that of *inventio* in a context of one's quest for self-knowledge. The passage which follows is one of the strongest among all his early writings, and it adumbrates the great Melanchthonian themes of later days, such as knowing Christ through His "benefits," rather than by an abstract cognition of His life and teachings.

> For what does it profit to know that the world was created by God, as Genesis indicates, unless you adore the mercy and wisdom of the creator? Furthermore, what will it profit to have known that God is merciful and wise, unless you take it into your own soul that to *you* He is merciful, to *you* He is just, to *you* He is wise? And that is truly to know God. Nor has philosophy followed this utmost method of knowing God. It is peculiar to Christians. [*Neque vero extremam hanc cognoscendi dei rationem assecuta est philosophia. Christianorum propria est.*][33]

This deepest and most urgent meaning of sacred history, whereby one knew in oneself the mercy, justice and wisdom of God, thus also defined what was unique about Scripture and made Christianity much superior to philosophy. His comments are suggestive of a new critical awareness of the limitations of philosophy in comparison with the powers of Scripture.

> Truly, the spirit of the Psalms pours out this sweetness on pious souls, and this is the heavenly harmony which the Spirit of God makes. What one boasts to me of the Gentiles' ancient songs, or the hymns of Orpheus, is nothing; the voice of this cithara, which so joins the souls of men to heaven that they are clearly transformed in divinity, is indeed far different.[34]

In this brief preface Melanchthon thus asserted a broad view of biblical authority, which revealed the formative power of Luther upon his thinking.

But it also revealed the formative power of his own linguistic system upon the new theological and hermeneutical ideas. His remarks on Romans as the interpretive center of Scripture surely reflected more the influence of Luther than it did his previous construal of the text, and the passage on Orpheus, while not entirely different from earlier sections in his writings, suggests a new tone of interest in a critique of the liberal arts as a means of "grace."[35] It is also evident that he had been spurred on by new ideas to think out his hermeneutical sense of what Scripture was about as a coherent whole, and one suspects aroused personal experience behind the words on the unrivaled power of the biblical text to change lives for good.

One must also notice, though, the idiosyncratic manner in which he had begun to develop Luther's ideas in connection with his own. In the *Operationes*, Luther had constantly put Christ before the eye, not in an uncontrolled collation of poetic images, but through a conscious use of tropology and metaphor in the context of Christian tradition.[36] Moreover (particularly on the first Psalm), Luther proved himself quite adept at sorting through the intricacies of Hebrew vocabulary and usually drew his theological points from exegetical arguments. Whether this theory and method were adopted from or merely confirmed by Melanchthon for him (or a bit of both) is difficult to tell. But Luther was constantly struck by the prophetic power and, thus, the unmediated present significance of these words in Scripture for all of God's people. Melanchthon's preface certainly does not suggest that he denied either the attentiveness to the literal sense or the present power of the text, but that these same notions seemed to him best expressed as arising from the Psalmist's sound *inventio*, or *usus historiae*, so that he instinctively construed the Psalmist as rhetorical historian. David had composed an *elenchthus*, or interpretive commentary, to disclose the *loci* or *gnesion* of sacred history by uncovering knowledge of laws and the grace of God. Whereas Luther did indeed consider the Psalmist a master of prophetic metaphor and treated each Psalm as an integral work with a theological coherence to it,[37] Melanchthon pushed this into systematic linguistic form by offering that the Psalmist had written in the more didactic rhetorical structure of persuasive *enarratio*. Thus Luther's pervasive occupation with the "literal sense" of the text disclosed a way of looking at and treating biblical language and truth that was markedly different from Melanchthon's (though not clearly contradicting it). The one man was instinctively drawn to the depths of metaphor, while acknowledging the value of clear dialectics. The other instinctively loved the modest language of pure propositions, while of course conceding that tropology was a valid form of speech. Even in the harmonies of the Psalms, Philip looked for the cognitive structures that held Scripture logically and semantically, and only then, theologically, together.

Perhaps Melanchthon's comments on the unity of Scripture are illustrative of this last claim. There is no doubt that Luther, too, believed there to be a coherence to Scripture, and that this coherence was literal, that is, came together, sometimes very loosely through multivalence and tropology, in a Christocentric biblical theology.[38] Melanchthon, however, held Scripture to a concept of literal unity in the context of his dialectical and rhetorical theory. His preface to Luther's *Operationes* suggests that it was important to him that all biblical assertions, while not of exactly equal importance or weight, be assertively true and that all Scripture cohere together in freedom from logical contradictions between texts, each writing contributing in its own way. Luther's approach to biblical unity was sometimes oblivious to the author's historical intent; the wholeness of Scripture was greater than the mere sum of its parts, its divine or theological meaning never reducible to grammar or even rhetoric. Melanchthon, too, believed in the divine, spiritual sense of Scripture, but it is doubtful that he ever imagined it apart from the rhetorical artistry of its human writers. As we shall see, his Protestant model (and for him this was no mere analogy) for biblical diversity and unity came directly from his idea of *antiquity* as a normative *tradition* (not a single book, but a whole literary tradition).

Luther, in the *Operationes*, worked on the assumption (possibly derived from the works of Athanasius)[39] that the Psalms, unlike other biblical books, not merely dictated *what* men ought to do in life, but *aroused* them to do it by inspiring within them the needed affections.[40] The Psalter was, after all, "oratio et laus dei, hoc est, liber hymnorum...."[41] Like a loving and good parent, God "produces in us, with this book, both word and affection...."[42] Luther connected this power with the literary form of hymnody, but in spiritual conjunction with the loving presence of God through Christ at work in the hearts and minds of His children. Melanchthon, it would seem, was the more deeply impressed by the power of the literature itself to rival even that of the "strings of Orpheus," his metaphor for the classical arts. Nevertheless, the power was genuine for him, was not merely a matter of the mind and was intensely involved in shaping the heart. For him, the great shaping power of Scripture was much more directly in its divinely inspired *oratio* than it was for Luther. (And *oratio* was more dialectically structured for him than it was for Erasmus.)

The result of these impressive developments during the six months at Wittenberg was the birth of a theology that was neither simply Erasmian [43] nor quite Lutheran.[44] Working in his own solid fashion within these frameworks, he adumbrated the unmistakably Melanchthonian style of the later *Loci communes*, in which he made famous the idea of going to the "benefits of Christ," rather than to the "mysteries of heaven." It is a blend of Socratic humanism and Lutheran common sense that comes through in what is perhaps the strongest passage of the preface. The progression, through use of the second person pronoun, from the wide and vast concept of a creator to that of a personal consciousness of His good will, not merely *pro nobis*, but most essentially *pro me, in oneself*, announces the birth of the premise upon which, in Harnack's terms, "the first Protestant dogmatics" would be built: "cognoscere Christum est, eius beneficia cognoscere."

Otho Germanus Pio Lectori

"I confess that the authority of Scripture itself is superior to the opinion of all mankind. Truly this concerning the scriptures is not controversial. Both of us receive and reverence the same Scripture, but the problem concerns the sense of Scripture." (Erasmus, *De libero arbitrio*, LB ix, p. 1219.I.)

Melanchthon wrote the preface to Luther's *Operationes* in March of 1519. From then until the time of the Leipzig Disputation which occurred in July, he intensified his scholarly study of Scripture. In a letter written on the third of April to John Lang of Erfurt, he mentioned not only the publication of Luther's Psalms,[45] but also his own lectures on the same writings[46] and, as we have seen, that "rather copious *scholia*" on Paul and James were in progress.[47] During these months he became better acquainted with Luther's theological positions. To Spalatin, in May of 1519, he wrote: "I am sending you [Luther's] sermon on double righteousness."[48] Maurer has shown that Melanchthon transcribed Luther's lectures on Genesis for future publication, as well,[49] and that he learned much of Luther's theology through sermons which, as John Doelsch recalled, caused the hearers to expend more tears than ink.[50] Indeed, the preface which Melanchthon wrote for Luther's commentary on Galatians indicated both a growing devotion to Luther's theological views and discontent with those of Erasmus.

The preface was published pseudonymously as *Otho Germanus pio lectori*, to which the postscript was added, *Paulus Commodus, Brettanus, lectori....*[51] Whatever the reason for his use of the pseudonyms (probably an attempt to be clever, as in "one commodious toward Paul," and not to conceal his true identity), a brief discussion of this preface will complement the preceding one by making somewhat clearer the strengthened tone, under Luther's influence, of asserting the uniqueness and superiority of Scripture over human letters, but also the manner in which he put his linguistic system into action to process and shape Luther's theological *sensus* in his own distinctive way.

"There is no doubt that the philosophy which is most agreeable to the Christian is one in which he more swiftly promotes and more nearly attains genuine felicity."[52] But where was one to find such a "philosophy?" "That which is taken from sacred letters, in particular evangelical and apostolic ones, is indeed of this sort."[53] "Whether you seek felicity [*felicitatem*] or beatitude [*beatitudinem*] or both, nothing is more expedient [*nihil est expeditius*], nothing more efficacious [*efficacius*] than this [Christian philosophy]."[54] Therefore, Melanchthon warned (in thought perhaps of what might have become of himself) against spending too much time with pagan literature. For those who neglect theology or take it lightly "waste away and grow old in the books of the Gentile philosophers."[55] Why, indeed, spend years laboring over and memorizing the volumes of Aristotle rather than "divine wisdom [*divinam sapientiam*]"?[56] "Will we Christians always ignore that the wisdom of the world is foolishness to God?"[57] Not only the users of Aristotle came under fire, as was always the case, but now the (unnamed but obvious) members of the growing school of Christian Platonism. Was Plato to be viewed as a god?[58] Although "...I attribute much to him...in his own realm of light...,"[59] when used incautiously he, too, is an "enemy of Christian philosophy."[60]

Melanchthon applied his principle of rigorous discrimination in a somewhat fresh manner to the brand of humanism that had been part of his own academic identity. The philosophy of Plato is confused by some with Christian truth: "...whatever is read in him [Plato] they bring without discrimination [sine iudicio] and inculcate it into the oracles of the Holy Spirit."[61] As a result, one is left either with no theology at all, or with too little room for it.[62]

Into this confused state of affairs strode Martin Luther, under severe attack by those who interpret sacred letters "as they will."[63] Beneath an ominous cloud of accusations and intimidation, Luther managed nevertheless to bring forth this commentary on Galatians; and if it should seem a little too vehemently written, one was advised to consider that "all men are liars...,"[64] the word of Christ is eternal and not mere tradition[65] and Paul's epistle was written with even greater vehemence than was Luther's commentary upon it.[66]

In this brief preface, Melanchthon expressed his favorable judgment of Luther in the context of biblical authority over philosophy. The vocabulary seems purposefully Erasmian (perhaps in an effort to project and strengthen an *esprit de corps* between Luther and humanists), but the direction was decidedly toward the more radical Lutheran theology. Scripture put forth its own unique kind of Christian "philosophy," *literae sacrae*, which aimed at defining and helping people to attain true *felicitas* or *beatitudo*. The main theme of the preface was that no other philosophy, not even that of the great Aristotle or Plato, could actually accomplish this goal, and that Scripture must thus, under no circumstances, be intermingled with philosophy. Finally, the strength of Martin Luther was foremost in his brave assertion of the offensive biblical truth that human beings are deeply sinful, and that the age was in dire need of an *eternal* word from Christ (in apostolic and evangelical *literae*) to stand as judge over and above the magisterial traditions of the church.

Luther's sweeping indictment of fallen human nature, and its concomitant erosion of confidence in the products of human culture (even ecclesiastical culture), had begun now to tip the balance of Melanchthon's perspective toward greater stress on the transcendence of biblical truth rather than on a positive mediation between it and the best of human philosophy. This intellectual and spiritual displacement brought him to Luther's side even as very dark clouds began to build on their horizon. With the election of Charles V and the nearly disastrous outcome of the Leipzig Disputation, things would get much darker still in the coming summer months. But as others, like Reuchlin, kept a safe distance from the "Saxon Huss" (and enticed Philip to do the same), Philip's allegiance to Luther as the "Saxon Hercules" only grew stronger.

As he took the Lutheran theological road, however, he did so as Melanchthon the rhetorician, in his own rhetorical style. The linguistic terms of this preface are generically humanistic and do not by themselves reveal the distinctive features of his rhetorical theology, but one ought nevertheless to notice them. Galatians was a source of Christian "philosophy," *literae sacrae*, *doctrina Christi* and *divinae literae*, thus giving precise form to the *sensus literalis*. Moreover, it was a source, not merely of true propositions, but of the kind of doctrine which was centered upon topics of the greatest possible concern to humankind. In the preface to Luther's *Annotationes*, he had made this last point by stressing the Psalmist's interest in the *gnesion* of sacred history, God's relation in Christ to human beings. In this second preface, he wrote that the main topic of Galatians, like great philosophy, was the attainment of genuine *felicitas* or *beatitudo*. Luther's emphasis on the sinfulness of human nature in contrast with the holiness and grace of God thus found expression in the vocabulary of Melanchthon's rhetorical theories of *inventio* and its larger context of classical values which stressed knowledge of the self as a moral being as the beginning of wisdom.

A more detailed outline of exactly what kind of rhetoric Galatians was, in Melanchthon's view, can be gained from the extraordinary little document that was uncovered by Kolde and published in Bizer's useful edition of early Melanchthon texts.[67] His comments in *De rhetorica* on the deliberative style and structure of Galatians make this document relevant to our present discussion, although it stemmed from work that he performed, most probably in his extracurricular *schola domi*, in the year 1520. The title of the writing, *Exegesis methodica in Epistolam Pauli pros tous Galatas Philip: melanx: Auctore*, is indicative of how he construed the text itself. Galatians belonged to that class of writings which he now termed the *genus didacticus* (which one recalls was another name for the didactic form of demonstrative rhetoric).[68] As such, it began with the usual *exordium*,[69] but one in which the apostle used several logical arguments, also, to demonstrate his qualifications and authority over his readers.[70] This was followed by his main proposition or *status*, that the foolish Galatians had departed from his doctrine of justification without works.[71] Paul next supplied two powerful deductions in confirming the *status*.[72] First was an inference from the premise that it had not been circumcision that had saved them, but hearing the gospel and receiving the Holy Spirit.[73] Second, the same conclusion was drawn from the example of Abraham by tight logical construction.[74] These were followed by a syllogism, constructed of premises from the Old Testament:

> "For however many are of the works of the law" is a syllogism. Anyone who does not keep the entire law is cursed. There are none among those of the work of the law who keep the entire law. Therefore, those who are of works of the law are cursed.[75]

There followed two more simple deductions that led to the same conclusions.[76] The apostle finished off his epistle with three *occupationes*[77] and a sixth argument *ab allegoria*: "The son is free. The people of the New Testament are the son. Therefore we do not require works of the law."[78]

Melanchthon had not merely begun to adopt Luther's theological doctrine of justification and the cluster of other doctrines that went with it, structurally. He had also gone into the very rhetoric of the biblical documents in order to demonstrate the claim of this theology to be properly grounded in the text. What is fascinating is the underlying picture of how the author of this text, Paul, grounded his own teachings in the truth. These were demonstrations, conclusions that followed inescapably from Christian premises. At one and the same time, Melanchthon claimed to have shown both that Luther was grounded properly in Paul and that Paul's authority was grounded properly in the truth. The authors of Scripture not only made inspired assertions, they defended and demonstrated them according to the rules of good rhetoric to render them incontestable to pious minds. Not only did Luther have the weight of Scripture behind him, the doctrines of Scripture were themselves propped up by the strength of rhetoric. To read Scripture aright was not merely to be *told*, on the "say-so" of the inspired author, but to be *persuaded* by incorrigible arguments. And of course to be persuaded in *this* way was also to be won to the position of Luther.

Which came first, the hermeneutic or the theology? The answer must be that they occurred together in a cyclical manner. *De rhetorica* suggested a confluence of earlier rhetorical theory and Lutheran intuitions in heightening Melanchthon's sensitivity to biblical books as whole compositions. Luther's theological insights gave impetus to his literary inquiry into these biblical texts, and the biblical texts confirmed the theology. Melanchthon emerged not merely as the public statesman of Protestantism, as is widely known, but more deeply as its *hermeneutical* apologist, as the one who erected its first systematic hermeneutical foundation. As the pressures mounted to judge Luther a heretic, Melanchthon's methodical, precise handling of the biblical text as *oratio sacra* would become all the more valuable an asset in building a protective scaffold around him and would greatly assist a rapid process of institutional reform. However, it would also bear the burdens and limitations of any theory which presumes that "theologies" can be proved both biblical and true through logical devices, that there is not a deeper epistemic mystery in interpretation that calls for greater subservience to tradition and ancient consensus. To the extent that Melanchthon's truth theory and methods became typical of Protestant dogmatics, its theology would be vulnerable to the very factionalism that he so detested among his contemporaries, and thus to attacks from enemies of Protestantism. Nevertheless, Luther would have been more vulnerable to exegetical refutation without Melanchthon than he was with him at his side.

A glance at Luther's commentary on Galatians shows that he was barely conscious of these demonstrative rhetorical structures in the epistle, if at all. There is no mention of conformity with a *genus*, no finding a *status*, no appeal to Paul's dialectical methods, nor even to his cleverly inductive use of allegory. The relationship between text and reader is not dialectical and argumentative, but homiletic, assertive and obvious. The Word of the gospel speaks at once to the Galatians and to us; its power is the deeply spiritual sense of freedom from the law and of justification by the pure grace of God. Biblical authority in this instance seems to transcend epistemic rationality by the mysterious power of the Spirit. Moreover, so far as we can tell, even Erasmus, who produced this Greek text of Galatians and who freely applied rhetorical tools to interpretation, never construed it systematically *as* demonstrative rhetoric, permeated on every level with the force of formal logic.[79]

One final observation ought to be made. Melanchthon, even as he traveled into the Lutheran theological world and made his commitment to a theology that divided between Scripture and human culture more sharply and daringly than in the Christianity of his younger days, created an intriguing problem, threatening what philosophers call a self-reflective contradiction (and partisan Protestant theologians call the root of heresy). His very concept of the "difference" or *discrimen* between Scripture and merely human letters was itself that of his rhetorical theory. His way of asserting Scripture's authoritative supremacy over philosophy entailed both the negative judgment of philosophy as in some sense really false *and* the positive assessment of its linguistic value system as, in its pursuit of "felicity," in some sense really true. Goethe's claim that "form is never without content" is appropriate to this problem, which transcends the seductively simple solution of saying that Melanchthon affirmed the *form* of philosophy, but rejected the logic of its *substance*. At best, the nature of this maneuver implied the existence of conceptual tension within his earliest Lutheranism, and it was the sort of tension that he, being Melanchthon, could hardly ignore. Its resolution would demand the full powers of his intellect. Whether the resolution was coherent, internally, and/or true to the principles of Protestant theology has been the subject of raging controversy from the sixteenth century down to the present. On this complex matter we shall offer our own opinions in due course. Meanwhile, we must follow Melanchthon to Leipzig and his fateful entry into the public theological forum, continuing to develop an interpretive context for assessing his concept of biblical authority on these levels.

Notes to Chapter 5

1. J. Camerarius, *De vita Philippi Melanchthonis narratio*, (ed.) G. Th. Strobel, Halle 1777, pp. 31ff.; Cf. W. Maurer, *Der junge Melanchthon*, Bd. 2, Göttingen 1969, pp. 43ff.; Melanchthon's references to Luther collated in S. Wiedenhofer, *Formalstrukturen humanistischer und reformatorischer Theologie bei Philipp Melanchthon*, Bd. II, Bern/Frankfurt/München 1976, pp. 84f., n. 62.

2. Cf. A. von Harnack, *Philipp Melanchthon: Akademische Festrede*, Berlin 1897, p. 8, "Wie der Mann im Gleichniss, der alle seine Habe verkaufte, um die eine kostliche Perle zu kaufen, so gab Melanchthon zunächst alles dahin, und wie er bisher in Erasmus gelebt hatte, so stellte er sich nun mit Leib und Seele in den Dienst Luthers." Also H. Maier, *An der Grenze der Philosophie*, Tübingen 1909, p. 40, "Bald hatte er sich dem Zauber des grossen Mannes ruckhaltlos gefangen gegeben. Die Revolution, die heraufzieht, hat für seine weiche Natur etwas Entsetzliches."

3. G. A. Herrlinger, *Die Theologie Melanchthons in ihrer geschichtlichen Entwicklung und im Zusammenhange mit der Lehrgeschichte und Kulturbewegung der Reformation dargestellt*, Gotha 1879, p. 72.

4. K. Sell, *Philipp Melanchthon und die deutsche Reformation bis 1531*, (Schriften des Vereins für Reformationsgeschichte, XIV. 3), Halle 1897, p. 15, found it "...bewundernswert, dass die gewaltige Inanspruchnahme durch diese ihm neu entgegendtretende Gedankenwelt ihn keinen Augenblick in der rastlosen Gelehrtenarbeit hinderte...."

5. Cf. *MW* VII/1, letters 4-21 for a good sampling.

6. *Ibid.*, letter to Spalatin, 13 March 1519, p. 63.4 on Galatians; to John Lang in Erfurt, 3 April 1519, p. 67.21ff. on the Psalms.

7. *Ibid.*, to Lang, p. 68.25ff.

8. We have consulted the superbly edited text in *D. Martin Luther. Operationes in Psalmos 1519-1521*, Teil II, Psalm 1 bis 10 (Vulgata), (hrsg.) G. Hammer und M. Biersack, (wissent. Leitung) H. A. Oberman, Köln/Wien 1981; WA 5; cf. other editions listed by H. Bornkamm, *Luther und das Alte Testament*, Tübingen 1948, p. 230; published segments between March and June 1519, cf. *MW* VII/1, p. 66, n. 10.

9. WA 2, published in Leipzig, September 1519.

10. Melanchthon's preface to Luther's *Operationes in Psalmos*, c. 27 March 1519, so *MB* I, p. 58; the best critical text in G. Hammer and M. Biersack, *op. cit.*, pp. 16ff.; other texts in WA 2, pp. 24ff.; *SM* VI/1, pp. 61ff.; *CR* I, pp. 70ff.; secondary discussions in H.-G. Geyer, *Von der Geburt des wahren Menschen*, Neukirchen 1965, pp. 180ff.; S. Wiedenhofer, *op. cit.*, Bd. I, pp. 122ff.; W. Maurer, *op. cit.*, Bd. 2, pp. 47f. Melanchthon's preface to Luther's commentary on Galatians, April (?) 1519, so *MB*, p. 60; text in WA 2, pp. 443ff.; *SM* VI/1, pp. 59ff.; *CR* I, pp. 120ff.; on the contents of the preface, W. Maurer, *op. cit.*, Bd. 2, pp. 51ff.

11. WA 5, pp. 3ff.

12. On Melanchthon's hope to publish a text of Proverbs with Boschenstein, *MW* VII/1, letter to Spalatin, 24 September 1518, p. 43.22ff. Boschenstein arrived in November and, disappointingly, departed from Wittenberg three months later, cf. *ibid.*, n. 13, and W. Maurer, *op. cit.*, Bd. 2, p. 42.

13. W. Maurer, *op. cit.*, Bd. 2, p. 42; *MW* IV, p. 10.

14. The issue of Melanchthon's influence on Luther has been handled at length by L. Green, *How Melanchthon Helped Luther Discover the Gospel*, Fallbrook 1980, *passim.* On Melanchthon's part in the betterment of Luther's ability to use ancient languages, see W. Maurer, *op. cit.*, Bd. 2, pp. 51ff.; and K.- H. zur Mühlen, "Luthers deutsche

Bibelübersetzung als Gemeinschaftswerk," in *Die Bibel in der Welt*, Bd. 18, (ed.) S. Meurer, Stuttgart 1978, pp. 91f.
15. G. Ebeling, *Lutherstudien*, Bd. I, Tübingen 1971, esp. pp. 3ff.
16. G. Hammer and M. Biersack, *op. cit.*, p. 13.12ff., "Nam et omnia, quae B. Augustinus, Hieronymus, Athanasius, Hilarius, Cassiodorus et alii super psalterium contulerunt, verissima sunt, sed a sensu litterae quandoque remotissima." Cf. n. 70 for similar quote from the Leipzig Disputation.
17. W. Maurer, *op. cit.*, Bd. 2, p. 47, "...bekennt sich Melanchthon nun zu den Prinzipien der lutherischen Hermeneutik."
18. WA 5, p. 24.
19. *Ibid.*
20. *Ibid.*
21. *Ibid.* On Karlstadt, cf. W. Maurer, *op. cit.*, Bd. 2, pp. 22ff. and 69ff.
22. WA 5, p. 24, "Plurimum puto efficiunt, qui in divinis scripturis enarrandis versantur...."
23. *Ibid.*
24. *Ibid.*, "Non hoc dico, quod e sacris et canonicis libris non sint pari apud me loco omnes, sed quia vulgo quidam frequentius leguntur, et quorundam talis est conditio, ut in reliquos vel *Elenchi* vel commentarii vice esse possint."
25. *Ibid.*, "Ut in Paulinis epistolis eius, quae ad Romanos scripta est scopus velut atticus Mercurius ad reliquas iter indicat, ita alios libros aliis cum vulgi usus tum argumentorum series praefert."
26. *Ibid.*
27. *Ibid.*
28. *Ibid.*
29. *Ibid.*, "...ut hac laude multo etiam David antecedat reliquos prophetas."
30. *Ibid.*, pp. 24f.
31. *Ibid.*, p. 25, "...quae animos nostros per Harmoniam Psalmorum expergefacit, et impetu quodam percitos rapit ad celestia."
32. *Ibid.*
33. *Ibid.*
34. *Ibid.*
35. Cf. the very penetrating discussion in H.-G. Geyer, *op. cit.*, pp. 180-187 on the rhetorical forms used in this preface; on the critique of philosophy, p. 186, "Ist die Absage an das humanistische Programm des Erasmus...darin nicht unüberhorbar...."
36. Cf. G. Ebeling, *op. cit.*, pp. 29ff.; also G. Hammer and M. Biersack, *op. cit.*, references in n. 2, "rhetorische Begriffe," p. 66, on Luther's disciplined concept of allegory, and esp. pp. 74.17-75.1ff., "Non autem allegoricum dico more recentorium, quasi alius sensus historialis sub eo sit quaerendus, quam qui dictus est, sed quod *verum et proprium sensum figurata locutione expresserit.*"
37. *Ibid.*, p. 65, n. C1ff.
38. Cf. G. Ebeling, *op. cit.*, esp. pp. 292ff.
39. G. Hammer and M. Biersack, *op. cit.*, p. 14, n. 77.
40. *Ibid.*, "In ceteris enim docemur et verbo et exemplo, quid agendum sit, hic non modo docet, sed et modum et usum tradit, quo verbum impleamus et exemplum imitemur."
41. *Ibid.*, p. 15.5ff.
42. *Ibid.*, p. 15.9f.
43. Contra A. Sperl, *Melanchthon zwischen Humanismus und Reformation: Eine Untersuchung über den Wandel des Traditionsverständnisses bei Melanchthon und die damit zusammenhängenden Grundfragen seiner Theologie,* (Forschung zur Geschichte und Lehre des Protestantismus, 10, XV), München 1959, p. 72; E. Mühlenberg, "Humanistisches

Bildungsprogramm und reformatorische Lehre beim jungen Melanchthon," *Zeitschrift für Theologie und Kirche*, 65, 1968, p. 440; and S. Wiedenhofer, *op. cit.*, Bd. I, p. 153.
44. W. H. Neuser, *Der Ansatz der Theologie Philipp Melanchthons*, Neukirchen 1957, p. 26, surely overstated the matter in asserting, "Im März 1519 hat er jedenfalls seinen humanistischen Standpunkt hinter sich gelassen." W. Maurer, *op. cit.*, Bd. 2, pp. 47ff., seems also somewhat premature in *equating* Melanchthon's stress on history and the affections (along with a new awareness of Romans) with Luther's hermeneutic.
45. *MW* VII/1, p. 67.21ff.
46. *Ibid.*, p. 67.22ff., "Ego hebraicum psalterium praelego."
47. *Ibid.*, p. 68.25ff., cf. n. 13, "Solche Scholien Melanchthons sind nicht bekannt." Also *SM* I, p. 62, reference to the same proposed work.
48. *Ibid.*, p. 73.18f., n. 7.
49. W. Maurer, *op. cit.*, Bd. 2, pp. 114ff.
50. *Ibid.*, p. 114, n. 97.
51. Texts in WA 2, pp. 443ff.; *CR* I, pp. 121ff.; additional notes in *SM* VI/1, pp. 59ff. and *MB* I, p. 53 with date c. April 1519 and not September, as in *CR* I, *ibid.*
52. *CR* I, p. 121, "Non dubium est, quin ea philosophia Christiano vel maxime conveniat, in qua et citius promoveat, et synceram foelicitatem propius contingat."
53. *Ibid.*, "Qualis est nimirum, quae ex sacris literis, in primis Evangelicis Apostolicisque petitur."
54. *Ibid.*, cf. W. Maurer, *op. cit.*, Bd. 2, pp. 50ff., on the "Erasmian" language used here by Melanchthon while subtly, but evidently, rejecting the substance of his theology.
55. *CR* I, p. 122, "...in gentilium philosophorum libris macerantur et senescunt."
56. *Ibid.*
57. *Ibid.*, "An semper christiani ignorabimus mundi sapientiam apud deum esse stulticiam?"
58. *Ibid.*
59. *Ibid.*, "Non sum adeo stupidus, pie lector atque malignus, ut ei philosopho in suo Albo non plurimum tribuam."
60. *Ibid.*, ". . . christianae philosophiae vere hostis..."; cf. W. Maurer, *op. cit.*, Bd. 2, p. 51, on the "new tone" of Melanchthon's critique of Plato and the indirect attack on Erasmus.
61. *CR* I, p. 122.
62. *Ibid.*
63. *Ibid.*, "...qui pro libidine sacris literis, praetextu religionis, abutantur...."
64. *Ibid.*, p. 123, "...omnes homines esse mandaces...."
65. *Ibid.*, "Christi verbum esse aeternum, nec de maioribus tantum nostris accipiendum."
66. *Ibid.*
67. E. Bizer, *Texte aus der Anfangszeit Melanchthons*, Neukirchen 1966, pp. 31ff.
68. E. Bizer, *op. cit.*, p. 34, "Epistola haec est generis Didactici...."
69. *Ibid.*, "Exordium est ab affectu indignationis Sicuti alias optima exordia sunt ab affectibus...."
70. *Ibid.*, "Rationes reddit propositi Exordii, & demonstrat doctrinam suam esse a deo Coniecturis aliquot [cf. note on this term, n. 1]. Non didici ab hominibus: *Ergo* per revelationem...."
71. *Ibid.*, p. 35, "Status seu propositio per obiurgationes O stulti Galates (Gal. 3:1) cur descivistis a veritate Constat autem unde desciverunt scilicet ab illa sententia Iustificationis per fidem."
72. *Ibid.*, "Idque probat esse Argumentis...."
73. *Ibid.*
74. *Ibid.*

75. *Ibid.*
76. *Ibid.*, p. 36.
77. *Ibid.*, p. 36, and p. 33, n. 1, from *De rhetorica*, "Occupatio est cum dicimus nos praetitire, quod tum maxime dicimus...."
78. *Ibid.*, p. 37.
79. Cf. W. Maurer, *op. cit.*, Bd. 2, p. 105, and here, below, on Melanchthon's use of Romans as rhetoric, chapter 7.

CHAPTER 6

Melanchthon and the Leipzig Disputation

"It would certainly be false should one wish to insist that he was no fighter." (R. Stupperich, *Der unbekannte Melanchthon*, p. 85.)

The Leipzig Disputation began ominously for the Wittenbergers. The trumpets of Frankfurt had scarcely stopped sounding their fanfare on the election of Charles V as all two hundred of them arrived in Leipzig for what was officially to have been a debate between John Eck and Andreas Karlstadt.[1] It had rained, and one of the two lead wagons broke down, pitching poor Karlstadt headlong into the mud, to the delight of the throng of local onlookers.[2] His hand and arm were badly hurt (no worse than his dignity), and he was not in top form during the disputation.[3] The whole affair began with a first performance of local musician George Rhau's *Mass of the Holy Ghost* (in twelve parts) and an exhausting, two-hour lecture by Mosellanus on the ground rules, only to be followed—as he left backwards, bowing repeatedly—by more musicians and, at long last, a final hymn and lunch.[4] In the afternoon, Karlstadt and Eck began what became an entire week of wrangling over the matter of grace and freedom of the will. The battered Karlstadt did not perform well, and his tedious habit of looking up every reference to every citation infuriated Eck and bogged things down so badly that the spectators, most of whom, perchance, had never before watched academics debating the finer distinctions of theological doctrines, grew restless in their desire for what they had really come to see—Luther.[5] On July 4 their interest revived as the squarely built man stepped onto the stage and took over for the tiring Karlstadt.[6]

It is well known that what happened next was far from dull. Luther defended his thirteenth thesis that the papacy was a human institution. Pouncing on the opportunity to expose Luther with a shibboleth, and perhaps to earn a Golden Rose for himself, Eck pressed him relentlessly to say just how his position differed from that of the arch-heretic John Huss. Luther stunned the audience by dropping his defenses and conceding that many of Huss's teachings were sound, and not to be condemned. He further conceded the implication that not only popes, but councils, too, may err.[7] The damage was done. Eck and others triumphantly assumed that they had reached the end of the matter, for what more was there to talk about? They underestimated the extent of the damage that had been done during the preceding three hundred years to the established norms for Christian authority in the society as a whole.[8] Luther's arguments were not so easily shunted aside, nor would the charge of heresy prove possible to enforce without great political difficulties. The kernel of the controversy was now most clear to everyone, Luther and Melanchthon included.

It seems that Melanchthon had a natural role to play in Leipzig. He had been in Augsburg in August, on his way to Wittenberg, when Eck published the initial attack on Karlstadt (who had earlier gone impulsively to Luther's defense). Eck's *Defensio* was published in Augsburg, and it is not likely that Melanchthon missed these literary skirmishes.[9] The connection with Eck for Philip went back to his days teaching dialectic at Tübingen. He had used Eck's textbook and, in the inaugural address and in *De rhetorica*, had made special reference to it as typical of that brand of barbarism which was in truth nothing more than "scholastic" wrangling.[10] Moreover, Melanchthon supposed it was Eck who had plotted to destroy his good relationship with Erasmus by whispering of negative things allegedly spoken about the *Paraphrases*.[11] Philip wrote to Eck's friend Christoph Scheurl that Eck's arrogance was typical of a godless generation, and that he marveled at his pompous attitude in debates with other members of the Wittenberg faculty, such as Paul Ricius.[12] As he watched his colleagues Luther and Karlstadt preparing for the great disputation, he had secretly fretted about where things would end, and yet he believed that Luther and others were doing what they must do.[13] He viewed himself as a follower, but as one who was once removed from the center of the stage.[14]

According to John Rubeus, a student from Wittenberg who observed the Leipzig Disputation, Melanchthon acted as a kind of encyclopedic secretary to both Luther and Karlstadt during the long debates, and thus managed to annoy Eck and the rest of the opposition.[15] When the disputation ended on the 15th of July, after eighteen days, both sides agreed to be silent until the Sorbonne in Paris and the theological faculty at Erfurt had given official judgments. It was during this "silence" that Melanchthon bravely (and shrewdly) provoked a continuation of the debate in public by writing an open letter to his friend Oecolampadius in which he launched a full assault on Eck.[16]

Melanchthon's entrance into public controversy was carefully planned. He knew well that Eck was no great favorite of the clergy in Augsburg, where

Oecolampadius was preaching,[17] and also must have known in advance that Eck would come at him like a wounded lion (which he did). Luther's camp obviously felt that bringing the *arguments* into the broadest public light possible, before the charges of heresy became an official litany, would help to hamstring the policy of intimidation that was sure to come. After hearing the arguments in Leipzig, Melanchthon seemed confident that he could hold his own with Eck and that the time was right for a reputable humanist like himself to claim Luther for their cause, just as they had done for Reuchlin in his hour of crisis.

Eck was not impressed by his adversary. He curled his lip in scorn at the very mention of this mere grammarian, who had neglected his store of Greek declensions and dared to match himself with theologians.[18] Melanchthon rallied with his usual gift for clarity, crispness and getting straight to the point of things, producing a rebuttal which was a good deal longer than the original essay.[19] Their literary exchange ended in no great triumph for either one of them. Eck had drawn more blood than Melanchthon cared to admit, particularly on the issue of free will and grace, and he was now irreversibly embroiled in controversy; his strident defense of Luther's anthropology left some in grave doubt as to his reputed faithfulness to philosophy and letters.[20] (And, of course, his urgent attempts to disprove the charge would cause him no end of trouble on the other side.) Eck suffered damage as well, since his hope was to play the champion of philosophy and learning; in fact, in the opinion of some, he instead revealed embarrassing bald spots in his knowledge of literature. And his rhetorical ploy of constantly repeating that Melanchthon had disclosed himself as a staunch ally of the heretic Luther, and that he was thus guilty by association, was so transparently to beg the questions of truth that it may have done more good than harm to the Lutheran side in the long run.[21]

The main points of contention were the issues of "good works," "freedom of the human will," "papal authority" and "purgatory." In their approaches to each of these topics, important differences surfaced between them on the nature of biblical authority: What was the theological center of Scripture? Was Scripture essentially distinct from patristic tradition? Did the apocryphal writings of the Intertestamental Period belong to the sacred text? This was Melanchthon's first systematic defense of his earliest Lutheran theology and of the concept of biblical authority which accompanied it. The documents are particularly useful in revealing how the Preceptor had begun to develop concepts of biblical perspicuity and unity, in the contexts of Luther's theology and his own linguistic theory, and how he viewed these properties of Scripture as evidence of its originality and *discrimen*, that is, as that which made Scripture unique amid all human tradition in the *degree* of its divine authority.

During the Leipzig Disputation, Karlstadt had argued that God alone, and not man, was the author of good works.[22] Eck had retorted that good works indeed were of God, but that man also played a part in their creation. Melanchthon ridiculed (rather than engaged) Eck's distinction (which rested on the conventional categories of *meritum de condigno* and *meritum de congruo*) between good works construed as a whole (*in totam*), on the one hand, and as a *totality*, on the other. He derided this distinction as "clever" (*argutum*), as "indeed worthy of the name of theological majesty" and as typical of the word-games being played in those days by theologians.[23] Why, after all, had Eck thought it necessary to invent new terms to vent the old, Occamistic doctrine of *meritum de congruo*?[24] Eck somewhat justifiably dismissed this response as a grammarian's derision and as amateurish question-begging.[25] He repeated the logic of his explanation that God's authorship of good works must not be taken to contradict the freedom of the human will; both acts happened simultaneously, and congruently together, not singly or one after the other.[26]

Whatever its actual merits, Melanchthon's response was a clear indication of his growing commitment to Luther's (and Karlstadt's) position on grace, works and freedom of the will.

> Karlstadt undertook to defend his conclusion...that the free will, prior to grace, does not have power except to sin [*non valere nisi ad peccandum*]; Eck opposed [him with] this conclusion which you see put forward on human powers and, indeed, human righteousness or congruent merit [*seu merito congrui*].... I believe what motivates him [Karlstadt] to say, and rightly so, that the whole work is from God, is the profane school of Eck which makes no distinction between works of grace and of nature except in respect to the ground [*nisi respectu rationis*], as they call it....[27]

In view of our earlier discussion of Melanchthon and the *via moderna*, it is interesting that he here detected the linguistic influence of "that barbarian" Scotus [28] and considered that Eck would have done better to have followed the Occamists, who allowed that certain acts were merely received from above.[29]

Melanchthon did not further elaborate his *own* position on the issue of grace, nature and freedom of the will, but rather limited his comments mainly to what he considered Eck's overly subtle and profitless scholasticism. It was very clear, however, that he had now joined sides with Karlstadt and Luther, and that he considered this subject one of several which, when disputed in public, would plainly reveal "how great a distinction there is between the ancient theology of Christ and the newly coined [theology] of Aristotle."[30]

A second main point of contention between them was that of papal authority.[31] In the seventh article of his *Excusatio*, Eck's argument in support of Roman papal authority had rested mainly upon the classic text of Matthew 16:18 with the received view that Peter was the "rock," upon which Christ would build His church.[32] Eck had solidified this view by citing extensively from authorities such as Augustine, Ambrose and Jerome,[33] and thus opened a tricky patristic issue. In order to respond, Melanchthon was forced to go into the literature himself and to sharpen his view of biblical authority with respect to the derivative status of theological tradition. "Since Eck so bravely boasts the authority of the holy fathers and places all hope of victory in them, behold what he accomplishes."[34] Philip claimed that the fathers must be respected, for "... I venerate and adore these many lights of the church [*tot ecclesiae lumina*], the most celebrated vindicators of Christian doctrine [*vindices Christianae doctrinae*]."[35] On the other hand, he cautioned, what was one to think when the fathers varied, or contradicted each other, as they often did? From the premise that the patristic traditions did not emerge as a logically coherent body of truth, he inferred that belief in an authoritative revelation implied the existence of a discernible, higher standard than was visible in the literature of the fathers.

> Moreover, I think it not indiscriminately done, when the opinions of the holy fathers are at variance, as they are accustomed to being, that they be received with Scripture as the judge; let Scripture not suffer violence from their wavering judgments.[36]

What was it, then, that gave Scripture a greater authority than that of the holy fathers? Here Philip applied one of the fundamental elements of his truth theory to the fathers in a way that seems perhaps inconsistent with its lack of clear application heretofore on the doctrine of election. Rather than the mere primacy and antiquity of Scripture, Melanchthon stressed its clear *unity* of presentation. Just how he defined this unity was evident from the assertion that followed:

> Indeed, there is one certain and simple *sensus* of Scripture (as heavenly truth is also most simple), which, after the Scriptures have been compared, can be attained from the connecting structure and thread of the oration.[37]

The simplicity and unity was that of the thread or *status* of a rhetorical composition. God had addressed His world in the manner of a good rhetorician on the premise that simplicity, clarity and coherence were in the essence of successful communication. And in that manner of picturing the canon, Philip wrote that the *sententiae* and decrees of men must be weighed against Scripture as against "a Lydian proofstone."[38] Knowledge of the "unus et simplex sensus" of Scripture would free one from the weaknesses to which all men are prone (including popes and those who misread Scripture to give them nearly divine status). The fathers were susceptible to errors of interpretation, because, like all human beings, they were taken hither and thither by diverse affections and concerns,[39] and we, confessed Melanchthon, experience the same thing: "...we understand Scripture variously, because we are variously affected...."[40] Oftentimes one encountered something among the fathers which, although there was clearly no malice of intent, "nevertheless, we little men are unable to square with the letter...."[41] He granted that sometimes the fathers, although not consistent with the letter, may have been successful in gaining a "sensus verus et non impertinens," and that this experience was perhaps what Paul called "spiritual understanding, which was easier to perceive than to explain in words."[42]

Without amplifying this last point, however, he returned to his theme of abuses and contrast between patristic tradition and the canonical writings:

How often do they disagree among themselves; how often do they retract their own errors? And why go on? Scripture, which they call canonical, is alone of the heavenly Spirit, pure and true in all things.[43]

That this was a war between fundamentally opposing construals of the text itself became clear in the words that he wrote in defense of Luther: "I believe in the fathers, because I believe in Scripture...."[44] In contrast to Luther and the noblest of the fathers, Melanchthon argued, Eck and his contemporaries were devotees of an Aristotle whom they but badly knew themselves[45] and were destroyers of the plain sense of Scripture:

> ...they [*scholastici*] transform them [*divinae literae simplices*] into allegorical, tropological, anagogical, grammatical, literal, historical senses and then pour them into I do not know what chasms.[46]

He concluded that even the fathers whom Eck had enlisted against Luther had expressed misgivings about this traditional rendering of Matthew 16:18, because a simple *enarratio* of the text failed to justify such an elaborate defense of papal power.[47]

The third and final issue of dispute between Eck and Melanchthon was that of purgatory. And that debate landed them in an intricate squabble over the actual definition of the canon that led Melanchthon to more radical criticisms still. In his defense of belief in purgatory, Eck had cited texts from the books of the Maccabees.[48] According to Melanchthon, doctrinal proofs from these writings were invalid, and Luther was correct to follow Jerome in not taking the books of the Maccabees as canonical.

> It seemed to Martin in the disputation, according to the judgment of Jerome, that the Maccabees are not valid. On the contrary, he [Eck] attributes as much [authority] to the book of Maccabees as to the gospel....[49]

In his *Excusatio*, Eck conceded the point that, indeed, the books of the Maccabees had not been in the Hebrew canon; nevertheless, according to both Augustine and Jerome, they had been *received* into the canon by the church.[50] Moreover, he argued that, just as we would not know which of the presumably many gospels written were of "indubitable truth [*indubiae veritatis*]" unless the church had stamped its approval [*nisi ex approbatione Ecclesiae*] upon the four canonical Gospels and rejected the others, "so also the books of the Maccabees ought to be of indubitable truth to the Christian because of the approval of the church."[51] Melanchthon accused Eck of misrepresenting Jerome, who indeed affirmed the value of Christians *reading* the books of Judith, Tobias, Maccabees and others, but did not consider them *canonical*:

...who [Jérome] says, just as the church, therefore, indeed reads the books of Maccabees, Judith and Tobias, but does not receive them among canonical scriptures, so also these two volumes, namely Wisdom and Ecclesiasticus, are for edification of the public, not for the authority of establishing ecclesiastical dogma.[52]

Melanchthon concluded:

There is therefore a distinction between the books of the church, which receives some books differently; so it does not follow that because a book is counted among our number, it is therefore Scripture of the Holy Spirit.[53]

He did not attempt to define the criteria for this *discrimen* between the books of the church; but his comments in the earlier sections of his letter to Oecolampadius and of the *Defensio*, when read in the light of his later development, would indicate a growing connection in his thought between the canonicity of Scripture and the continuous, thematic "thread of the oration" which set it apart from patristic tradition. As will become clear, the debate over this "thread" was not merely the formal question of literal sense versus allegorical construals of Scripture, but the substantive one of what that sense *was*, and whether Luther's critique of recent Christian theology was correct, or not. Melanchthon, however, obviously believed by now that a proper hermeneutic would vindicate Luther's theology and set the church back on the right course. This part of the debate also illustrates plainly how the issues pertaining to canon became entangled with the matter of *sense* and interpretive problems. Melanchthon's rigorously logical truth theory exacerbated the troublesome quarrels on that subject, and he obviously helped the Lutherans to refine their own definitions of authoritative text.

Perhaps the most striking thing about Melanchthon's defense of Luther in these writings is the manner in which his linguistic theory and his newly born theology had become bonded together in a fresh treatment of the Bible and the nature of its authority. Before coming to Wittenberg, within the context of his South German humanism, he already professed a doctrine of biblical authority that stressed its uniqueness as "pure evangelical teaching." This "purity" was the essential property of its "literal sense," not some imagined, homiletic symbolism on the part of recent interpreters. And, for Melanchthon, this "literal sense" comprised several sub-properties, such as its primacy as ancient and original tradition, but particularly its semantic propriety, logical coherence and force of arguments, and its rhetorical powers of "invention," "disposition" and "elocution." The precise contents of this "literal sense" are difficult to determine accurately, but his language was typically about the shaping of morals and behavior that was appropriate to being a Christian. There is no clear evidence that he had completely worked out a theory of biblical unity and clarity along the substantive lines of, say, Erasmus, and it is just possible that he was still in the stage of inquiry on the matter when he encountered the works of Luther. When he met Luther and became convinced that his reading of Romans was correct, that Paul removed *all* grounds for asserting human merit of any kind, including even the *freedom* to receive the gift of grace, and that this theology was basic to the entire theology of the Bible, the "literal sense" of Scripture became for him an even more powerful critique and subversion of human culture than it had been. It destroyed not merely the pretense of human achievement at its damnable worst, but was most critical of it when it was at its best and, thus, most in danger of prideful affections and ideas. The focus shifted from the moral responsibility of humans to the moral sovereignty of God in Christ. The concept of *humilitas* would seem to have lost all downward limits.

If the "sense" of Scripture had now become evident to him in radical, Lutheran terms, the "literalness" of it remained something of the same conceptual order that it had been before. Melanchthon fused these two sets of terms into the concept of biblical authority that was peculiar to him. This was really a cluster of concepts that radiated from a complex linguistic core. The matters of biblical unity or coherence, clarity or perspicuity, and uniqueness or supremacy as the Word of God emerged together as distinct but logically interdependent members of the same large notion. That Scripture possessed a unity and clarity was integral to its uniqueness and supremacy; that it coherently and clearly presented the doctrine of God's unmitigated *grace*, something which was to be found nowhere else, magnified the uniqueness into a sense of a *divine* author behind the human books and a powerful critique of the sinful humanity behind all others. Nevertheless, without even a trace of equivocation, Melanchthon began to hammer out this "radicalized" notion of biblical authority on the anvil of his classical theory. This procedure has helped to make him a problematic, microcosmic study of faith and reason in Protestantism.

In the writings against Eck, one begins to have a clearer view than before of the tangled mass of problems that the young Melanchthon somehow would have to unravel. Perhaps of the very deepest order of magnitude was the difficulty of adhering to Luther's "sense" of Scripture while at once asserting its perfection as rhetorical "invention," "disposition" and "elocution," taking these terms directly from a secular tradition. The annihilation of all human cultural pride came to the world as *truth* in its very highest cultural modalities. When the Spirit of God spoke through divinely chosen human beings, He properly used the philosophical system of antiquity to get the truth across. Indeed the very concept of "truth" was nearly identical with that within the chain of great rhetoricians from Plato and Aristotle, through Cicero and Quintilian, to the present revival of letters. The essential meaning of all the various books of the Bible could be thus simply and rightly reduced to the "thread of an oration." The problem of "natural theology" would arise not so much from Philip's theory of natural law, as is commonly thought, but from deeper, epistemic roots. His nearly uncritical use of ancient rhetoric reflected an a priori commitment to the ontological paradigm underlying it. This ontology comprised analytical and moral intuitions which are not obviously consistent with the radical elements of Lutheran doctrine on the varied levels of revelation, grace and sin. Even in the context of his most critical assessments of philosophy, Melanchthon would maintain that pagan philosophers did not merely catch the truth in a fractured manner, but they did so with ontologically right intentions, reasons and (sometimes) results. God Himself honored the integrity of their search for universally important truths, emulated their linguistic techniques in expressing the truth and called human beings to self-knowledge and blessedness.

The problem of "intellectualism" in Lutheran history had also sprouted. It took shape in Melanchthon's manner of setting forth Luther's idea of the unifying scope of Scripture as *das Wort Gottes*. His way of construing Scripture as a whole is deeply connected with the great many battles that have raged over his actual place in history next to contemporaries such as Luther or Erasmus. By "intellectualism" is usually meant his overuse of logic to articulate the Christian faith, a style which is thought to have reduced theology to a set of propositions for our intellectual assent, and thus to have slain the spirit of Luther's original proclamation.[54]

There is no doubt that Melanchthon's construal of Scripture as the Word of God differed importantly from Luther's. Ebeling has included a most valuable discussion of biblical unity in the context of Luther's general hermeneutic.[55] Luther inherited from his medieval forebearers a belief in the inspiration and unity of the biblical canon. As with Melanchthon, the renewed stress on the singularity and authority of Scripture was formally "nothing but a radicalized medieval legacy...."[56] Moreover, when Luther wrote of the simple, clear unity of Scripture, he did so not out of what Ebeling called the recent problem of an "external perfection" (*äussere Vollkommenheit*) and "freedom from contradictions" (*Widerspruchslosigkeit*).[57] "In this respect, he exhibited an astonishing nonchalance. He was free of an anxious striving for harmonization...."[58] According to Ebeling, Luther thought of the Word of God as being essentially the core of Scripture: "... die Sache der Bibel selbst, ihren Generalskopus, das Eine, Einzige, worauf alles in ihr abzielt. Die Einheit der Bibel hat nicht die Art einer Summe, sondern ist die Spitze, in der alles zusammentrifft, das Ziel, auf das alles hinausläuft. Das hatte mit dieser Schärfe niemand zuvor erfasst." Luther's view of Christ as the larger theme of the scriptures to which individual texts must be hermeneutically related was not, it seems, a matter of atomistic rational coherence.[59] The formal logic of his concept of biblical unity perhaps bore greater resemblance to Erasmus's than it did to Melanchthon's. When Erasmus considered that Scripture was a divine *oratio* and that Christ was the *sermo Dei* and *scopus* of the whole, he had in mind the navigational metaphor of "sighting," as with the polar star.[60] Indeed, (as with Melanchthon) Christ was the Ciceronian "commonplace" to which all the various lines of discourse must be referred by the *interpreter* of Scripture,[61] but to do this is a profoundly deductive, hermeneutical action, a controlled but conceptually "loose" association of meanings by analogy, rather than by more or less straightforward logical induction. It would seem that Erasmus and Luther, albeit with very different *senses* of the letter in hand, despaired of scholastic theology in its hermeneutically fractured state and offered the simplicity of a Christ-centered method, by which to bring the diversity of the canon, and thus the culture, into homiletical and theological harmony.[62] In spite of his protestations against scholastic theology, Melanchthon had the mind of a technical logician. He challenged the scholastic community (as well as fellow humanists) to become even more rigorous than they had been in using Aristotle and pure logic. As we shall see more clearly in his exegetical works, the great diversity of Scripture seemed more an illusion to be cut through by inductive analysis than it was a mystery to be suspended by changed focus upon simpler, clearer and more practically useful themes or dissolved through the deep "multivalence" of texts. Once one grasped the rhetorical patterns of individual books, the unity of Scripture was visibly demonstrable through arguments as a univocal, positive assertion, in varying degrees of structure and clarity, of the same general *scopus*. His concept of Scripture as *oratio* thus brought a distinctive shape to his Lutheran theology and concept of biblical authority.

Perhaps this is a good time to bring up still another issue that is connected with Melanchthon's alleged "intellectualism." His rhetorical construal of biblical unity and the accompanying notions of perspicuity and freedom from extensive contradiction also invite suggestions of influence upon later generations of Lutheran theologians, who became obsessed with showing the logical perfections of the Bible.[63] There can be no doubt that Melanchthon introduced certain dogmatic methods into Lutheranism, or that he at least pioneered a style of theology through the use of *loci communes theologici*. It is perhaps also true (though in need of careful documentation) that he is partly responsible for inducing a whole generation of students to think of Scripture in the terms of dialectical unity, perspicuity and freedom from contradiction.[64] Nevertheless, just as there were subtle but important differences between Luther and Melanchthon, so were there between Melanchthon and the later dominant tradition. His rhetorical construal of Scripture included a strong belief in the *human* artistry and creative composition of the texts. They were interrelated not merely on the level of a deterministic theory of inspiration and dictation, but rather in the manner of a classical literary *tradition*. This made his conceptual structures much more complex than most of theirs, and certainly much more adaptable to the complexities of life in the culture. His rhetorical construal of the canon also brought forth other differences that will emerge in writings yet to be discussed.[65]

However one finally assesses him, the writings against Eck show that Melanchthon's earliest construals of Scripture, in the context of the Lutheran theological "sense" of the letter, searched for a way of sustaining the whole by the sum of all the various parts. Rhetoric was not simply a method by which to "find" the *theology* of the canon, but was the essential identifying structure of the canon *itself*. In that respect, he was very different from Luther. Nor did Melanchthon construe Scripture at all in the manner of what O'Rourke Boyle called Erasmus's "skepticism" in handling the exegetical data of the grammatical texts in the context of murky doctrinal debates. The dialectical framework of rhetoric in Melanchthon brought along an easy confidence in human powers of perception, once properly steered on course, to discern truth directly (something that O'Rourke Boyle suggests was in the essence of scholasticism, and antithetical to Erasmus's disposition). The irony is that this epistemic optimism was strangely compatible with Luther's thundering, "prophetic" certainty that, on the matter of grace and freedom, he was absolutely right and that there simply was no room for disagreement between Christians.[66] There was thus little in Melanchthon of what Manschreck has most unsatisfyingly suggested is the master key to understanding him: "...his recognition that human beings are finite, that no human being has final truth..., and the gospel cannot be absolutely translated into human thought...."[67] On the contrary, from the very earliest years his truth theory was a philosophically "realistic" brand of Aristotelianism, and this he applied unapologetically to the activities of exegesis and hermeneutics. He believed that the meaning of the text was clearly knowable through right methods, and that the use of right methods must inevitably lead to knowledge of the truth about Scripture. It was not a stoic *skepsis* or a modern epistemic relativism that made him the agent of diplomacy that he would soon become. The truth is that, beneath his modesty, he had a stubborn and unfailing confidence, to the very last, in the possibility of consensus and rapprochement between the warring factions, if only they would be reasonable and look fairly at the text. It is obvious by now that Luther's doctrine of sin, while it had immense meaning to Melanchthon both personally and philosophically, held a very ambiguous position in relation to the core of his general epistemology, and to that of his special hermeneutic. But his theology was barely on its first legs. His career as theologian had only just begun; the adaptability of his rhetorical system (and the pliability of his theology) was yet to be explored as one day it would be. His response to the Leipzig affair was to bring himself up to speed in theology, to become a professional. We must follow him now on his course, through Paul, toward forging the "first Protestant dogmatics."

Notes to Chapter 6

1. Cf. E. G. Rupp, *Luther's Progress to the Diet of Worms*, New York/Evanston 1964, pp. 67ff., for a superbly written summary of the proceedings.
2. *Ibid.*
3. *Ibid.*
4. *Ibid.*
5. *Ibid.*
6. *Ibid.*
7. *Ibid.*
8. *Ibid.*
9. W. Maurer, *Der junge Melanchthon*, Bd. 2, Göttingen 1969, pp. 54ff.
10. *MW* III, pp. 34ff.; W. Maurer, *op. cit.*, Bd. 2, pp. 55ff.; *Philippi Melanchthonis de rhetorica libri tres*, Wittenberg 1519, D1v.
11. *MW* VII/1, p. 55; and W. Maurer, *op. cit.*, Bd. 2, p. 55.
12. *MW* VII/1, p. 44, n. 1; no. 22, pp. 73ff.
13. *MW* VII/1, p. 73.25ff.
14. *Ibid.*, p. 70.25f., to Wolfgang Capito, May 1519: "Credo, non nihil Martinus et Carolostadius efficiunt. Hos ego, sed longo sequor intervallo."
15. For a complete text of the disputation, O. Seitz, *Der authentische Text der Leipziger Disputation*, Leipzig 1903; also WA 2, pp. 254-383; in English translation, D. Ziegler (ed.), *Great Debates of the Reformation*, New York 1969, pp. 3ff.
16. The text of the letter: *MW* I, pp. 4ff.; on Melanchthon's rebuttal of the Sorbonne's final verdict, in which he, in the year 1521, made many similar points to those which he made against Eck, cf., *MW* I, *Adversus furiosum Parrisiensium theologastrorum decretum, Philippi Melanchthonis pro Luthero apologia*, pp. 146ff.
17. W. Maurer, *op. cit.*, Bd. 2, pp. 54ff.
18. *Excusatio Eckii ad ea, quae falso sibi Phil. Melanchthon Grammaticus Wittenbergo super Theologica Disputatione*, CR I, pp. 97ff. The general tone of the work is suggested adequately by the title.
19. *Defensio...Philippi Melanchthonis contra Joh. Eckium, M W* I, pp. 12ff. Stupperich, *ibid.*, p. 13, remarks: "Melanchthon erteilt dem berühmten Disputator eine solche Abfertigung, dass Eck sich nicht mehr an ihn herantraute." This statement is somewhat biased in Melanchthon's favor, for Eck continued to peck at Melanchthon and even attempted to undermine him during the ten years which passed before they clashed again at the Diet of Augsburg in 1530. See below, on Eck's attack on Melanchthon's *Baccalaureate Theses* in theology, chapter 7. Furthermore, we do not think it is at all clear that Melanchthon engaged Eck's arguments on freedom of the will fairly or successfully, or even on a level that comported with his own logical values.
20. Cf. the open letter from Martin Cellarius to Melanchthon which is the preface to Eck's *Excusatio*. Cellarius wrote with amazement that (he had heard) Melanchthon was now an enemy of philosophy. *M B* I, pp. 65ff. and reference to K. Schottenloher, *Zentralblatt für Bibliothekswesen*, 32, 1915, no. 6, p. 256.
21. Cf. esp. W. Maurer, *op. cit.*, Bd. 2, pp. 58ff.
22. *MW* I, p. 7.1ff.
23. *Ibid.*, p. 7.7ff.
24. *Ibid.*; on the concept of *meritum de congruo*, cf. esp. H. Oberman, *The Harvest of Medieval Theology*, Grand Rapids 1962.
25. *CR* I, p. 99.

26. *Ibid.*, "...sic bonum opus est totum a Deo, non tamen sic quin etiam sit ab libero arbitrio, quia simul agunt, non vicissim; mixtim, non sigillatim...."
27. *M W* I, pp. 16.9ff.
28. *Ibid.*, p. 16.34ff., "Hic vero tutandos seu excusandos Barbarus ille Heraclitus Scotus, quem, meministis, in rhapsodiis suis quam Christiana hac de re doceat."
29. *Ibid.*, p. 17.17ff., "Porro, quid necesse erat novis glossematis et plane fictitiis asserere vim liberi arbitrii, qua bonum efficiat, cum receptissimum sit et apud scholasticos vel summae notae, nempe Occamicos, quosdam voluntatis actus tantum recipi." It is most doubtful that Melanchthon really thought that the Occamistic theory of "prevenient grace" could be taken as normative for his soteriology. But, in view of his later predestinarian theory (cf. chapter 11), it is intriguing that he would mention it in a favorable light.
30. *Ibid.*, p. 5.4ff., "Haec vero disceptandi provincia primum non ob aliud suscepta est, nisi ut palam fieret, inter veterem et Christi theologiam ac noviciam et Aristotelicam quantum intersit."
31. P. Fraenkel, *Testimonia Patrum: The Function of the Patristic Argument in the Theology of Philipp Melanchthon*, Geneva 1961, esp. pp. 272ff., on the importance of the Leipzig Disputation to the development of a patristic argument at Wittenberg.
32. *CR* I, p. 100.
33. *Ibid.*
34. *M W* I, p. 17.30ff.
35. *Ibid.*, p. 17.35ff.
36. *Ibid.*, pp. 17.36-18.1ff., "Deinde puto non temere fieri, sicubi sententiis S. patres variant, quemadmodum solent, ut iudice scriptura recipiantur, non ipsorum nempe variantibus iudiciis, scriptura vim patiatur."
37. *Ibid.*, p. 18.1ff., "Quandoquidem unus aliquis et simplex scripturae sensus est, ut et coelestis veritas simplicissima est, quem collatis scripturis e filo ductuque [cf. Lewis and Short, *in loco* II, A] orationis licet assequi."
38. *Ibid.*, p. 18.4ff., "In hoc enim iubemur philosophari in scripturis divinis, ut hominum sententias decretaque ad ipsas ceu ad Lydium lapidem exigamus."
39. *Ibid.*, p. 18.10-30.
40. *Ibid.*, p. 18.12f., "...varie nos scripturam intelligere, quia varie afficimur...."
41. *Ibid.*, p. 18.32f., "...quem tamen nos homunculi ad literam quadrare non videmus...."
42. *Ibid.*, p. 18.29ff., citation p. 18.32ff., "...quod puto Paulum intellectum spiritalem vocare, quae facilius sit percipere, quam verbis delineare."
43. *Ibid.*, p. 19.16ff., "Quoties ipsi inter se dissentiunt, quoties suos errores retractant? et quid multis? una est scriptura coelestis spiritus, pura et per omnia verax, quam canonicam vocant."
44. *Ibid.*, on Luther's freedom to depart from patristic teaching, p. 19.20ff.; citation here, p. 19.34ff., "Patribus enim credo, quia scripturae credo...."
45. *Ibid.*, p. 19.13ff.
46. *Ibid.*, p. 19.6ff., "...eas in allegoricos, tropologicos, anagogicos, literales, grammaticos historicos sensus transformant et transfundunt in nescio quas lacunas."
47. *Ibid.*, cf. pp. 20.3-24.
48. *CR* I, p. 101, article 4.
49. *M W* I, pp. 9.38-10.1ff., "Martino visum est in contentione iuxta Hieronymi sententiam non valere Maccabaeos. Contra ille, tantum deberi Maccabeorum libro quantum Evangelio...tenuit."
50. *CR* I, "Nam ad contentionem valere libros Maccab. adduxi, quia S. Augustinus Lib. 18 de civitate Dei, et Hieronymus...dicant, librum illum non fuisse in canone apud Hebraeos, sed Ecclesiam recepisse in Canonem...."

51. *Ibid.*

52. *MW* I, pp. 20.38-21.1ff., "... qui sic ait, sicut ergo Judith et Tobiae et Maccabaeorum libros legit quidem ecclesia, sed inter canonicas scripturas non recipit, sic et haec duo volumina sc. Sapientiam et Ecclesiasticum ad aedificationem plebis non ad auctoritatem ecclesiaticorum dogmatum confirmandam."

53. *Ibid.*, p. 21.5ff., "Est ergo inter libros Ecclesiae discrimen, quae alios libros aliter recipit, ut non sit consectaneum: hic liber est in numero nostrorum, igitur est scriptura Spiritus sancti."

54. Cf. below, chapter 11, our discussion of "intellectualism" in Melanchthon.

55. G. Ebeling, *Lutherstudien*, Bd. I, Tübingen 1971, pp. 292ff.

56. *Ibid.*

57. *Ibid.*, p. 293.

58. *Ibid.*

59. *Ibid.*

60. M. O'Rourke Boyle, *Erasmus on Language and Method in Theology*, Toronto/Buffalo 1977, pp. 88ff.

61. *Ibid.*, p. 93.

62. Cf. *ibid.*, pp. 96, 124ff., on Erasmus's rejection of an atomistic word-theory in favor of *oratio* in Christ on a much looser associative paradigm.

63. So R. Preus, *The Inspiration of Scripture*, Edinburgh/London 1957, p. ix, "Just as Melanchthon was an ardent disciple of Luther and wrote his *Loci communes* as an exposition of Luther's doctrine, so also the *Loci theologici* of Chemnitz and that of Hutter were both amplifications of Melanchthon's eminent work...." According to Preus, the connecting link was "their unanimous conviction that Scripture was the source of theology." Preus left the impression that there was a more or less continuous line of development from Melanchthon's concept of biblical authority through that of the dogmaticians of the 17th century.

64. For a useful summary of this pervasive theology in the 17th century, cf. *ibid.*

65. Cf. below, esp. chapter 8 on the perspicuity and efficacy of Scripture.

66. Cf. O'Rourke Boyle's superb discussion of this debate and their differing epistemic orientations, *Rhetoric and Reform*, Cambridge, Mass./London 1983.

67. C. Manschreck, *Melanchthon: The Quiet Reformer*, New York/Nashville 1958, p. 18.

CHAPTER 7

Melanchthon's Beginning as a Theologian

"That little Greek surpasses me, even in theology." (Luther, WABr I, p. 597.)

The Baccalaureate Theses of 1519

To a perfectionist like Melanchthon, there is no deeper wound than that inflicted by the taunt of "amateurism." He must have known deep down that, in answering Eck's arguments, he had sometimes resorted to the very sort of rhetoric which he detested in others, and that the polish of eloquence had hidden more than a little logical ambiguity. In any event, he no longer followed his comrades "from a distance." In the months after Leipzig, his interest in Luther and Luther's theology grew into a consuming passion. The letters, furiously written in the wake of the disputation, reveal a gripping bitterness towards Eck and equally intense devotion to the cause of Luther.[1] To John Lang he wrote in August, "If I love anything in human affairs, I vehemently love and embrace Martin, Martin's zeal and [his] pious letters with my whole spirit."[2] A few months later, in December, he wrote to John Schwebel:

> We are completely [immersed] in sacred letters, and I wish that you also would apply yourself wholly to these. There is in them a wonderful delight, nay rather a certain ambrosia of heaven is poured out upon the soul which is occupied with them.[3]

Melanchthon gave this testimony in connection with reports of his recent lectures on both Romans and the gospel of St. Matthew. "Through this time we have interpreted the epistle of Paul to the Romans, by far the weightiest of them all, serving as a *scopus* in all sacred Scripture...."[4] "Likewise we are now at work in Matthew, and perhaps we shall publish commentaries on Matthew."[5]

Melanchthon was a "mere grammarian" no more. In September, concentrated study of Scripture and theology had culminated in defense of a series of theses for the degree *Baccalaureus Biblicus*.[6] The *Theses*, which he drafted and defended before the theological faculty, provide a glimpse into his theological development up to the autumn semester of 1519 and are a path that lead to the more massive lectures, commentaries and theological summaries that were soon to follow.

Melanchthon's *Baccalaureate Theses* made it clear how the issues debated at the Leipzig Disputation in July had captured his theological imagination. Bondage of the human will,[7] opposition between faith and meritorious works,[8] the doctrines of law and gospel, faith and justification[9] and the final authority of Scripture to overrule the decrees of church tradition[10] appear as a set of unified Lutheran convictions about Christian soteriology: there is no capacity on the part of humans to love God; we can only hate Him in "servile fear"; righteousness is a gift or *beneficium* (Melanchthon's first public use of this important term) of Jesus Christ, and our righteousness is given us by grace and not by works.[11]

Besides a later letter to John Hess, to be examined in the next chapter, there are no existing records of how Melanchthon explained and defended his theses; thus, one can but imagine how he developed such views as those expressed on the sacrament of Holy Communion or on laws of nature and the essence of God.[12] The sources do indicate, however, that he passed the examination easily. Luther wrote: "He answered the questions in such a way that it seemed to all of us exactly what it was...a miracle."[13] We also know that his eighteenth thesis, on the lack of biblical support for belief in transubstantiation, caused him some grief when Eck pursued it in a letter to Elector Frederick.[14]

One may wonder why Melanchthon never aspired to a doctorate in theology. Perhaps it was for him a matter of principle not to give implicit validation to the system that had produced those scholars to whom he referred regularly as "that herd" and, derisively, as "nostri magistri." His later edition of *Loci communes theologici* was clearly aimed at destroying, rather than building upon, the principles underlying standard examination texts such as Lombard's *Sentences*. This modest academic rank was enough to unleash Melanchthon for theological lectures, and it was more than enough for his students, who turned out in droves for his classes—in excess of a thousand attended his lectures on the gospel of Matthew. Luther sincerely regretted that everyone could not be there to see the young scholar at work.[15] As Melanchthon had indicated in the letter to Lang, he was also occupied with lectures on Paul's epistle to the Romans. Texts related to the lectures on Romans and on Matthew have been preserved and are available in scholarly editions. The one is Melanchthon's *Theologica institutio in epistolam Pauli ad Romanos* (which was a predecessor to the great *Loci communes* of 1521); the other is entitled *Annotationes in Evangelium Matthaei*. The rest of this chapter will be devoted to discussing the fundamental ideas that emerged from his study of Romans, particularly biblical authority and its rhetorical properties. The *Annotationes* on Matthew will be the main subject of the next chapter.

The Lectures on Romans

On the 3rd of April in 1519, as we have seen, Melanchthon wrote of his plans to publish *scholia* on several epistles of Paul and on James.[16] Among these epistles must have been Romans, for during the summer and autumn of 1519 he had given unofficial lectures at his home through the entire text.[17] Melanchthon's *Institutio theologica* and the *Summa* of Romans attached to it were in part the harvest of these first private lectures.[18] Although the text of the *Institutio* may be imperfect, there is nearly unanimous judgment that it is a largely accurate sample of Melanchthon's earliest Lutheran theology.[19] Maurer has convincingly shown[20] that the *Institutio* was indeed among the *scholia* on "several epistles of Paul" and, thus, was written during and after the summer of 1519. Our references are to the edition published by E. Bizer,[21] who re-edited and corrected the *Codex Hessius* used by Plitt and Kolde.[22]

We shall see that Melanchthon had worked out a highly systematic outline for construing Romans as sacred rhetoric of a peculiar kind. It was "sacred" in that its authority had about it a transcendent quality or "difference," which one simply *knew* to be from God. But of course this "difference" was not *simply* obvious; it was obvious only when one at long last had a clear grasp of its complex (Lutheran) doctrinal structure. This *was* Scripture in its *sensus literalis*. Its *authority* was contingent first upon *knowing* that this was so and then grasping and believing its claims in a context where one *sensed* the presence of a "divine difference" from merely human systems of thought. This "divine difference" or *discrimen* of Scripture was perhaps the most striking and important theme of the *Institutio*, which positively exudes a sense of wonder and amazement at the transcendent quality of the (Lutheran) text.

The question of biblical authority is not just an exegetical matter, but is a most complex *modal* problem about the actual properties of that authority. In our judgment, the second most interesting feature of this early writing was the *rhetorical* modality of Scripture and its authority, or the manner in which, for Melanchthon, the divine power of Scripture operated with the modal functions of human rhetoric as he distinctively defined them. Not just its "perspicuity," to use the relevant traditional term, but also its "efficacy" upon the full human epistemic system, convicting mind, heart and will of its truth, was rhetorical in his precise sense of the art. Thus, the semantics of biblical authority in Melanchthon were not at all simple and straightforward, in spite of his claim that this was so, but were very complex on the levels of knowing *what* the sense of Scripture is, *that* what it says is *true* and that this truth is *divinely* grounded. The almost a priori sense in which he asserted the clarity or obviousness of such truth-claims occurred only after these complex conditions for truth had been satisfied by interpretation. The entire modal structure of truth and authority, for both the text and the processes of thought that were required for a proper epistemic relation to it, was that of rhetorical persuasion.

Melanchthon thus took Luther's theology in his own peculiar direction. From very early on, there were people in the Lutheran fold who felt the difference and did not like it. The historiography is filled with judgments against Philip's chilly, clinical "intellectualism." What he made of Luther's system has been laid accusingly at his feet as the slain corpse of a great beginning. It is said that his was the theological miscreant of Luther writ small—reduced to mere doctrine to be grasped through the powers of reason. These complaints are legion in the literature. Too frequently, however, judgments on Melanchthon's "intellectualism" were made without clear knowledge of how he pictured right intellectual processes as rhetorical in kind. Our discussion of the *Institutio* and later writings will help us to gain clearer perspective on these judgments and to assess Melanchthon in a fresh way.

There is a deeper question that has occurred to us in sorting through Melanchthon's earliest theological writings. And we simply put the question here for consideration, before going into the technical exegesis of Melanchthon's text. The question is whether such qualifying points about the rhetorical modalities of *what* Scripture conveys and *how* it does so with authority might have caused Luther's "fine, brash hypothesis," in Flew's oft-quoted phrase, "to die the death of a thousand qualifications." One thinks not so much of that sort of death which comes through overuse of definition and systematic structures as of a somewhat different process. It would seem that Melanchthon made the validity of Lutheran theology a matter of straightforward exegetical induction, imagining the text as a logically direct and solid foundation for it, and that he thus placed this theology upon a foundation of inductive evidence and arguments from the text, rather than leaving it to some simpler form of self-disclosure. To use modern jargon, as a theologian, he was a *hermeneutical* (as well as an epistemic) "foundationalist." To the young Melanchthon, there seemed nothing at all ambiguous about asserting the Lutheran sense of Scripture that might call for a mystical, spiritual or authoritarian element in the process of believing and *coming* to belief in the claims of the new theology. He sincerely thought that a rational reading of this rationally written text would inevitably lead to rational theological consensus among *vires boni et literati,* to vindication of Luther and to a golden age of flourishing among God's people. Of course this never happened, nor could it have. Catholic fears (and Melanchthon's worst) would all be realized. The principle of *cuius regio* had all the ring of "every man for himself" in socio-political form. There was no consensus even between himself and someone as affable toward his literary theories as was Erasmus. Catholics and Protestants alike seemed to experience, here, on the level of hermeneutics, something like what A. Plantinga called the "de-ontological fatigue" which has settled upon metaphysics in our century, and they retreated variously to forms of dogmatism and spirituality to authorize their warring claims about the literal sense of Scripture. Melanchthon stood amid these rushing streams, rather stranded on his island of theory, crying, "come let us reason together," while a whole generation of Christians marched inexorably toward war, parochialism and the sort of fragmentation that bred modern relativism in religion. It is a hard thing to know how he ought to be judged, fairly, in his own historical context, for having this disposition and holding these beliefs to the end (for which he suffered much). For now, we are still clarifying the question and will undertake a response to the matter of Melanchthon's "intellectualism" in the course of discussion. It is obvious, however, that through Melanchthon, on this level, one has come up against the problem of theological pluralism and of the fractured state of human religious knowledge in the context of interpreting and using texts. And how one rates Melanchthon's interpretive practices will depend in part upon one's stance toward modern metaphysics and hermeneutical theory.

In our discussion of the *Institutio* and *Summa,* we shall center upon the large themes which Philip brought forth with all the exuberance of a proselyte, rather a pedagogical prophet to an unconverted generation: the sacred "difference" of Scripture and the rhetorical nature of that "difference." First, we shall discuss the *Summa* of Romans, because it clearly reveals the technical senses in which he judged this writing to have been a work of rhetoric. Next, in the *Institutio,* we shall observe how he used this foundation to erect a basic theology that was stridently Lutheran in its assertion of the transcendental qualities of biblical doctrine. Relevant historic doctrines here pertain generally to the difficult matter of saying how the divine and human traits of Scripture are together engaged in its "perspicuity" and "efficaciousness" as the Word of God in the words of men. And we shall concern ourselves with the rhetorical modalities of those properties of Scripture as Melanchthon imagined them.

The Summa *on Romans*

Attached to Melanchthon's *Institutio* was a most interesting outline of Paul's epistle to the Romans.[23] The document begins with Melanchthon identifying the *status caussae* of the entire writing: "...righteousness comes from faith without works, i.e., no work can transform an affection, but faith alone attains righteousness, that is, our renovation."[24] Romans was not merely *oratio* in the metaphorical sense of being part of the divine Word to humanity; it *was* an *oratio.* "The oration [*oratio*] is of the *genus iudicalis*; it has an *exordium, narratio* [and] *confirmatio*; it is aptly composed."[25] In the *exordium,* Paul used the rhetorical *loci* of *benevolentia,* by which he conveyed to the reader his good will towards them, and of *attentio,* whereby he caught their attention with a personal statement related to the main theme, "For I am not ashamed of the gospel."[26]

In the *narratio,* or development of his main theme, beginning at verse 1:18, "for the wrath of God from heaven is revealed upon all impiety,"[27] Paul prudently ordered his discussion according to a thematic plan.

This is the counsel of the *narratio*: since indeed Paul wished to prescribe the source and anchor of righteousness to Gentiles as well as to Jews, he rightly *begins* from this place, that there was law among both the Gentiles and Jews—to the one natural, to the other divine; but the law was useful neither to Gentiles nor to Jews for subduing the affections, since all will have perceived in themselves that the affections resist the law, that they do not attain what the law requires.[28]

Paul's *narratio* consisted of "these axioms,"[29]

1. That the Gentiles have the law of nature.
2. That the Gentiles, although they have the law of nature, nevertheless have sinned.
3. The Jews have divine law.
4. That the Jews, although they have divine law, nevertheless have sinned.
5. And so all men sin, that is both Gentiles and Jews; nor are they helped by the law, that they might sin less.
6. Righteousness is truly through Christ; it is not prepared by any works.[30]

This *narratio* lasted until the end of chapter four, and it comprised several "digressions" about the universality of sin.[31] The first of these occurred "from the beginning of the second chapter, 'Therefore there is no excuse,' up to the verse, 'Behold, you are called a Jew'...[v. 17]."[32] The "second began at the third chapter and continued up to this *locus*, 'We are all, Jews and Greeks, accused under sin' [v. 9]."[33]

With chapter four, however, Paul got to the substance of his argument, the all-important *confirmatio*, in which claims and assertions received *authoritative* backing from logical arguments. In this instance, Paul put forward "six of them...."[34]

1. Abraham was justified by faith, not by works; therefore, we, the sons of Abraham, are not justified except by faith.
2. David says that blessedness [*beatitudo*] is through the non-imputation of sin [*per non imputationem peccati*]; therefore it is not of works.
3. Abraham was justified prior to circumcision; therefore justification is not of works.
4. The promise [*promissio*] is not through the law, i.e., justification was prior to the Mosaic law; therefore justification is not of works of the law.
5. If the inheritance is of the law, i.e., if the law is sufficient for justification, the promise of Christ is in vain [*frustra et promissio Christon*], i.e., if it is of us we have no need of Christ.

6. The law works wrath, therefore it does not reconcile; the law creates hatred of God [*lex facit odium Dei*], not, therefore, love [*amorem*].[35]

After "amplifying" these conclusions by an equally strong indictment of Gentile morality,[36] Paul scoped in on the precise sense of his message. One might say that, to Melanchthon, chapter five was the semantic lexicon of the terms that were flying about in contemporary theological debate. The knowledgeable reader will catch straightaway that Philip introduced here the doctrinal triad of "sin," "law" and "grace" that would become famous as his distinctive summary of fundamental theology.

> There he begins a *locus*, really independent from the ones above, by which he compares [*comparet*] sin, law and grace; and it is a *locus didacticus*, in which he teaches what sin, law and grace are, and whence [*unde*] they come [*quo, quid et unde peccatum, gratia et lex sit, docet*].[37]

This *locus didacticus* comprised a series of propositions:

> Through Adam is sin.
> Through sin is death.
> There was sin even before the Mosaic law.
> But it was not known.
> Through Christ is grace.
> Through grace, life.
> Through the law, sin abounds.
> As sin was known, grace also abounded.
> Therefore, is the law the cause of sin?
> No.
> The law is good.
> We are evil.
> We use a good thing badly; as reins are a cause of raging to a horse, they do not rage by themselves. [*Re bona male utimur, ut frenum est equo causa saeviendi, ipsum per se non saevit.*] [38]

Paul handled these themes up to chapter seven, to the fourteenth verse, "'We know, moreover, that the law is spiritual and I am carnal.'"[39] The entire sixth chapter, with the beginning of the seventh, up to the *locus*, "What therefore do we say? That the law is evil?" was a digression which contained a moral disputation (*moralem disputationem*) and the distinction (*discrimen*) between the kingdoms of sin, law and grace.[40] Paul concluded "That we are not under the law, but under grace; and this *locus* destroys freedom of the will [*arbitrii libertatem tollit*]."[41] From the seventh chapter, wrote Melanchthon, Paul argued that the powers of sin are so great that "before someone is in Christ, it is impossible that he do anything of the law."[42] Through the ninth chapter "are exhortations and consolations...."[43] Chapter nine "contains predestination and the call of the Gentiles"[44]; chapter ten, "a *comparatio* between the righteousness of faith and Pharisaic righteousness"[45]; chapter eleven, an "exhortation,"[46] and "The rest are moral teachings."[47]

In the *Summa* one gains a clearer view than in any previous writing of how Melanchthon used his rhetorical system to set up a biblical *foundation* for Lutheran theology and, in the process, created a concept of biblical *authority* that drew upon his older structures of thought in connection with the new ones. Romans was rhetorically structured oration on the doctrine of justification apart from works, where that meant the destruction of human freedom to seize upon any affection *for* God. That Romans belonged to the *genus iudicale* (and later to the *genus didacticon*) was seemingly obvious to him, in spite of its general lack of *pure* syllogistic structure and the roughness of its seams at some places. Paul had inventively selected topics from the very core of the tradition (this application of the "invention" of *loci communes* would be stressed more in the *Institutio* than it was here); he had "disposed" his oration by "scoping in" on a main thesis, or *status caussae*; he had "confirmed" it through the use of special logical and rhetorical techniques of inferential reasoning; he had deepened his arguments by rigorous dialectical definition, using the typical *quaestiones* or *loci* for that purpose, and he had finished off his discourse by exhorting his readers to assertive action that was consonant with belief in the truth of his position. Much of the power and authority of Romans was quite human, and quite clearly human, in Melanchthon's best classical sense of that term. Hence, the doctrine of Romans ought to be just as apparent, hermeneutically, as Paul was successful in putting it down.

Let us look but briefly at Melanchthon's view of Paul's use of inference and the modality of biblical authority connected with it. It would seem that Paul was non-authoritarian in this writing. No appeal was made to his unique station as an apostle, or to private, "inspired" revelations within that larger body of tradition. His authority derived mainly from what Melanchthon evidently took to be clear inferences from a shared body of truths that emerged from both the Old Testament and the moral experience of the Gentiles. Through the modalities of logical implication, these inferences connected the old truths incorrigibly with the new interpretive claims. The major premise of his argument, that justification is not by works, was the *logical* implication of Old Testament history and theology. The *meaning* of Scripture here emerged in the rhetorical relation of Paul to his Old Testament text and it to him. Thus, the perspicuity and power of Scripture as a *unity* shaped up in the classical terms of orators standing within traditions. We shall return to this theme in another chapter, but it deserves to be noted that Melanchthon was perhaps one of the first Christian theologians (at least in post-medieval times) to construe Scripture as a diachronic, organic *tradition*, rather than as a synchronic and flat sourcebook of truth for "glossing." One should perhaps also mention his utterly uncritical stance toward Paul's inferences, some of which he might well have wondered about with respect either to their actual validity or to their validity in deducing a clearly Lutheran position. This receptivity indicates not only a disposition to believe that Scripture was "inspired by God," but also to believe that agreement with Luther was the inescapable, clinching outcome of rational engagement of Paul's text. The reader was finally bound by *logic* to agree, and that this was so for the young Melanchthon is important to discussion of the aforesaid problems of intellectualism and foundationalism, which we shall take up in later contexts.

Perhaps this is also the place to take up again the issue of Melanchthon's originality in construing and using rhetoric in forming a doctrine of biblical authority. We cannot pursue the subject here to the full extent that it deserves. Nevertheless, our own research, taken in the light of secondary literature on the history of rhetoric in sixteenth-century Christian humanism, permits us to venture a tentative judgment. The research of Maurer,[48] O'Rourke Boyle,[49] J.W. O'Malley,[50] J. Aldridge [51] and H. Sick[52] is variously suggestive of important differences between Melanchthon and Erasmus on the use of rhetoric in theology. In Maurer's view, Melanchthon's practice was unique among Christian humanists. "To concentrate the content of Romans in this manner upon a few central concepts [*loci*], as Melanchthon did, lay entirely outside the horizon [*Gesichtskreis*] of the biblical humanists; he [Erasmus] did not seek systematically to grasp the whole [*das Ganze*], but rather, philologically compared the particulars of the text."[53] Maurer concluded, "It would never have occurred to him to pursue the structure of the epistle from the rhetorical *genus iudicale* into all the details, as we find it in Melanchthon's *Summa*."[54] In his *Paraphrases*, Erasmus treated Paul's assertions individually, often applying the devices of *tropi* and biblical allegories, and drew from them spiritual and ethical meaning, in accord with his own "philosophy of Christ."[55] One might call this technique a kind of humanistic, Christ-centered glossing. Sick has also argued that Melanchthon was very different from Luther and from earlier humanists, such as Erasmus, not in his mere use of rhetoric to comprehend the letter of the text, but in his passion for finding a presumed didactic and logical unity in and between particular writings, and for stressing the dialectical methods of the biblical writers themselves to prove their central propositions.[56] We have already mentioned the intriguing text in which Erasmus argued against the Pauline authorship of Hebrews, as he wrote to Cardinal Matthew Skinner in the preface to the *Paraphrases*, on the ground that "it was written in a more truly rhetorical than apostolic style."[57] Melanchthon's strongly Greek metaphysics, theory of truth, language and method helped produce a peculiar kind of rhetorical theory that now served as the handmaiden of Luther's peculiar kind of theology. As Schnell has argued, together they created a method that was without solid precedent in any previous tradition.[58]

Melanchthon's Theologica Institutio in Epistolam Pauli ad Romanos

Melanchthon divided his *Institutio* into thirteen sections, which followed nearly as much from his own systematic interpretation as from the order of Romans itself. (No doubt that is why the *Summa* was appended to it, and Melanchthon was disenchanted with the independent publication of the *Institutio*.) A rough outline of his conceptual framework is that of law and righteousness, the nature of sin, the doctrine of grace and justification through faith, the difference between pagan and Christian righteousness, and predestination (which received no systematic treatment, but obviously constituted much of the substructure for his arguments).

This outline expressed Melanchthon's fresh discovery of the gospel as applied to academic theology. Readers who are familiar with the *Loci communes* will notice straightaway the historic emergence of his distinctive language.

> Among the theological *loci*, on God as one, [as] triune, [and as] creator; on man, sin, the law, the incarnation of the Word; on grace, the sacraments, the church, the keys; on the power and nature of men, there are some in particular which are of the very greatest importance to us [*vel praecipue sunt et qui nostra maxime referunt*]: SIN, LAW, GRACE, so that the rest contain disputations more inquisitive than useful. For in these three the *summa* of our justification is comprehended [*Nam tribus his summa iustificationis...comprehenditur*]....[59]

This was perhaps Philip's schoolmasterly way of stating Luther's "theology of the cross." Forever after, he would view the essential core of Christianity as consisting of this little theology in triplicate—law, sin and grace—rather than in the sacred mysteries of the triune and incarnate Son of God. From the *Summa*, we may gather that Melanchthon took this to be the point of Paul's great *comparatio* between Christ and Adam in Romans 5. Of all theological *loci* (and notice that he did not dispute the fact that the others *were* theological *loci*), these were the ones that "mattered most to us," that is, had the most to do with *us* as broken human beings in search of truth and virtue.

One cannot but detect here the outlook which Melanchthon had considered essential and most basic to *inventio* in its broadest sense. All great authors (*auctores*), those with real *authority*, were blessed not merely with fine logical minds and skills of writing and delivery. They had a universal sense about them of what really counted in life, a sense of where the *core* of all matters came to focus. By imputing this virtue to Scripture, Luther, Erasmus and Melanchthon all alike brought forth a streamlined, simpler theology than what typically emerged from the schools. One suspects that Melanchthon, who attributed it not merely to *Scripture* as "God's text," or *oratio*, but systematically to the self-conscious strategy of each human author, surpassed both of his heroes in constructing a principled literary model for writing Scripture. Nevertheless, the great clue for all three was the quest for true righteousness, rather than "studying the hairs on the nose of the elephant while it is standing on the baby," to use John Gardner's description of "immoral" studies.

One of the pronounced themes of the *Institutio* was the divine "difference" of Scripture with respect to human philosophy.

On this [*iustificatio nostra*], philosophers have trifled many things so variously, that indeed, from these so very many opinions, it will be obvious that all philosophy is lies and darkness [*tenebras et mendacia esse universam philosophiam*]. As I pass over the matter itself, it is enough to make the accusation that the dialectic of philosophy is inefficacious for changing the hearts of men, for renewing men's affections [*satis coarguere, ten dialexin philosophou inefficacem esse ad immutanda hominum pectora, ad instaurandos hominum affectus*]. All of these *loci* are handled above by Paul in this epistle.[60]

This theme of the divine "difference" or *discrimen* of biblical theology emerged most clearly in the third section of the *Institutio*, on the nature and power of sin, and in the thirteenth, on the distinction between the righteousness of Christ and the Gentiles. Each section helps to show how Melanchthon's idea of the "divine" element of Scripture emerged in a confluence of Luther's theology and his own rhetorical linguistic theory.

In this third section, Melanchthon asserted, "All of us men judge, by the counsel of natural reason, that it is preferable to live with virtue than among so many vices."[61] On the other hand, "Truly, we apprehend in ourselves a certain love for vices which is such that it causes us to be content in vices, not likewise in virtue."[62] Universal human experience testifies to the fact that "our conscience always contends with the cupidity of nature; although it may see what is good, right, pious, it nevertheless does not attain it."[63] Philosophy thus attempted various solutions:

When the pagans were seeing these things, they variously prescribed the method of righteousness or perfect virtue [*IUSTITIAE sive perfectae virtutis rationem varie praescribebant*]. One judged that virtue was produced by nature, another by habit [*assuetudine*], another by some different method. Then, when they had determined that virtue was produced by habit, they were seeing that it is not so sweet as vice. It was debated how they might insert such delight into the souls of men. Plato, in the second book of *Laws*, judged that felicity could not be attained by perfect virtue unless it was agreeable [*Plato...in perfecta virtute censet esse felicitatem non posse, nisi eadem iucunda sit*]....Wherefore, from the pagans it is plain that the form of righteousness that might be both sound and constant was not known [*Proinde palam est a gentibus eam iustitiae formam ignoratam esse quae et solida et constans esset*]....And it is well known that Plato admitted this fact.[64]

The history of the Jews was not unlike that of the Gentiles: they, too, believed that by keeping moral precepts they had made themselves righteous.[65] But their efforts were in vain, because "no works of this kind are so efficacious that they are able to change the inner propensity of our hearts."[66] For this reason, "Christ died for our justification."[67] Christ fulfilled the hope of all the prophets "that God would rain righteousness upon the earth."[68] And this too must be the prayer of every pious person; "when they condemn themselves and plainly sense that they cannot attain what they desire, they sigh in longing for God to supply a spirit to cleanse, illuminate [and] justify [them] hereafter through Christ [spiritum purgantem, illustrantem, iustificantem praeterea per Christum]."

Similarly, Melanchthon wrote in the thirteenth section that pagan righteousness (iustitia gentium) "is that by which we perform the external appearance of works,"[69] while nonetheless being motivated by love of self (amor nostri), "the root of all evil."[70] In contrast, Christian righteousness "is that in which we are seized by voluntary spirit [ultronco spiritu] toward the good, even had there been no law."[71] In one of the most stirring passages of his early Lutheran writings, Philip wrote:

> ...faith alone [sola fides] lifts the burden of law and sin, faith alone gives peace to suffering consciences, faith alone conquers death and hell. Believe in Christ, call upon Christ through faith; now the Spirit, [our] justifier and cleanser [iustificator et purgator], is present. Now peace is granted the conscience, now the horror of death may cease, now the threats of hell have been ended.[72]

Thus, Melanchthon defined "Christian righteousness," in contrast to pagan ethics, as a divinely given affection for the good, an inner power which gives peace to the mind and an altogether new love for what is good, no matter the cost to oneself. "O immense benefit!" he wrote, "O blessed ones, to whom it is granted so to know Christ!"[73]

In disputing theology with Eck, Melanchthon had stressed the rhetorical-dialectical unity of Scripture as a main element of its authority, in contrast to the contradictory nature of patristic theological traditions. In the Institutio, perhaps aiming at a readership of people who, like himself, were infatuated with classical literature, he stressed the profound efficacy and power of biblical teaching to effect genuine virtue, in contrast to the powerlessness of philosophical traditions. And, once more, a rhetorical virtue became a deeply ingrained element of biblical authority. In the Summa we have seen how this auctoritas comprised various logical mechanisms. In the Institutio one begins to gain a somewhat more complex and perspectivally deeper picture of how Scripture worked in the world. In his sixth and seventh sections on the nature and power of the law, Melanchthon wrote of how the law of God "killed," or caused us to hate ourselves, to hate the law and to hate God.[74] In his following sections on the nature of grace, faith and justification, he eloquently described the power of Paul's metaphor (tropus) of justification to lead us into a new relationship with God through His gracious gift of fresh, new affections for good.[75] As we shall see, the rhetoric of Scripture moved not merely the mind, although this was essential to the process of being justified, but was instrumental in the spiritual work of God to change the heart. One senses that this final movement into the divine grace was not merely the work of the Spirit, but was on some level *also* a quite human psychological process, not entirely foreign to the experience of moral philosophers when they failed to effect the desired changes in their souls. Nevertheless, there is an emerging doctrine of Word *and* Spirit, albeit shaped by the forms of his rhetoric (and not entirely at peace with the assertion of a thorough determinism).

These last points suggest that the epistemic problem of an "intellectualism" in Melanchthon requires very careful consideration. For his rhetorical horizons were here, as elsewhere, much grander than those of simple preoccupation with theory and theoretical knowledge. They also suggest a perspective on the related issue of "natural theology." For Melanchthon's very conception of the divine "difference" of Scripture (something that he constantly brought to the forefront of the discussion) had all the shape of classical rhetorical doctrine about it. This was not simply a matter of recognizing "truth" within pagan systems, or even of acknowledging its knowledge of "law, but not gospel," as is frequently alleged in this context.[76] It is rather the systemic affirmation of what pagan philosophy stood for in the world. Its status was that of an authentic search for and, in part, penetrating discovery of the essential universal truths. The strenuous critique of human philosophy as "lies and darkness," as having a "powerless dialectic" and as thus having failed its adherents turned out also to affirm that the philosophers had "inventively" put the right, universal question of righteousness, that they had intuitively deduced that attaining it was a matter of disposition, or "habit," and that a sense of moral futility that was analogous to the moral fatigue of Old Testament Judaism had finally come upon them in their searchings. Melanchthon left these affirmations of philosophy in an unqualified state, suggesting that the epistemic root of pagan wisdom was in human reason itself rather than in some sort of indirect revelation (described, say, as "common grace," to use the Calvinistic term). The rhetoric of the scriptures was very much that of their own philosophy and the "difference" something they could well have understood, and welcomed with gladness, had they but known about it. Both God and the ancients had come at the question of our existence in much the same way and were thus bound together by their shared topical *inventio* and rhetorical *dispositio* (and, therefore, by a shared ontology, to an important extent). The divine "difference" of Scripture was in rightly conveying, mainly through Paul's *disputatio exacta*, the "form of righteousness that might be both sound and constant...." Quite aside from the question of proving God's existence, this common bond in rhetoric certainly constituted, for Melanchthon, a kind of "natural theology" that was (as yet) not entirely worked out with respect to his general critique of scholasticism or to his Lutheran anthropology[77] and theory of free will and predestination.[78]

In the *Institutio* and *Summa*, one thus gains a much clearer view of how Melanchthon used the various thought-forms of his rhetoric systematically to interpret, express and even verify hermeneutically the theological views which he had adopted from Luther. He praised Paul for his wisdom in selecting the right themes for discussion; Paul had a view of humankind's deepest need to know itself and to see the avenue to virtuous living. Towards that end, the apostle developed the *loci* of law, sin and grace, rather than those of a more abstract nature and of doubtful intelligibility. He selected and developed themes which would reveal the essential meaning of *all* sacred history and of Christianity itself; his doctrine was both intelligible and urgent to mankind.

In developing and forming these topics into *doctrine*, Paul was successful in bringing forth their native rational and affective power. He defined the nature of human sin, *peccatum originale*, but he also reminded us of our common experience that sin was an affection which imprisoned us all. This teaching should, therefore, guide the readers fearfully and despairingly to knowledge of themselves as prisoners. Paul defined the law and the nature of the good, but he also wrote of the law's power to sharpen our knowledge of sin and to increase the weight of such knowledge to that of an unbearable burden, a sense of guilt which would lead to desire for grace. Finally, he defined the grace of God, but also reminded his readers that grace was itself an "affection," which was gotten through a living faith, not merely through an intellectual *fides historica*, and he inspired them to seek spiritual change which could come from God alone.

Melanchthon thus wove the strands of Luther's doctrine together with his rhetorical theory to produce the first dogmatic theology from Wittenberg and Lutheranism. Luther's consuming desire as monk, professor and preacher to define and to attain true righteousness found a counterpart in the Socratic-humanistic (and not entirely "unscholastic") concerns of Melanchthon; moreover, Luther's overpowering passion for a righteousness which penetrated deep beneath the surface of thought and action to the inmost movements of the heart became beams of light in Melanchthon's rhetorical vision of a moral truth which would redeem one's affections from the power of sin and from the weight of despairing hypocrisy. Both believed they had found answers to their different longings for moral truth in the biblical conflict of law and gospel which resolved itself happily in gaining grace through faith. Finally, Luther's much-discussed belief in Scripture as alone the Word of God, *sola scriptura*, in its power to effect these things found expression of a different sort in Melanchthon's rhetorical idea of *doctrina efficax* and *sermo proprius*, Scripture alone as sacred oration.

Notes to Chapter 7

1. *MW* VII/1, p. 76.25ff.; also *ibid.*, p. 83.75ff., pp. 92f. for references to Eck.
2. *Ibid.*, pp. 76.35-77.1ff.
3. *Ibid.*, p. 79.15ff.
4. *Ibid.*, p. 78.7ff., "Per aestatem hanc intrepretati sumus Epistolam ad Romanos Pauli, omnium longe gravissimam et ceu scopi vice fungentem in universam scripturam sacram...."
5. *Ibid.*, p. 79.14ff.; cf. *MW* IV, p. 10 for references to these and other theological lectures that would follow yearly.
6. Cf. W. Maurer, *Der junge Melanchthon*, Bd. 2, Göttingen 1969, pp. 102ff.; K. Hartfelder, *Philipp Melanchthon als Praeceptor Germaniae*, Berlin 1889, pp. 68f.; J. Camerarius, *De vita Philippi Melanchthonis narratio*, (ed.) G. Th. Strobel, Halle 1777, p. 37.
7. *MW* I, p. 24.4ff.
8. *Ibid., passim.*
9. *Ibid.*, mainly, p. 24.7ff.
10. *Ibid.*, pp. 24.29-25.10ff.
11. *Ibid.*
12. Cf. W. Maurer, *op. cit.*, Bd. 2, pp. 102ff., who has argued (we think rather unpersuasively) that only the last section of the theses (nos. 12-24) came from Melanchthon's hand.
13. WABr I, p. 514.
14. W. Maurer, *op. cit.*, Bd. 2, p. 103.
15. *Ibid.*
16. *MW* VII/1, p. 68.25, letter to John Lang.
17. Letter to John Schwebel, *MW* VII/1, pp. 78.7ff., "During this time we have expounded Paul's èpistle to the Romans...." Maurer has argued that these were not formal lectures, but rather private studies which Melanchthon offered, working "overtime," in his *schola domi*. W. Maurer, *op. cit.*, Bd. 2, p. 104, and his articles, "Zur Komposition der Loci Melanchthons von 1521," in *Luther-Jahrbuch*, 25, 1958, pp. 148ff., and "Melanchthons Loci communes von 1521 als wissenschaftliche Programmschrift," in *Luther-Jahrbuch*, 27, 1960, pp. 2ff. On the subject of Melanchthon's first lectures in theology, L. Green, "Die exegetischen Vorlesungen des jungen Melanchthons und ihre Chronologie," in *Kerygma und Dogma*, III, 1957, pp. 141ff. Green's proposal that Melanchthon held lectures on Romans in 1518 has not found much support. Cf. P. Barton, *MW* IV, pp. 10ff., for the most recent table of Melanchthon's early exegetical lectures, and, by the same author, "Die exegetische Arbeit des jungen Melanchthon, 1518/19 bis 1528/29: Probleme und Ansätze," in *Archiv für Reformationsgeschichte*, 54, 1963, pp. 52ff.
18. W. Maurer, above references, esp. "Melanchthons Loci communes von 1521 als wissenschaftliche Programmschrift," pp. 2ff. For texts of the *Institutio*, cf. G. L. Plitt and D. Th. Kolde (eds.), *Die Loci communes Philipp Melanchthons in ihrer Urgestalt*, 4th ed., Erlangen/Leipzig 1925, pp. 29ff.; *CR* XXI, pp. 1ff., 49ff.; E. Bizer, *Texte aus der Anfangszeit Melanchthons*, Neukirchen 1966, pp. 88ff., which we have used. For studies of the theology of the *Institutio*, E. Bizer, *Theologie der Verheissung: Studien zur theologischen Entwicklung des jungen Melanchthon, 1519-1524*, Neukirchen 1964, pp. 34ff., W. Maurer, *op. cit.*, Bd. 2, pp. 104ff.
19. To our knowledge, no one except L. Green has accepted the view that the *Institutio* must be considered, among other early writings, a source of the "third rank." L. Green, "Formgeschichtliche und inhaltliche Probleme in den Werken des jungen Melanchthon,"

Zeitschrift für Kirchengeschichte, 84, 1973, pp. 30ff. A detailed discussion of Green's position seems unnecessary, since it has not been acknowledged generally as a valid one, or as posing an important revision of textual criticism in the study of the young Melanchthon. But, briefly, his argument is that a "perfect" (*einwandfrei*) source must (1) be written in Melanchthon's *own hand* and (2) be "acknowledged" by Melanchthon himself. Both of these criteria lead to rather unfortunate possibilities, such as classifying a work as "second" or "third" rate simply because no original manuscript is known, even though a well-attested "family" of copies and editions has survived (as in the instance of the *Institutio*, cf. W. Maurer, "Melanchthons Loci...," pp. 2f., and G. L. Plitt and D. Th. Kolde, *op. cit.*, pp. 29ff.). Moreover, the term "acknowledge" is vague. Does one dismiss a source as third rate simply because a direct citation of Melanchthon approving it cannot be located? Does one dismiss a source (such as the *Institutio*) simply because others may have published it and Melanchthon later replaced it with a new edition? In the instance of the *Institutio*, assuming Maurer's judgment correct, i.e., that it was the *lucubratiunculae* replaced by the *Loci* of 1521, W. Maurer, "Zur Komposition...," p. 148, n. 5, Melanchthon replaced it, not because it was unrepresentative of his thought, but because it was not intended for reading apart from the text of Romans, *MW* II/1, p. 16.7ff. In which event, one cannot but be inclined to agree with Maurer's conclusion, "As a witness of his theological development, it is of inestimable worth to us." W. Maurer, *Der junge Melanchthon*, Bd. 2, p. 104 and references in n. 67.

20. W. Maurer, *op. cit.*, Bd. 2, p. 104.; cf. E. Bizer, *Theologie der Verheissung*, pp. 36ff., for comments on Maurer and discussion of the *Institutio*.

21. E. Bizer, *Texte*, pp. 88ff.

22. *Ibid.*, p. 88; E. Bizer intended his text to be an improvement over both Plitt-Kolde and *CR* XXI, pp. 49ff.

23. E. Bizer, *Texte*, pp. 97ff.; also discussion by W. Maurer, "Melanchthons Loci communes...," pp. 2f.

24. E. Bizer, *Texte*, p. 97, "Status causae. Iustitia ex fide sine operibus, id est, nullum opus potest affectum immutare, sed sola fides impetrat iustitiam, hoc est innovationem."

25. *Ibid.*, "Oratio est generis iudicalis, habet exordium, narrationem, confirmationem, apte compositam."

26. *Ibid.*, "Exordium: Primum quidem gratias ago Deo meo....Secundo habet locos benevolentiae aptos a principio. Deinde sequitur attentio: 'Non enim erubesco Evangelium.'" Note the qualifier, "Id est res pudenda est lex, quae non efficit, quod imperat. Evangelium res minime pudenda, nempe efficax est ad iustificationem...."

27. *Ibid.*, "Narratio: Revelatur enim ira Dei de coelo super omnem impietatem."

28. *Ibid.*, pp. 97f., "Consilium narrationis est: quandoquidem volebat Paulus praescribere fontem et anchoram iustitiae tam gentibus quam Iudaeis, recte inde coepit et gentibus et Iudaeis legem fuisse, illis naturalem, his etiam divinam, sed neque gentibus, neque Iudaeis profuisse legem ad opprimendos affectus, quin omnes senserint in se repugnantes legi affectus, non adsequi se, quod lex praescribit."

29. *Ibid.*, p. 98, "Summa vero narrationis constat his axiomatis."

30. *Ibid.*

31. *Ibid.*, "Hanc narrationem Pauli extendit ad caput usque quartum, et miscet ei aliquot digressiones, quas nisi quis observet, non facile putem adsecuturum disputationis."

32. *Ibid.*

33. *Ibid.*

34. *Ibid.*, "Confirmatio quae in capite quarto est, argumenta habet sex."

35. *Ibid.*

36. *Ibid.*, "Post hac in quarto capite sequitur amplificatio, qua ad gentes causam detorquet."

37. *Ibid.*, p. 99.
38. *Ibid.*
39. *Ibid.*
40. *Ibid.*
41. *Ibid.*
42. *Ibid.*
43. *Ibid.*, "...adhortatoria sunt et consolationes...." Cf. E. Bizer, *Texte*, p. 24.
44. *Ibid.*, "...praedestinationem et vocationem gentium continet." Cf. also Melanchthon's fuller rhetorical outline of chapters 9-11 in the *Artifitium epistolae Pauli ad Romanos a Philippo Melanchthone*, in Bizer, *Texte*, pp. 10ff. which was published in 1520 or 1521 (*ibid.*, p. 19). This section of the epistle was a "new disputation," p. 27, built upon a *discrimen* between works' righteousness and faith, p. 28, concluding with a rhetorical exhortation, *ibid.* Bizer rightly observed how Melanchthon had by then modified his rhetorical classification of Romans, so that he now construed it as belonging to the *genus didaktikon*. This was not a principled change for him, but merely a more precise way of saying about Romans what he had said before. Cf. p. 17. One should notice, too, that Melanchthon was not entirely oblivious to the segmented character of Romans and that he proposed a somewhat relaxed position on its structural unity, particularly at the apparent "breaks" at chapter 5 and then at 12. Cf. *ibid.* However, Bizer's assertion that this text and other later ones exhibit a "giving up" of an earlier concept of rigid unity in Romans seems somewhat too strongly put, in view of Melanchthon's statement that Romans 5 was "really independent" (and in view of the similarity between this statement and the later ones, cf. *ibid.*). And there can be no doubt that he continued to be impressed by the *theological* unity of Romans, and of all of Scripture, on the level of internal logical consistency.
45. *Ibid.*, "...comparationem iustitiae fidei et iustitiae pharasaicae."
46. *Ibid.*, "Caput XI adhortationem."
47. *Ibid.*, "Reliqua moralia sunt."
48. W. Maurer, *op. cit.*, Bd. 2, p. 105.
49. M. O'Rourke Boyle, esp. in *Erasmus on Language and Method in Theology*, Toronto/Buffalo 1977, pp. 59ff. on *ratio*.
50. J. W. O'Malley, "Grammar and Rhetoric in the Pietas of Erasmus," *Journal of Medieval and Renaissance Studies*, Spring 1988, pp. 90ff.
51. J. Aldridge, *The Hermeneutic of Erasmus*, Richmond 1966, esp. pp. 57ff. on "Erudition as the Means to Interpretation."
52. H. Sick, *Melanchthon als Ausleger des Alten Testaments*, Tübingen 1959, p. 41.
53. W. Maurer, *op. cit.*, Bd. 2, p. 105.
54. *Ibid.*
55. *Ibid.*
56. H. Sick, *op. cit.*, pp. 41ff.
57. J. Aldridge, *op. cit.*, p. 64.
58. U. Schnell, *Die homiletische Theorie Philipp Melanchthons*, Berlin/Hamburg 1968, pp. 123ff.
59. E. Bizer, *Texte*, p. 90.
60. *Ibid.*
61. *Ibid.*, p. 91, "Omnes homines censemus pro naturalis rationis consilio satius esse cum virtute vivere quam inter tot vitia."
62. *Ibid.*, "Verum in nobis deprihendimus amorem quendam ad vitia, talem, qui efficit, ut per illum nobis bene sit in vitiis, in virtute non item."
63. *Ibid.*, "Pugnat ergo semper cum cupiditate naturae conscientia nostra, quae, quamquam videat, quid bonum, rectum, pium sit, tamen non assequitur."

64. *Ibid.*
65. *Ibid.*
66. *Ibid.*, "...nulla eiusmodi sunt opera tamque efficacia quo intimam pectorum nostrorum propensionem mutare queant."
67. *Ibid.*, "Christus vero mortuus est propter iustificationem nostram."
68. *Ibid.*
69. *Ibid.*, p. 96.
70. *Ibid.*, "AMOR NOSTRI radix omnis mali est."
71. *Ibid.*
72. *Ibid.*
73. *Ibid.*, p. 91.
74. *Ibid.*, p. 93.
75. *Ibid.*, pp. 94ff.
76.· Cf. below, chapter 11, on "natural theology."
77. On original sin, pp. 92ff., "PECCATUM ORIGINALE est genuinus ardor, impetus, raptus quo trahimur ad vitia." The model is here quite clearly a deterministic one.
78. *Ibid.*, "Voluntas potest comparari vel ad praedestinationem, sic nullo modo est libera, sed huius est ratio, quam ut a nobis comprehendi queat, aut sua tantum natura consideratur...."

CHAPTER 8

The Annotations on
St. Matthew's Gospel

"It grieves me that I cannot send all the brethren to Philip's lectures on Matthew...." (Luther, WABr I, p. 597.)

Melanchthon's lectures on Matthew lasted from the autumn of 1519 until the end of the winter semester of 1520.[1] We cannot be certain why he broke them off at the end of chapter twenty-six, nor exactly how to interpret his expressed dissatisfaction with them as "too brief" and less a proper commentary than a prelude to one.[2] Luther, on the other hand (as perhaps the only person who constantly overestimated Melanchthon), humbly confessed that the "little Greek" now surpassed him in theology, too, and arranged to have these lectures published from notes without Melanchthon's knowledge or approval.[3]

Others have offered broad, thematic discussions of the *Annotationes* as a whole.[4] Our purpose will be to use them in approaching Melanchthon's concept of biblical authority from a perspective other than that of the writings of Paul. In this way, we shall enrich our larger thesis that Melanchthon shaped the various "properties" of Scripture by the thought-forms of his rhetorical theory in the context of classical tradition. Of special interest are the manner in which he used this theory to conceptualize the teachings and actions of Christ in relation to the literary methods of Matthew the writer and the actual *modes* of this Gospel's authority in its engagement of the entire biblical tradition. Melanchthon's treatment of Matthew is particularly relevant to the traditional doctrines of biblical unity and divine efficacy and, through them, to the broader range of historiographical questions about faith and reason in the young Melanchthon.

In a brief preface, Melanchthon introduced his main themes and hermeneutical framework for handling Matthew's Gospel. For the first time, we now observe him applying the conceptual scheme of law and gospel to the biblical literature, and it is very clear that he did not consider this to be merely a "conceptual scheme." Rather, as with his handling of Paul in the terms of oration, the distance between theologian and text seems so thoroughly absent from mind that Matthew's very purpose in writing a "Gospel" must have been that of *the* gospel, now of course interpreted as the *Lutheran* gospel.

Melanchthon's preface to Matthew was a summary of the fresh Lutheran dialectic between morality and the power of God's grace. This interpretive framework, he believed, must control one's initial construal of the text. "First of all, it is crucial to know what the gospel is, and what it confers upon the human race...."[5] And "We shall grasp the nature and power [*vim et rationem*] of the gospel most truly if we compare it with the law."[6] Here, Melanchthon inserted his views on "natural law," "insculpted in our minds,"[7] and divine law, "that God gave through Moses,"[8] both of which made moral demands "which the powers of human nature cannot carry out."[9] Instead of redeeming us from original sin,[10] the law simply exposed the severity of sin and the hard fact that a much greater power than that of moralism must intervene.[11] "And so the law is wont to declare sin, to coerce, to terrify and to instill fear in us, to cause us to hate God the lawgiver and, finally, to flee from God [*ut fugiamus Deum*]."[12] Against the darkness created by law and sin, however, we behold the bright goodness of God in Jesus Christ, who imparted to us the Spirit (*spiritus rapiens*) and "a certain power by which we are seized towards good with the same ardor and spirit as we are accustomed to being seized by concupiscence towards evil [*per concupiscientiam rapi ad mala*]."[13] To empower human beings to become virtuous was the essential purpose of the incarnation of Christ.[14]

Melanchthon's comments on chapter one make it certain that he believed this dialectical message about Christ to be the central theme of Matthew. Verse twenty-one, "He will procure salvation for His people," was in fact "a clear oration about Christ, who He is and what He will have come to accomplish, so putting forward in a few words a summary of the whole Gospel."[15] To view Matthew's Gospel in this way was merely to apply what had become a nearly analytical proposition about "Scripture": "Evangelical Scripture always impresses upon us this very proclamation of Christ...."[16] Scripture simply *was* for Melanchthon "evangelical," where this comprised Luther's theology in the shape of clear methodical (*quis? quid?*) oration. In the course of our discussion, we shall see exactly what kind of rhetoric it was and in what ways Matthew executed his mission as an author and theologian (for Melanchthon's rhetoric helped him to make a distinction of some sort between the history and the text, and between the doctrines of Jesus and those of Matthew).

Matthew and the Rhetoric of Christ

Melanchthon quite intuitively took Matthew's Gospel to be a work of history in his rhetorical sense of that term. The text, a composition of collected *exempla*, was constructed to teach fundamental truths or *loci communes* that were thematically related to and clustered around a main proposition. One of the striking features of this early Lutheran writing is the extent to which Philip detected in Matthew's Gospel a narrative theological structure that supported the Wittenberg movement. The scope of the Gospel was, above all, to fashion from the events and teachings of Jesus a clear *contio* of Christian doctrine. Through this rhetorical method, Matthew had captured the essence of *Jesus'* mission on earth to instruct us unto salvation by grace. The historical actions, such as His various miracles and, finally, death and resurrection, gave us a harvest of doctrines, a point of view. These doctrines mediated between the reader and the realities behind the events in such a way that they (the events, words and realities behind them) became the means of one's own salvation in the present. As we shall see, Melanchthon's *Annotationes* on Matthew are illustrative of his rhetorical vision, in which ideas and concepts of reality were logically necessary and antecedent to the experience of salvation, but were never an end unto themselves. The shape of Melanchthon's hermeneutic was that of a word-event, a rhetorical progression from *verbum et res* to *res gestae* or morally virtuous feeling and action.

One can gather from Melanchthon's text that he judged the thematic structure of the Gospel to begin with a kind of introduction, through the *historiae* on Christ's birth, which aimed at teaching *why* it was that He entered our world and *whence* we might expect to find salvation.[17] The intricate weave of dialectic with conventional rhetoric was evident in the constant progression from the *quid* of doctrine to the affective dimension of the *quid pro nobis*, that is, to the active power of doctrine as *doctrina efficax*. The story of the Magi contributed to explaining the significance to *us* of Jesus' life; in this story of God calling the wise men, "he [Matthew] taught *why* Christ will have come; He foreshadows *our* vocation."[18] The star of Bethlehem signified "a certain heavenly light which, when it cuts into the darkness, places us before our own eyes [*nos nobis ante oculos ponit*].... And He [God] shows us *ourselves*, since nature's power of comprehension still does not see what the way to God might be [*captus tamen naturae non videat, quod ad Deum iter sit*]...."[19] Wicked King Herod entered the stage as an *exemplum impietatis*, to convict *us* of *our* sinfulness and to accuse *our* piety of being mere pretext and appearance.[20] This entire section of the Gospel was interspersed with *exempla* containing *loci* or *argumenti* on faith and hope in the grim face of other *exempla* which reminded of moral evil and, thus, of the doctrine and reality of sin.[21] Melanchthon concluded that the stories of Jesus' birth and infancy had a major strategic purpose; they answered briefly the questions "why He was born and in what manner we are called,"[22] and they taught us that "we are reborn in Christ and that the first rudiments of Christ's life are to suffer adversities and exile."[23] Using his rhetorical framework, Melanchthon thus gave his own sort of meaning to Luther's sacramental vision of history: the story of Christ's temptations were designed "indeed not only for the sake of example, but also that, through this victory, *we* have won; for all the victories, all the triumphs of Christ, are victories and triumphs of all believers."[24]

After this introductory lesson, Melanchthon judged that the section including chapters five through eight (mainly the Sermon on the Mount) had been structured to follow the logic (one is reminded here of his term *gnesion*) of Christ's historical mission; that is, His actual life and the development of His own teaching reflected the progressive movement from law to grace. In this place one notices that Melanchthon's Jesus introduced His great discourse with the theme of *beatitudo*, "because the longings of all men strive for this."[25] The pursuit of "beatitude" was universal, because "we pursue nothing from which we do not wish to...be blessed...."[26] These pressing human concerns had made themselves "the *scopus* of philosophy."[27] Melanchthon thus placed Jesus (as he had Paul) at the center of philosophical tradition with respect to one's "inventive" sense of the question that really counted among all human questions. These great rhetorical intuitions had guided the greatest of the philosophers; they guided Paul, Jesus and now Matthew, too, in focusing properly on the core of history. And, like the philosophers, Jesus and Matthew rightly perceived that the core of this largest question about self-knowledge was one's ontological theory of human nature.

The structure of the Gospel and the logic of Jesus' teachings thus unfolded. "The oration of this chapter [five] is a certain exposition of divine law...."[28] The topical order comports logically with the final aim of the sermon: "...Christ begins with it [divine law] for this reason: since He came to forgive sin, He was necessarily putting forth the law, by which He might condemn us, that is, show that we are sinners and that we need His grace."[29] He would bestow the spirit of grace upon those who were terrified, broken and trembling before the law.[30]

In his treatment of this section on the law, Melanchthon wrote of Jesus as if He were a Lutheran master of rhetorical doctrine. The saying in Matthew 5:13, "You are the salt of the earth," is a *locus* intended for "all who teach the gospel."[31] The teaching on perfection in Matthew 5:19ff. is a *locus* which "demands perfection from us" and leads into Jesus' attack against Pharisaic ideas of righteousness.[32] Melanchthon believed that Jesus here used methods of rhetorical argument and ornamentation, as in Matthew 7:7, where, for example, He spoke on the need for prayer "by a certain amplification [*quadam amplificatione*]," and when He taught about our need to approach God as sons, "He argued from an *exemplum* [*ab exemplo arguit*]...." [33] Jesus' purpose in teaching about the law, finally, corresponded with the oratorical convention of relating one's doctrine to the human affections: "Christ transfers the whole law to the affections...."[34]

Melanchthon believed that chapter eight marked a new seam in the thematic structure of the text, as one now moved from the theme of law to that of grace. It is intriguing, though, that the rhetorical medium shifted from that of Christ's discursive teaching to that of His historical actions and Matthew's handling of them as *exempla* for theology and life. Matthew, he wrote, now inserted a series of *exempla*, or *historiae*, showing forth God's mercy, to follow after Jesus' shattering words on the law. The "examples" of Jesus healing the leper and of His coming to the aid of the Roman centurion were subject to, and illustrative of, the general principle that "all the histories of Christ are sacraments, that is, promises by which we are certain that God will give grace to everyone who believes."[35] Obviously, Philip had latched onto Luther's concept of the promise, *promissio*, and his sacramental view of sacred history, and he had given it the shape of rhetorical doctrine, most particularly through the literary device of *exemplum*. Not only the words of Jesus, but His actions, His *res gestae*, if you will, conveyed the native powers of truth.

In reference to the healing of the leper, following the strong words on keeping the law to perfection, Melanchthon wrote, "It is not gratuitous [*non temere*] that this example [*hoc exemplum*], in which there is the promise of Christ [*pollicitatio Christi*] that He wishes to make the leper clean, was recorded at the very beginning, so that He might strengthen [*confirmet*] the faith of all who would beseech Him."[36] The actual subject of the "recording," or "commemoration," would seem to have been Matthew at work logically with the plan of real events. We read Melanchthon to be asserting that Matthew correctly perceived the intent of Christ's actions and that he thus rightly "disposed" his composition to convey that intent as powerfully as possible. As an "example" in the true sense of that term, the story served not merely to demonstrate Jesus' mercy towards one person in the past, but also to show forth to all men at all times that He promises to be gracious towards them, too. "Now when Christ says 'I will,' He does so not only for the sake of the leper [*non propter solum leprosum*], but that He might succor the trust of many, that they might be certain that Christ wills to save all those who cast themselves upon Him through faith [*quicumque in ipsum per fidem se coniecerint*]."[37] The modality of this power of Scripture to cross the centuries from one person and circumstance to endless others was in part the universality of its *topoi*, which was amplified and piercingly disclosed as one penetrated into the *particular* actions of Christ. Of course all this depended upon the antecedent knowledge of Matthew's plan and the linear structure of the Gospel itself.

The next story, the healing of the centurion's servant, worked in the same mode as the previous one: "...also here, just as in the *exemplum* above, it is promised that, when He has come, He will heal."[38] This *exemplum*, too, taught the manner in which Jesus would come to heal us, "for He comes through the Word [*Venit enim per verbum*]. Then He will heal by faith [*medetur fide*].... All of which pertains to this: that faith be more agreeable to us, and that we might embrace the evangelical history as the pledge and guarantee of *our* salvation [*historiam evangelicam complectamur ut arram et pignus salutis nostrae*]."[39] As genuinely shaped (not fabricated) histories, Melanchthon judged that they pertained to us in a very direct way, which he imagined to be that of the rhetorical *locus* or commonplace.

In this context, a few words to adumbrate our later discussion of "intellectualism" in Melanchthon are in order. The point has often been made that, for Melanchthon, Scripture was *doctrine*, and the inference drawn that this was the root of "intellectualism" of all sorts in his theological practice and teaching. Until recently, however, the complexity of the concept *doctrina* has not been acknowledged adequately or defined precisely for assessment. But the complexity of its structure, as mainly that of rhetoric, requires a corresponding complexity of inference and judgment. Not to deny the antecedent theological framework of law and gospel, the fact remains that Melanchthon's typically Erasmian[40] concept of historical *exempla* was strongly emotive and performative. The typically Lutheran doctrine of Word *and* Spirit found coherent, if not fully satisfying, expression in the rhetorical categories of Melanchthon for writing human history. It seems fair to say that, for Melanchthon, the teachings of Christ about law, sin and grace went to the heart quite directly under the proper conditions. Nevertheless, the precise nature of those conditions and their relevance to his hermeneutic and religious epistemology seem still very difficult to set free from important ambiguities. All the examples conveyed universal, urgent truth directly *to us*, a Lutheran emphasis (*pro nobis*) which comported well with Melanchthon's rhetorical theory. This was the great, transcendent power of God at work in the words of Scripture and the spirits of men and women. On the other hand, however, one might say that Melanchthon viewed the rhetoric of Matthew and Jesus as "second-order doctrine," that is, as operating in a manner that was *contingent* upon the conditions set up by the systematic writings of Paul. The entire shape of biblical authority as *doctrina efficax* seems to have been, diachronically, a nearly straight rhetorical line of argument, moving progressively from Paul, to Jesus and the Gospels and on to the remaining books of the canon. Such a diachronic rendering of biblical meaning and authority would seem to require that revelation, in its essential forms, was available only through the deductions of those who were in a historical position to see the entirety of the text. Viewed synchronically, the hermeneutical process seems to have been ambiguously imagined, if at all. There is nothing of Erasmus's (or later Calvin's) interest in the historical circumstances, intent and perceptions of the original players themselves, and so one is left to speculate how Melanchthon might have responded to the question, how did they understand the gospel without Paul? The documents which we shall discuss as the basis for our next chapter will enable us to offer a cautious proposal on the matter. The problem of "intellectualism" thus also arises in the context of Melanchthon's diachronic model of biblical unity and sense.

The *Annotationes* on Matthew's Gospel is simply too large a work for us to treat as a whole in this context. Thus, we have selected passages that help to illustrate how Melanchthon pictured the conceptual shape of the text after the Sermon on the Mount and the examples of grace. Three such sections on chapter eleven show how he operated on the presumption that every teaching, and every history, was, by comparative association, about the controlling themes of law and grace. Introducing his comments on chapter eleven, he wrote, "The *locus* of this Gospel [vv. 1-4] pertains to confirming faith, for we all sometimes doubt with the disciples of John...."[41] The *exemplum* of John and his followers was barely related in Melanchthon's mind to a *Sitz im Leben* or an original historical-theological problem in Judaism. The story worked associatively and existentially in the life of the contemporary Christian, who doubted along "with" these ancestors in the Lord and whose faith was confirmed along with theirs. In his comments on Matthew 11:5, "the poor have the good news preached to them," Melanchthon (perhaps correctly) related Jesus' saying to the issue of spiritual, rather than material or monastic, poverty. "The poor are all those afflicted in spirit;...evangelical poverty is not mendicancy...."[42] Further, he interpreted Jesus' famous prayer of thanksgiving in Matthew 11:25-27 as a *locus* or doctrine against freedom of the human will.[43] The great invitation at the end, "Come all ye who are heavy laden," was a *sententia* or "teaching" on "mortification of the flesh" under the weight of trying to keep the law.[44] In each instance, Melanchthon's hermeneutical vision was controlled by two presumptions: that the text and the teachings of Jesus Himself were structured by the rules and devices of proper *oratio*, and that Scripture, as *Scripture*, everywhere taught the Lutheran sense of the gospel.

Melanchthon's handling of the death of John the Baptist illustrates his manner of applying his rhetorical literary theory, together with Lutheran theological assumptions, to the text. In this way he "invented" or discovered *loci communes theologici* that arose as "deeper senses" from beneath the surface of the document and its plain historical or literal sense. This was a "memorable *exemplum*" of the evil sort of death that all too often came upon the prophets of the Lord.[45] The narrative must therefore be taken in the context of the thematic structures that pertain to human evil: "these *loci* pertain to original sin."[46] Finally, Philip construed all the various histories of Christ in the middle chapters as *exempla* of the grace and goodness of God to us. "All of these are precious examples of our salvation [*Haec sunt exempla omnia pignora quaedam salutis nostrae*] which we have through Christ, if we believe."[47] That he operated with a systematic theory of the text that guided his interpretations is obvious. Our point is that this underlying system expressed the confluence of literary theory and theology, rhetoric and Lutheranism, the budding Protestant idea of Scripture as the Word of God and the Preceptor's image of the text as *oratio*. The outcome was an idea of biblical authority that one may rightly call "sacred oration," *oratio sacra*. That he himself imagined this procedure as liberating the simple and plain sense of the text is one of the many ironies that make him an interesting figure in the history of doctrine.

One should also notice Melanchthon's treatment of the parables. He regarded them as symbolic in all details, but also as having a *scopus* or main teaching which was itself related to the large themes of the Gospel and of Jesus' teaching as a whole. One might say that he considered them to be orations in miniature. Commenting on Matthew 13:33ff., where Jesus compared the kingdom of God with leaven, Melanchthon wrote,

> The woman is the church, the leaven the Word of God [*fermentum verbum Dei*]. The three measures are many men, for three is the number of perfection according to Chrysostom. And this parable adumbrates the power of the Word of the Lord [*vim verbi Domini adumbrat*]..., and so it attributes the beginning of our justification to the Word of faith [*principium iustificationis nostrae verbo fidei tribuit*].[48]

Thus, the parable emerged from the symbolism as a teaching about the power of the Word of God, and it expanded into the larger hermeneutical context of *loci communes* on faith and justification through the primacy of the Word. The same was true of his comments on the parable of the kingdom and the foolish virgins in Matthew 25:1-13. Instead of interpreting it in the immediate context of teaching on the Last Things, Philip related the parable directly to the doctrines of sin and self-righteousness. "The *scopus* of the parable [*scopus parabolae*] is commendation of vigilance and the renunciation of hypocrisy. For, as human righteousness is condemned in the *whole* Gospel, it is especially condemned in these three chapters...."[49]

Although his formal treatment of the parables as allegories was typically Erasmian[50] and the theology that he mined from them was Lutheran,[51] the underlying sense of Scripture as having a straightforward, linear unity in the doctrines of law, sin and grace was the trademark of Melanchthon. On this level, he would seem to have found his own way.[52] Maurer was quite correct in his view of Melanchthon's construal of Matthew: "He cannot apply the *loci*-doctrine to the gospel narrative as a whole. But he has it in sight at all times...."[53] The first "systematic theologian" of the Protestant era was about to emerge upon the stage of history and, with him, the first Protestant *concept* of biblical authority.[54]

In summary, we have shown how Melanchthon applied the full breadth and depth of his rhetorical system to his new theological understanding. Luther, too, treated the biblical histories as "Beispielhaft,"[55] and it was he who taught Melanchthon to refer the entire biblical text to its theological sense—a radical doctrine of sin and law in dialectical tension with Christ and the promise of grace.[56] Bornkamm has written eloquently on Luther's "unmediated [*unvermittelt*]" entry into the world of Scripture. Luther particularly loved and felt the christological power of the Old Testament.[57] That the histories of Israel were written as examples for *us, pro nobis*, and for all times, seemed as obvious to him as the sky above and the earth below. And, on that existential intuition, he used the text, relating it constantly to Christ, with great genius. All this passed without formal *linguistic* or philosophical defense.[58] It is true that he often used rhetorical devices in interpretation and that he sometimes compared biblical writings (such as the book of Job and the Psalms) with classical texts.[59] But one finds in Luther nothing like Philip's use of theory to determine the rhetorical scope and logical point of each writing, even to the extent of viewing Jesus' teaching as a didactic system.[60]

From our modern point of view, it seems evident that Melanchthon was not a genius at theological interpretation. His field of hermeneutical vision was pressured, and he in turn pressed the text through narrow straits. In contrast to Luther's wide-ranging literary intuitions as expressed by his deep love for the Psalms and the great Prophets, Philip's favorite book in the Old Testament was Proverbs with its carved and ordered view of the cosmos.[61] And the appeal of Matthew's sermonic Christ fits with Melanchthon's own love for contained moral discourse. Moreover, he made this Gospel even more manageable than it is by portraying Christ as perhaps an inspired Socrates and Matthew as His

Plato, who together gave us a logically structured oration on the elements of the faith. One is tempted to downgrade him for making these oversimplified judgments. Whatever our final evaluation, however, he must be weighed in reference to the intrinsic difficulties of working without clear precedent behind him. Between Luther and Melanchthon were differences of the sort that one might expect between a great preacher, on the one side, in whose nature it was to *proclaim* the truth, and a born teacher, on the other, whose instinct was to *ground, clarify* and *demonstrate* everything as clearly as possible to his students.[62] If Germany was Luther's *Gemeinde*, it was Melanchthon's school.

Other Considerations on the Coherence of Scripture as a Whole

Melanchthon's *Annotationes* on Matthew help one to penetrate still further into his concept of Scripture as a coherent whole, and they reveal just how rigorous he had become in applying a terminological model of unity to the Bible. Two sections of this writing are of particular relevance to the subject of biblical coherence. The one is an independent segment entitled "Agreement between Luke and Matthew." This little digression is evidence of how very far removed his outlook was from that of an allegorist, and how bothered he could become by apparent conflict within Scripture, such as inconsistencies between Matthew and Luke on several matters.

The main issue was apparent conflict between the two genealogies of Christ. Melanchthon resolved the problem by proposing that Matthew had permitted some gaps to remain in his family tree, "not so much recounting those who were born of Solomon as those who were in whatever way the successors in the kingdom."[63] Luke, on the other hand, "traces more exactly the genealogy through Nathan, the son of David...."[64] Other apparent inconsistencies could be resolved by proposing that Luke and Matthew had used different names to describe the same person: "so that it is not a discrepancy of persons, but only of names...."[65] Finally, allowing room for some theological creativity on the part of the author, he suggested that "sometimes...fathers of the *law* were written down instead of fathers of nature."[66] In each instance, Melanchthon searched for some way of harmonizing the two genealogies on a literal level. He simply could not believe that the one Gospel might contradict the other, and he believed that discrepancies were the result of various *human* differences between literary plots.

Melanchthon was also bothered by Matthew's apparently inaccurate citation (in Matt. 2:6) of Micah 5:2. The "reading is plainly different from the reading of the evangelist."[67] He attempted to resolve the discrepancy (as to whether Bethlehem *was* or was *not* "least among the leaders of Judah") by asserting that Matthew "here rendered the meaning [*sententia*] more than the words [*verba*]."[68] In support of this harmonization he claimed that Micah had used the rhetorical device of *emphasis*, and that his statement about Bethlehem being "too small to be counted" must be read in the Hebrew as a question that implied a tone of admiration.[69] "The evangelist rendered this *emphasis* with the added negation, since what the prophet had earlier foretold was now fulfilled. For the rest, little is Bethlehem in appearance, great in spirit, just as the church is in appearance contemptible, in spirit glorious."[70] One sees thus that Melanchthon was deeply interested in lining up every detail of the text, that even prophets used rhetoric to get their messages across (and keep themselves free from error) and that the New Testament writers presumed such rhetorical structures in transferring the meaning of the Old Testament to the Christian church. In this context, however, one must warn against a facile connection between Melanchthon and later Lutheran dogmaticians who made the conceptual unity of Scripture into a shibboleth. The driving power of Melanchthon's doctrine, here, was a truth theory that emerged as much from a model of *human* authorship as it did from a theory of divine inspiration that amounted to dictation of propositions by the Spirit.[71]

During the course of these lectures on Matthew, it would seem that Melanchthon's sense of theological unity between the two testaments also grew in the direction of increased theological and literal harmony. In the preface, he had written almost dualistically that God was present to Israel mainly through law and, thus, toward a response of fear and trembling.[72] One must wonder whether he would have left these comments to stand in a more carefully edited text. Bizer has shown that Luther preached a powerful sermon about the "covenant" on Easter Sunday of 1520, about the time Melanchthon neared the end of his lectures.[73] In this sermon, Luther treated the "covenant" as essentially God's "promise" to redeem His people.[74] He concluded that the God of the promise was one and the same, first to the Jews, then to the Gentiles, and that justification by grace, through faith in God's promise, rather than in human works, was always the basic biblical teaching.[75] Luther's doctrine of the covenant as *promissio* seems to have helped Melanchthon to articulate his position on the coherent relation between the two testaments.[76] On the twenty-sixth chapter of Matthew, Melanchthon now defined the concept of "testament," "contract," "pact"[77] as best understood in the sense of *promissio*: "the divine promises are signified by these words."[78] The concept of God's promise was to be related to the histories of Noah, Abraham and the prophets, from whom God required faith.[79] He judged that the two covenants were distinct from one another, since the promises of the one were of a material nature, the other spiritual.[80] But there was also theological coherence between them, since in both covenants men were justified through faith in the diverse promises,[81] and we have seen how Melanchthon used his rhetorical system to solidify this position with respect to the literal sense of individual authors. We shall see the full development of this profoundly Lutheran idea in our treatment of the *Loci communes* of 1521.

Matthew and the "Divine Difference" of Christ's Doctrine

The *Annotationes* on Matthew also help to clarify Melanchthon's growing sense of the *discrimen* or "divine difference" between Scripture and secular philosophy. Of particular interest is the section at the end of chapter seven where he included brief comments on the natural moral order. Alongside his strong view of Scripture and its sacred "difference" (and perhaps underlying the world view in which he asserted it) was his belief in a universal natural system of law. We have seen how Melanchthon quite intuitively placed Christ in line with the great teachers of history in centering upon the deepest question, true beatitude. Throughout the sections on the Sermon on the Mount, he also stressed the greatness of Jesus, in comparison with the philosophers of antiquity, and the difference between His doctrine and theirs. "Christ prescribes the way and nature of beatitude [as being] plainly in conflict with natural and philosophical reason."[82] Jesus' teaching in the Beatitudes (here Matt. 5:3) made the distinction clear enough through a contrast between the piercing *locus* of sin (*peccatum*), in Scripture, and the much weaker notion of vice (*vitium*), which the philosophers hoped to eradicate through virtue.

> And so here we little men may place ourselves before our own eyes, about to see completely both how miserable we are and, moreover, how we may have sinned, and how great the divine kindness towards us may be.... No natural powers of man will have been so acute that they can discern the true nature of beatitude [*Nulla quippe hominum ingenia tam perspicacia fuerunt, quae veram beatitudinis rationem cernere potuerint*], nor are they able to attain what they themselves prescribe.... Philosophers prescribe a certain fictitious way of beatitude [*Philosophi quandam beatitudinis viam praescribunt ficticiam plane*], for the philosophical virtues are fictitious. Christ truly overthrows at once all the desires of our nature and all the comments of the philosophers, when He says, "Blessed are the poor in spirit."[83]

Once again Melanchthon thus expressed the sacred "difference" of Scripture in the terms not merely of its *doctrine*, but of the *power* of that doctrine to help change the human motivational centers. In the *Annotationes*, the ideas were still fresh and near enough to that first flush of discovery to exude an emotional warmth that one seldom detects in the later writings. On the seventh chapter, noting Jesus' initially terrifying statements about perfection, Melanchthon wrote eloquently of the power of the Word to release us from terror and guilt.

> Now it is fitting here to observe how powerful a thing the Word of God is [*quam efficax res sit verbum Dei*], and that there is much difference between the Word of God and the word of men [*multum adeo inter verbum Dei et verbum hominum interesse*]. Therefore, in the churches, that powerful Word of God [*potens istud verbum Dei*] must be preached, not that broken and lame word of men [*non fractum et elumbe hominum verbum*].[84]

From the conceptual interplay between rhetorical philosophy and Luther's biblical theology, Melanchthon's doctrine of the *verbum efficax* thus emerged. Scripture was sacred oration. Nevertheless, he added a qualifying sentence (that was more typical of Luther than it would be of his own theology): "...the power is not in the language [*verbum*], but God is present in the language, and through the words He softens the hearts of men."[85] In the main, however, Melanchthon's stress would fall upon the intrinsic rhetorical power of the *doctrine*.

Melanchthon's comments on natural law occurred in the context of this critique of legal and philosophical morality. Here he defined "natural law" as

> ...certain judgments [*sententiae*] or thoughts [*cogitationes*] to which all men assent [*quibus assentiuntur omnes homines*], just as there are, in visible affairs, certain principles known by nature. The whole is greater than the part. So in actions, there are certain principles known by nature [*Ita in agendis quaedam sunt principia natura nota*]....[86]

The most fundamental principles were: to worship God, defend the privileges of life, bear children, feed one's family, do unto others as to oneself, not use force against another and use all things in common, (except) that one has the right to own property.[87]

These texts indicate, once again, Melanchthon's belief in the existence of natural moral order and in the essential agreement between it and the law of God. The precise theoretical status of these beliefs, with respect to the principles of his theology, is not at all clear yet. The more obvious point is that, in Melanchthon's new theological view, natural law did not lead to the desired self-knowledge, through guilt and spiritual regeneration. He regarded their philosophical embodiment as *doctrina inefficax*. And yet, such principles simply pervaded his own theological system; he understood that Christ Himself made constant rhetorical appeal to them and to the sensitivities that one expected universally from people. They were evidently not wholly "lies and darkness," nor simply *inefficax* unto our salvation. Great care is needed in trying to state exactly how Melanchthon related the philosophical universals of the moral order to his theology. If fair judgments are to be made about his own internal coherence on this matter and, what is a somewhat separate issue, his fidelity to genuine Lutheran principles, then we must first examine the theological writings that preceded the *Loci communes* and, finally, relevant sections of this monumental work itself.

Notes to Chapter 8

1. Cf. P. Barton, *MW* IV, p. 133; *eodem*, "Die exegetische Arbeit des jungen Melanchthon, 1518/19 bis 1528/9: Probleme und Ansätze," in *Archiv für Reformationsgeschichte*, 54, 1963, pp. 52ff.; E. Bizer, *Theologie der Verheissung: Studien zur theologischen Entwicklung des jungen Melanchthon 1519-1524*, Neukirchen 1964, pp. 86ff.; W. Maurer, *Der junge Melanchthon*, Bd. 2, Gütersloh 1969, p. 104, contra L. Green, "Die exegetischen Vorlesungen des jungen Melanchthons und ihre Chronologie," in *Kerygma und Dogma*, III, 1957, pp. 141ff., whose suggestion that the lectures occurred in 1518-19 has received little support.

2. *MW* VII/1, letter to John Hess, 27 April 1520, "Matthaeum nondum absolvi. Nec est, quod annotationes seu scholia nostra desideres. Brevius aequo tractavimus Evangelistam, magis *proimiadzomenoi* ac praeludentes justae narrationi," p. 79, n. 5, reference to *CR* I, p. 158; *SM* I, pp. 98f.

3. Cf. P. Barton, *MW* IV, p. 133. We have used the text in *MW* IV and have followed the vast majority in taking the text as a generally reliable source, in opposition to L. Green, "Formgeschichtliche und inhaltliche Probleme in den Werken des jungen Melanchthon," in *Zeitschrift für Kirchengeschichte*, 84, 1973, pp. 30ff. On this matter, P. Barton, *op. cit.*, p. 133; W. Maurer, *op. cit.*, Bd. 2, p. 107; E. Bizer, *op. cit.*, pp. 88ff.

4. Cf. E. Bizer, *op. cit.*, pp. 86ff., on the text. For the most comprehensive survey of its main themes, pp. 96ff., on doctrines of "Christology," baptism, forgiveness, "Word and faith," the promise and justification; W. Maurer, *op. cit.*, Bd. 2, pp. 107ff., whose discussion of influences on Melanchthon (Erasmus and Origen, p. 108, Hilary, p. 109, Chrysostom, p. 109, all of whom Melanchthon cited in the work) is brief but valuable. Both Maurer and H.-G. Geyer, *Von der Geburt des wahren Menschen*, Neukirchen 1965, pp. 189ff., briefly discuss Melanchthon's view of the Gospel as rhetorical.

5. *MW* IV, p. 134.22.

6. *Ibid.*, p. 135.7f.

7. *Ibid.*, "Lex quaedam insculpta est animis nostris, quam naturalem vocant, estque consilium rationis nostrae...."

8. *Ibid.*, "Est et quam Deus dedit per Mosen."

9. *Ibid.*, p. 135.11f., "...quae assequi humanae naturae vires nequeunt."

10. *Ibid.*, p. 135.13-20.

11. *Ibid.*, p. 135.20ff.

12. *Ibid.*, p. 135.23ff.

13. *Ibid.*, p. 135.30ff.

14. *Ibid.*, p. 135.35-136.1ff.

15. *Ibid.*, p. 141.7ff., "Haec prima est et perspicua de Christo contio, quis nam sit, et quid collaturus venerit, paucis item verbis proponens totius evangelii summam."

16. *Ibid.*, p. 141.10ff., "Hoc ipsum Christi praeconium nusquam nobis non inculcat scriptura evangelica...."

17. *Ibid.*, p. 142.21ff., "...quid Christus venerit, docuit, adumbrat vocationem nostram."

18. *Ibid.*

19. *Ibid.*, p. 142.23ff.

20. *Ibid.*, p. 143.28ff., "Sic solemus pietatis speciem omnibus nostris cupiditatibus praetexere."

21. *Ibid.*, p. 144.8ff.

22. *Ibid.*, p. 145.6f., "In Christi natali et infantia paucis tractatum est, cur genitus sit, quomodo nos vocemur stella duce...."

23. *Ibid.*, p. 145.8f.

24. *Ibid.*, p. 147.11ff., "Neque vero tantum exempli causa, sed et in hoc, ut per hanc victoriam nos vinceremus; omnes enim victoriae, omnes triumphi Christi omnium credentium sunt...."

25. *Ibid.*, p. 150.15ff., "Principio a beatitudine orditur, quod huc omnium hominum vota tendant."

26. *Ibid.*, p. 150.16f., "Nihil enim agimus, quin inde nobis bene beateque esse velimus...."

27. *Ibid.*, p. 150.17f., "...qui philosophiae quoque scopus...."

28. *Ibid.*, p. 149.27ff., "Contio huius capitis explicatio quaedam divinae legis est...."

29. *Ibid.*, pp. 149.28-150.1ff.

30. *Ibid.*, p. 150.2ff.

31. *Ibid.*, p. 153.4ff.

32. *Ibid.*, pp. 154.19ff. and 160.10ff., on Matt. 5:42.

33. *Ibid.*, pp. 164.6ff. and 164.14.

34. *Ibid.*, p. 154.30ff.

35. *Ibid.*, p. 166.14ff., "Omnes historiae Christi sunt sacramenta, id est: promissiones quibus certi sumus Deum daturum omni credenti gratiam." Cf. E. Bizer, *op. cit., passim,* esp., pp. 119ff.

36. *MW IV*, p. 166.16ff.

37. *Ibid.*, p. 166.29ff.

38. *Ibid.*, p. 167.10.

39. *Ibid.*, p. 167.13ff.

40. The difference between Melanchthon and Erasmus here is that Melanchthon believed dialectical and theological structuring had been employed by Matthew to unfold the sense of Christ through the law first, and then the gospel. Cf. n. 52, below.

41. *Ibid.*, p. 173.30ff.

42. *Ibid.*, p. 174.14ff.

43. *Ibid.*, p. 175.4ff.

44. *Ibid.*, p. 175.22ff.

45. *Ibid.*, p. 180.18ff.

46. *Ibid.*, p. 180.19ff.

47. *Ibid.*, p. 181.19ff.

48. *Ibid.*, p. 178.20ff.

49. *Ibid.*, p. 204.18ff.

50. Melanchthon clearly used Erasmus's *Annotationes* on Matthew of 1516; cf. W. Maurer, *op. cit.*, Bd. 2, pp. 108f. on points of reference to this work in Melanchthon's text and on areas of agreement and disagreement between their theologies.

51. Cf. particularly *ibid.*, p. 109 on Melanchthon's use of Luther's Athanasian Christology, and the reference to Chrysostom on this subject. Luther and Melanchthon had been drawn to the idea of "exchange" as support for their radical distinction between the righteousness of God and the unrighteousness of humanity, against the libertarian notions of Erasmus.

52. *Ibid.*, p. 108, "In diesen versuchen, mit dem Rustzeug, das die antike Rhetorik bot, den biblischen Text aufzugliedern und seiner Struktur nach zu erfassen, war Melanchthon schon in der Institutio über Erasmus hinausgegangen; indem er diese Versuche in dem Matthauskolleg fortsetzte, verfolgte er weiterhin seinen eigenen Weg."

53. *Ibid.*

54. The term "concept" here implies conscious structure, as in "doctrine." Luther obviously had a view of biblical authority, but his was largely unsystematic and implicit in his exegesis, rather than worked out in theoretical detail. Cf. ref. to H. Bornkamm, below, n. 59.

55. H. Bornkamm, *Luther und das Alte Testament*, Tübingen 1948, esp. pp. 15ff.
56. E. Bizer, *op. cit.*, esp. pp. 119ff.
57. H. Bornkamm, *op. cit.*, pp. 15f.
58. *Ibid.*
59. *Ibid.*, p. 30.
60. Esp. *ibid.*, p. 30; cf. Luther, *Commentary on the Sermon on the Mount, LW* 21, pp. 2ff., who relates the text (in his preface) to the "vulgar pigs and asses, jurists and sophists" (p. 2), rather than to classical moral philosophy, and who explores, develops and applies every detail of the text, quite ingeniously, without any reference to its theological structure as a whole.
61. Melanchthon's first major Old Testament work was the *Paroimiai on Proverbs*, cf. *MW* IV, p. 11, which he made tidier still by pressing his system of law and gospel onto it; cf. his introduction, 1525 edition, Cambridge University Library, aaii, "Universa scriptura legem alias, alias Evangelium docet. Idem et hic libellus agit, quanquam peculiari orationis figura, proponit enim vulgares sententias, seu adagia, quibus breviter ea monentur, quae pluribus leges aut evangelicae promissiones tractant."
62. It should also be kept in view that modern scholars frequently defend a structural model of Matthew's Gospel that is not so very different, theologically, from that which Melanchthon proposed some centuries ago. E.g., E. Jüngel, *Paulus und Jesus: Eine Untersuchung zur Präzisierung der Frage nach dem Ursprung der Christologie*, Tübingen 1972; and R. Guelick, *The Sermon on the Mount: A Foundation for Understanding*, Waco 1982. The issue of literary structure and influences of classical rhetoric upon the Gospel traditions and composition is presently a matter of considerable debate. Cf. G. Kennedy, *Classical Rhetoric and Its Christian and Secular Tradition from Ancient to Modern Times*, Chapel Hill 1980; and *eodem, New Testament Interpretation Through Rhetorical Criticism*, Chapel Hill 1984.
63. *MW* IV, p. 139.26ff.
64. *Ibid.*, p. 139.30-140.1ff.
65. *Ibid.*, p. 140.9ff., "...ut non personarum, sed nominum sint discrimina tantum...." Cf. the lengthy list of double naming, p. 140.10-23; note Melanchthon's guarded skepticism about one of them! p. 140.15f.
66. *Ibid.*, p. 140.32ff., "Opinor...alicubi...legis patres pro naturae patribus conscriptos fuisse."
67. *Ibid.*, p. 143.16ff., "...quae lectio plane diversa est ab evangelistae lectione."
68. *Ibid.*, p. 143.17f., "Sed hic sententiam magis quam verba retulit."
69. *Ibid.*, p. 143.18ff., "Nam si legas apud prophetam per interrogationem admirationis notam: Tu ne Bethlehem?, quasi dicat: certe non. Quare non? 'Quoniam ex te mihi egredietur, qui sit dominator in Israel.'"
70. *Ibid.*, p. 21ff.; on *emphasis*, cf. *MW* III, p. 383, "Quintilian 8, 3, 83: *emphasis*, altiorem praebens intellectum, quam quem verba per se ipsa declarant...."
71. See R. Preus, *The Inspiration of Scripture*, Edinburgh/London 1957. The strong impression given is that the human element was almost lost from view in these later discussions of the origin and various properties of Scripture. Cf. esp. pp. 26-86.
72. *MW* IV, p. 141.24ff.
73. E. Bizer, *op. cit.*, pp. 123ff.
74. *Ibid.*
75. *Ibid.*
76. Also, W. Maurer, *op. cit.*, Bd. 2, pp. 114f.
77. *MW* IV, p. 206.13.
78. *Ibid.*, p. 206.13f., "...quibus vocibus divinae promissiones significantur."
79. *Ibid.*, p. 206.19ff.

80. *Ibid.*, p. 207.8ff., "In veteri vero testamento fuerunt promissa bona temporalia. Novo testamento promissio facta est rerum spiritualium." For a similar framework, cf. Calvin, *Institutes of the Christian Religion*, (ed.) J. T. McNeill, (tr.) F. L. Battles, Philadelphia 1960, Book Two, ch. X-XI, pp. 428ff. The translator's list of reformers who advanced the doctrine of the covenant before Calvin has omitted the names of Luther and Melanchthon.

81. *MW* IV, p. 207.3ff., "Abrahae promisit Deus semen, in quo benedicerentur omnes gentes..., credens huic Abraham iustificatus est. Sic nobis promissa est peccatorum condonatio...."

82. *Ibid.*, p. 150.18f., "Christus beatitudinis viam atque rationem plane pugnantem cum naturali et philosophica ratione praescribit."

83. *Ibid.*, p. 150.20ff.

84. *Ibid.*, p. 166.4ff., "Iam vero et hic convenit observare, quam efficax res sit verbum Dei, et multum adeo inter verbum Dei et verbum hominum interesse. Proinde ecclesiis potens istud verbum Dei praedicandum, non fractum et elumbe hominum verbum."

85. *Ibid.*, p. 173.2f., "Non est autem illa vis in verbo, sed Deus adest verbo et per verba corda hominum emollit."

86. *Ibid.*, pp. 164.19ff.

87. *Ibid.*, pp. 164.25-165.1ff.

CHAPTER 9

The Orations on Paul's Doctrine

One of the more pleasing ironies of history is that the Apostle Paul was the patron saint for the University of Wittenberg. On the twenty-fifth of January in the year 1520 the dons, students and other dignitaries gathered, as they did every year, to commemorate his conversion. That Melanchthon was invited to give the plenary address must have seemed as appropriate then as it does now.[1] He would publish his oration almost immediately afterwards as *Declamatiuncula in Divi Pauli doctrinam*;[2] to this he appended a letter to his friend John Hess in Nuremberg which was, in reality, a pointed attack on the exalted status of extra-biblical church tradition.[3] In May, he wrote a précis announcing to the students his forthcoming lectures on Romans. This second brief summary of Paul's great significance, the *Admonitio ad Paulinae doctrinae studium*, came into print, too, and circulated among the general public.[4] Geyer was correct in his judgment that these documents, although they have been largely neglected in the secondary literature, are of great value to understanding the emergence and development of Melanchthon's theology, and toward precise definition of widely used catch phrases such as his "neues Paulusverständnis" and "Rezeption des reformatorischen Erkenntnis Luthers."[5]

The orations on Paul are particularly important to our study of Melanchthon on biblical authority. First, they help make clear the fundamental distinction that he now stressed between the divine status of Scripture and the merely human character of classical philosophy. Once again, we shall observe that this very distinction was itself intelligible only in the terms of his rhetorical world view, so that the force of its negation of philosophy was always, also, an affirmation of ancient wisdom. The two essays thus enable us to advance our discussion of Melanchthon and his problematic doctrine of *sola scriptura*, in the context of Greek thought, with respect to the modalities of the

Bible's uniqueness. Of special importance here is the theoretical scope of the *gospel* and its actual power or efficaciousness in Scripture.

Secondly, these texts show more comprehensively than any of his earliest writings the contours of his foundational biblical theology, the *sensus literalis* of Scripture as a whole. The issue here is not only *what* Scripture proposed, in Melanchthon's view, but also the modalities of that "proposing" and the kind of proposition that he had in mind. We shall see in some detail that he pictured the sense of Scripture as a single thread of argument, as a *status* that emerged from the many and various biblical writings and functioned as the *scopus* of the entire canon. Perhaps the most fundamental theme of this chapter is Melanchthon's way of seeing the single sense of Scripture in the context of its many writings and circumstances. His interpretive model (although it never occurred to him that this was at all his own construction) was the linear historical idea of an unfolding, authoritative literary and social tradition, actualized through its histories, poetry, wisdom and moral codes. Most important, though, were the Apostle Paul and his works of systematic rhetoric. Moreover, we shall see that this rhetorical vision of the canon generated Philip's peculiar concepts of biblical unity and perspicuity. In this light, we shall be better placed to comment on strengths and weaknesses of his distinctive doctrine of revelation through Scripture.

The formative processes by which he shaped what one might call his meta-textual theory, that is, how he brought the full set of his conceptual convictions to the text and how the world of the text thus emerged for him, are by themselves of great interest to us. They bring to mind the complex analogy that obtains between the general problem of knowledge and the special problem of interpretation, or knowing what Scripture conveys and how to *know* that it does convey just that meaning. In Melanchthon, the problem of theological consensus arises to confront us rather disturbingly with the interpretive issues that pertain to the survival of Christianity and Western civilization in any discretely unified form. In view of the disintegration of European institutional Christianity that followed upon Melanchthon's best efforts to the contrary, his exuberant *orationes* in 1520, with their ringing affirmations of Paul and the clear theological unity of the canon, elicit a great range of thoughts and emotions about the status of Protestant theology. Moreover, his manner of rhetorically shaping and constructing these essential concepts is also of critical historiographical importance. For how is one to assess him in the context of Lutheran history unless one has heard him in the context of his own conceptual terms in his own time? Issues to consider here are his contact with the methods of later dogmaticians and the pertinence of certain criticisms, such as that of a pervasive intellectualism or scholasticism. In this chapter, we shall advance our discussion of all of these topics.

Finally, his earlier public criticisms of transubstantiation now called for public explanation and defense. This forced Melanchthon to give a clear statement of his underlying views on the status of extra-biblical tradition, and, thus, to give a fuller account of his doctrine of *sola scriptura*, with respect to the traditions of the church. Therewith, he stressed not only the rhetorical (epistemic) powers of Scripture on the human side of its authoritative function in the world, but also its formal ontological status as originating in the mind of Christ and as inspired by the illuminating power of the Holy Spirit. It thus became clearer how Melanchthon imagined the process of divine inspiration in the context of his view of Scripture as human *oratio*. Because of his greater clarity here than elsewhere on the subject of Scripture as *revelation* (something which he very rarely broached directly), the continuity of his intellectual and religious movement from a particular Catholic paradigm of biblical authority to that of his early Lutheranism also emerges more vividly than before.

In the *exordium* to the *Declamatiuncula* (itself written in the style of the *genus demonstrativum*), Melanchthon proposed that his encomium on Paul was more deeply, also, a defense of Scripture itself.[6] Prince Frederick was sitting conspicuously in the audience, and so was the imperial emissary, Jerome Brunner, who had come from an electoral meeting in Zerbst for the occasion.[7] Melanchthon wisely dedicated the speech to Brunner and used the opportunity to put in a good word for Luther, "a man both pious and learned, and truly a theologian...."[8] He thus began what would become a lifetime of standing before the powers of the age to offer a clear and rational account of the Wittenberg theology. In circumstances like these, Melanchthon was usually at his best, and the *Declamatiuncula* is an early sign of his genius for clear, contained thought under the pressures of a most dangerous time.

The speech consisted of two main parts. The first was mainly a *comparatio* between Paul's doctrine and that of classical philosophy. In the second, he turned to the subject of scholastic theological method. In the letter to Hess, the main topic was the status of Scripture with respect to tradition, particularly that tradition which had emerged from Christian sources other than Scripture. The *Admonitio* mainly handled the problem of philosophy, but, as in the *Declamatiuncula*, this discussion developed alongside the deeper, hermeneutical matter of what the message or *sensus* of Scripture was. To put this more precisely, it developed alongside the hermeneutical-epistemic question of how this *sensus* might be known as an objective truth or as a structured complex of truths. In the lectures on Matthew and Romans, we gained some idea of how he treated this question, but the orations on Paul are the first instances of a consciously systematic statement. At the risk of distorting Melanchthon's own presentation of the issues, we shall handle them individually and topically, since we judge that such an approach will avoid needless repetition and will be in the best interest of advancing our analytical project. We shall, nevertheless, make every effort to bring the topics up in their proper contexts.

Scripture and Its Divine Difference from Philosophy

Paul's virtues were many: love of Christ, faith, knowledge of things hidden, contempt for this life, majesty of doctrine, great courage.[9] Here was one greater than words could express.[10] Nevertheless, one virtue stood out: "Among these [virtues], truly, I judge that his doctrine takes first place. For he himself enjoyed the remaining ornaments privately; the fruit of the doctrine, indeed, is ours."[11]

Making use of the rhetorical *locus argumentorum* of what is "useful," *utile*,[12] Melanchthon summed up the nature and importance of Paul's writings.

> ...I am of the opinion that Christ, and the *summa* of our salvation, can be known in the letters of no one, in the commentaries of no one, more nearly than those of Paul [*nullius commentariis propius cognosci posse Christum atque adeo salutis nostrae summam quam Paulinis*]. There is no praise which can commend Paul to the human race more forcefully than this.[13]

In tones now familiar to us, he stressed the connection between good studies and the quest for felicitous self-knowledge: "those [arts] which show forth the way of salvation, the nature of perfect felicity, ought by right to be sought after by all men."[14] This was the intuition of all great philosophers since antiquity.

> Antiquity [*vetustas*] also embraced philosophy mainly for this reason, that it might thence seek the form of a better life [*ut inde vitae melioris formam peteret*], and, in the consensus of all wise men, this most noble kind of discipline has always been held in esteem, because it was best accommodated to emending morals and the desires of life [*quod ad mores vitaeque studia emendanda accomodatissimum fuit*].[15]

As he had done in the *Annotationes* and *Institutio*, he now proposed the qualitative superiority of Scripture. "It is fitting that Christians seek a plan of life [*vitae formam*], not from the philosophers, but from the divine books [*ex divinis libris*]."[16]

Once again, the irony of Melanchthon's fresh Lutheran disparagement of classical metaphysics comes to the fore. Philosophy had failed to attain its stated goal; it had not managed to find true felicity. Instead, the "divine books" of Scripture give us such a "plan of life." Still, the essential aim of philosophy was a sound one. And that aim took the form of questions that expressed truthful intuitions about deep levels of our human ontology. The *organon* of Aristotle and others was itself the product of deep wisdom about the nature of human being as a moral teleology. Both Scripture and ancient philosophy had these *loci* in common; both relied upon genuinely human intuitions that were presumably grounded in our common human nature. But how was this positive body of metaphysical truth related to Melanchthon's Lutheran view of human nature and its concomitant doctrine of biblical exclusivity, or *sola scriptura*, in reference to the philosophers? The orations on Paul will start us on a course toward answering this question and engaging the common accusation that there was something simply self-defeating about Melanchthon's attempt at asserting Lutheran doctrine without a more fundamental critique of human intuition.

In the *Declamatiuncula*, Philip constantly returned to the issue of Paul and philosophy. He asserted that it is good to know and emulate the higher laws of morality, but better to have a heart which is readily inclined to *do* the things of the law. His great stress on the uniqueness of the biblical answer to our common human questions might at first suggest a lack of awareness of other deontological matters. "Laws for living well were not lacking among the pagans; they were not entirely lacking in examples [*non deerant omnino exempla*], but they *were* lacking someone who could teach them *whence* a soul might be sought [*unde petendus sit animus*] which might be at peace with the laws."[17] Here Melanchthon introduced what would become one of his most renowned and distinctive ideas, that of the "benefits of Christ." "Philosophers also placed beatitude in perfect virtue and perpetual tranquillity of the soul...,"[18] but they knew not "...whence they might find such a soul; the philosophers were not seeing—for that is the mystery hidden for so many ages—the benefit of Christ [*id ipsum est mysterium tot absconditum seculis, Christi beneficium*]."[19] The impression is left that Melanchthon viewed the doctrine of the *beneficium* as the distinct difference between biblical teaching and that of ancient metaphysics, but that on other points of moral-ontological analysis they agreed. However, as we shall seek to show here and in a later chapter,[20] this commonly held interpretation is not quite adequate to stating the nuances of his understanding.

In this context of comparison between Scripture and philosophy, Melanchthon also formed his concept of biblical efficaciousness and power. It is evident that, for him, this power was not grounded merely in the objective truth and uniqueness of biblical doctrine, or in the sovereign spiritual use of it by God, but very much in its human rhetorical force, in its self-actualizing truthfulness and power. And it was Paul who held the master key to unleashing it in full measure. Melanchthon's Paul was to the biblical tradition what Socrates, Lysia, Pericles and Ulysses were to the ancients.

> I cannot express in human words by what figures of rhetoric [*rhetorum figuris*], by what embellishments [*quibus floribus*], by what ornaments of oration [*orationis ornamentis*] he captivates the reader. Alcibiades attributed a certain unalterable power [*ratam quandam energian*] to the Socratic orations, Socrates to Lysia, the ancient comedies to Pericles, the poet Homer to Ulysses.... But by how many steps does our Paul surpass these— the one whom the admiring pagans called Mercury![21]

Melanchthon illustrated his claim about Paul's powers by giving what was for him a very rare personal testimony.

> In my own experience, indeed, after I gave my mind over to him [Paul] for direction [*formandum*], I know well enough what he will have done. And would that all men might prefer to experience the matter itself rather than trust in my words. As a youth I did much harm to the soul in the literature of the philosophers [*Nonnulli animi iacturam in Philosophorum literis puer feci*], which I hope Paul's doctrine will one day heal

[*olim doctrina Pauli sarciet*]. For in my judgment they are wandering entirely from the path who think that the doctrines of the Christian life are helped by the literature of the philosophers [*qui Philosophorum literis iuvari vitae Christianae rationes censent*]. For Christian doctrine *alone* is efficacious for arousing and inspiring souls [*Sola enim Christiana doctrina efficax est ad excitandos inspirandosque animos*]; that is what the apostles were confessing when they were calling Christ's word of eternal life a "philosophy" which alone is the way, the truth, the light and the life....[22]

So for Melanchthon biblical (Pauline) doctrine was transcendentally more powerful than even the greatest of human philosophies. One issue that arises here is the question of how to express the difference. Was it, as some have thought, that human reason and Scripture interlocked on the level of moral truth or law, but diverged on the issue of grace. On this view, the law was not by itself distinctively a divine revelation, whereas the gospel was. This would seem an inadequate way of putting it, though, since, in Melanchthon's view, these existential deficiencies of reason were grounded in the metaphysical problem that philosophers may have "prescribed laws of living ..., but those of the heavenly Father were much purer [*multo sanctiores*]...."[23] But what made the *laws* of Scripture purer or holier than those of moral philosophy? Melanchthon explained:

...namely, since philosophy did not know exactly the nature of humanity [*nondum exacte genium norit hominis philosophia*], how could it guard against moral vices with laws? Philosophy teaches that virtue is produced by practice and habit, but do we not yet see in experience how nothing is of help to the warring affections of nature? For as an ape remains an ape [*simia semper est simia*], even when clothed in purple, so by no counsel, by no art, will you have conquered the sickness of the soul [*nullo consilio, nulla arte, animi morbum viceris*].[24]

Part of his answer was, thus, that one's moral theories or laws were inseparable from one's basic ontology of human nature. This is a proposition that we shall explore more fully in the next chapter. It will suffice for now to have observed that Melanchthon proposed something different from a simple model of moral synthesis on the basis of natural law.

There is also another level on which this synthetic model of interpretation is inadequate in asserting the absolute distinction in Melanchthon between the gospel and the moral intuitions of classical philosophy. If one listens to the undertones of his critique of the ancients on this very question, it becomes subtly evident that, in his view, even the philosophers had certain "gospel-intuitions" that took them to the limits of simple moralism. There was, as he had indicated in the *Institutio*, "need for another certain master of souls [*alio quodam animorum magistro*], namely the heavenly Spirit, who would occupy the inward hearts of men [*intima hominum pectora*], renew, inspire, seize, inflame and transform [them]."[25] This was a conclusion, he argued, which was in agreement with the Platonists, who "were seeing that there is need in human minds for a certain interior 'catharsis' [*opus esse humanis mentis interiore...katharsei*]..., a cleansing [*purgatione*], without which they were denying that perfect virtue could be obtained."[26] Only in Scripture would one find this "certain power [*quaedam vis*]" for such a transformation; only in "sacred oration [*sacro sermone*]" will the hands of the gods be present to us.[27] So even the Platonists intuited something "gospel-like" through reason and experience; what they lacked was the *power* of the gospel. How did Melanchthon imagine the semantic dimension of this unique power? How exactly was it distinct from the intuitions of moral inadequacy, the need for catharsis by higher powers than the mundane or merely human? A simple model of interlocking at the level of law, and absolute distinction at the level of grace, seems not quite appropriate to the structures of Melanchthon's view.

In concluding the *Declamatiuncula*, he reiterated his main themes and continued his critique of moral philosophy as qualitatively inferior to sacred Scripture. Paul had given the world what, in its noblest philosophies, it had sought after for centuries. He disclosed our true ontology as moral beings (presupposing the Greek ontology that pictured humans as rational and moral creatures) and thus consummated the quest for self-knowledge.

> Many men love philosophy because it puts man before his own eyes [*quod hominem sibi ipsi ante oculos ponat*], and the ancients considered [this] the fruit and end of philosophy: to know oneself [*fructum et kolophona Philosophiae censerunt, sese novisse*]. But how much more felicitously has Paul surpassed this; in whom it is to see, as in a mirror, whatever has been placed in the inner recesses of man [*ceu in speculo est cernere, quidquid est in intimo hominis secessu positum*].... It seems that philosophy pours out a certain darkness before the eyes of men; and in judging the nature of man, which it usually does first, and in determining definitions [*finibus*] of virtues and vices, it is everywhere frigid, hallucinates and is blind [*passim frigere, hallucinari et caecutire*]. [28]

In the *Admonitio*, Melanchthon gave a similar line of argument, adding subtle but important qualifications about the distinction between pagan and biblical moral analysis.

> There exist rules of living [*vivendi formulae*], some divinely produced [*aliae divinitus proditae*], others written by ingenious men [*ab ingeniosis hominibus conscriptae*], such as the poems of Homer and Hesiod, the commentaries of philosophers and the many laws of the noble cities, the memory of which, by the benefit of histories, has been propagated in our time. Truly, among these, the divine laws are much holier than the human

ones [*divinae leges tanto sanctiores sunt humanis*]; for how
much more nearly do they portray both the author and the
archetype of all good things [*quanto propius effingunt tum
autorem, tum archetypum omnium bonarum rerum*], who
without doubt is nowhere more certainly expressed [*nusquam
certius expressum*] than in those letters which He, by His
inestimable kindness, insculpted on tables of stone with His own
hand [*in iis literis quas suis ipse digitis*].[29]

Melanchthon's stress in the above passage was upon actual ontological
differences between the origin and propositions of moral and divinely revealed
law. As noble as pagan law may have been, the contrast fell this time, not
immediately upon the anthropological question, but upon that of knowledge of
God. His premise was that biblical law did not merely reveal what was morally
right and wrong, but carried with it an epistemic connection with the true
source, "author" and "archetype" of right and wrong. The term "law" was
contextually different for Christians than it was for non-Christian philosophers.
So biblical law was not simply identical with moral or philosophical law.

There followed a critique of philosophy as being "not holy," but "blind," "a
kingdom of trifles, its dogma insane and delusory," something that
"hallucinates when it discusses the definition of good and evil...."[30] The Stoics
themselves wrote of how ineptly philosophy handled virtue, and even
"Socrates...was seeing that there was nothing of certainty in the entire order of
philosophy...."[31] The young readers must turn to Christ, "since indeed He is the
oration of the great Father,"[32] and "Our souls will express Christ more certainly
by no other method than by study of sacred doctrine, in which His image shines
forth as if in a looking glass."[33] Nearing the conclusion of his *Admonitio*,
Melanchthon wrote:

Now also from Paul one can know...appropriately what the
distinction is between Christian doctrine and philosophy [*inter
Christianam doctrinam, et Philosophiam proprie quid intersit*]....
Truly, I would wish every Christian mind persuaded of this: that
Christianity is something altogether different from philosophy,
or from the theology of our men [*prorsus aliud esse
Christianismum, quam vel Philosophiam, vel nostrorum
hominum Theologiam*]. The way to virtue is different, the
definition of the good, the felicity of man which Paul prescribes is
different from what is taught in the schools of the philosophers.[34]

Finally, he once again added the dimension of Paul's rhetorical method as
essential to the whole matter of what was not only powerful, not only uniquely
powerful, but transcendentally powerful about Scripture.

And so with what weighty, lucid, elegant oration [*quam gravi,
quam dilucida, quam eleganti oratione*] does he set forth all these
things. Indeed, briefly, but so that nothing is lacking.... They say

that the oration of Pericles usually left arrows holding fast in the souls of his hearers; it cannot be said of him that he bends, turns, seizes and inflames the soul of the reader [*huius dici non potest, ut flectat, ut verset, ut rapiat, ut inflammet legentis animum*].... There is no panacea so powerful as the Pauline oration [*Neque ulla tam efficax Panacea est, quam Paulina oratio*], no moly so salutary against magic potions as is the doctrine of Paul against the sicknesses of the soul....[35]

Melanchthon thus hammered away at philosophy and praised Scripture for its rhetoric, as if to say, "philosophy is dead, long live philosophy!" The majesty of Scripture was inseparable from the modalities of human rhetoric. And this affirmation of the *methods* of rhetoric illustrates Goethe's truism that "form is never without content." To affirm these methods in that comprehensive manner was also, implicitly, to affirm the basic intuitions behind them. It was to affirm the instincts and insights, the deeply important *loci communes* or universal truths that shaped proper *inventio* in the human quest for self-understanding and lives based on truth. It was to establish a solid, created common ground between the Word of God and the word of man.

Awareness of Melanchthon's image of Scripture as *oratio sacra* has already helped us to see the problem of "natural theology" in the peculiar form that it developed in his early, formative writings. It seems that he did not make a simplistic *distinction* between Scripture and philosophy, on the level of "gospel," and then a *synthesis* on the basis of common morality, on the level of "law." For there was a sense in which the world of classical philosophy foreshadowed all the essential doctrines of the Christian canon, the truths of law, sin and grace. There were in classical metaphysics analogies to the Word of God as a whole, just as Scripture as a whole was qualitatively distinct from philosophy. It is difficult to find precisely the right way to express this relationship between them. In our final chapters, we shall seek to show that, within the framework that we have set up and with certain qualifications about what counts as true Protestantism in its historic sense, Melanchthon did successfully relate Scripture and philosophy to each other, even though he departed in some ways from the trends in Luther's method, to the dismay of certain members of the fold.

Here, we must finally comment on the manner in which his concept of biblical efficaciousness, or transcendental power, emerged. One of the commonest criticisms of Melanchthon is that he centered biblical authority on its doctrine, or propositional truth, and that this emphasis led to an "intellectualism" that drained Luther's grand, emotionally powerful message of its initial life force. Begging the question of comparisons with Luther (remembering that not many could compete with him for literary genius), we must again notice that Philip's image of Scripture as rhetoric presumed a notion of "doctrine" that is not always considered by those who accuse him for giving us too much of it. Melanchthon most certainly believed that Scripture was, in its very essence, a library of doctrine. However, he also presumed that a rightly formed doctrine, or "truth" (*locus*), was a complete elocution. It was more like what modern hermeneuticists such as Hans Frei have called a "word-action" or "word event" than it was the simple inscription of cognitive propositions and terms. That is not to say that he was never tedious, a man who loved filing systems and indices to an extent that seems remarkable. In weaker moments, Philip lapsed into spells of pedestrian sterility. But it was not always so. His stress on the heart and on the emotional power of the text was often, as here, quite strong and well expressed, and deserves greater respect than it has received until recently. In our final chapter, we shall argue that the typical forms of criticism are generally not sensitive enough to Melanchthon's thought-forms and their effect upon people in his own context. In our next section, here, on the sense and perspicuity of the canon, we shall undertake to show how specific "intellectualistic" problems did arise. Nevertheless, his emphasis on the heart should be kept in view, as should the peculiar rhetorical modalities of Scripture, since they enable us to see these problems rightly, in their particular conceptual shape, before attempting critical judgments. This section will also help to clarify the problem of biblical uniqueness, insofar as we now come to a still fuller account of what Melanchthon imagined Scripture to be, essentially, in making its claims about God and the world.

The Sensus Scripturae—Its Perspicuity and Coherence as a Whole

In the *Declamatiuncula*, Melanchthon developed the concept for which he is perhaps best known, the *beneficia Christi*. This was obviously a teleological notion in keeping with his classical principles of invention which centered all knowledge upon self-knowledge. The great rhetoricians uncovered and exposed the true meaning of events and circumstances. They shaped and proclaimed the universal *caussae communes* to their own people, but also to human beings in all times and places. In Melanchthon's view, that is exactly what Paul did for people trying to understand biblical revelation. He exposed and proclaimed its universal relevance as divine truth to our common humanity. In this context, Melanchthon's idea of the text as a coherent whole emerged. The orations on Paul are an invaluable resource for viewing his emerging idea of biblical unity and perspicuity with respect to the diversity within the canon.

He began his discussion of Paul's contribution to the unifying structures of the whole by making literary distinctions of genre or kind between the various biblical writings. Notice that all of them fit in one way or another into a literary form. "In the number of divine volumes, some [contain] laws, some examples of life and morals, some obscure prophecies concerning Christ; others commemorate the histories of Christ."[36] The biblical canon was a repository of structured ideological tradition. It was the Apostle Paul, however, who narrated the *beneficium*, the true meaning of *all* God's work wrought through Christ: "Who explains more gravely, more accurately, more copiously than Saint Paul the *beneficium* which Christ prepared for the world by His own blood?"[37] One notices how Paul's function mirrored the full range of rhetorical actions within a tradition. To know moral laws was not unimportant,[38] and it was indeed of great value to meditate upon the best examples of virtue among those whose lives were recorded in the histories, especially the life of Christ, who was "the example of perfect virtue."[39] "But it is of the very greatest importance to know what the true glory of Christ is, *wherefore* He came down to the earth, *how* the incarnation of the eternal Word may be of profit to the world...."[40] For in these things "the *summa* of salvation has been placed."[41] Paul defined and expressed the quintessence of what God was all about, in Christ, in relation to the deepest concerns of humankind. The "wherefore" and the "how" were essential conditions for the "profit" and the power of the event, and the "profit" and the power were the scope and end of stating the "wherefore" and the "how."

Melanchthon stressed the troublesome epistemic-hermeneutical implication of such a model. It was a matter of the greatest possible urgency that the "...Pauline epistles be added to the laws promulgated through Moses, to the oracles of the prophets and to the histories...."[42] For it was in the writings of Paul that "the beneficence of our savior [*beneficentia servatoris*] is described..., whence perfect felicity [*absoluta felicitas*] must be sought."[43] Melanchthon might seem, here, to have proposed a very strong doctrine of a "canon within the canon," to the point even of reducing non-Pauline tradition to the status of a mere legal corpus. He conceded that Paul also taught morals, and that he did placed him in line with the other biblical books,[44] but "we know peculiarly from Paul the *nature* and *power* of Christ's benefit...."[45] To know this "benefit" was truly to know Christ: "...not only to hold onto His historical deeds, but with a grateful soul to embrace His benefit, which the heavenly Father pours out through Him upon all the earth...."[46] We have seen elsewhere that Melanchthon's truth theory inclined him to modify this stance and to preserve an inductive exegetical unity throughout Scripture. And, in later sections, we shall see that his concept of *loci communes* served him in trying to preserve the unity of Scripture on the level of gospel and grace, in addition to that of law. But the orations on Paul make it clear that tension remained. For Paul's letters were essential to knowing the benefits of Christ, and these were essential to a knowledge of God properly speaking, that is, in the sense that made Christian knowledge distinct from other forms of knowledge. It would seem that this was not merely the consummation of that knowledge, as its crown or capstone, but really its core, its essential condition and context. It was knowledge of this *beneficium* "by which alone the distinction was made between impious pagans and truly Christian souls."[47] For it was in Jesus Christ, known only in reference to this immense *beneficium*, that "...God has most perfectly expressed...His goodness...."[48]

Melanchthon reached to express his conviction that true knowledge of God was available to people through the other biblical texts apart from Paul, but it is ambiguous as to what sort of knowledge that might have been. The sacred mystery was known, but dimly, to the patriarchs and prophets of the Old Testament. "The patriarchs knew this benefit of Christ from certain secret oracles, as many as were saved.... Likewise also the prophets sing a hymn of peace and a song of a new Sabbath."[49] In later writings, he would use the language of "promise" to work out the objective content of pre-Christian biblical knowledge of Christ and the dialectical interaction of law and gospel.

But here he did not make use of it. The *beneficium Christi,* as explained by Paul, was also the central teaching of the New Testament which, like John the Baptist, pointed us to the "...Lamb of God who takes away the sins of the world."[50] In our examination of his lectures on Matthew, we have seen the manner of this "pointing" through inventive rhetoric in the context of a Pauline pre-understanding. The dilemma was as dangerous in Melanchthon's and Luther's circumstances as it is theologically troublesome today. If one failed to press the inductive unity of the Bible on something so radical and revolutionary as this Lutheran concept of grace, one was vulnerable to the charge of having invented a new interpretation, a sure sign of heresy. However, to press the matter was to run the perhaps greater risk of proving the suspicion true through strained exegesis. The fact that Melanchthon could write the following words is some indication of the difficulty that he was up against without seeming to be very conscious of it. If the examples of virtue put forward by the philosophers showed signs of imperfection that were unsettling even to themselves, [51] the other sacred writers, although they "made mention of this benefit everywhere," did so "too obscurely to be understood unless Paul had elucidated the *universal theme* with so many epistles, so many *disputations.*"[52]

In the *Admonitio,* too, Melanchthon asserted the absolutely essential role of Paul in the history of revelation and knowledge of God, that apart from Paul there would be no such knowledge in the fully Christian sense of the term. Here also he saw the difference between Paul's writings and the other biblical books as being both in his singular position with respect to the incarnation of Jesus Christ (*a successione fidelium*) and in the theory of truth and method which he used to bring out the essential meaning of this revelatory event. Finally, the linguistic successes of Paul comprised not only the *sensus scripturae* but also the logical *discrimen* between it and human tradition, whether that of the church or philosophy. Biblical authority in its full sense, that is, as exerted in the world and known savingly by people, was logically and therefore diachronically dependent upon the teachings of Paul.

In this little "Exhortation" to the study of Paul's doctrine, Melanchthon began by setting forth a comparison between what one might call "legalism" in moral theory and "evangelicalism." His remarks conveyed briefly how he related Scripture and philosophy to each other and also the manner in which he now pictured the canon as a diverse but coherent whole.

> In the divine scriptures, human laws have been surpassed [*humanae leges divinis scripturis vincuntur*], since evangelical letters which display Christ to mankind have been added to them, imparting a spirit by which human souls, inflamed, spontaneously desire nothing [that is] not of heaven.[53]

Directly following his assertion that in Christ we have to do with the saving *sermo* of God, he exhorted his readers to consider the place of Paul among the diverse writers of Scripture.

For, since some volumes prescribe laws, others narrate the history of past deeds [*historiam rerum gestarum*], our Paul, by a certain methodical disputation [*methodica quadam disputatione*], examines those *loci* without which it will not have profited at all to have learned the laws [*eos locos persequitur, citra quos non admodum profuerit leges didicisse*]. Neither the predictions of the prophets [*Prophetarum vaticinia*], nor the evangelical histories [*Evangelicae historiae*] can be entered into, unless you follow his commentaries, as accompanying a river to the sea, serving as a method [*methodi vice*]. For in discussing human nature, the tyranny of sin, the kingdom of the law, the origin and propagation of perfect virtue, the sacraments ..., Paul alone places these *loci* plainly before the eyes of mortals [*unicus Paulus hos locos palam ob oculos mortalium posuit*].[54]

Had it not been for Paul, we should not have known Christ Himself, as indeed we must if we are to be redeemed.

In brief, for the sake of our redemption, indeed, we would not have known Christ Himself [*Christum ipsum ignoraremus*], had God withheld Paul from the world. For to know Christ is not to hold to the history of things done by Him, but to know His immense benefits [*Neque enim Christum novisse, est historiam rerum ab ipso gestarum tenere, sed agnoscere ingentia beneficia*]....

In vain will you have learned the evangelical history, unless you observe the scope and use of the history [*nisi historiae scopos et usum*], demonstrated by him. Where he writes on the abrogation of the law, sin, the flesh, spirit, the sons of adoption, liberty, servitude, what else does he do but bring light to all Scripture as by a certain method [*ceu methodo quadam, universae scripturae lumen adferat*]? I omit what mysteries and sublimities he teaches....[55]

Taken together with similar statements in the *Declamatiuncula*, these sections help expand our picture of biblical authority in Melanchthon's early writings. We observe here how every level of Scripture's authority, from its intrinsic relation to the incarnate *sermo Dei*, to its final scope in transforming the lives of people, was contingent upon its rhetorical forms or modes. Of particular importance was the nature of biblical diversity and unity as a whole, or the manner in which Scripture "carried" its authoritative truth as a completed whole. Not merely Paul's writings, but also the remaining volumes of Scripture, fell into specific literary classifications. Some were books of laws, some contained *exempla vivendi*, others gave us *res gestae* of great persons. Still others held forth "obscure prophecies," and we have seen how, in his treatment of the Psalms, he combined the concepts of literature with those of predictive prophecy. Our main concern here is to clarify his distinctive concepts of biblical unity, diversity and perspicuity by identifying the rhetorical modalities of these properties of the canon. The shape of Melanchthon's biblical canon seems strikingly the same as that of his literary canon. Revelation from God and truth from the ancients unfolded along the same historical-literary lines with similar conceptual values. The unity of these canons was not immune to historical process and diversity, and the phenomenological *appearance* of that unified *sensus literarum* was not a flat, entirely synchronic perspicuity. The perspicuity of the canon as a unified whole required knowledge of this vast historical process, knowledge of the development of the tradition and, most especially, awareness of Paul's position as the one who "scoped" the essence of the whole. Like one greater than Pericles, Paul explained the sacred tradition and constructed from its diverse elements a systematic sense of the whole, without which we would not have known Christ in the manner that makes us truly Christian.

Melanchthon thus entered the great power struggle of the age for control over the sense of Scripture and, thus, over the soul of Christendom. His main instrument was an astonishing facility with rhetorical constructions in service of Lutheran theology. It must be stressed that his approach was a world removed from that of a Chemnitz or a Hutter, whose methods typify a powerful obsession with the doctrine of inspiration on a model of divine dictation. As we have indicated, to assert a chain of tradition from Luther, through Melanchthon, to these theologians is to invite distortion through oversimplification.[56] But how ought one to evaluate this model of revelation and biblical authority with respect to its basic assertion that everything depended upon a clear view of Paul and his rhetorical-theological *oratio*? The problem of a "canon within the canon" seems acute, here, and Melanchthon is very vulnerable to the charge that a completely artificial unity has been imposed on the text as a *pretext* for making Lutheranism out to be true. But it would be unfair to accuse him of intellectual dishonesty; he was incapable of power-mongering. To an extent unlike Luther, Melanchthon quite believed that they could stand theologically, digging their heels into purely exegetical ground. Everything unfolded from Paul outwards, or ought one to say backwards? This approach would prove unsatisfying to both sides of the controversy, as each sought an ever-greater perspicuity claim to warrant absolute control over the text and the church. There is nothing in Melanchthon of the ready appeal to authority in the tradition that one found in his Catholic adversaries; nor is there anything of the desperate attempt to combine the perspicuity of biblical truth with private spiritual vision and a deterministic theory of inspiration that is typical of later Lutherans, like Chemnitz and Hutter. His honest effort to deploy his rhetoric in recovering the lost sense of Scripture is to his credit as a person and scholar. Evaluating the extent of his success, however, is a somewhat more difficult matter. Can the Pauline writings really reinterpret all of Scripture so radically? We have already commented on the rather strained way in which Melanchthon sought to counter this problem through a "tight" exegetical system, rather than by appealing more loosely to tropological and spiritual intuitions for support, as in the writings of Luther. Melanchthon was not interested in a *sensus plenior*, unless that really was in the structure or *locus* of the text itself. His claim seems to have been that Paul did not create new meaning, nor did he simply evoke meaning. He *found* and disclosed it in pure elocutionary style, and brought it forth in the context of Jesus Christ and the gospel of justification by grace through faith. The underlying premise verged on circularity. *Since* Paul had taught these things, and since there must be a cognitive unity within the revealed texts, the non-Pauline texts *must*, on some level, teach the same things as Paul taught. In his *Loci communes* of 1521, as we shall see, Melanchthon set out to prove that this was so, and to vindicate Luther and Lutheranism. Initially, this quest to demonstrate the unified, literal sense of Scripture went on in the context of a radical Lutheranism; eventually it evolved into something more moderate and, thus, more capable of sustaining its norms and accomplishing its aims. Given the truth theory behind Melanchthon's construal of the text, there had to be great pressure upon his doctrine of predestination (and everything related to it) to square with everything else that had been revealed in Scripture and passed through Christian intellectual tradition.

Let us explore this matter of the perspicuity of Scripture in Melanchthon a bit further. This property of biblical authority has to deal with the modality of biblical unity. The claim is not simply that the Bible has a unity, but that this unity manifests itself clearly, perspicuously. This was something that he now stressed in making his criticisms of reigning theological methods. It is interesting to note his attempt to ground this claim about the Bible and its sense, not only philosophically, in the terms of his rhetoric, but theologically, as a presumption about the nature of God as good and about the fact that the Spirit of God was the spirit of light, not darkness. Melanchthon imagined the combined work of Christ and the Spirit as an original, sacred and rhetorical action that continued in the works of the Apostle Paul. The implication would seem to be born of a kind of theodicy: a good, wise and powerful God would not just grant us truth, but also understanding.

In the *Declamatiuncula* and the letter to John Hess, Melanchthon launched a vigorous assault on what he took to be the prevailing hermeneutical abuses of Scripture. He pinned the failings of these systems upon their inability to handle the teachings of Paul, and this he attributed to their flawed theory of truth and its very construal of Scripture. His Lutheran sense of Scripture's "difference" from human theory now amplified his intuition that Scripture alone, because of its original purity, ought to have the status of universal authority over all Christians.

In the *Declamatiuncula*, Melanchthon refined his critique of contemporary theology. His argument was that theologians neglected the essential doctrines of Paul and that they instead "embraced Aristotle."[57] The implication was that by neglecting the core of Paul's doctrine, they omitted Christ almost entirely.[58]

> Nor do I go on about what kind of language there is in the schools, how impure and sordid is the method of teaching and writing [*quam impura et sordata docendi disserendique ratio*]....

As it is commonly said, "no cup was to be found unmixed with bad water." So neither in the scholastic theology [*potum non inveniri ex aqua coeno turbata. Ita nec in scholastica Theologia*]....[59]

The metaphors of impurity and sordidness were conceptually linked to the fact that scholastic theologians preferred "a more sublime theology."[60] The fundamental problem was of course in the intuition of their method; they did not just neglect Paul, they neglected him because they failed to apprehend his proper status within the world of Christian discourse. They failed to place Paul properly, because they failed to interpret him correctly. And they failed to interpret him correctly, because they brought the wrong system of interpretation to the text. Thus, they came with all the wrong questions and structures of mind and affection. "Perhaps...the difficulty of the oration [*difficultas orationis*] and what appears to be an encumbered method of writing [*ratio disserendi impedita*] frightened some away from Paul...."[61] But how much more easily, and with how much less peril, could one unravel the meaning of Paul's disputation [*disputationem*] than that of their "impious and contentious little questions [*contentiosas et impias...quaestiunculas*]..."![62]

> ...that Pauline writings are less understood we owe to those distinguished masters of ours, who, since they are unacquainted with all of the ancient literature and with sound learning, first dissect the divine oration of Paul—tightly arranged by rhetorical members, and united by its own joints [*divinam Pauli orationem et rhetoriciis vinctam membris, et suis compactam articulis*]—with their new interpunctuations; then, having dissected it, they interpret it in their own manner according to Aristotle, so that not even verse coheres with verse [*ne versus quidem cum versu conveniret*].[63]

Melanchthon attributed the entire theological breakdown to a mentality of dissection that was itself the product of unfamiliarity with "sound learning." Without a disposition tempered by "all classical literature," a profoundly destructive process unfolded. The "divine oration" of Paul, with all its perfections of rhetorical coherence, was sliced into parts and then, piece by piece, interpreted in "their own" manner, that is, in view of a corrupt Aristotelianism. The loss of *oratio* spelled doom for everything else.

But the process went beyond even this splintering of Paul and Christianity into pieces. The scope of the text now came through the artificial method of finding four senses of meaning,[64] rather than "the certain and, what is the same thing, plainest [meaning], according to the figures of grammarians and rhetoricians, just as Erasmus advises in his Method...."[65] Here Melanchthon introduced a supporting argument that had not been typical of his earlier positions. The event of inspiration itself entailed belief in something like the literary premises that he described. "...Scripture was not put forth that it be misunderstood; nay, rather, the benevolent Spirit of God, who is light, intended that it be understood commonly by all pious men...."[66]

His logic was that the event of inspiration by God implied a revelatory intent, and this intent implied (on the assumption of God as "light") clarity of the sort that all "pious" people could apprehend. What better vehicle for clarity was there than that of classical *oratio* as Melanchthon defined it? The question did not arise as to how the opposing theologies of Erasmus and Luther could have arisen from similar methodological commitments to the plain sense of the text. It seems Melanchthon believed that adoption of his method would in the end bring to the controversies the sort of objectivity that would make it possible, even necessary, to resolve the differences and bring about a consensus between the warring parties. His comment that the objective truth of Scripture was known only by "pure minds,"[67] uncorrupted by philosophies which obscured the sense of Scripture, suggests that he harbored such dreams.

Several sections in the letter to Hess also reveal an intense conviction about the basic perspicuity of Scripture. The argument that the office of interpreting Scripture belonged only to the few simply did not hold. Once more, he appealed to the intentions of God, who had revealed Himself to the world. "Nay, rather, the benevolent Spirit of God intended this: that He might be understood by all pious men with as little difficulty as possible."[68] Thus, not only the "light" or truthfulness of God, but also His benignity or disposition toward the good was a ground for believing that Scripture was a clear book, not to be contorted into "Egyptian hieroglyphics."[69] And again he appealed to the logic underlying the act of incarnation on the part of Christ. "The Son of God came down in the flesh, lest He be unknown; how much more did He wish to be known through letters, which He left as an image of Himself that would endure forever?"[70] The act of the incarnation was motivated in part by the didactic concerns of a teacher. Hence, Christ exhorted His disciples to believe and to care for "His doctrine [*suam doctrinam*],"[71] implying that we must "give first place to sacred letters...."[72]

These passages from the *Declamatiuncula* and the letter to Hess show not only that Melanchthon asserted the peculiar, rhetorically shaped doctrine of biblical unity, but also that this coherent sense of Scripture was to him clearly evident. It is widely recognized that he stood among the many Protestant theologians who staunchly defended the principle of biblical perspicuity.[73] Nevertheless, we cannot agree with Fraenkel's statement that, for Melanchthon, Scripture was "'clear,' in the sense that God has clearly revealed these mysteries for us ...and has not left anything to our initiative to find out."[74] Nor can we agree with Breen that the meaning which one attains through proper theological method (using commonplaces) is "not to be found [*invenienda*] as a result of search; it is ready at hand in Scripture and needs only to be selected, arranged, defined and so on."[75] Melanchthon's concept of biblical perspicuity was contingent upon a series of complex commitments. The *sensus* of Scripture as a whole was not *perspicuous* to one until one had an adequate grasp of Paul's method. And Paul's method was as daunting at first as it was complex. Moreover, one required this model of Scripture as a vast, unfolding literary tradition, in which the Pauline *scopus* appeared clearly only when one recognized the interplay between various kinds of texts. It seems that there was no "royal road" that went straight to the sense of Scripture, but only this rhetorical one. It was true, as Fraenkel wrote, that for Melanchthon the perspicuity of Scripture was "an aspect of divine grace,"[76] but this was grace executed by means of processes analogous to those which operated between a classicist, his books and the human realities of the universe. Once again, the differences between Melanchthon and a Quenstedt or a Gerhard are quite profound on the human level of things. [77]

No doubt, all these hermeneutical-epistemic commitments could be squared with a carefully qualified doctrine of perspicuity. One could argue that the coherent, literal sense of Scripture was clearly evident to all those who had access to Paul, interpreted him rightly and had a grasp of how his texts functioned in the aforesaid rhetorical manner. However, this approach would seem self-defeating, since the lucidity of Scripture is tied to a literary application that is known only to a few scholars, and only in recent times, at that. Aside from the fact that even they failed to agree on *what* was perspicuous about Scripture, one may wonder about the grace and light of God during the hundreds of years when such literary theories and applications were obfuscated by allegories and Aristotle. And, of course, there is the canonical manner of texts, both pre-Christian and Christian, which contain the Word of God in its redemptive sense "too obscurely" to be of help by themselves. Difficulties here are related to those involved in sustaining the unity of Scripture through Paul's *inventio*. Philip had not yet, as he would to some degree do in the *Loci communes* of 1521, come to substantial answers to such questions.

And what of Melanchthon's own setting, the horizon of his own readers and the actual force of his remarks to Hess about giving Scripture back to the Christians? He seems to have believed that replacing contemporary linguistic models with Ciceronian ones was to deliver the text from the interpreter's "own manner" and to secure it objectively in itself, purely and simply. Had he not badly underestimated the extent to which this involved an act of interpretation on the part of Lutherans, and overestimated the extent to which adopting a theology was simply a matter of employing the right method in the right way? Again, how did he account for Catholic humanism? Was this for him simply an anomaly, or a wrinkle that properly reasoned exegesis would eventually iron out? If there was a sense in which Melanchthon was unusually "ecumenical" for his time, it was in part because of an epistemic realism in this facet of his hermeneutics. And, again, a doctrine of perspicuity grounded in method, rather than in the fideistic response to the Spirit, must feel the pressure to modify and change in the course of rational negotiation. Melanchthon may have been largely fideistic on the epistemological matter of recognizing the truth-value of Paul's biblical doctrine, but not on the hermeneutical matter of its content and proper function within the canon, for these were to be secured through reason and method, or at very least by recognizing the reason and method employed by Paul himself.

In conclusion, he wrote that the reader must beware the methods of contemporary theology[78] and know that "apart from Paul's doctrine, it was impossible to know Christ exactly...."[79] Not merely knowledge, but the force of that knowledge, its power to console, came through the uniquely powerful rhetoric of the apostle.

> The power to comfort the soul and to meditate on Christ as your own [Christum tuum meditari]..., the power to be cheered; the oration is full of charms, [it is] pure, sinewy, elegant, polished, clear [oratio est plena illecebris, pura, nervosa, elegans, nitida, plana].... Here you have an argument [argumentum] which you can compare with the philosophers, one in which you may accuse the theologians of this age.... You have, also, that by which you may discuss the many remaining mysteries [de quibus disseras reliqua mysteria pleraque]....[80]

In this final passage of the Declamatiuncula on Paul, one has a view of the various lines of Melanchthon's complex concept of biblical authority as sacred and rhetorical. In spite of our critical remarks, it must also be said that he thus championed something much more estimable than a mere "theology of definitions." The young Melanchthon aimed early on at supplying his age with a sure evidential-textual foundation for the Lutheran viewpoint, showing this to be the clear sense of the whole Bible, and thus to be the truth. "Showing" here involved reasoning, demonstratio rather than mere indicatio. "Clarity" was thus contingent upon the propriety of the noetic relationship between Christian and text. The strength of his approach was that theologies could be weighed against the letter of the text, and people on both sides saw this as a contribution and an improvement over medieval hermeneutics. His weakness was in a tendency to think (unlike Luther) that this was theology, and that the history of theology could be controlled through exegetical perfection. Melanchthon's initial concepts of biblical unity, diversity and perspicuity thus remind us of the complex social and intellectual history of which his life and work was but one important expression.

Scripture and Church Tradition

In the letter to John Hess, Philip mainly defended the line of reasoning which he had pursued in the Baccalaureate Theses, particularly in reference to the controversial assertions about transubstantiation and the authority of church traditions that had no clear biblical warrant. One will recall that these statements had made him vulnerable to Eck's accusation that the whole faculty of Wittenberg had become heretical.[81] The document gives one a rather detailed view of how Melanchthon applied his idea of biblical authority to the element of extra-biblical Catholic tradition. What is intriguing here is the way in which his Lutheran sense of the "difference" of Scripture magnified the force of his pre-Lutheran commitment to sola scriptura on logical and empirical grounds. Melanchthon thus exemplified not merely the more obvious sort of continuity that existed between certain strands of Northern European humanism and the Reformation, but also that which Oberman has identified between the basic assumptions of Protestants and certain late medieval doctors of theology. Melanchthon's earliest Lutheran idea of biblical authority indicates how he was himself a microcosm of the historical forces and revolutionary intellectual syntheses which produced the Protestant mind.

The letter to Hess explained to the public that he, Melanchthon, had derived his critique of transubstantiation from two premises which he now undertook to prove true. The first was that only articles approved by Scripture were "catholic,"[82] the second, that the authority of councils was inferior to that of Scripture itself.[83] On examining transubstantiation, he wrote, "...I was seeing that everywhere the authority of sacred letters was diminished by human decrees; human [decrees] were not only made equal to the divine, but preferred to them...."[84] Even the ancient Greeks knew better than to ignore this essential distinction between divine and human authority. "Plato wrote that there was an Egyptian law that no new song be received among the sacred ones [*ne quod in sacra novum carmen reciperetur*]."[85] Of how much greater concern to forbid "that doctrine of sacred things, divinely produced, whose author is the very Son of God, be changed by the traditions of human commentaries."[86] Melanchthon's views rested mainly on appeal to the divine authorship of Scripture. The divine origin of the text implied, for him, an exclusive authority. Since Scripture alone had this divine origin in the revelatory acts of God, it alone had universal authority over Christians. But why make this initial claim about the exclusivity of Scripture as a divinely given authority? Why exclude the possibility of other divinely inspired truths, such as those which appeared in the later traditions of the church? Oberman has shown that a doctrine of *sola scriptura* was not the original property of Protestantism, but that it was basic to a reforming Catholic tradition among people like Brivicoxia, Wyclif, Hus, Gansfort and Gerson.[87] Their reasoning was not quite that of the humanistic historical judgment *primum et verum*, which Fraenkel rightly noted as one of Melanchthon's principles.[88] It was rather that of the dialectical judgment (with its intense method of discrimination) *divinum solum et verum*. The ontological status of Scripture as divine revelation, supported by better understanding of many biblical texts than had been possible before (and thus of the discrepancies between Scripture and tradition on some critical teachings),[89] implied the doctrine of exclusivity.[90] The development of Melanchthon's concept of "Tradition I" was perhaps not unlike that of his predecessors: a deeply ingrained dialectical sense of discrimination, improved understanding of the literal sense of Scripture as a coherent whole and growing awareness of need for a standard of judgment and criticism with respect to the history of the extra-biblical tradition combined to form the basic premise of exclusivity.[91] This premise, as we have seen, Melanchthon carried with him to Wittenberg and his destiny with Martin Luther. The freshly developed theology of grace and justification, with its correlative doctrine of human depravity, gave new semantical and affective power to the term *sola scriptura*. He wrote of his previous training in theology as a kind of "shipwreck," which he had survived only by recovering the delights of sacred writ.

I appeal to you, Hess, you who have navigated the unhappy ocean of questions; now, as it were, having recovered from shipwreck, in safety you have enjoyed the delights of divine letters. What do you think of the counterfeit schools and human traditions? Do you not seem to yourself now to be in another world? [*Nonne in alio nunc tibi mundo esse videris?*] Does not the Spirit of Christ form you differently from the way in which those schools once did? Do we not owe the destruction of Christianity and of sacred letters...to human doctrines?[92]

Melanchthon's point seems to have been that the exclusively divine authority of Scripture, besides being an inference from its inspired origin and the lack of same for extra-biblical tradition, was evident in the "difference" of its formative powers. He had dared to test things for himself and had discovered a new world of spiritual reality through his new interpretive method.

He confessed that he had once retreated from interpreting the sacred scriptures on his own,[93] but now, "This is my goal, that judgment of sacred things be taken from divine letters alone [*e solis divinis literis*], not from the determinations of men."[94] What about the claim that the Spirit of God protected holy councils from error?[95] The classification of Scripture as *divinum et primum* was not merely an empirically or logically derived principle, but a biblical one. In 2 Timothy, Paul made it clear that such perfection was given to the canonical writings alone.[96] On that basis, "We know that what is published in the canonical books is the doctrine of the Holy Spirit. We do not know that what is decreed by councils is of the Holy Spirit, unless it agrees with Scripture."[97] Moreover, to the Corinthians (1 Cor. 3:11) Paul wrote that there was no other foundation than the one which had already been laid; this foundation, to which nothing need be added, argued Melanchthon, was "canonical doctrine [*canonicae doctrinae*]."[98] He concluded the letter to Hess: "Scripture has been divinely produced; it is, as I use Paul's word, a pattern [*hypotyposis*] and exemplar of faith, against which it is fitting that councils decree nothing."[99]

In summary, then, the letter to Hess gives an expanded picture of how Melanchthon used the resources of his pre-Lutheran system to form a Protestant doctrine of biblical authority. In his own style, he systematically combined the concerns of the principle *primum et verum* with those of the *divinum et verum* to form a doctrine of exclusivity. Scripture alone was of divine origin and weight, the final standard and measure of doctrine and practice. One could not only not contradict Scripture; the doctrine of exclusivity meant that one could not add to it either (for that would be, in principle, to contradict its logic and nature as revelation in a fallen world, and even its occasional claims about itself). We have seen that the force of this formal position was strengthened by what he now judged was the demonstrable unity and power of its message. With respect to the conciliar and confessional extra-biblical traditions of the church, there was very little ambiguity in his assertion of biblical exclusivity. Later controversies over *adiaphora* would not seem to have exposed logical changes in this early line of thinking, for he never claimed that all church practices must be derived from Scripture alone, but only that beliefs and practices that were universally binding must be so derived.

Notes to Chapter 9

1. Cf. *MW* I, p. 26, on this event.
2. *Ibid.*, pp. 27ff., for the text of this oration.
3. *Ibid.*, pp. 43ff., for the text of this letter.
4. *CR* XI, pp. 34ff., for text and text-critical discussion; also *MB* I, p. 76.
5. H.-G. Geyer, *Von der Geburt des wahren Menschen*, Neukirchen 1965, p. 13. Geyer was the first to make the connection between the theology of these writings and the rhetorical concept of *doctrina* within Melanchthon's humanism. Our own independent research has come to similar conclusions, which we have developed in the context of the Preceptor's concept of biblical authority and the larger historiographical question of faith and reason.
6. *MW* I, p. 27.27ff., "Suscipies igitur non modo orationis nostrae, sed omnino sacrarum literarum...patrocinium...."
7. *Ibid.*, pp. 26f.
8. *Ibid.*, p. 28.2f.
9. *Ibid.*, p. 28.32ff.
10. *Ibid.*, p. 29.10ff.
11. *Ibid.*, p. 29.13ff., "Reliquis enim ornamentis ipse privatim fruitur, doctrinae vero fructus noster est."
12. Cf. above, chapter 4, on this rhetorical *locus*.
13. *MW* I, p. 29.24ff.
14. *Ibid.*, p. 29.33ff., "...sed quae salutis viam, quae rationem absolutae felicitatis monstrant, eae demum ab omnibus expeti iure debent."
15. *Ibid.*, pp. 29.35-30.1ff.
16. *Ibid.*, p. 30.5ff.
17. *Ibid.*, p. 30.34ff.
18. *Ibid.*, p. 32.7ff.
19. *Ibid.*, p. 32.11ff.
20. Cf. chapter 11.
21. *MW* I, pp. 33.38-34.1ff.
22. *Ibid.*, p. 34.8ff., "philosophy"—quotation marks ours.
23. *Ibid.*, p. 34.26.
24. *Ibid.*, p. 34.26ff.
25. *Ibid.*, p. 35.2ff.
26. *Ibid.*, p. 35.11ff.
27. *Ibid.*, p. 37.13ff.
28. *Ibid.*, p. 41.12ff.
29. *CR* XI, p. 36.
30. *Ibid.*
31. *Ibid.*
32. *Ibid.*, p. 37, "Siquidem sermo maximi Patris Christus est."
33. *Ibid.*, "Non alia ratione Christum certius expresserint animi nostri, quam sacrae doctrinae studio, in qua illius velut in speculo relucet imago."
34. *Ibid.*, pp. 38f.
35. *Ibid.*, p. 39.
36. *MW* I, p. 30.8ff., "In numero divinorum voluminum, alia leges, alia vitae morumque exempla, alia obscura de Christo vaticinia, alia res Christi gestas memorant."
37. *Ibid.*, p. 30.10ff., "Beneficium vero, quod sanguine suo Christus universo peperit orbi, quis gravius? quis accuratius? quis copiosius divo Paulo explicat?"

38. *Ibid.*, p. 30.14ff.

39. *Ibid.*, p. 30.17f., "...nempe absolutae virtutis exemplar...."

40. *Ibid.*, p. 30.18ff., "...sed multo maximum est, quae vera est gloria Christi, quare is in terram delapsus sit, quid mundo sermonis aetherni incarnatio conducat, scire...."

41. *Ibid.*, p. 30.21, "...in eo summa salutis posita est."

42. *Ibid.*, p. 30.37ff., "Tantum referebat et legibus per Mosen promulgatis, et vatum oraculis, et historiis addi Paulinas epistolas...."

43. *Ibid.*, pp. 30.39-40.1ff.

44. *Ibid.*, p. 31.1-4.

45. *Ibid.*, p. 31.5ff., "...peculiariter e Paulo cognoscimus *rationem* ac *vim* beneficii Christi...."

46. *Ibid.*, p. 31.11ff., "Siquidem Christum novisse non modo est res eius gestas tenere, sed grato animo beneficium complecti, quod per ipsum coelestis pater in universum terrarum orbem effudit...."

47. *Ibid.*, p. 31.14ff., "...quo solo inter impias gentes et vere Christianos animos internoscitur."

48. *Ibid.*, p. 31.20ff., "Bonitatem suam...tam in Christo absolutissime expressit...."

49. *Ibid.*, p. 32.23ff., "Norant e secretis quibusdam oraculis hoc Christi beneficium patriarchae, quotquot servati sunt.... Idem et Prophetae canunt, hymnum pacis et novi sabbati *paiana.*"

50. *Ibid.*, pp. 32.30-33.1ff.

51. *Ibid.*, p. 33.15-29ff.

52. *Ibid.*, p. 33.35ff., "Meminerunt huius beneficii passim et reliqui sacri scriptores, sed obscurius, quam ut possent intelligi, nisi *universum argumentum* tot epistolis, tot *disputationibus* illustrasset Paulus."

53. *CR* XI, p. 35.

54. *Ibid.*, pp. 37f.

55. *Ibid.*, p. 38.

56. R. Preus, *The Inspiration of Scripture*, Edinburgh/London 1957, pp. 26ff., and many citations; and his suggestion of continuity with Melanchthon, p. ix.

57. *MW* I, p. 37.21f., "Posteaquam enim contempta huius doctrina Aristotelem complexae sunt...."

58. *Ibid.*, p. 37.22f., "...vix Christi nomen reliquum est...."

59. *Ibid.*, pp. 38.30-39.1.

60. *Ibid.*, p. 39.7.

61. *Ibid.*, p. 39.12ff.

62. *Ibid.*

63. *Ibid.*, p. 39.18ff.

64. *Ibid.*, p. 39.25ff.

65. *Ibid.*, p. 39.29ff., "...certa quaedam eademque simplicissima iuxta Grammaticorum et rhetorum figuras, perinde atque Erasmus in Methodo monet...." The reference is to Erasmus's *Ratio seu Methodus.*

66. *Ibid.*, p. 39, "Neque enim prodita scriptura est, ne intelligatur; immo hoc agebat benignus dei spiritus, qui lux est, ut ab omnibus piis communiter intelligeretur...."

67. *Ibid.*, p. 40.15, "Nam sacrae literae, ut per sese purae sunt, ita in puras infundi mentes amant."

68. *Ibid.*, p. 47.36f., "Immo hoc benignus dei spiritus agebat, ut omnibus piis quanto minimo negotio intelligeretur."

69. *Ibid.*, p. 48.1ff., "...ex divinis literis Agyptia hieroglypha fieri?"

70. *Ibid.*, p. 48.2ff., "Delapsus est in carnem dei filius, ne ignoraretur, quanto magis per literas cognosci voluit, quas ceu effigiem sui perpetuo duraturas nobis reliquit."

71. *Ibid.*, p. 48.17f.
72. *Ibid.*, p. 48.36f., "Primas itaque sacris literis damus."
73. Cf. P. Fraenkel, *Testimonia Patrum: The Function of the Patristic Argument in the Theology of Philipp Melanchthon*, Geneva 1961, pp. 208ff., esp. n. 4 and references.
74. *Ibid.*, p. 209.
75. Q. Breen, "The Terms Locus and Loci Communes in Melanchthon," *Christianity and Humanism: Studies in the History of Ideas*, (ed.) N. P. Ross, Grand Rapids 1968, p. 205.
76. P. Fraenkel, *op. cit.*, p. 209.
77. R. Preus, *op. cit.*, pp. 156ff.
78. *MW* I, p. 41.24f.
79. *Ibid.*, p. 41.37f.
80. *Ibid.*, p. 42.11f.
81. Above, chapter 5, and *MW* I, p. 23.
82. *MW* I, p. 44.15ff.
83. *Ibid.*
84. *Ibid.*, p. 44.32ff.
85. *Ibid.*, p. 46.30ff.
86. *Ibid.*, p. 46.33ff., "...ut doctrina sacrorum divinitus, ipsoque dei filio autore prodita, commenticiis hominum traditionibus mutaretur."
87. H. Oberman, *Forerunners of the Reformation*, Philadelphia (1965), 1981, pp. 53ff., 67ff.
88. P. Fraenkel, *op. cit.*, pp. 162ff. The author stresses this as perhaps the guiding logic of Melanchthon's argument for biblical primacy.
89. H. Oberman, *The Harvest of Medieval Theology*, Grand Rapids 1962, p. 374 and n. 40.
90. *Ibid.*, p. 378, and Oberman's intuition that Melanchthon represented methodological concerns that were not simply Erasmian, but larger in theological horizon, n. 48 and references.
91. *Ibid.*, pp. 277ff., for references to a similar pattern in Huss and Gerson.
92. *MW* I, p. 47.3ff.
93. *Ibid.*, p. 47.22f.
94. *Ibid.*, p. 47.26ff.
95. *Ibid.*, p. 49.14ff.
96. *Ibid.*, p. 49.19ff.
97. *Ibid.*, p. 49.20ff., "Scimus spiritus sancti doctrinam esse quae est canonicis libris prodita. Non scimus spiritus sancti esse, quod conciliis statuitur, nisi cum scriptura conveniat."
98. *Ibid.*, p. 49.27-35; Melanchthon appealed on these points to Augustine's writings against the Donatists, *ibid.*, pp. 50.14f., n. 15, in reference to *De Baptismo contra Donatistos*.
99. *Ibid.*, p. 51.19ff., "Divinitus prodita est scriptura, quae sit, ut Pauli verbo utar, hypotyposis ac exemplar fidei, contra quam conciliis nihil statuere fas est." Cf. 1 Tim. 1:16; 2 Tim. 1:13.

CHAPTER 10

Didymi Faventini adversus Thomam Placentium pro Martino Luthero Theologo Oratio

The great chess game between the papacy and the Lutheran insurgents came ever nearer to stalemate and trenchancy. Comprehensive reports on Luther, a series of commissions sponsored by the Curia and the devoted energies of Miltitz, Cajetan, Prierias and John Eck all combined to force Pope Leo X into action.[1] The resulting bull of excommunication, *Exsurge Domini*, carefully avoided mentioning Luther by name, and its distinction between what was actually heretical in his writings and what was simply offensive was calculated to give him some room to maneuver toward retraction with dignity.[2] However, on the most basic matters, the church remained intractable. If Huss had been a heretic, which he must have been, then so was Luther, since he agreed with Huss on the essential problem of authority. This Luther now freely admitted, but called the church under God to submit to Scripture and true tradition: "I have been teaching all that John Huss taught, unawares," he wrote; "...we are all Hussites, though we have not known it, even Paul and Augustine." In his spirit Luther had now broken with Rome, believing that Rome had broken with God. Six months later, shortly before Christmas, the university would gather around a huge bonfire, into which would be thrown papal decretals and the volumes of canon law. Finally, Luther would dramatically toss the papal bull itself into the flames, symbolizing the gravity of the matter. The symbolism of Philip's break with Rome was less inspirational than Luther's, but it was genuine. He posted a public notice, inviting the "pious young students" to "attend this pious drama," whereby "the Antichrist must be revealed."[3]

During these months, Luther had written some of his most stirring works, so that it seemed for a time that the entire German nation might be fused around him to form an irresistible power for independence of identity. It was precisely to quench such fires, and to gain support for the papal action, that Roman theologian Thomas Rhadinus wrote an essay entitled *Oratio ad principes et populos Germaniam in Martinum Lutherum nationis gloriam violantem*.[4] Rhadinus portrayed Luther as a barbarian, whose manic actions would inevitably bring Germany to ruin.[5] The idea was to sway the nobility, but also the opinions of academics like Erasmus, whose pens could wield a mighty influence, as they had during the Reuchlin affair.[6] In Wittenberg, the essay was mistakenly thought to have been written by Jerome Emser, secretary to Duke George of Saxony.[7] In an earlier pamphlet, Emser had fancied himself a Danielic figure, "the ram of Leipzig," who would see Luther chased out of the flock of God's people. That is why Philip's response is full of derogatory references to "the goat" (*Hircus*) as the adversary.

When Rhadinus's essay appeared, it must have seemed strategically shrewd for the grandnephew of Reuchlin to come out against it. The response was written, for some overcalculated reason, under the pseudonym Didymus Faventinus, even though everyone knew that Philip was its author.[8] Karl Sell called it "Melanchthon's first reformation writing."[9] It was certainly his most direct and comprehensive defense of Luther, and that in the ominous shadow of Worms, which was to convene in only a few weeks. When one contemplates all that has been written of Melanchthon's diffidence and even cowardice, one should call to mind that in Luther's hour of danger Philip came to his side with his sword drawn. One can be sure that Luther never forgot the honest bravery of his faithful friend. It was the rapier rather than the bludgeon that suited his style of combat, but combat it was, with all the deadly dangers thereof, and Philip stepped into it with little regard for his personal safety or reputation.

The attack on Luther covered a multitude of alleged sins. His views on scholastic theology and philosophy,[10] public magistrates,[11] indulgences and penance,[12] the Turkish wars[13] and the authority of the Roman pontiffs[14] all sufficed to back the papal judgment. Nearly half of Melanchthon's response was devoted to the delicate issue of philosophy and theological method. This section of the essay will help us to begin engaging the widely discussed historiographical matter of the values that guided Melanchthon's selection of theological topics. Profound questions emerge on Melanchthon's opinion about the nature and status of theological concepts. Did he operate by a principle of "double truth," so that some Christian concepts or *topoi*, such as the *mysteria coelestia*, simply violated logical norms? Was he in full agreement with Luther's theology of paradox? And, to raise a somewhat different question, was he acting on the instincts of an anthropocentric humanism that made him a precursor to the Kantian theology of a later age with its premise that human concepts do not apply at all to the nature of God, and with its thoroughly pragmatic approach to religious knowledge and truth? These issues arise in the context of Philip's acerbic rejection of speculative theology. Here we can develop a framework for the proposals that will receive systematic treatment in our final chapter.

A second major issue that arises for continued development is that of the literal sense of Scripture as a whole in relation to the doctrines of moral philosophy. In a main section of the essay, Melanchthon used his rhetorical idea of the *scopus caussae* to define the distinction or *discrimen* between philosophical and Christian thought on morals. Thus, besides being of value to seeing how he looked upon the internal logic of Christian topics and propositions, this is a work of considerable importance to seeing how the formation of a doctrine of *sola scriptura*, in the context of pagan ethics, had progressed. Here, again, we can build a framework for understanding his problematic language of the *discrimen* between Scripture and philosophy as entire paradigms of thought. To see the relation in his mind between the rhetorical concept of *scopus* and the literal theological *sensus* of the canon is essential to understanding both his approach to the logic of Christian concepts and his approach to natural law and the *ius gentium*.

The Logic of Christian Concepts

Melanchthon began by praising what he viewed as Luther's cautious, discriminating allegiance to the cause of philosophy.

> Luther does not condemn that part of philosophy which describes mathematics, the natures of stones, plants and animals. For he admits that knowledge of these things is necessary for sacred studies [*Nam horum cognitionem fatetur ad sacra necessariam esse*], and he is accustomed to use it in its place, whenever the topic requires it [*quoties res postulat*]; he approves, I say, the fruitful description of things…. In brief, Luther commends what has been…written about the nature of things [*collaudat Lutherus, quae de rerum natura…conscripta*].[15]

On the other hand, Luther had grave doubts about metaphysics, speculation about the non-empirical nature of things, their origins and meaning.

> He condemns, if you do not know it, that part of philosophy which invents strange nonsense about the principles of things [*quae de rerum principiis…prodigiosas nugas comminiscitur*], the causes of winds and rivers and, indeed, whatever it is that Aristotle calls…metaphysics…. [16]

Moreover, "he condemns whatever has been published by philosophers on morals."[17] Luther's opponents had demanded an explanation of these criticisms, and Melanchthon promised now to give one.[18]

It is fascinating to see how Melanchthon, with his peculiar philosophical-rhetorical vision, came to the defense of Luther's concept of revelation and his theology of the cross, with its underlying epistemic nominalism.[19] As we have sought to show, neither of these elements was entirely alien to the intuitions of the young Christian classicist, even with his strong passion for philosophy and ethics. Everything in his nature and rhetorical philosophy inclined him toward clean ontological and epistemic distinctions and toward a focus upon what was both a properly delimited object of cognition *and* was of central existential importance; in his own terms, this was *sermo proprius*. But the very energy that he spent systematically explaining this critique of reason was itself clear evidence of his concern that great care and responsibility be exercised, lest what was good about the human mind be denigrated. We do not believe that he was at any stage capable of simply dismissing the deliverances of metaphysics, as Luther would seem to have been. And it is obvious that, with his attack on human moral theory, he also felt a deep sense of obligation to explain himself to moral philosophers. On both counts, he felt obliged to manufacture a systematic definition of the relation between theology and non-Christian ontologies. And of course the need for systematic coherence on these questions was something that he felt deeply in his spirit. This disposition was very much a part of what made him the man that he was and set him apart from Luther. Even as he defended his older friend and agreed with his doctrines, the modes of Philip's propositions belied differences between their views of the world. The strand of realism in Melanchthon's epistemology and truth theory must have made it impossible for him not to resist the idea that truly illogical propositions (in either intensive or extensive senses) could also be true. And, in contrast to the regnant interpretation, we believe that this remained true of Philip even through the early Lutheran years, when he often sounded a little more like Luther than himself.

Thus, he began his treatment of the Christian and metaphysics with his usual criticism of contemporary theologians who permitted the speculative theories and vocabulary of Aristotle to replace "the oracles of heaven, namely, those in which He expresses Himself as in a relief."[20] He decried the widespread use of human concepts to carve into the very being of God.

> The ones whom they call metaphysicians write about God, about those things which are attributed to God by men: on [His] unity, intellect, will, simplicity.... From this [method] the factions of Thomists, Scotists, Occamists were born as if from a Demogorgean chaos. Here the great mass of theologians is divided into contrary studies..., while each asserts his own dogma. [21]

Melanchthon explained his criticism. What these "Aristotelian" theologians have written about God's nature was not simply inappropriate, but was at its core the expression of an irreligious spirit. "First,...it is irreligious [*irreligiosem esse*] to dispute in a juvenile manner [*juveniliter digladiari*] about the divine majesty and about the things which are properly attributed to Him...."[22] He even insinuated that it was perhaps a Faustian lust, rather than a merely human quest for truth, that lured men to go beyond their proper human boundaries into regions where they would surely die the death of spiritual arrogance. "...I am not entirely certain that it ought to be attributed to a human curiosity that we search out mysteries hidden and unapproachable by creatures [*quod abscondita illa et inadita creaturis mysteria quaerimus*]."[23]

Here we behold Melanchthon giving his own expression to Luther's theology of the cross and its epistemic value system. "God desired indeed to be known, but in order to be known He came down in the flesh, nay rather, He was made flesh."[24] Philip looked upon this act of incarnation as pointing to the epistemic values that we have been describing.

> For, since that immense majesty could not be comprehended, He put on that person which the human mind, in one way or another, was able to understand; for the common opinion of the fathers was that those who had seen God would not survive.[25]

The majesty of God was immense, unapproachable; one could not survive in its presence. For Melanchthon, the incarnation would seem to have been an event that affirmed the epistemic value of *finitio* and intensive coherence of terms, but which also burst the canons of logic into pieces. Whether this was quite so remains to be discussed. Nevertheless, he professed great sympathy for Paul's confession that it pleased God to be known through foolishness rather than wisdom. [26]

At this point, Melanchthon put his rhetorical concept of the *scopus* to use in trying to picture the proper way of reading God's purpose in clothing Himself with human flesh.

> Christ has been proposed to us as a *scopus* upon whom the human mind could successfully fix its eyes. When we despise this *scopus*, about to fly upwards to heaven, it is inevitable that reason be imperiled, that it wander like a vagabond. That is what we see to have happened to that race of theologians, when each imagines for God a new form, who, though He is the simplest of beings, has been so dissected by opinions that Proteus among the poets is not more variously put forward.[27]

To have said that in Christ God gave us a *scopus*, particularly when one considers Melanchthon's individual use of that term, now seems a somewhat different thing from saying that in Christ God gave us a logical paradox, or that this event implied that human concepts in no wise apply to the nature of God. A change of one's scope does not always mean that other objects are in themselves beyond description, nor that one ought never to talk about them, but only that one has shifted the focus to first-order objects of knowledge, to the *loci causae* that are at the heart of the matter. Whatever his purpose, it is an essential part of the received historiography to interpret Melanchthon's mature doctrine of God (from the 1530s on) as a major deviation from the norms and practices of his earliest teaching. But what did he mean to say when he completed the thought of this section on the majesty of God by writing these words, seldom, if ever, cited in the discussion?

> But as I grant that it is a pious thing to investigate those incomprehensible mysteries, it is certainly impious and perilous to attempt such a thing by human cleverness rather than by the divine scriptures....[28]

What was pious about investigating the sacred mysteries? What was it to investigate them? In what sense exactly were they incomprehensible? And what is one to make of his distinction between such examination either by the perilous route of using reason alone, or by the divine scriptures? It would seem that, just as he could unabashedly assert the simplicity of God as a property of His nature, once the proper *scopus* had been located, the possibility remained of moving outwards toward the limits of theological discourse, even to investigation of the *mysteria coelestium*.

The logical problem for theology was not only in the transcendence of God. It was also in the limitations of a human mind that was both creaturely and fallen: "...since both nature and reason stand in dread of this light, and indeed the mind of man is otherwise never consistent with itself, so that not even a chameleon is more changeable."[29] The inability of the human mind fully to explain the divine nature had often led to atheism. The Stoics, Democritus and the Epicureans all fell into this titanic trap.[30] "Your Aristotle, O 'Goat,' is an atheist, with whom as your leader, you wage war against heaven. O Titanic arrogance!"[31]

This "war against heaven" was an assault of unsuitable concepts and language upon the divine being:

> These [philosophers] were following the methods of human reason [*Sequebantur hi rationis humanae methodos*]; they were seeking after that "immensity" [*immensum illud*] which they heard was called "God" by their forefathers. Now, since they could not comprehend it, as the Apostle says, they were made vain by disputation. Among these things are those demonstrations of yours [*illae vestrae apodeixes*] on infinity, on the unity of God, on divine knowledge, on fate, on contingencies and on other questions of this kind....

> ...I am not accusing now the barbarism of the "theologists" [*Non accuso iam Theologastrorum barbariem*], nor that unskilled and confused sophism, which no one of sound mind would approve, but that very wisdom of language [*sed illam ipsam sapientiam sermonis*]; I accuse, I say, that by which alone you seem to yourselves to excel in Christian matters, by which you call Christian minds away from the scriptures to reasons [*qua Christianas mentes a scripturis ad rationes revocastis*], by which

you wrest the sword of the spirit from the hands of the simple [*gladium spiritus e manibus simplicium extorsistis*]....[32]

It is not altogether clear what doctrines Melanchthon had in mind when he wrote these words. The dominant thought, though, was that improper rational methods were applied to God, something that elevated men above God. Their concept of God was an idol, not the true God. "Since that race of theologians lacks [Christ] as its guide, what opinions, what portents, nay rather what idols has it not imagined [*quae non idola confingit*]?"[33] How different from these theological vanities, wrote Melanchthon, was the "doctrine of the Spirit, another certain light, by which the darkness of our minds is wont to be divinely dispersed."[34] In closing this section of the essay, he appealed to his audience to consider what an unchristian thing it was "to refer the divine mysteries to philosophical reasons...."[35]

Somewhat later in the essay, Melanchthon again took up this line of criticism, singling out the Thomistic tradition as the main culprit, but also pointing to deficiencies in Occam and his followers. His comments seem to support our earlier judgment that his earliest loyalties in religion were more with the epistemic-linguistic and practical engagement of Steinbach's nominalism than they were with the methods of Jacob Lemp and realism. He placed "Hircus" in a long line of people who had used Thomistic methods, which he portrayed as a colossal failure: "You attribute solid learning to Thomas, while the dogmas of no one are more contradictory [*inter se pugnant*]."[36] Melanchthon then punned on the name of Duns Scotus that the term "dark" befitted his writings.[37] Albert the Great, too, was a great barbarian. In Cicero's words, "in the whole corpus, there is not one grain of salt."[38] The general problem in this school was its application of reason to the mysteries of God. Giving a preview of things to come in the *Loci communes* of 1521, Philip concluded, "it was not to the advantage of Christianity to summon those sublime mysteries of divinity to the standards of reason."[39]

> They say, "we have forced philosophy to be the handmaid of theology," while in philosophizing they destroy the gospel. They say, "we have tried to make the human intellect captive in obedience to Christ." What is it that I hear? Does Christ occupy a mind which approves nothing but what human reason attains?[40]

In terms that would one day become controlling ideas in his dogmatic theology, and would come to be associated as much as any others with his name and place in the history of theology, he concluded his critique of Thomism. "The sublime mysteries of the trinity, of providence, of the incarnation want to be worshipped and believed, not to be penetrated by human reason."[41]

Moreover, Melanchthon professed that he had once held Occam in high esteem, but certain criticisms now emerged.

> Even you, Occam, once our delight [*deliciae quondam nostrae*], what did you mean when you were arguing that neither

Scripture, nor reason, nor experience testifies that grace is necessary for justification? You know, I think, your own dogma.[42]

It is impossible to know just which texts in Occam Melanchthon was thinking about, much less whether he had fairly interpreted them. Nevertheless, the central thought was not so much that Occam had failed consciously to separate between the being of God and the rational concepts of men, but that his doctrine of justification had broken down in some fateful manner. Within the Lutheran paradigm which Melanchthon now defended, the distinction between faith and reason was quintessentially dependent upon a right doctrine of grace, rather than works, as the core of our salvation. This was the central intuition of the *sensus literalis* and, thus, of the *discrimen* between Scripture as revelation and everything else as merely human. Here the critique reminds one of Philip's bewilderment in response to Erasmus, who used right methods but came, oddly, to the wrong conclusions. Occam's school may have used judicious language, but it had failed in the end to see what Luther, Melanchthon and others believed that they saw clearly in the text.

In summary, let us consider briefly the idea of biblical authority that was behind this critique of theologians. It is obvious that Melanchthon held a strong view of God's transcendence, that this was magnified epistemically by his Lutheran view of man, that he was incapable of a strong realism in theology (at least with respect to the being of God) and that he was greatly troubled by the philosophical theology of the schools. His language at times verged on an affirmation of the view that God is beyond our puny concepts altogether. But would Melanchthon have wanted to put it quite that way? Was there not a rather different controlling logic to his criticisms from that of a precursory Kantianism? Was he not motivated less by a theory of double truth in the strongly nominalistic sense than by the rhetorical notion that, in Christ, God the Father had given humanity a *scopus* of His self-expression? His basic approach to divine revelation was to imagine it as exhibiting the patterns of proper *inventio* and *dispositio*. As an interpreter of God's *oratio*, one's first and most essential obligation was to locate the *scopus* and *loci* which were of the highest hermeneutical magnitude. That is not to deny our own point about Philip's dispositional religious nominalism, but one must take care not to ignore his creational realism, either. Unless Melanchthon was in fundamental contradiction within himself, this rhetorical vision of revealed truth enabled him to give some (we are not saying how much) room to a "pious investigation" of the mysteries. As he put it, such an investigation would be guided "by the divine scriptures." In his terms, Scripture as *oratio sacra* gave place to the theological intuitions of both nominalism and realism, first the one, but then the other, also. As we read him, it seems that Melanchthon's leading concern was not that theologians had used human concepts to form a doctrine of God, but that they had failed miserably in their initial *ordering* of theological topics and concepts. Ignoring the *scopus* (and, thus, the heart of the matter), they flew to heaven with their axioms, predicates and doctrines. Had they first considered the doctrine of justification by grace alone, perhaps a pious, no doubt more deeply humble and cautious, investigation of the mysteries would have been possible. While sounding strongly nominalistic in this essay, particularly under the influence of Luther's personality and the (in his view) abysmal state of things in theology, Melanchthon's views on the logic of Christian concepts seem still in a process of formation. Clearest is his ringing call for a proper beginning in the proper "places," putting "first things first." With respect to the specific question of the logic of Christian propositions, his biases were very much with those of Luther, but, in systematic terms, he had not yet found his way into the clear as to how to apply *all* his principles regarding truth and knowledge to his new religious consciousness. Our judgment, here, finds support in his treatment of philosophical ethics, to be discussed below.

Christian Doctrine and Moral Truth

Melanchthon's greatest concern in *Didymi Faventini* was that readers approach Scripture in the right hermeneutical context, by beginning where it began and with what set its teaching apart from every other authority. "The part of philosophy which shapes morals must be discussed here, whence you may understand not a little more clearly how philosophy and human reason disagree with Christian doctrine [*quam non conveniat philosophiae aut humanae rationi cum Christiana doctrina*]."[43] The metaphysical issue was important, but the problem of ethics was the matter that weighed most heavily upon him.

> For I condemn metaphysical theories, since I judge it of much peril to measure heavenly mysteries by the standards of our reason. [I condemn] *ethics*, however, because these plainly contradict Christ.... I do not argue, here, "peril," but rather deplore a present calamity....[44]

Confusion between philosophical and biblical concepts of God was perilous, but mixing the ethical teachings of Scripture with those of the philosophers was to obscure Christ Himself.

> Nor indeed is this simply sin; but immediately after the ethics of philosophers were received, one from the other, as it usually happens, error was born, indeed—O horrible darkness!—the entire doctrine of Christ was obscured.[45]

Melanchthon thus devoted the rest of the essay to the purpose of showing more precisely than in any previous writing the distinctions between the biblical *loci morales* on law, sin and grace and their counterparts in philosophy.

> As I see it, there are three supreme *loci morales* in Christian doctrine. They are law, sin and grace. Everything that can be said about vices, virtues...[etc.] is taken from these as from a fountain.

> They [modern teachers] have weighed these *loci* according to
> philosophical dogmas, and in discussing...moral life they have
> been devoted to this only: that the Spirit, the divine author of
> Scripture, must always agree with Aristotle.[46]

He treated each of these first-order concepts individually and systematically
with respect to philosophy.

Law

Melanchthon used three arguments to show that biblical conceptions of law
could not be reconciled with philosophy. First, he argued, to reveal something
implied that it had been hidden; God revealed the law. Therefore, the law must
have been hidden before it was revealed: "...why, I ask, was there need for
divine laws, if reason was teaching the same things?"[47] Melanchthon could not
have meant to say here that God's law had nothing in common with pagan
morality, since he explicitly affirmed this common conceptual ground
throughout the essay and elsewhere generally. The point was that the concept
of revelation implied a dialectic of some kind between these two realms of
legislation. Precisely what kind of dialectic this was remained to be stated.
Nevertheless, because the event of divine revelation itself implied an
antithesis of some sort, an ignorance of some dimension on the part of unaided
reason, the two could not simply be intermingled. "If they are in conflict
[*diversa*], why have you mixed them into theology [*cur admiscuistis
Theologiae*]?"[48]

A second argument was empirical: one needed only to look at the morals
taught by philosophers to see the disagreement between biblical and pagan
ethics.

> Divine law commands that we love our enemies; reason
> [commands] that we hate them.... Divine law says that we act well
> towards everyone; reason denies that good should be done to
> anyone but those who repay..., as Hesiod commands.... There are
> certain impulses of the soul [*motus animi*] with which reason
> flatters itself, such as those by which it is born to "glory," or to
> that false "tranquillity of spirit," which Democritus called
> *euthumias*, others *analgesia*.[49]

The dialectic was thus between deep underlying construals of reality, between
paradigmatic structures. His critique of moral reason had to do with what he
considered a certain lack of grace in pagan ethics, and also a manner of pride
that was inconsistent with biblical principles. A third kind of argument
emerged. The dialectic or difference between them was rooted in conflicting
teleologies: "...what a war there is with these in divine law, which ceaselessly
reproaches this depravity of human nature."[50] False premises about human

nature and moral reality attached themselves to moral laws. Such laws were merely moral justification for what was in reality wickedness.

Quite aside from clearly observable contradictions, however, Melanchthon made the point that any construal of law that was rooted in false beliefs about human nature and the moral universe was itself in some way false. One might say that, for Melanchthon, when there was empirical agreement between divine and human law, there was still this fundamental disagreement between two paradigms, the one essentially self-justifying, the other inseparable from the doctrines of sin and grace. His theory of meaning or sense in relation to that of one's essential *scopus* would enable him coherently to affirm the empirical truth of a moral precept, while at the same time to construe it as paradigmatically false, as "lies and darkness." The lie was not in the proposition itself, but in its deeper sense, in its paradigmatic goal of contributing to one's perfection through self-discipline.

Thus, Melanchthon placed the sense of biblical law in an inseparable relation to the *loci* of sin and grace and to proper knowledge of oneself and God. Without a context of correct self-knowledge, and of the divine response, law absorbed false meaning from the self-justifying *loci* that emerged naturally from depraved people. Thus, part of the meaning of biblical law was that "the law does not justify, but condemns and drives us to Christ." Melanchthon believed that, by failing to see this distinction and carelessly adopting pagan ethics into the Christian family, theologians had naively adopted a world view which obscured Christ. In spite of all appeals to Christian language, they created a state of affairs in which "you cannot distinguish Christianity from Judaism."[51] Melanchthon made this argument from the *scopus* or aim of the law clearer in the related discussions of sin and grace.

Sin and Grace

"On the subject of sin, the gospel does not agree with philosophy...."[52] The source of disagreement was clear: "...philosophy reckons the most despicable evils in place of the best virtues."[53] Once again, it seems that Melanchthon's point was not on the level of straightforward conceptual conflict between assertions, but between construals of moral reality. Moral philosophy itself was erected on the premise that ethics depended upon proper ontology, and it rightly instructed us that ethical beliefs, if they are true, must follow upon a correct understanding of human nature.

> Plato, whom you, "Goat," worship as some divinity,...judges that the *summa* of philosophy is contained in that Delphic opinion *gnothi se auton*, and that philosophy clearly is the method of knowing the self....[54]

Once again, we observe how Melanchthon's appeal to philosophy in support of his critique of moral reason implied that the common ground between revelation and philosophy went deeper into his Christian paradigm than he perhaps knew. Nevertheless, as elsewhere, he insisted that philosophers, and the theologians who followed them, had missed the mark or essential *scopus*, whereas Scripture had hit upon it to perfection. The language here is comparative.

> How much more correctly, as in a mirror [*ceu in speculo*],...may we contemplate ourselves in divine letters, which alone place us clearly before our own eyes. For how philosophy fails to offer what it promises, I think, is well known, since it shuts its eyes to certain horrible vices.[55]

Melanchthon's point was not merely that philosophers frequently approved the wrong moral values, but, more deeply, once again, that philosophical ethics emerged within an idea of moral reality which was paradigmatically off the mark.

> I am not saying, only, how Aristotle approves shameful acts, first in his *Ethics* and then in his *Politics* ..., but am complaining that certain tacit vices of souls [*tacita quaedam animorum vitia*] have been approved by human reason and by all philosophy....[56]

The crucial concept was the radical biblical idea of *peccatum*, sin, in contrast to philosophical theory on the imperfections of humans.

> Only with the help of divine letters could one avoid this fatal error. Divine letters consider the very nature of man to be corrupt [*vitiosam esse*]. Philosophers and their followers, the scholastics, deny that anything more absurd can be imagined. Divine letters condemn whatever affections of concupiscence you will [*quosvis concupiscentiae adfectus damnant*]. These are counted, for the most part, by philosophers and pseudo-theologians among things indifferent [*in mediis rebus*], that is, among those things which deserve neither the name of virtue, nor of vice. Furthermore, divine letters place the universal forms of sin plainly before our eyes; philosophy deceives the human mind, as with a juggler's tricks, lest it see its own sicknesses.[57]

Philip advanced what had become the Augustinian-Lutheran view that human nature was not only imperfect and fallen, but was itself morally evil, so that the very propensities of men must merit their damnation. The moral agent was not distinct (say, by virtue of his lack of freedom) from his moral nature; one's moral identity was not mere corruption, but *peccatum*, sin. Therein was a wholesale critique of the philosophical paradigm as Melanchthon knew it and the foundation for the terrible doctrine of predestination by decree. It would be some time before he would work out the moral and logical intricacies of that doctrine to the satisfaction of *all* of his principles. For the moment, he was driven to show that to fail to appreciate the gravity of biblical *peccatum* invariably obscured the relationship between biblical law and grace. Once this absolutely basic distinction had been made, however, he would make the adjustments which he deemed necessary to a genuinely moral universe.

He turned next to the subject of grace, the third in this essential triad of doctrines which constituted the *scopus* of Christianity.

> There remains the third *locus*, "grace," as they call it.... Philosophers believe that perfect virtue in man is produced by discipline [*adsuetudine*]; on the contrary, divine letters teach that everything human is polluted by sin [*humana omnia polluta esse peccato*], nor are they cleansed except by the Spirit, whom Christ merited for the human race. Philosophers attribute everything to the powers of human nature; divine letters deprive them of everything in creating perfect and genuine virtue.[58]

Scholastic theology was pagan moral philosophy dressed in biblical language. Instead of grace, the teachers of the age taught "that virtue can be acquired by human powers, that the Spirit is added on..., after we have purged ourselves by our own strength [*nostro Marte purgatis*]...."[59] Melanchthon concluded: "By which dogma, who does not see that Christ has been entirely obscured, whom divine letters exhibit [*exhibeant*] as the author of a good spirit and [as the] purifier of human minds...."[60]

Melanchthon, no doubt, represented the positions of contemporary theologians too simplistically and thus unfairly. The doctrine of grace in the Catholic church in Luther's time and earlier has been the subject of much recent discussion.[61] Moreover, it seems that he remained untroubled (theoretically) by the positive intuitions that defined classical philosophy. He would never offer a systematic mechanism (such as "common grace") to explain the occurrence of such wisdom as that of Socrates on knowledge of the self. In our view, Lutheran doctrine never spoiled his love for the creation and true *humanitas*.[62] At any rate, we must not miss the overall shape of his argument, which was framed by his rhetorical idea of the *scopus* as the biblical *status*, or sense of the whole. The sense of the biblical law was determined by its relation to sin and grace. Law existed hermeneutically in the context of this biblical ontology, wherein human beings were mightily depraved and vitiated, but God was gracious nonetheless. The relevant point for us is that Melanchthon viewed the *loci* of law, sin and grace as a single *locus didacticus* (as he had earlier described it) or *status causae*, which constituted the *scopus* of divine revelation. Just as it had given him some freedom to deploy a Christian metaphysics, this rhetorical theory of meaning also gave him a certain flexibility in developing a powerful critique of moral reason without denying obvious parallels between biblical and pagan ethical tradition. How this last observation contributes to one's assessment of him on the subject of natural theology remains for our final chapter.

Notes to Chapter 10

1. See *The Cambridge Modern History*, Vol. II, New York 1907, pp. 134ff., for a useful summary.

2. See E. G. Rupp, *Luther's Progress to the Diet of Worms*, New York/Evanston 1964, pp. 80ff.

3. Cited in R. Stupperich, *Melanchthon*, (tr.) R. H. Fischer, Philadelphia 1965, p. 42.

4. *MW* I, p. 56, published in August of 1520.

5. Cf. *SM* VI, pp. 116ff.; *CR* I, pp. 212ff., for introductory comments and text of Rhadinus's essay; also F. Lauchert, *Die italienischen literarischen Gegner Luthers*, Freiburg 1912, pp. 178ff.; and (ed./tr.) F. Ghizzoni, *Orazione Contro Filippo Melantone*, (intro.) G. Berti, Brescia 1973, pp. 44ff.

6. Cf. W. Maurer, *Der junge Melanchthon*, Bd. 2, Göttingen 1969, pp. 132ff.

7. *Ibid.*

8. On the meaning of this pseudonym, *MW* I, p. 56; W. Maurer, *op. cit.*, Bd. 2, p. 132. Because the author had compared Luther with the ram of Daniel 8:1ff., wounded by the he-goat, both Luther and Melanchthon presumed the writing to be the work of Luther's opponent Jerome Emser, "Der Bock von Leipzig," and wrongly believed Rhadinus to have been a pseudonym. Thus, Wittenberg responded with a false name of their own, perhaps suggesting the faith of Didymus in contrast to that of his doubting brother, Thomas, and a "favorable" disposition toward Luther and his theology.

9. In R. Stupperich, *op. cit.*, p. 42.

10. *MW* I, p. 57.

11. *Ibid.*

12. *Ibid.*

13. *Ibid.*

14. *Ibid.*

15. *Ibid.*, p. 72.16ff.

16. *Ibid.*, p. 72.26ff.

17. *Ibid.*, p. 72.30f., "...damnat, quidquid de moribus a philosophis proditum est."

18. *Ibid.*, p. 72.31f. We cannot go into the complex subject of faith and reason in the early Luther. But Melanchthon's summary of Luther's basic position squares with that of K.-H. zur Mühlen in *Luther: Sol, Ratio, Erudio, Aristoteles*, Probeartikel zum Sachregister der Weimarer Ausgabe, Sonderdrücke aus "Archiv für Begriffsgeschichte," Bd. XIV, Heft 2, und Bd. XV, Heft 1, Bonn 1971, pp. 192ff.

19. *Ibid.*, p. 193, on the structure of Luther's distinction between *ratio* and *fides*.

20. *MW* I, p. 75.8f., "Atqui hanc opinionem [of Aristotle] ad divinorum oraculorum studium adferre, quis non videt perniciosum esse? nempe in quibus velut *ektypois* sese divinitas expressit."

21. *Ibid.*, p. 75.13ff., "De Deo, de iis, quae deo tribuuntur ab hominibus, de unitate, de intellectu, de voluntate, de simplicitate disserunt metaphysici, quos vocant.... Hinc natae sunt factiones illae Thomistarum, Scotistarum, Occamistarum, velut ex chao demogorgoneo. Hic Theologorum vulgus studia in contraria scinditur..., dum suum quisque dogma adserit."

22. *Ibid.*, p. 75.24ff.

23. *Ibid.*, p. 75.27ff.

24. *Ibid.*, p. 75.29ff., "Voluit sane cognosci se deus, sed ut cognosceretur delapsus est in carnem, immo caro factus est."

25. *Ibid.*, p. 75.31ff., "Nam cum immensa illa maiestas comprehendi non posset, eam induit personam, quam complecti mens humana utcunque potuit; vulgaris enim patrum sententia fuit, non victuros, qui deum videssent."

26. *Ibid.*, p. 75.35ff. We have chosen not to include a chapter on Melanchthon's annotations to 1 and 2 Corinthians. Cf. *MW IV*, pp. 15ff. In his comments on 1 Corinthians 1-3, however, he did not develop the idea of incarnation as logical paradox, but rather centered upon its spiritual and practical difference from philosophy and legalism in the context of law and gospel, working together. The foolishness of the cross is primarily in its claim that our lives are not ours to control. Cf. pp. 20.16ff., and 20-35 *passim*, "...philosophy attributes everything to our powers and works, and the gospel takes everything away...." p. 20.19.

27. *MW I*, p. 76.1ff., "Scopus nobis propositus est Christus, in quem oculos defigere humana mens feliciter posset. Quem scopum cum contemnimus evolaturi ad coelestia, fieri non potest, quin periclitetur, quin erret vagabunda ratio, id quod accidisse videmus isti Theologorum generi, cum adfingit deo novam quisque formam, qui cum sit simplicissimus istorum, opinionibus ita dissectus est, ut non magis varius sit apud poetas Proteus."

28. *Ibid.*, p. 76.8ff., "Sed ut donem, pium esse, incomprehensibilia illa mysteria vestigare, certe et impium est et periculosum, humanis argutiis potius, quam divinis scripturis rem tantam tentare...."

29. *Ibid.*, p. 76.12ff., "...quod hanc lucem et natura reformidet et ratio et alioqui adeo nusquam constet sibi hominis ingenium, ut ne chamaeleon quidem sit mutabilior."

30. *Ibid.*, p. 76.18ff.

31. *Ibid.*, p. 76.20ff.

32. *Ibid.*, pp. 76.21-77.1.

33. *Ibid.*, p. 77.9ff.

34. *Ibid.*, p. 77.17ff., "Est enim alia quaedam spiritus doctrina, alia quaedam lux, qua tenebrae mentium nostrarum divinitus discuti solent."

35. *Ibid.*, p. 77.25ff., "Intelligere vos opinor, principes, quam non sit ex re Christianorum divina mysteria ad philosophicas rationes referre...."

36. *Ibid.*, p. 94.28ff.; also p. 93.22ff. Melanchthon's criticism of Aquinas was that he failed to understand the clear sense of New Testament theology and that this led him to use improper language about God, namely Aristotelian language. See *ibid.*, pp. 93-96.

37. *Ibid.*, p. 94.28ff.; also p. 86.20, "...he shall have deserved the name of darkness, for the doctrine of no one is more confused than his."

38. *Ibid.*, p. 95.4ff.

39. *Ibid.*, p. 95.28ff.

40. *Ibid.*, p. 96.7ff.

41. *Ibid.*, p. 87.10ff.

42. *Ibid.*, p. 96.26ff.; also p. 98.5f.

43. *Ibid.*, p. 77.34ff.

44. *Ibid.*, p. 77.38f., "Damno enim *metaphysikas theorias*, quod periculi plenum arbitror, mysteria coelestia ad nostrae rationis methodos exigere, Ethica vero, quod plane ex diametro cum Christo pugnant.... Non hic periculum accuso, sed praesentem calamitatem deploro...."

45. *Ibid.*, p. 78.7ff., "Neque vero simpliciter hic peccatum est, sed postquam recepta sunt philosophorum Ethica, alius ex alio, ut solet, error subinde natus est, adeoque obscurata, o horrendas tenebras, universa Christi doctrina."

46. *Ibid.*, p. 79.5ff.

47. *Ibid.*, p. 81.17ff.

48. *Ibid.*, p. 81.19f.

204 • *Oratio Sacra*

49.   *Ibid.*, pp. 80.35-81.1ff.; cf. n. 7 on the reference to Democritus's *Peri euthumias*, "On Cheerfulness."

50.   *Ibid.*, p. 81.8f.

51.   *Ibid.*, pp. 79.37ff.

52.   *Ibid.*, p. 81.28f.

53.   *Ibid.*, p. 81.29ff., "...deterrimas fere pestes optimarum virtutum loco numeret philosophia."

54.   *Ibid.*, p. 82.4ff.

55.   *Ibid.*

56.   *Ibid.*, p. 82.15ff.

57.   *Ibid.*, pp. 81.30-82.1ff.; cf. also *ibid.*, pp. 82.25-83.1ff.

58.   *Ibid.*, p. 83.10ff.

59.   *Ibid.*, p. 83.19ff.

60.   *Ibid.*, p. 83.23ff.

61.   Cf. H. Küng, *Justification: The Doctrine of Karl Barth and a Catholic Reflection*, Philadelphia 1981.

62.   Cf. chapter 11 on "natural theology" and Melanchthon.

CHAPTER 11

The Loci Communes
of 1521

"He who desires to become a theologian has the Bible, and after that he can read the *loci* of Philip. When he understands both, he is a theologian, and to him all theology will stand open." (Luther, WA, *Tischreden*, vol. V, no. 5511.)

Melanchthon finished the proofs of his deeply influential work, the *Loci communes* of 1521, while the winds surrounding Luther were building to cyclonic force. The summons to Worms, the historic moment before the assembled powers of the age, the terrifying judgment that Luther was to be banned as a criminal in imperial lands followed by the abduction and refuge within the cold walls of the Wartburg, a riotous atmosphere developing in Wittenberg, war and rumors of war throughout the territory—all this was going on as Philip wrote his book.[1] "Nevertheless," Maurer wrote, "one notices scarcely anything of the burden which nearly crushed the friend and spokesman of Luther."[2] Indeed, that he could write Spalatin for permission to accompany Luther to Worms and scan Rhineland libraries for books along the route is evidence of his remarkable powers of detachment and academic concentration in the midst of a troubled and rapidly changing world. One suspects that this was not as much the measure of his naiveté as it was an instinctive response to danger. He was quintessentially academic, but unafraid to expose himself to deadly peril.

The troubles in Wittenberg during Luther's exile are well known: uproar at the Augustinian monastery over the issues of celibacy and monastic vows,[3] confusion over forms of worship appropriate to the gospel[4] and public chaos on the entrance of the "Zwickau Prophets."[5] Before leaving, Luther had made it clear that Philip was heir to the prophet's mantle, naming him "his Elisha," blessed with a double portion of the Spirit. As Maurer put it, "...he positioned the young humanist as heir to his mission as reformer; he laid the entire burden of his own world-historical responsibility on the shoulders of his friend."[6] The burden weighed upon Philip terribly, and some remember him mainly for buckling under it. The mood of his letters, which had almost always vibrated with the lightness of being in a new age of possibilities and hope, became heavy with thoughts of responsibility and the fragility of life. For those of us who have learned to idealize the Reformation, it is important to take note here of how the movement, like war, had already begun to exact its living sacrifices from the best and brightest of the young.

It has become part of Melanchthon's story that, despite his passion for the great orators, he simply could not lead from the pulpit, as Luther could. He was a bookworm, who learned to see the world from his granduncle's library; his tools for reform were the paradigms of grammar and the structures of contained thought. Nevertheless, it has too often been neglected that, if his performance as a public leader was mediocre (although that, too, ought to be debated, considering his role at the Diet of Augsburg in 1530),[7] his part as a thinker and teacher behind the scenes was played with such extraordinary skill that anyone who knows academic life firsthand must stand in simple wonderment. He labored ceaselessly as the prime mover of sweeping curriculum reform at the university[8] and carried not only his own full load of lectures, crossing the two disciplines of languages and theology, but stood in for the absent Luther, besides. Notably, he lectured on Romans through the entire academic year.[9] Remarkably, however, in spite of all his other duties, he published more in 1521 than in any previous year, and it must rank as one of the most productive times in the life of any scholar in any era. Polemical tracts in defense of Luther, brief essays on the mass, priestly marriage, piety and good works, a spate of Greek texts on New Testament writings, a new edition of his rhetoric and a dozen or so classical editions—all came flooding forth in that year.[10] Among them, however, the *Loci communes rerum theologicarum seu hypotyposes theologicae* stands out as the harvest of his years with Luther. If he had written that book alone, his reputation in the history of theology would have been solidified. With problems swirling all about him, he somehow found the discipline to stay a steady course of writing until the last manuscripts went to the press in December.[11]

Maurer's careful research into the composition of the *Loci communes* has greatly enhanced our sense of their worth as original work in the history of Christian theology.[12] Indeed, discrediting the legendary view that he was a sort of "Luther's Boswell," the *Loci* of 1521 grew from many roots that Melanchthon had cultivated with varying degrees of independence from Luther. On the 27th of April 1520, he wrote to John Hess about his latest undertaking, a volume of "obelisks" (*obelisci*) on the *Sentences* of Peter Lombard.[13] In this book he would "show in which teachings on the nature of man those 'three-penny masters' have hallucinated."[14] Maurer attempted to reconstruct the textual history, showing that the plan to publish this critique of the *Sentences*, while never finished as an independent writing, in time emerged as a constructive textbook on doctrine.[15] Melanchthon combined the "obelisks" with his *Institutio theologica*, and the result was a volume which he entitled *Rerum theologicarum capita seu loci*.[16] The *Capita* then matured into the *Loci communes* of 1521, which Philip envisioned as a normative theology for his generation and, thus, as a challenge to the systems of either Lombard or Erasmus in his *Ratio seu methodus*.[17] Indeed, the work was much more than a summary of Luther's thought.

Two modern Latin editions of the *Loci communes* may be recommended. The one is the famous work of Plitt and Kolde,[18] the other the work of H. Engelland in the superb *Studienausgabe*.[19] A useful English translation of the 1521 *Loci*, with a brief but insightful introduction, is the work of Wilhelm Pauck in the Library of Christian Classics.[20]

A comprehensive discussion of the contents and influence of the *Loci communes* cannot possibly be undertaken here, and so the reader may be directed to secondary sources.[21] Our main purpose in this final chapter is to show how Scripture functioned for Melanchthon as a whole, that is, how its *sensus* came from God to the world. In discussing the *Loci communes* of 1521, we can bring various elements of our book into something like a summary. The rhetorical shape of Melanchthon's views on the properties of biblical topics and doctrine as we have discussed them—the properly grounded invention, the contained and flawless disposition, the transcendent effect upon both mind and heart, the inspiring power to action—will serve our interpretive efforts to picture the underlying norms for his theology. The *Loci communes* gives the large picture of how Melanchthon defined the essential topics of Scripture, how they emerged from the diverse canonical writings into conceptually unified doctrines and how these doctrines each connected with the others to form the *sensus scripturae* as a coherent, perspicuous, powerful Word from God, unequaled in authority on earth. The book will also help us to assess the historical judgments that have been passed in secondary literature on his approach to biblical authority. The major historiographical debates are about "double-truth theory," "anthropocentrism," "intellectualism" and "natural theology." All of these issues are at the center of intense controversy over his rank and place in history. In the light of our previous discussion of Philip's view of Scripture as *oratio sacra*, we shall propose that considerable revisions of established traditions on all these crucial levels of his thought are needed.

We have divided our discussion into two main parts, corresponding to the structure of Melanchthon's conceptual vision of the Word. The first is centered upon the topical *inventio* behind biblical doctrine; here we shall develop our thoughts on the logical order and status of biblical *topics* as *loci communes*. In this context, the historiographical issues of "double truth" and "anthropocentrism" naturally arise, so that applications of our method may be made to influential secondary literature. The second part is devoted more to the *modalities* of the doctrines themselves, or to their structured *dispositio* as developed teaching. In the context of this rather extensive, but necessary section, the deeply important questions of "intellectualism" and "natural theology" finally emerge for critical discussion.

The Topics of Scripture and Biblical Inventio

"...the study of philosophy is [for me] most profane. I would like to have exchanged it...for theology—that theology, I say, which looks at the core of the nut, the kernel of the wheat and the marrow of the bones." (Luther, WABr, to John Braun, 14 March 1509.)

In the letter of dedication to Tilman Plettner,[22] Melanchthon stated that his main purpose in writing was to insure "that the chief *loci* of Christian discipline might here be indicated. . . ."[23] The larger goal was to assist the youth in knowing which were the most urgent topics of theology and to show "how horribly they have hallucinated everywhere in theological study, who have produced for us the cleverness of Aristotle instead of Christ's doctrine."[24] He wished to outfit students with a sort of "index" for learning the "nomenclature" of Christian theology, a guide to those wandering through the biblical landscape without proper direction.[25] It was not to be a *summa* of the faith, but an index to show on what "the *summa* of Christian doctrine depends."[26] His was thus a hermeneutical work, an exercise in proper method, which for him meant proper invention of topics.

This work also showed his deep convictions that the meaning of Scripture was "perspicuous" and that a "pure" biblical theology was possible, uncorrupted by human thought and method. The epistemic positivism that was intrinsic to his rhetorical theory was also essential to his belief that Scripture might function alone as the Word of God. He seemed never even to suspect that his contact with Luther and his peculiar theories of language, with all their variety of constructive force, constituted anything like an overlay upon the objective text. Once the right moves of *inventio* were made, the job of managing a consensus among good men ought not be difficult. These thoughts, rather than a naked biblicism, were behind the assertions of biblical authority that abounded in the preface alongside scathing criticisms of theological authorities and their impure creations.

Nay, rather, I wish for nothing as much as, if it be possible, that all Christians be most freely versed in divine letters alone and be plainly transformed into their image. For since, in these, divinity will have expressed the most perfect image of itself, it can be known neither more certainly nor more intimately from any other source. He errs, who seeks the true form of Christianity from a source other than canonical Scripture.[27]

This "most perfect image" of the deity, expressed in canonical Scripture alone, was thus superior in purity to human commentaries or philosophy.

For how greatly distant are commentaries from the purity of this [Scripture]? In this [Scripture] you will discover nothing that is not worthy of honor; in those [commentaries] how many things there are which are based upon philosophy, from the judgment of human reason, [and] which are in direct conflict with the judgment of the Spirit.[28]

The non-biblical writers, Melanchthon explained, could not adequately repress their human "flesh," "so that they breathed nothing except 'spiritual things.'"[29] Men like Origen, whom the Greek theologians followed by consensus, as did Ambrose and Jerome, were considered pillars of the Latin West.[30] One might think it almost a rule that "the more recent one is, the more unauthentic. . . ."[31]

Nevertheless, Philip's famous section on the nature of Christian knowledge which followed these remarks on the purity of Scripture made it clear that a correct method of *inventio*, rather than Scripture "alone," was the primary matter. Our previous discussion enables us to appreciate the underlying sense of those oft-quoted words. "In the single arts," he wrote, "certain *loci* are usually looked for, in which the *summa* of each art is comprehended...."[32] This *summa* would act *scopi vice*, in the place of a *scopos*, "toward which we may direct all [our] endeavors. . . ."[33] Recent theological authorities had neglected their methodological duties. "For Damascus philosophizes too much; Lombard prefers to accumulate the opinions of men rather than to set forth the judgment of Scripture."[34] It is therefore necessary, he argued, briefly to indicate which are the essential *loci*, from which the *summa* of doctrine could be known.[35]

Melanchthon began where any good rhetorician would begin, by "finding" the essential *loci* of the subject matter. His list of topics proper to the study of theology was mainly conventional: God as one and as triune, creation, man and man's powers, sin and the fruits of sin, law, promises, regeneration through Christ, grace and the fruits of grace, faith, hope, love, predestination, signs of the sacraments, the status of men, magistrates, bishops, judgment and beatitude.[36] We should not forget that he included all of these as *loci*, so that his procedure of limiting the focus to a selected few will not be mistakenly viewed as exclusivistic, but as based on principles of some other kind. "Among these," wrote Melanchthon, "on the one hand, just as certain ones are incomprehensible, so, on the other hand, there are those which Christ wished to be most certainly known by the entire Christian multitude."[37] In this context came the now-famous declaration: "The mysteries of divinity are more rightly worshiped than investigated."[38] To enter upon study of the mysteries was as difficult as it was perilous. "Nay, rather, they cannot be handled without great peril; that is what even holy men not infrequently have experienced."[39]

As in the *Oratio* by Didymus Faventinus, Melanchthon argued that the "logic" of the incarnation itself was against speculative theology. "And the Most High God clothed His Son with flesh that He might invite us from contemplation of His majesty to contemplation of our flesh and, indeed, our fragility."[40] Therefore, he concluded, "there is no reason why we must put great labor into those supreme *loci*, on God, on [His] unity, on the trinity of God, on the mystery of creation, on the mode of the incarnation."[41] For what have scholastic theologians accomplished when "versed in these *loci* alone?"[42] Have they not been made vain, to use Paul's words, in their disputations?[43] Nonetheless, Melanchthon's important concession must also be recorded, that "their foolishness could perhaps be left unnoticed, if these . . . disputations had not, in the meantime, obscured to us the gospel and the benefits of Christ."[44]

If study of the mysteries was dangerous, knowledge of "the power of sin, law, grace"[45] was the way to the truth. Another now-famous declaration emerged in this context. "For from these, Christ is properly known, since to know Christ is to know His benefits, not, as they teach, to gaze upon His natures, the modes of the incarnation."[46] Nor was knowledge of Christ merely about the history of His coming, but rather in understanding the use of these events: "If you do not know why [*in quem usum*] Christ put on flesh and was nailed to the cross, what will it profit to know His history?"[47] Not to know the use and power of sacred history would be like a physician knowing the colors and shapes of his herbs, but nothing of their power to heal diseases.[48] Proper *inventio* was the master key.[49] He thus devoted his work to the essential topics: on the powers of man and freedom of the will,[50] on sin,[51] on law,[52] on the gospel,[53] on grace, justification and faith,[54] on the distinction between the Old and New Testaments,[55] on signs (or sacraments)[56] and brief segments diversely on love, magistrates and scandal or offense.[57] Only in later editions of the *Loci communes* would Melanchthon expand its scope to include doctrines of God, trinity, incarnation and the Decalogue.[58]

These words of introduction to the *Loci communes* have been at the center of controversy among theologians for more than a hundred years.[59] Since the second half of the nineteenth century, it has been common for Lutheran theologians and historians to view the early Melanchthon as opposed to speculation in a manner that contributed to the emergence of modern liberalism and its anti-metaphysical values. The principle that guided his anti-speculative practice is frequently identified as a logical one in the context of a strong view of revelation. In *Justification and Reconciliation*, Albrecht Ritschl declared that orthodox dogma on such subjects as the trinity and incarnation was for Luther and Melanchthon logically unintelligible.[60] Ritschl believed that Luther had shattered the "scholastic impasse" to which belief in such logically absurd propositions had taken them.[61] Moreover, in Ritschl's view, Melanchthon's *Loci communes* of 1521 helped open the way into a modern approach to theological coherence and pragmatism:

> Melanchthon, in his first epoch, interpreted the thought of Luther to mean that the formula of the two natures of Christ is not important so long as Christ is acknowledged in his saving benefits. Thus, the *loci theologici* of the year 1521 read: *Hoc est Christum cognoscere, beneficia eius cognoscere*.[62]

Ritschl's interpretation and assessment of Melanchthon has been transmitted in one form or another through the writings of both Continental and American thinkers. Quirinus Breen blamed Melanchthon for the very thing that Ritschl praised. In Breen's view, the Preceptor was "tarred with the stick of double-truth theory" and, thus, helped establish the modern premise that orthodox Christian propositions are logically incoherent.[63] In a similar light, Swiss theologian Emil Brunner argued that Melanchthon's early Lutheran writings were a prelude to the rise of "modernism" and the widespread abandonment of orthodoxy among Western theologians. He asserted that Melanchthon's statement on knowing Christ's benefits was "not only well known but epoch-making."[64] Brunner's focus was not upon the idea of logical paradox, but upon a pervasively "anthropocentric point of view," or pragmatism, that would dominate the theological mind of Lutheran liberalism in later centuries. No account of the nature of Melanchthon's subjectivism was offered, but one might venture to say that Brunner held it as grounded in the utilitarian, humanistic tradition that Philip was heir to.

> How Christ speaks to us, not what we think about Him, is the problem for faith. This is evidently the real meaning, which not only could lead one astray, but actually has done so. It contains the germ of the whole anthropocentric point of view of later Lutheranism. Man occupies the center of the picture, with his need for salvation, not God in His glory, His revelation; thus God becomes the one who satisfies the needs of man. Not in vain has Ritschlian pragmatism so often appealed to these words.[65]

Roman Catholic theologian Walter Kasper agreed. There was in Melanchthon a strong "principle of *pro me*," that became the basis of Schleiermacher's Christology:

> In his introduction to the *Loci communes* of 1521 there is the famous sentence "Hoc est Christum cognoscere, beneficia eius cognoscere...." This principle became the basis of Schleiermacher's Christology, and via Schleiermacher, of "neo-Protestantism."[66]

Others, such as Karl Barth,[67] H. Thielicke[68] and Paul Wernle,[69] have given their own variations on the same theme.

Some of these interpreters draw attention to an anti-metaphysical, logical principle in Melanchthon; others center upon an anthropocentric disposition. In either event, all of them judge that Melanchthon was responsible in part for the development of modern theology in the context of Schleiermacher's dogmatics. (Apparently none of them had the elder Melanchthon in mind, who is regularly accused of injecting too much logic and theocentric language into Lutheran dogmatics!) Whether one judges this a favorable development or not obviously depends upon one's own basic principles. Ritschl considered the young Melanchthon's anti-speculative approach something to be praised; Barth and others viewed it as greatly unfortunate insofar as it detracted from God and centered upon human life. However, a more fundamental question has to deal with the nature of influence itself. Similarities do not necessitate the conclusion that there has been an influence, and there is the question of what constitutes a genuine similarity at all. One can speak of cognitive similarities between actual principles and assertions, or one might think more ambiguously of influence occurring through one's "tendencies," or psychological *Geistesorientierung*. But it is obvious that similarities of some kind must be present for there to have been a genuine influence of one thinker upon another, in the sense that the other carried on in a manner continuous with the tradition of his forebearers. Can we detect important similarities between the principles or tendencies of Melanchthon and those of post-Kantian modernists? Let us explore that question, which is so very crucial to Melanchthon historiography, somewhat more deeply in view of our own previous discussion.

For Ritschl and Breen the issue was clearly one of principle, that is, Melanchthon's anti-speculative principle was continuous with that of post-Kantian modernists for whom propositions about God's being had no cognitive value or objective referent. Did Melanchthon in 1521 believe either that our propositions about God had no cognitive value or that they signified nothing in external reality? Secondly, barring a positive answer to the first question, did he view such doctrines as impractical and, to that extent, as unimportant?

Many sources and secondary studies make it entirely obvious that Melanchthon viewed propositions about God as referring to an objective reality. That there really was a God, that God really was triune, that in Christ God really was both human and divine and that God really was the good creator of the world with many real perfections were all beliefs held firmly by him.[70] Melanchthon's belief in the cognitive and externally "real" referent of theological language is beyond dispute. That fact alone ought to establish a principial suspicion of theories that connect him semantically with post-Kantian metaphysics and modernism. He would have fought against it every bit as intensely, on primary metaphysical grounds, as did Barth, Brunner and the others. The issue for discussion is, what kind of cognition of the "mysteries" did he affirm? To what extent, in Melanchthon's view, can our language take us toward knowledge of divine reality? To what extent does the divine reality conform to the logic of human concepts?

Meijering was no doubt right in viewing Melanchthon's reticence to speculate, in 1521, as largely the outcome of a renewed biblicism, with humanistic overtones.[71] And it is quite evident that the young Melanchthon did not wish to go very far at all in explaining the *mysteria coelestia* in rational terms. As Brüls so aptly put it of Melanchthon's lifelong approach, "He is rather the theologian who thinks existentially."[72] But what was the force of his "biblicism," and how did he construe biblical language and concepts as personally relevant? Exactly what were the "humanistic overtones" of this critique? Did a nominalistic notion of "double truth" enter quietly into his Lutheran biblicism, however problematic that may have been for his belief in the referentiality of biblical language? If it did, as it seems to have done with Luther, then connecting him, on at least one important level, with the neologies of later Lutheranism is conceivable. His dogmatic values would have been to the Kantian theologians something akin to what the Moravian pietism was for men like Schleiermacher, who once said that he was merely "a Moravian of a higher type." But, if not, the connection becomes weaker, and the nature of an alleged influence is more difficult to pin down. We believe that it did not, and that there are better ways of construing his principles in the early *Loci* than to view them as "tarred with the stick of double-truth theory" or "anthropocentric" in a manner that one would predict might fuel the ontological developments within liberal Lutheranism.

In our view, Philip's emphases on the soteriological *loci* emerged from the application of his rhetorical principles on *inventio* to what he regarded as a very grave situation in the state of theology. And these principles do not quite conform to either of the influential models of assessment in the literature. Clear awareness of the principles which Melanchthon applied to his theology helps make better sense of the entire network of problems surrounding his selection of topics—the alleged "intellectualism," the development of a "natural theism" and the varied matter of his evolution from this period to the later ones.

Indeed, as we have just seen, Melanchthon wrote in his introduction that some theological *loci* were "incomprehensible,"[73] that we shall worship the mysteries more rightly than investigate them,[74] that to know Christ is to know His benefits[75] and that the master of theologians is the Apostle Paul, who wrote not on mysteries of creation and incarnation but on the *loci* of law, sin and grace.[76] Moreover, it is also true that Melanchthon appealed to the act of Christ's incarnation as an implied warning against presumptuous and disastrously inappropriate uses of philosophical language, condemning the foolishness of such human "wisdom."[77] In our previous discussion, we have sought to show that the principles behind these latest assertions were not derived simply from his freshly won Lutheran biblicism, but, more deeply, that they emerged from a linguistic vision which he had systematized in his pre-Lutheran rhetorical theory and applied to his entire world view. The metaphysical and linguistic foundations of this theory expressed a synthetic approach to the concerns of philosophical realism and nominalism alike. The realism manifested itself most powerfully in his approach to natural science, but we have seen that it was also connected to his theology in the shape of a *Naturfrömmigkeit* that presupposed conceptual and logical continuity between God, the creator, and the world, His creation. The Lutheran impulses shook his world view in foundational ways, particularly on the subject of human nature, and gave Philip a strong push in the direction of his already-present inclination toward the discipline and practical virtues of religious and theological nominalism. Nevertheless, even if Luther's theology may have caused his realism to bend, we see no clear evidence, even in the *Loci communes* of 1521, that it ever completely broke apart. The processes here are analogous to those which we detect in his approach to the epistemological matter of proofs and evidence of God's existence.[78]

It has generally gone unnoticed that in this anti-speculative introduction to the 1521 edition of the *Loci communes*, and elsewhere in earlier writings, Philip granted that a theology of the mysteries might indeed be warranted, under the right conditions, "if they had not, in the meantime, obscured the gospel and the benefits of Christ."[79] In *Didymi Faventini*, he had also asserted that "to investigate those incomprehensible mysteries is a pious thing...."[80] What was impious was to investigate them "by human cleverness rather than by the divine scriptures...."[81] His point was that such investigations are perilous, because human language has a very tenuous application to the deeper things of God, as Scripture constantly warns, but not that human language has no significant application, or that a doctrine of God is absolutely invalid, or that we should think of the *mysteria* as involving us in logically contradictory claims about a God who is simply "beyond God." If one can identify a principle at all in his mass of criticisms, it seems largely to be one of proper focus or *inventio*, "picking up the right end of the stick."

There is also the very slippery question of Melanchthon's own development, wherein it is well known that doctrines of God, incarnation and creation all emerged in considerable detail as he expanded the scope of his *Loci communes*.[82] Within scarcely more than a year after the first edition of the *Loci*, in a commentary on St. John's Gospel, he stressed the ontological reality, the importance and the biblically framed sense of the trinity in a manner that would lead naturally to the use of neo-Platonic concepts to articulate a doctrine of God.[83] An older Melanchthon (in part, under pressure from the spread of anti-trinitarian movements) would deploy all sorts of philosophical terms in application to the nature of God, in order to exact some sense of logical meaning from the biblical language on these lofty themes.[84] The thesis of strong nominalism (or puritanical biblicism) in the young Melanchthon requires the conclusion that he changed his most basic principles, within a very short time, mainly for tactical, occasional reasons, and this without any evidence of being conscious that he was undergoing a monumental shift of epistemic norms. On balance, the occurrence of such a process in the steady, methodical and methodologically self-conscious Melanchthon seems improbable.[85] Taken as a whole, the data invite us to seek a better explanation for Melanchthon's theory and practice in selecting and developing theological topics.

If one looks at Melanchthon's anti-speculative assertions, and the occasional qualifications thereof, in the context of his doctrine of *inventio*, then a certain coherence emerges between the nominalistic and realistic strands of his theology, and between the young and the older Melanchthon. The picture that emerges is such that parallels with the epistemology and human-centeredness of modernism become difficult to sustain. One can imagine his theological system to have unfolded rather like a properly constructed oration. In the early years of his Lutheranism, in what he saw as the gravest of circumstances, Philip (like Luther) was preoccupied with defining the essential *scopus* of the theological discipline. In later years, under somewhat different circumstances, he would expand his message to include topics that were further removed from this center and were finally to be interpreted against the *scopus* and, thus, in their proper logical places as parts within the whole. The distinction here is not between logically meaningful and logically meaningless Christian claims, but between first- and second-order themes in an oration.[86] No doubt, in following this "inventive" procedure, Philip considered the majesty of God as cause for reverence and epistemic humility, but that is very different from the assertion of principles that connect readily with those of Ritschl and others. The young Melanchthon, in collaboration with Martin Luther, was devoted more to reforming contemporary methods of theological *inventio* than to excluding traditional language about God. Taken in this way, Melanchthon's famous dictum on knowing the benefits of Christ hardly seems suited to the purposes of Schleiermacher or Ritschl. The mere fact that they cited him, to gain support from their public, is not evidence enough to show a positive influence. And if "influence" simply means that there were vaguely comparable tendencies, such as an "anthropocentric" bias, then Philip was merely a member of a vast company of pre-modern thinkers who were heir to the forces of the Renaissance, and he ought not be singled out, as if his early (not later!) *Loci* influenced Schleiermacher in anything like the measure of a larger critical tradition, going back through Kant and Hume, to Descartes, Bruno, Galileo and an irreducibly complex sum of socioeconomic and conceptual forces that brought us from the Middle Ages into modernity. We believe that it would be easier to build a case for seeing Melanchthon as the ally of rational, culturally penetrating orthodoxy than to brand him as its enemy. And of course, on other levels, this is exactly the way he has been received and the reason he has been condemned by many. The question for orthodox Protestants is, as Hildebrandt put it, whether Melanchthon, with his affirmation of rational structures and the importance of an orthodox idea of God, is an "alien or ally" of the true faith. Furthermore, that he is attacked on both levels (sometimes by the same people), first as having abdicated metaphysics and rational epistemology *and*, second, as having caved in to the cultural demand for a "natural theism," is really quite extraordinary. That one and the same man might be quoted approvingly by both Kant and Thomas Jefferson (or Queen Elizabeth I) would suggest a misunderstanding of some sort, unless Philip turns out to be two completely different people.

In our view, then, the introductory words of Melanchthon's early *Loci communes* mainly expressed his attempt to reform the value-order, the *inventio*, of theologians in the selection of topics. Since the time of the orations on Paul, in which he had introduced the concept of Christ's benefits, he had carried on a steady attack against the inventive methods of scholastic theology, arguing that, apart from knowledge of the true *scopos* of revelation, there was little value in teaching the doctrines of the mysteries. The little piece of paper discovered after Melanchthon's death is a moving expression of what had always been a deeply rooted hunger and thirst for metaphysical knowledge, combined with profound awareness of the fact that, in this life, "we see through a glass darkly." Reflecting on his own impending death, he wrote:

> You come to the light, you will look upon God and His Son.
> You will understand the wonderful mysteries which you could
> not understand in this life,
> Why we were made in this way and not in another,
> And in what the union of two natures in Christ consists.[87]

These are assuredly not the ontological sentiments of a Schleiermacher, nor are they evidently inconsistent with the first principles of Melanchthon in 1521.

The Doctrines of Scripture and Biblical Dispositio

"Philippus canit eandem cantilenam." (Cited in P. Fraenkel, *Testimonia Patrum*, p. 145, a refrain from Melanchthon's theological students.)

"Ego aliquando audivi ex Philippo, quod tota scriptura nihil aliud sit quam certamen serpentis et seminis." (Luther, WA, *Tischreden*, 5, p. 5585.)

In this part of the chapter we shall expand our thesis that, for Melanchthon, the authority of Scripture resided in its doctrine. We shall consider the *loci* not merely as topics, or as first principles, but as ideas that have been shaped into theological concepts, propositions and teaching in its complete sense as *oratio*. We shall seek to look, as it were, through Philip's exegetical and theological doctrines to see the underlying construal of Scripture in its unity (in reference to individual doctrines and to the coherent relationships between the doctrines), perspicuity and powers as the Word of God. This will enable us to gain important critical perspective on Melanchthon's notorious reputation for having unleashed a deadly "intellectualism" upon Lutheranism, and it will position us to discuss the issue of "natural theology" in the context of his peculiar notion of how Scripture alone was the source of truth about God.

On the Powers of Man and Freedom of the Will

Melanchthon began writing on this subject believing that, besides Augustine and Bernard, precedents for doing so were not numerous.[88] This was no great matter, though, since his aim was not to follow "opinions of men," but instead to explain the subject "as plainly and simply as possible...."[89] Both ancient and recent authors mostly obscured it, "as they wished to satisfy, at the same time, the judgment of human reason."[90] Indeed, there was much to offend. It seemed "too little civilized to teach that man sins by necessity, cruel to reproach the will, if it had not been free to return to virtue."[91] And so human philosophy "crept into Christianity,"[92] bringing with it a concept of freedom that would obscure the beneficence of God in Christ.[93] One must begin by re-introducing a biblical model of human nature.[94] For Melanchthon, that was the basic function of this doctrine and the reason he began the *Loci communes* with a treatment of it. Moreover, it "was necessary to advise of these things, so that the distinction between law and grace might be shown more clearly, afterwards...."[95]

One might think that Melanchthon's belief in the bondage of the will indicated a clear commitment to a theory of double truth and thus supported some of the theories which we have rejected in the foregoing part of this chapter. He did, in fact, write as if the biblical doctrine of predestination generated logical contradictions. At this time in his development (one must consider that he had been with Luther for about two years), he still viewed the doctrine of human nature and its connecting soteriological concepts in sharply polarized terms. The established theology which provided the rationale for the elaborate system of merit and indulgences stood on the one side, Luther's powerful presentation of God's absolute grace on the other. On this level, Philip's fresh biblicism (temporarily) drowned out his older and deeper epistemic and ontological beliefs. However, in time he would think the matter right through, according to his *own* metaphysical norms. The result was to be an analogical, rather than simply paradoxical, model of language. We have rightly insisted on viewing Melanchthon as his own man and as having been underestimated as a hermeneutical theologian and communicator. Nevertheless, in these early and exciting days, Luther caused a tremor that shook his Hellenic pride in moral discipline and forced him into a position that was not yet altogether his own. The later changes in his thinking on the doctrines of God and the human will seem much more the products of his own mind and fundamental world view than do these earliest outbursts of excitement over the Lutheran "breakthrough."

Nor was it the mystery and paradox of predestination that inspired Melanchthon to treat it as the touchstone of Christian theology. In contrast to someone like Calvin, the young Philip blithely ignored the *decretum horribile*, the seemingly gratuitous damnation of people—to the glory of God. In later years, when this problem did trouble him, his response was to find a humane synthesis, not to revel in the *mysterium tremens* of God's majesty. The idea that inspired Melanchthon was not that faith embraced the logical absurdity of Christian doctrine, or that we should picture God as being an abstract, absolute power, *potentia absoluta*, beyond all human reckoning. His essential concern was that we come to an honest awareness of *ourselves* as being absolutely powerless to merit the goodness of God. Thus, his initial point was that, in spite of the difficulty and offense of the doctrine, and that it *seemed* "uncivilized" and "cruel," we must persist in teaching it for its salutary value. His main reason for beginning with this unsettling subject was to create the context for self-knowledge through the doctrines of law, sin and grace. His aim, once again, was to follow the inventive and dispositional pattern of the biblical *oratio*. He would, in time, abandon the strongly Lutheran determinism, but never the thesis that we are powerless to merit God's grace and that this knowledge of ourselves is essential to everything else that we profess as Christians. The core of the gospel was not the absolute sovereignty of God or the insignificance of human choices, but rather knowledge of oneself as a sinner in the context of God's immense goodness and grace. And, of course, his powerful commitment to the proposition that God really is good hardly comports with a radical nominalism (or with the thesis of "anthropocentrism"). That is how this doctrine functioned in the *dispositio* of the *Loci communes* of 1521, and it would continue to do so till the last edition came out in 1555.[96]

Our question now is, how did this idea of human powerlessness emerge through Scripture as a biblical *doctrine*? On this fundamental and heated question, Melanchthon wrote as if everything was simply obvious. The irony, as we have pointed out, is the elaborate philosophical and theological system that he himself brought to the text, while seeming to believe that he stood outside the interpretive process. In contrast to the *inventio* of Paul, whom he claimed to be following simply and plainly, his theological index would begin with the topic of free will (Rom. 9-11) rather than with God, creation, morality, law and grace (Rom. 1-8). Later editions would eventually correct this interpretive overlay on the text, but throughout his life he would constantly suffer disillusionment and frustration at his chronic failure to convince opponents of what seemed self-evidently true to him.

Indeed, Philip believed that the powerlessness of humankind to merit grace implied a doctrine of no free will; that the one idea did not imply the other had not yet occurred to him. Moreover, he believed that this basic doctrine emerged from a great variety of texts, most clearly in the New Testament, but also in the Old.[97] We cannot tarry over individual passages and Melanchthon's obvious proof-texting. A cursory reading reveals that, here, he offered no exegetical arguments to support his interpretations of controverted texts, but simply gave the individual verses as evidently teaching the *locus* that human beings have no freedom to redeem themselves from the passions of sin. Scripture was absolutely clear on this; only the corrupting influence of philosophy could cause one to miss the point. In fact, the terse exegetical sections of the *Loci communes* often leave the impression that Philip was less sensitive to diversity and development in the canon than he in fact was. His approach in the *Loci* was, no doubt, due in part to an overriding interest in *claritas et brevitas*. He wished to hasten on to his *scopus*, which was to reach the affections of people with the insight that God is gracious to sinners. Moreover, he believed this doctrine was simply inherent in, and would be confirmed by, treatment of the remaining *loci communes theologicae*.

Of interest here, and throughout the writing, is the manner in which he construed the nature and function of Scripture as a book of sacred *loci communes*. Like secular *loci communes*, biblical doctrines centered upon the deepest existential questions, conveyed the clearest cognitive truths and brought about transformation in the hearts of receptive readers. Satisfied that he had secured the doctrine of predestination as a biblical *locus*, he exhorted his readers to heed the fatherly wisdom of Solomon: "For nowhere will you learn either fear or faith in God more certainly than where you imbue the soul with this doctrine [*sententia*] of predestination."[98] Melanchthon pointed to Christ's pastoral use of the doctrine among His disciples: "Does not Christ, in this one place [Matt. 10:29ff.], most efficaciously console His disciples, when He says, 'All the hairs on your heads are numbered'?"[99] The point of the doctrine was not to send us on a syllogistic course which ended in resignation before God's transcendent majesty, but that we might better understand ourselves before God and that God loves us. Thus, as already indicated, Melanchthon viewed this doctrine as a means of entering properly into the *oratio* of God, with its *loci* on law, sin and grace and its *scopus* of justification by faith apart from works of the law. In his view, this doctrine of human freedom was a *locus* that unified biblical teaching as a perspicuous whole, and it could thus function as a premise in the logic of biblical oration.

On Sin

Melanchthon's subdivisions for handling the doctrine of sin reflected not merely his own methodological patterns, by which he applied dialectical invention and *divisio* to the biblical text. More deeply, they manifested his construal of the very structures of biblical oration itself. The structure of this biblical *locus*, as a coherent whole, emerged in three logical stages: *Quid peccatum*, *Unde peccatum originale* and *Vis peccati et fructus*. In view of our previous analysis of his rhetorical categories, the teleological connection of the cognitive aims of dialectic with the affective ones of rhetoric was the linguistic key to what the Word of God was; it developed along the logical and practical lines of *sermo proprius*. He believed that Scripture communicated to us by that same linguistic pattern. We shall sum up his main points briefly, showing how he drew them from the text of Scripture and developed them into a structured *locus de peccato*. Again, our main concern is not with the content of his doctrine, although this must be summarized, but with its rhetorical patterns as *oratio sacra* as a canonical whole.

Critical of contemporary *somnia*,[100] Melanchthon vowed to write sparingly, "and we shall use the word 'sin' in the manner of Scripture." Under *Quid peccatum*, he defined original sin as "a native propensity and a certain inborn force and power by which we are drawn to sin....''[101] Under *Unde peccatum originale*, he interpreted the fall as a loss of God's inner light and life, and the incursion of a burning self-love.[102]

Melanchthon judged that the existence of original sin is a matter of lucid biblical doctrine throughout the canon. The constitutive texts were Genesis 6:3, Romans 8:5-7, Ephesians 2:3, the whole *figura sermonis* of Christ and Adam in Romans 5 and 1 Corinthians 15, Psalm 50 and John 3:6. All these texts were "*loci*, testifying that there is original sin."[103]

Under *Vis peccati et fructus*, Melanchthon asserted the Lutheran critique of "new Pelagians [*novi Pelagiani*]"[104] who had entered the stage of contemporary history; these theologians did not deny the existence of original sin, but rather its power to render all human works sinful.[105] Against this weakened form of the doctrine, Melanchthon advanced the Lutheran view that all men, no matter how civilized, with their "satisfactions and philosophical virtues," produced works which were impure and sinful.[106] He granted that there was a kind of virtue in men such as Socrates, Xenocrates and Zeno,[107] but all their good works—tolerance in Socrates, chastity in Xenocrates and so on—grew from a profoundly deep and evil love of self.[108] Even the weightiest among the pagan moral philosophers—Cicero, Plato and Aristotle—manifested this selfishness and self-directed *amor*. Cicero, indeed, believed that all reason for virtue stemmed from love of self;[109] Plato promoted an inflated and arrogant spirit which was contagious upon reading him,[110] and the doctrine of Aristotle was "in general a peculiar lust for wrangling [*quaedam libido rixandi*]...."[111]

We shall keep these comments in mind when we come to the matter of "natural theology" in Melanchthon. They also contribute further to our picture of how he construed the sense of Scripture as a perspicuous, coherent and efficacious doctrinal whole. Biblical support for these assertions on the scope and power of original sin could be compressed "into a compendium: All men are, by the powers of nature, truly and always sinners, and they sin."[112] He began with the texts on the evil antediluvian human race, applying them directly to human nature. From the Pentateuch, he cited Genesis 6:5 and 8:21, the second of which he preferred in the German translation—"depraved," rather than the weaker phrasing of the Vulgate, "prone to evil."[113] From the book of Isaiah, Melanchthon honed in on texts such as 9:16, 49:21 and 53:6-12, each of which was taken (no doubt through Paul) to refer to the entire human race.[114] The texts in the fifty-third chapter of Isaiah were construed as a summing up of the gospel of Jesus Christ and as a stern warning to those who would attribute something of value to their own moral powers. The "rich" mentioned in this text were "plainly those who would assert the human righteousness of free will, philosophical virtues, in brief, human powers...."[115] He concluded, "You see how Isaiah, in a brief sermon, has described the entire power of the gospel."[116] The thirteenth Psalm of David, wrote Melanchthon, "The fool hath said in his heart . . . ," was a statement not merely about human sins, but about sinful human nature, leading to the (Lutheran) view that bad trees do not yield good fruit.[117] On the basis of the Psalm and the other texts cited, Melanchthon affirmed a great *discrimen* between philosophy, or human reason, and sacred letters (*sacrae literae*). Philosophy had a view only of the external appearance of the person, whereas sacred letters observed the deepest affections which reigned in the heart.[118] In interpreting Romans 8, Melanchthon accused scholastic theologians of ignoring the "phrasing and metaphor of Scripture."[119] The point of controversy was the meaning of Paul's term "flesh," which was commonly taken to mean "the appetites,"[120] whereas Melanchthon, in support of Luther, took it as "the whole man."[121] Besides the fact, he argued, that Paul "splendidly and grandly teaches from the testimonies of the prophets [Rom. 3]," showing that all men were under sin, his *"argumenta* in the whole epistle to the Romans would not be consistent," were the scholastic rendering of the "flesh" true. For Paul argued that the flesh could not keep the law, therefore the Spirit was required for righteousness. But if there was a part of man able somehow to fulfill the law, "in what manner is Paul's *enthymema* consistent?"[122] He concluded: "Truly they have forgotten not only the meaning [*sententia*] of Scripture, but also the language [*sermo*]...."[123] Just as Israel, according to Ezra 10:2, had married foreign wives and adopted their languages, so had contemporary theologians adopted the language of self-righteous moral philosophy in developing a doctrine of the flesh.[124]

Melanchthon continued to argue, along similar lines, that fallen humans had no *sensus dei* (since the mind is also fallen flesh)[125] and that the clear sense of the text destroyed the validity of *actus eliciti,*[126] *meritum de congruo*[127] and penitence.[128] Against these doctrines, all of which attributed some measure of power to man in turning to God, he placed such predestinarian texts as

Jeremiah 31:19 and John 6:44. If passages such as Zechariah 1:3, "Be converted to me, and I will turn to you," were to be used in support of a counter-argument, Melanchthon responded that nothing would be gained. For this text must be viewed next to the others which clearly removed the power of repenting from human control; there were two sides to conversion, "Duplex est conversio": God's turning to us and our turning to God. Zechariah taught merely the second, not the first; and so the dispute was settled.[129]

This part of the *Loci* of 1521 is rich with ideas that reach into several levels of our study, not least into how, in Melanchthon's view, biblical doctrine emerged as a unified whole. He considered the discovery of this doctrine of the nature and power of sin to be a matter simply of "indicating" the literal sense of Scripture. Underlying this view was the deep conviction that the Holy Spirit worked in much the same way, as a rhetorician or good teacher. Toward the end of this section, he wrote:

> The divine Spirit is one and the same, the very simplest and most certain teacher [*doctor*], who has expressed Himself accurately and most simply in sacred letters, in which, when your mind has been transformed, as it were, then you will comprehend perfectly, simply, exactly the nature of this *locus*, as well as of the other theological subjects.[130]

This last citation helps to frame the extended summary of Melanchthon's points that we have just given. It illustrates the extent to which Philip looked upon the Lutheran doctrine of sin as a biblical *locus* that emerged mainly in direct ways from the entire biblical canon. We can now see how much energy he had put into solving the basic problems within the Lutheran diachronic model of biblical meaning and truth, centered as it was upon the hermeneutical works of Paul and New Testament Christology. Melanchthon believed himself to have shown that the sense of Scripture on this doctrine was not simply the result of Paul's normative or constructive theology (much less Luther's), but rather was a simple consequence of reading Scripture according to its literal sense, that is, its straightforward terms and propositions, the logical force of its imagery or tropology and the consistency of rhetorical argument or *enthymemata*. Of course, Melanchthon was barely conscious of the power that Paul, in reality, exerted upon him in handling individual passages. In the light of the many, complex interpretive decisions that Philip had made, it now seemed obvious to him that there was no room for debating the unified sense of the text on this subject. Genesis, David, Isaiah, Jesus, Paul and John all made exactly the same assertions about the fallen nature of man.

As we have seen in earlier documents, this *locus* operated for Paul as a major *sedes argumenti* in proving his *status* that we are justified by faith and not works. Melanchthon recognized that, for Luther's interpretation to succeed, this *locus* must be established as unambiguously biblical. So deep was Melanchthon's belief in both the soundness of Luther's view of human nature and the propositional unity of the text, that he was unencumbered by the thought of "counter-texts." Zechariah simply must agree with the main force of the biblical sense and tropology; he simply must have been thinking of the second stage of conversion to the Lord. Without going into the details of his exegetical reasoning (which are largely missing from view) or denying validity to many of his proposals, we dare say that his superficial treatment of the Zechariah text, in the same manner that we observed in some of his exegetical writings, exposed a grave danger of circularity and sectarianism in the early Protestant hermeneutic. The propositional unity and consistency of Scripture on the subject of human nature operated much more as an axiom than as the conclusion of an argument. Room for discussion and debate on the subject of the fall was at first all but eliminated, the issue presented as closed, the opposition as irresponsible or even foolish. It seems somewhat gratuitous, if not passing strange, that the exegetical dogmatism of Philip's early doctrine of sin is generally held up as normative for his Lutheranism, whereas his later exploration of a modified, more biblically balanced and ecumenical position is seen as degenerative.

Our main point here is not to debate the doctrine of sin, but to show how Melanchthon construed Scripture as a unified and perspicuous whole on this matter and that, for him, the biblical *locus de peccato* was thus identical with the Lutheran one and that he underestimated the extent to which these interpretive beliefs controlled his use of the text. On the whole, this section of the *Loci communes* leaves one with a badly oversimplified sense of what Scripture teaches on that subject.

To further pursue the question of the *nature* of doctrine, in Melanchthon, and its *modalities* as *oratio*, we judge that, besides comprising a perspicuous doctrine of sin, Melanchthon's canon gives us the sort of "doctrine" that was very much a *locus communis* in nature and operation. It settled the primary question of self-knowledge by capturing the powers of metaphysical reality. The cognitive concept of sin, its "what" and "when," was only the beginning of this elocutionary event; the "power and fruit of sin," to be discussed next, expressed the structural unity in his concept of doctrine of cognition and affection, doctrinal propositions and their connections with the inner recesses of human life. Scripture did not simply teach, it transformed—in the most important way that humans can conceive. The power originated in the contact between words and reality, between human language about sin and its powers and the reality that we do sin and are by nature sinners. Our own experience, he wrote, teaches us that this is so. Philip's tendency to over-systematize things should not make us forget this emotive, spiritual power that he constantly stressed as an essential mode of biblical authority.

Finally, a brief point ought to be made about the qualitative difference between Scripture and philosophy in this part of the *Loci communes*. The *discrimen* between the biblical *locus* of sin and the philosophical idea of *vitium* or vice was both analytical—philosophy looks only at the external form of the action—and a matter of experience. He could not imagine how moral philosophers failed to feel their own moral bondage. In this context of deep self-awareness, Melanchthon could say that humanity had no *sensus dei* or natural knowledge of God, for one could not properly know God without also knowing the self. The context of this remark must be kept in view when we discuss his position in reference to modern debates about his "intellectualism" and "natural theology." Meanwhile, the line of his own reasoning, toward sacred self-knowledge, now took him to his *locus* on the law.

On Law

Melanchthon introduced the topic of law: "The *locus* on laws will make known not a little more clearly the nature and power of sin, since the law is said to be knowledge of sin."[131] On this subject, "How much...more certain is that which the scriptures prescribe than what is gathered from commentaries."[132] Melanchthon made his well-known distinction between three classifications of law: "Some of the laws are natural, some divine, some human."[133] Once more asserting his belief that pioneering work was being done, he declared that, till now, nothing of great worth had been written on the entire topic of natural law,[134] since "human reason has been taken captive and blinded."[135] On the other hand, the Apostle Paul did teach, "in a wondrously elegant and learned argument [*enthymema*],...that there is in us a natural law."[136] In this section, besides Melanchthon's biblical doctrine of the divine, revealed law, we shall include a summation of his extended treatment of natural law. His ideas on that important subject will thus emerge in their context, and we shall be able to recall them as such in our final section on "natural theology."

Melanchthon affirmed, albeit in much more developed form, the view which we have observed in his earlier writings: "And so [on the basis of Paul] a law of nature is a common knowledge [*sententia*] to which all men equally assent and, indeed, which God has insculpted on the mind of everyone...."[137] He cautioned his readers against creating a system of natural laws by reason alone, for this was Cicero's procedure, "imitating Plato,"[138] and, in spite of what may have been of value, "many impious things...fell upon that disputation...."[139] That is what happens "when we follow the method and compendia of reason rather than the prescription of divine letters."[140] The judgment of the human mind erred (*fallax humani captus iudicium*) because of hereditary blindness (*propter cognatam caecitatem*).[141] These laws had indeed been insculpted within each of us, "but they can only scarcely be known."[142] It must also be stressed, wrote Melanchthon, that such law was from God and was not our own invention (*non inventam a nostris ingeniis*).[143]

Instead of the nine rules listed in the *Annotationes* on Matthew, Melanchthon now gave three principal (*capita*) laws of nature and discussed each in relation to biblical morality.

    I. God must be worshiped.

    II. Since we are born in a certain community [*vitae societatem*], no one should be done harm.

    III. Human society demands that we use all things in common [*omnibus rebus communiter utamur*].[144]

Melanchthon derived the first natural law from Romans 1:17ff.[145] On the question whether one might prove God's existence through reason, he equivocated in anti-speculative terms: "...that it might be possible by human syllogism to demonstrate that there is a God is more for the curious than the pious to dispute...."[146]

The second law of nature emerged from "the common necessity [*ex necessitudine commune*] that all of us are born bound and united with everyone else...."[147] He hastened to add that Scripture confirmed this universal apprehension of social law. Genesis 2:18 taught that it was not good for a man to be alone.[148]

The third law "plainly arises from the nature of human society."[149] He now affirmed the validity of Aristotle and Plato, both of whom believed that friends ought to have all things in common and that all men ought to strive for this ideal in society.[150] Melanchthon made one concession to practical realism, allowing that this third law must be modified by the standard of the second, which prohibited injury to anyone, and that the "sharing" required by this law could be expressed through legal contracts rather than in a literal manner.[151] Plato himself had observed, foreseeing practical difficulties, that society's sharing would be merely an approximation of what might occur among friends.[152] Melanchthon, noticeably, did not relate this third law of nature to the practice of the Christian community in the book of Acts (Acts 5-7), although this text may have been in the back of his mind, but viewed it rather as a Greek philosophical ideal.

He concluded his section on natural law by enlarging the topic to include "individual sayings...from the poets, orators, historians, which are usually referred to as an *ius gentium*...."[153] Pagan thinkers had written *sententiae* on marriage, adultery, giving thanks, ingratitude, hospitality and other subjects.[154] He cautioned, however, against unthinkingly accepting common beliefs which had arisen from "depraved affections of our nature...."[155] Among these false beliefs were Hesiod's sayings that one should offer love only to those who love in return and that one should give only to those who reward our giving,[156] the popular saying "give and take!"[157] and Euripides' view that one owed no kindness to an enemy.[158]

Next, Philip offered his doctrine of the divinely revealed law, "sanctioned by God through the canonical scriptures...."[159] He made conceptual distinctions between moral, judicial and ceremonial orders of divine law.[160] This section on divine law is of special value to seeing how he related the Old and New Testaments to each other and sought to solidify his belief in the doctrinal coherence of Scripture. "Moral laws," he wrote, "are those which are prescribed by the Decalogue, to which the studious person shall refer all the laws which have been put forth on morals in Scripture as a whole."[161] Building upon Luther's *Sermon on Good Works*, he related the Great Commandment to the affections, rather than merely to outward behavior.[162] And, perhaps building upon Erasmus,[163] he rejected the standard distinction between biblical "commandments" and "counsels."[164] In response to the rumblings which now threatened to break into riots among the monastic orders, including the Augustinian cloister at Wittenberg, Melanchthon bravely published the view that Luther had recently worked out in consultation with him:[165] such vows were certainly not divine commands, nor even counsels, but outgrowth from complete misapprehension of the gospel. "The reason why the tradition of making vows has been received is that it has happened only in ignorance of faith and evangelical freedom."[166]

The distinction between three kinds of divine law was essential to Melanchthon's developed view of Scripture as a coherent theological whole, particularly in reference to the weight and authority of Old Testament legislation for the Christian. The judicial laws of the Old Testament, he wrote, were put forth for the Jewish people[167] and were ignored by "evangelical letters" in the New Testament, "since legal claims have been forbidden to Christian people...."[168] The Old Testament contained many ceremonial laws, too, "rites of sacrifice, special days, vestments . . . and other things of this nature."[169] These laws "adumbrated mysteries of the gospel, as the epistle to the Hebrews teaches."[170] Several *loci* in 1 Corinthians and the letters of the prophets (*prophetarum literae*) also related types (*typos*) of the law allegorically (*allegorikos*) to the evangelical mysteries.[171] The Psalms, too, must often be taken as allegorical, though one ought to proceed "prudently."[172] He summed up his systematic principles on typological interpretation (as stated mainly in *De rhetorica*) in a few words. "Now he will handle allegories unfelicitously, who is not most well trained [*peritissimus*] in *all* Scripture [*universae scripturae*]."[173] When handled well, allegories would contribute not a little to our understanding the "power [*vim*] of the law and the gospel."[174] That is indeed what the author of Hebrews accomplished by comparing Aaron with Christ (*Aaronem cum Christo comparens*); ". . . it is remarkable how clearly he puts Christ before the eyes, how appropriately he teaches"[175] the benefits of Christ, His priestly ministry and the idea that we are saved through gracious justification and not by our works.[176]

Melanchthon's handling of the divine law in 1521 reiterates not only his deep conviction that Scripture was *one* word from God and that this "oneness" was a unity of propositions, but also his philosophical practice of finding warrant for this conviction in the context of diverse biblical traditions. It was not enough for him to use New Testament Christology and soteriology in an intuitive or loosely tropological manner, as it seems sometimes that it was for Luther. For a doctrine to be "biblical," in Melanchthon's terms, it had to be pervasive in a literal sense throughout the canon. Since the *texts* were rhetorical letters and *the* text was an oration from God subject to all the values that governed the truth theory of rhetoric, the interpreter was obliged to find and indicate the *foundation* of his doctrine in the letter of every relevant text. Since the structure of the biblical *sensus* really unfolded according to the logic of *inventio* and *dispositio*, so also must the theologian be controlled by sound technique in apprehending that *sensus*.

In this context, we may again affirm the received view that Melanchthon's use of texts presupposed and employed a concept of unity that was much more systematic than was Luther's.[177] We have sought to show the precise rhetorical nature of the "unity" for Melanchthon. If any of the central *loci* had created difficulty for his interpretive model, it would have been the complex teaching of the Old Testament on law and its relation to the grace of God. How was one to "find" the sense of Scripture in such texts without simply violating their literal meaning? By making his distinctions between moral, judicial and ceremonial law, and by viewing Old Testament rituals as "adumbrated mysteries" (on the authority of Hebrews), Philip sought rigorously to give the Old Testament text its share of control over theology. On these assumptions, he believed that the prophets themselves *related* "types" of the law, allegorically, and that the Psalms, as literature, gave *literary* justification for reading them in the light of the New Testament person of Christ.

The movement of Melanchthon's hermeneutical mind was not simply from *scopus* to individual text (as Luther's often was), but also, rigorously, from the individual text to the *scopus*—toward "finding" the foundational *loci communes* in those texts on a human literary level, rather than simply "seeing them as" the larger theological sense of the divine Word. This is possibly another reason he would eventually begin to feel the force of problem-texts that people used against Luther. There is also a suggestion of difference between them on their approaches to Moses and the moral law of the Old Testament. Bornkamm has argued that Luther took the laws of the Old Testament which conformed with "natural law" to be normative,[178] but that he disregarded much of it, even parts of the Decalogue, as crude folk-morality.[179] Melanchthon's norm was that all the laws were divine in origin and intent, and so could not be dispensed with easily as relative to a historical-cultural situation and purpose. He asserted that the entire Decalogue was moral in kind and that it was, therefore, universal in its application. The result was that, in Melanchthon, one sees a powerful instinct to recover a lost textual unity between Moses and the New Testament and, perhaps, a stronger commitment to the original intent of Old Testament texts than what seems typical of Luther. Further, his approach was less artificial than those of many later Lutheran dogmaticians.[180]

The modern Old Testament scholar may find Melanchthon's attempt to affirm the authority of both Testaments a mixed blessing. That he affirmed the Old Testament itself as God's Word to the church is a welcome departure from the Marcionite drift of Latin Christian theology. But to unify biblical ethics through the distinctions between judicial, ceremonial and moral law will seem too much the facile procedure of a systematician. And, ironically, the modern theologian may see in Melanchthon's system the strains of an "epicyclic" mentality, in vain defense of a dying orthodoxy, that is grist for the mill of hermeneutical and epistemic relativism, today.[181] Nevertheless, in its own setting—emerging from medieval practices into the new era of humanistic studies, and under the impact of Luther's equally revolutionary ideas about the sense of the text—it was an impressive use of available thought-forms to bring together and contain the most unsettling crosscurrents of the time in a solid and stable framework for teaching and preaching. The full depth and breadth of his position on the unity and power of the biblical doctrine of the law emerged in the following section on the gospel, for, as he put it, "that disputation cannot be grasped, unless the law is compared with the gospel."[182]

The Gospel

"There are, in general," Melanchthon wrote, "two parts of Scripture, law and gospel."[183] His preoccupation in the *Loci communes* with the systematic unity of the normative biblical sense was perhaps due, in part, to the fact that Luther's theology still lacked obvious exegetical grounding and justification.[184] Both Ebeling and J. S. Preus have shown that for Luther the Bible, particularly the Old Testament, was not essentially a book of doctrine. "It is a book which places man himself *coram deo*, and exposes and subjects him to God's concrete justice and mercy."[185] Although he had made the critical step of connecting his tropology with the letter of the text, construed as *promissio* or *testimonium*, it is not clear exactly how this procedure enabled the Old Testament to support his radical doctrine of justification apart from works of the law or showed Old Testament texts to apply in that *sense* directly to Christians in the present.[186] This section of the *Loci* is further evidence of Melanchthon's passion for unshakable textual foundations that would place doctrinal matters beyond reasonable dispute, as well as bring the teachings of Scripture directly to bear upon present-day readers. For him, the Old Testament was not simply a book of promise; it was a literary collection of *loci* or doctrines which lined up logically behind Luther's metaphor. This literature, as *litterae rhetoricae*, was aimed at people in all times and places; it was sacred oration. The entire canon reflected the classical structure: the strands of teaching on *quid evangelium, de vi legis* and *de vi evangelii* formed a tightly wound elocutionary braid of truth. The essential vehicle of thought was not simply a concept of "promise" in the context of a theological tropology that verged on allegorical typology, but was rather the literary structure that identified and conveyed the true sense of the language as the promise of the gospel. His sections on the nature and power of law and gospel were among the most forceful and convincing of his writings, because of the sheer power of his compendia, or assembly of biblical *exempla* and the *loci* embedded within them.

He began on a note of clarification about the use of "law and gospel" to classify the entire Bible. This, he affirmed, was a doctrinal nexus, not two separate and distinct doctrines, but a structural whole that was to be found throughout Scripture.

> Nor in truth does Scripture transmit law and gospel in such a way that you should consider the gospel only that which Matthew, Mark, Luke and John wrote, that the books of Moses are nothing but law. But the plan of the gospel is strewn, the *promises* are strewn in all the books of the Old and New Testaments [*sed sparsa est evangelii ratio, sparsi sunt promissiones in omnes libros*]. Moreover, laws are also strewn in all the volumes both of the Old and the New Testaments [*leges etiam sparsae sunt in omnia...volumina*].[187]

Nor ought one think of separate "times," one for the law and another for the gospel,[188] for, "Every time . . . is a time of law and gospel, just as in all times men have been justified in the same manner; sin has been shown through the law, grace through the promise or gospel."[189] Even before the giving of the law, Adam, Cain and their offspring possessed knowledge of natural law, which Melanchthon now (rather uncharacteristically) called a tradition [leges acceptas a patribus] rather than an "inner law," known intuitively, "not some inborn judgment, implanted or inscribed by nature on men's minds...."[190]

But first, what was the gospel? Melanchthon offered his definition: "...God's promise of grace or mercy and, indeed, the forgiveness of sin and testimony of God's benevolence towards us...."[191] He wrote, "Christ is the pledge [pignus] of all of those promises, so that all the promises of Scripture must be referred to Him [in eum referendae sunt omnes scripturae promissiones], who at first is revealed obscurely, afterwards more clearly."[192]

To appreciate the precise sense, for Melanchthon, of this "referring," both the clear and the obscure, one must see how he construed the promises as loci communes on the grace of God that emerged from biblical histories and teachings. The promise of grace sustained Adam after the fall, for the promise of the woman's seed was "the first gospel, by which Adam...was justified."[193] Next, the promise was made to Abraham, fulfillment of which the Old Testament constantly viewed in the coming of the Christ (Deut. 18:18, Ezek. 34:23).[194] "On the whole [In totum], the prophets repeated the law and promise of the Christ."[195] New Testament texts such as Matthew's genealogies or statements, such as in Romans 1:2, on Christ as the fulfillment of the prophets' message encourage us to think that such promises of temporal things [rerum temporalium] are not mere "figures of spiritual promises [non modo figurae sunt]," but are "by themselves [per sese] testimonies of God's grace and mercy...."[196] One could observe the "counsel of the divine Spirit in the Scriptures, how carefully [blande], how sweetly [suaviter] He educates [erudiat] the pious, as He has no other aim than that we might be saved."[197] All Scripture had been written with this eruditio in mind, "sometimes law, sometimes gospel."[198] Melanchthon wished to stress the point (which he would then seek to prove beyond question), that the plain letter of the Old Testament taught these doctrines in the Lutheran sense. Although "in all the letters of the New Testament the discourse is more evangelical,"[199] the writings of the Old Testament, taken according to their plain letter, teach both law and gospel. "I am not speaking at all about figures, but about those things which the letter itself plainly brings forth."[200]

His use of the term testimonia was more philosophically mechanistic than Luther's apparently was.[201] For Melanchthon, the eruditio and testimonia of the Old Testament came as rhetorical exempla with all the inventive and dispositional properties of that kind of writing. The rhetorical concept of exempla was his main tool for connecting passage with passage, text with text and writer with reader. Not only the Mosaic writings, but also the "sacred histories are examples, first of laws, then of the gospel."[202] Saul was an example of the law,[203] David of the gospel.[204] The Prophets contained many similar instances,[205] just as in the New Testament the examples of the centurion (Matt. 8:5ff.), Zacchaeus (Luke 19:1ff.) and the Syrophoenician woman (Mark 7:24ff.)

were of the gospel, and those of the Pharisees were of "the fury...and wrath of God."[206]

Within this literary context, the Lutheran way of asserting the continuity and distinctions between the Old Testament and the New could be articulated clearly as evident in the text itself. The difference between the Old and New Testaments was that Christ, in the New, had already come, and thus the promise was fulfilled and set forth most clearly, didactically [didaktikos], by the Apostle Paul in Romans.[207] Logical differences between them ought not be recognized. Moses taught the law with reference to the affections, not merely with the aim of influencing "external works,"[208] and Christ never taught the gospel apart from the law, "for grace cannot be preached apart from the law...."[209] Even the commandment to love one's enemy, stressed in the New Testament by Jesus, was part of the Old Testament moral teaching: Leviticus 19:17ff., in the better Hebrew texts [in nostris codicibus],[210] Isaiah 58:6ff. and Proverbs 20:22 all made it clear that love of enemies was required. Melanchthon puzzled over the issue of the Canaanite conquest, finally denying a conflict of moral propositions and offering the rather bland solution that, before Christ, love of enemies was required only between Jews, but afterwards between Jew and Gentile.[211]

In Melanchthon's view, this biblical doctrine or sensus of law and gospel was proper to both Old and New Testaments. The concepts of locus and exempla provided the systematic tools for showing that it was so. But beyond this indicative process of finding the essential loci communes of texts, Melanchthon developed the view that, as it is in the nature of loci communes and exempla, we must also find ourselves within them. The issue was not merely with the truth of the doctrine, but with its final scope or power to transform one's life. His ultimate concern was with doctrine as a living power.

In his section on the power of the law, Melanchthon characteristically stressed the disagreement between philosophy and true religion. Scripture viewed the law as something which brought forth fear of God; human reason viewed it as the means of acquiring a virtuous life.[212] One either viewed the law "carnally," and therefore as means of self-justification,[213] or one sensed the power of the law to reveal the sins of the flesh before God.[214] This power was not dependent upon New Testament doctrine; it burst forth from the text of the Old Testament. The Psalms,[215] the Prophets[216] and Moses[217] together indicated that the law brought out affections of guilt and fear. They confirmed the views expressed by Paul in Romans 7, describing the power of the law to reveal sin.[218]

Some of these texts on the law thus contained straightforward moral assertions, or loci, which, when taken alongside the teachings about sin ("Among hypocrites the law accomplishes nothing")[219] and not by themselves ("mere shadows of the law"),[220] brought dreadful things to heart and mind. Biblical references to God's wrath and threats of judgment all referred to this spiritual context of sinfulness, instead of to simple disobedience, where escape might be had through discipline.[221] Sometimes this deduction itself was incorporated into a locus, that before God we are always sinners under judgment.[222] The power of the law was thus both a biblical doctrine and a present, personal reality for the honest reader. This doctrine and its power, of course, came forth as the major premise of Paul's Romans.[223]

Sometimes this truth and reality was mediated through "types," such as the people Israel who shuddered in fear before the fire and thunder on the mountain (Exod. 19:16)[224] and whom the "evangelist" Moses relieved mercifully, saying, "be not afraid. . . ."[225] This shows that, for Melanchthon, the distinction between "type" and "example" was not a very clear one. In both instances, the texts were histories, which contained *loci communes* that referred to the larger world of biblical thought and applied directly to the horizon of the present reader and to justification before God. Perhaps a "type" related more properly to the affections and how one ought to act, whereas an "example" referred one more directly to doctrines, such as law and gospel, but the difference was not unambiguous. Melanchthon treated this "type" as something that both afflicted and comforted the heart at the same time by its *loci* of law, sin and grace. Doctrines they were, indeed, but, as *loci communes*, they were doctrines in which to find oneself and to find oneself before God.

In summary, Melanchthon viewed the law as the means by which God enabled His people to know themselves as sinners; such knowledge would be impossible to attain otherwise.[226] But then there was the "power of the gospel."[227] Those whose consciences were terrified by the moral law would have fallen in despair had it not been for the promise of grace and the power of the gospel. By this power, "as *exempla* declare wondrously," they were revived and given life.[228] Nothing—no garment, no pretext—could cover the sin of Adam and Eve; in God's presence they could but flee and give voice to their fear that the Lord might behold their nakedness.[229] Melanchthon's speculative comment on the text is revealing. Adam wrestled bitterly with himself, until he heard the "promise of mercy..., 'her seed will crush the head of the serpent.'"[230] The attempt was made, nonetheless, to ground this interpretation in a deduction from Adam's words to the Lord, "I heard your voice in the garden, and I was afraid because I was naked, and I hid myself." Melanchthon drew the conclusion, "Behold the confession and admission of the conscience."[231] Hence, here emerged the *locus* of sin. By giving them clothing to wear, which clearly signified the incarnation of Christ, the Lord also was doing much to repair their damaged consciences.[232] The *locus* of the gospel thus emerged, and, allegorically, the text reminded *us* (presumably not Adam and Eve) of the incarnation of Christ.[233] Likewise, King David was morally shaken by the voice of Nathan the prophet, and "he would have perished, indeed, if he had not immediately heard the gospel: 'The Lord will forgive your sin, you will not die.'"[234] Melanchthon again anchored his interpretations with an appeal to the literary construction of the text. Those who have fallen in love with allegories should look for truth in the "histories of the Old Testament."[235] The *exemplum* of David provided a helpful lesson: "....you see, here, how much erudition there is in this single example of David, if you consider the letter alone [*si solam literam consideres*]."[236] Histories are not allegorical, but are rather events, as in this instance, pictured in words: "What word could conceivably be more evangelical than this: 'The Lord will forgive your sin'?"[237]

Events and words must be searched for their lessons on the dominant *loci communes*. That would seem to have been Melanchthon's logic in asserting that one ought not look for allegories when dealing with such texts. "Nay, rather, that alone must be observed, in which the Spirit of God bountifully exhibits first the works of His wrath, then of mercy."[238]

Through the entryway of proper textual restraint and construal, the unified sense became clear and powerful. This same teaching emerged from an accumulation of histories from the New Testament:[239] the woman who wiped the feet of Jesus with her tears,[240] the story (*historia*) of the prodigal son,[241] Peter's declaration that the Lord should depart from him, a sinful man,[242] all were *exempla* which taught the nature and power of law and gospel.[243] These *exempla* or *historiae* in the New Testament referred to the theme of promised joy prominent in the writings of the Prophets, such as Isaiah 32:18; 51:3 and Jeremiah 33:6ff., all of which describe the future of God's people as one of jubilation. The joyous voices of the prophets "describe Christ and the church."[244] A king would one day come whose word would be different from the word of law, one who, unlike Moses, could bear to look upon the divine majesty without being afraid, and who would come proclaiming the joyful news of the gospel.[245]

On Grace, Justification and Faith

In this crowning section of the *Loci communes*, Melanchthon began by setting the "phrasing of Scripture"[246] against scholastic doctrines of grace as a "quality" (he rather liked Lombard's association of grace with the Holy Spirit),[247] for grace was about a disposition in God, "...God's favor, mercy, gratuitous goodwill toward us."[248] Without this distinction, the concept of justification by faith was obscured, for "only faith [*sola fides*] in the mercy and grace of God in Jesus Christ is righteousness [*iustitia*]."[249] Romans 3:22; 4:5 and Genesis 15:6 affirmed the truth that faith was our righteousness, but not the "faith" of the sophists who called it "assent to those things which are put forth in the scriptures...."[250] Melanchthon wished to speak of a different order of belief, with a different nature and power.[251]

Asserting the spiritual dimension of the problem, Melanchthon made what one can call a distinction between faith and belief or knowledge. "That there is a God, the wrath of God, the mercy of God are spiritual things [*spiritualia sunt*]; therefore, they cannot be known by the flesh."[252] To have faith is not the same thing as to have knowledge through the natural faculties, for "whatever nature knows of God, without the Spirit of God renewing and illuminating our hearts, is frigid opinion [*frigida opinio est*]...."[253] A few pages later, he commented on the passage in Hebrews 11, which said that it was "by faith" that we know that the world was made. One senses in his comments an underlying distinction, common among rhetoricians, between bare *scientia* and *sapientia*, and Melanchthon placed this in the context of law and grace. Mere "historical faith" concerning the creation of the world, "that common opinion which was established even among the Gentiles," was not faith. Faith was "knowledge of the goodness and power of God gathered from the work of creation."[254] Christian faith in a creator was "not frigid opinion, but a very living knowledge [*sed vivacissima cognitio*] of both the power [*potentia*] and goodness of God...."[255] "I ask you, is the flesh able to interpret the mystery of creation in that manner?"[256] With this picture of faith as a spiritual passion, he, not surprisingly, resisted the ideas of *fides acquisita* and *fides informata*, even for the sake of teaching, for "you should know that Scripture used the word 'faith' most simply...," as trust (*fiducia*) in the divine mercy promised in Christ.[257]

Again the rhetorical shape of biblical doctrine emerged in Melanchthon's treatment of Christian faith. Not only was faith a passionate trust in God's grace, but the biblical *locus* of faith, comprising a great variety of *loci* on faith, had a power of its own to evoke a passionate response. This rhetoric was the human dimension of the spiritual events that together formed true faith. Several *exempla* would bring forth the power of faith better than could detailed theological discussion.[258] Abraham believed not merely that God existed, but in God's promise, and he "declared that faith by an eminent example, when he was about to sacrifice his son, never doubting that God would grant him a posterity. . . ."[259] The Hebrew people, caught between the Egyptians and the sea, did not stop like scholastics to debate the situation, but "believed in the divine voice, the divine miracles...and so committed themselves through faith to the bottom of the sea."[260] Melanchthon judged that the power of these examples was purposeful; "these *exempla* indeed have been displayed to *us*, that we might learn to believe...."[261] The words of Moses in Deuteronomy,[262] the *exempla* of Israel's battle victories recited in the Psalms,[263] the prophet Hanani's strong demands that Asa trust God,[264] Jehoshaphat conquering his enemies with but a song ("I truly doubt that Scripture displays the power of faith by any more powerful example....")[265] and many others[266] were there for the "pious and learned reader" to learn the "nature [*ratio*] of faith" and gain strength of conscience.[267] And again, "I am not seeking allegories, but I mean that the *history* promises mercy in the very fact that corporal benefits have been promised."[268]

The New Testament, of course, abounded with such examples for us. Underlining the inspiration and didactic unity of Scripture, Melanchthon wished to record several of them, "so that it might be known that the spirit of each Testament is the same."[269] These *exempla* included Peter's speech in Acts 15:9ff., in which all the works of Old Testament saints were declared sin, to demonstrate that even they—David, Isaiah, Jeremiah—were justified through faith alone.[270] The epistle to the Hebrews defined faith and then gave a series of illustrative examples to form the subject into a powerful doctrine: "...so he defines faith; 'faith is the substance of things hoped for'...."[271] Never mind that the "sophists in their glosses twisted this 'sketch' [*hupographe*] of faith according to their private imaginings [*ad sua somnia*] and by that carnal little opinion which they call 'faith.'"[272] Let us "render the simplest words by the simplest proposition: faith is certitude of those things that do not appear."[273] And to this most plain definition the author added *exempla definitionis*, which proved that faith was the way in which all men had to approach God from the time of Adam to the present.[274] Cain and Abel exemplified the requirement of an inner, heartfelt faith in contrast to sophistic frigidity.[275] The *exempla* of Enoch,[276] Noah,[277] Abraham,[278] Moses[279] and the rest proved the proposition (Heb. 11:6 *cum* Rom. 14:23) that no one can please God without faith.[280] Indeed, the *exemplum* of Abraham and Isaac was a prelude to the entire New Testament.[281]

Melanchthon thus used his rhetorical construal of the text to find and elaborate what was for him a coherent, forceful presentation of biblical doctrine in Lutheran terms. The gathering together of histories and examples pertaining to the *locus* of faith made it clear that the pervading idea of all Scripture was to refer us to the promise of grace in Jesus Christ. The concept of divine inspiration was fused with that of the rhetorical shape of the message. "And so, through the history of the entire Scripture, He [God] is completely devoted to teaching us [*totus incumbit, ut doceat*] and making us accustomed to trust in His goodness...."[282] Not to believe merely in the history of Jesus, but to penetrate to the "why" of His history, "to believe why He put on flesh, why He was crucified, why He returned to life after death,"[283] was in the essence of having real faith, something that went beyond knowledge and words, and must be one's very own action of "hearing" the doctrine within.[284]

For Melanchthon, biblical doctrine was an elocutionary, rhetorical event, by which a truth moved within both the analytical and affective realms of existence, between mind and heart, thought and affection, understanding and action. There could be no division between theory and practice, no wise practice without wisdom, no true wisdom without practice. The biblical writers used words in a way that tapped into and unleashed the "nature and power" of God's Word to His people, as a coherent, didactic whole.[285] The essential proposition or *sententia* of the text became a source of power for both God and human beings. For God, our teacher, the rhetorical word was the agent for self-disclosure and establishing the kingdom of faith. For human beings, in ignorance and sin, it made possible the reality of the "justification" which it proposed as *oratio sacra*. As in the diplomacy of human affairs, for Philip, rhetoric was the bond by which God and human beings might be reconciled. The sense of Scripture was not merely a proposition, then, but was something like a "word-event," to use Hans Frei's term, wherein the things signified by the words, operating between reader and text, became ontological realities that obtained between the person and God.

Melanchthon's presentation of the doctrines of the gospel, faith and justification reinforces the points that we have already made about his position on the unity and perspicuity of the biblical canon. The overall unity of Scripture was that of a classical tradition, its lucidity that of a rhetorician's *inventio* and *dispositio* of its common truths, its truths analytically and morally-affectively inherent in the eternal nature of things. We have said as much as we wish to say on the complex matter of strengths and weaknesses of his approach to the coherence of the canon and on comparisons with Luther on the structure of the Word. We have mainly tried to show what is distinctive about Philip's construal of the text. And we cannot possibly undertake an evaluation in the light of contemporary biblical theology, bedeviled as it is by forces of fragmentation in its construals of biblical tradition. In what remains of this book, we should like to engage two of the most widely debated issues in the historiography. The preceding sections on law and gospel, with their impressive picture of the power of Scripture, have placed us now to consider Melanchthon's alleged "intellectualism." Second, the systematic references to the qualitative, divine *discrimen* of Scripture in reference to philosophy complete the textual foundation that we require for tackling the question of "natural theology" in the young Melanchthon. In the balance is the consistency of his metaphysics with a truly Protestant interpretation of Scripture, whether he was an alien or an ally to the cause of genuine Lutheranism. By applying the interpretive framework set forth in the previous chapters, we shall seek to show that scholars have typically underestimated Melanchthon on both of these levels of his approach to human reason.

Melanchthon and "Intellectualism"

In the mid-nineteenth century, three hundred years after his death, fresh theological winds in Germany brought with them a chance for new confessional slants on the name and reputation of Melanchthon. More than a century of denunciation on every essential level (as evidenced, not least, by the ritual destruction of his portrait in Wittenberg) had at long last reached the point of silent repudiation.[286] Heinrich Heppe searched the original sources for a more reasoned point of view on Melanchthon than had yet come to light. His work set the standard for the important studies that followed afterwards. An age that had grown tired of religious war (and warlike religion) was seeking peace between Christianity and culture. It came to a more balanced assessment of this "Preceptor of Germany."[287] But still there were debates. As it had been from the beginning, the heart of contention was, and has remained, the relationship between faith and reason in the structure of his thought. Did reason corrupt faith, or faith reason, or did each corrupt the other—the worst of both worlds? Or did Melanchthon perhaps manage to accomplish the rare feat of successfully affirming both Protestant Christianity and human rationality? The dominant side of the question has been the theological one. Was Philip, after all, the "ally" of Lutheranism, as in Hildebrandt's little volume,[288] or did he rather breed a "blight" that spread upon its youthful shoots, to use Caemmerer's unflattering metaphor?[289]

The discussion of faith and reason in Melanchthon may be divided on at least three levels. We have already examined his metaphysical and epistemological commitments in the selection and treatment of topics. Ironically, it is usually his "anti-intellectualism" that is suspected there. As we have sought to show, his procedure is best placed in the setting of rhetorical *inventio*. Rather than seeing a principle of "double truth" or an anti-theistic "anthropocentrism," we have chosen to view his procedure as that of proper rhetorical method, whereby one starts with the existential core of universal truths or *loci* and then works outwards from the center to doctrines that are hermeneutically contingent upon it. His was neither an "anti-intellectualism" nor an "intellectualism," strictly speaking, but a fusion of dialectical and rhetorical structures to select *loci communes*, which were by nature intellectually and affectively powerful when placed in their logically and existentially correct order.

There is a second level of the question, however. The less dogmatic age was also the more romantic, worldly one, an era whose theologians were often the children of Kant, and whose theologies were the harvest of Kantian metaphysics. Religious truth was to be found, not in cognitive propositions about divine reality, but in "practical assertions," in "spirit," in a "consciousness of God." Barth and others have made the litany of such norms during that time a familiar one.[290] In the historical theology which then emerged alongside higher criticism as a self-conscious theological *Wissenschaft*, there was both infatuation with the spiritual genius of Luther and appreciation of the practical side of Melanchthon. But there was also the sentiment that Philip's entire conception of theology and theological language exhibited a pervasive and degenerative "intellectualism." The list of writers who have taken this tack, and who have made it, as Fraenkel wrote, "one of the most respectable traditions of Reformation historiography," is very long and well known and need not be covered here.[291]

The kind of "intellectualism" in question is not primarily a metaphysical one. It touches, rather, upon Melanchthon's theory of doctrine, its nature and function. The broad critique is that he viewed Christian revelation in the terms of "mind-to-mind" communication. Everything began with proper cognition, and it ended with that. There are compelling reasons for rejecting this view and replacing it with a better explanatory model. In our discussion of topical selection in Melanchthon, we sought to show that his procedure is best judged within the conceptual field of his theory of *inventio*. Already implicit in this procedure is a theory about the nature of doctrines. They are not essentially propositions, but structures of *truth*, *loci communes*, which contain the seeds of wisdom and moral power that inhere in the created universe, or in divine reality. Moreover, these precious, sacred *loci* have been revealed by God and put to use by the Spirit of God. The modality of this revelation is hardly limited to knowledge of propositions. Sacred truth emerged in a great variety of ways, never independent from history, life and action on the part of God's people. The "propositions" emerged, rhetorically, from the holistic life-structures that God established for human beings. The charge of a reductionistic "intellectualism" is thereby weakened by its failure adequately to consider what Philip meant by "doctrine" on the level of topical truth-structure.

To take this analysis a step further, we propose that his method of arranging and presenting his topics, that is, his conception of theology and theological language, is best understood and assessed as a kind of rhetorical *dispositio*. There has been, in recent decades, a growing sense that Melanchthon's style had more to it than merely defining and organizing (Luther's) propositional truths.[292] Our purpose here is to support this growing view and to define more precisely than has been done how rhetorical *dispositio* (and its presumed basis in *inventio* of *loci communes*) was, for Melanchthon, the linguistic model of things like "propositions," "definitions," "doctrines" and "truths."

It will do no good to deny that there was, in Melanchthon, a passion for the proposition, for the proper terms, for the contained thought. His grounding in dialectic and logic reflected not merely a metaphysics of rational order, but a great love for that order itself. He was very much the expression of the Greek universe which he believed himself to inhabit. Luther's reference to him as "that little Greek" was a good description. And Philip's image of the sacred text expressed his deep, personal conviction that the mind of God was itself logically ordered, *mens aeterna*. The world of the biblical text could no more reflect logical disorder than could the world of nature. We have examined and discussed his concepts of biblical perspicuity and unity in enough detail to make the truth of these claims apparent, and, of course, to assert his passion for thought is hardly to invite contention in our discipline. We are rather interested in gaining an appropriate perspective on this dimension of his nature and work, on what he himself meant by "thought" and "order" in the world of Scripture.

The intrinsic connections in his thinking between dialectic and rhetoric on all levels are essential to grasping the theory and practice of *doctrine* which he employed in the *Loci communes* of 1521. His work was not really a "theology of definitions," as Troeltsch wrote of it, for that is too narrow a construal of his purposes and thought-forms. It was essentially a work of theological *inventio* and *dispositio* (with a minimum of effort put into garnished elocution) of *loci communes*. Simply to think of theological doctrines as *loci communes* was to picture them as something much more exalted than mere definitions or cognitive propositions. As developed ideas and doctrines, *Loci communes* did, indeed, have cognitive meaning, and rhetorical *inventio* included using the instruments or "questions" of definition. But the teleological reference of the *quid sit?* was always, through that, to unleash the *vis rei*, the power of the thing. And that power was no mere artifice, but was connected with something intrinsic to our existence, a *vis nativa*. As we have seen, Melanchthon was deeply committed to the belief (so much so that, to our knowledge, he never felt the need to defend it) that each writing of Scripture, and Scripture as a whole, had been put together by both God and men as a literary tradition of this kind. The theologian was thus a rhetorician once removed from the original rhetorical events that produced the text. The theologian was not very different from the classical scholar and teacher, "finding" and "indicating" the meaning and native power of the great human literature.

Each topic, beginning with the most basic teachings on self-knowledge, was handled to reveal the cognitive and human power of the truth contained within the *locus*. On the models of Romans and Hebrews, Melanchthon carefully set down the *quid* and then *vis* of each *locus*, using propositions collected from the sacred traditions and also examples and types, which he thought were particularly effective for conveying both meaning and the energy for motivation and Christian action, eventually that action which rendered us to God and God to us. The superbly written sections on law, gospel, faith and justification represent something very different from merely logging definitions or simply putting Luther's proposals into a tidy form, like the dull work of a theological amanuensis. Aside from the criticisms that we have made of his over-systematizing, we believe that these must rank among the finest of early Protestant summaries of biblical theology.

And, if this "first Protestant dogmatics" was imperfect, it was also a success. Luther's famous comment must have expressed the feelings of many others who were its first readers in its time, under circumstances in which a new world was being born and new Christian ideas were bursting forth from all directions in a desperate effort to cope. Martin rated the *Loci communes* as second in stature only to the canon and claimed that one could find "no other book under the sun where the whole of theology is so excellently explained...."[293] The widespread influence of the work, so far as one is able to trace it, would also weigh in favor of seeing the *Loci* as having communicated with a simple charm and power that may elude the modern reader.[294] Nevertheless, if the recent writings of people like Hauerwas, Hartt, Thiemann and others are to be taken seriously, there is much to praise in Melanchthon's ontological union of cognitive realism and moral teleology. For this is precisely what they believe is most urgently needed in our own time.[295] We dare say that it has ever been so, that such a union is required of the academic theologian in every time. Furthermore, in rating Melanchthon, one cannot stress enough the difficulty of his calling as Protestantism's first dogmatician. In Luther's words, "...at first it was not so easy as it is now."[296]

Melanchthon, indeed, viewed Scripture as a textbook of doctrine; its authority was in essence its doctrine. But for him "doctrine" was a grand elocutionary event between God and honest people. It was *oratio sacra*, not a theologian's lexicon or dictionary. We have been critical of Melanchthon for his lapses into overly crafted exegesis and his habit of forcing a unity upon the canon. Nevertheless, this criticism must be taken in the context of his own horizon as a rhetorician. He possessed a greater passion and theological imagination than he has been given credit for in the mainstream of the discipline. If Melanchthon fell short of Luther's "prophetic" stature, then he was not without company. Our study has called for a measure of respect and admiration for him in his own right that has not always been considered his due.

Melanchthon and Natural Theology

We have proposed that Melanchthon's concepts of rhetorical *inventio* and *dispositio* were underlying agents that shaped the deep structures of his thought on faith and reason. Our discussion has mainly concentrated on his idea of biblical doctrine and, particularly, its rhetorical authority as human language, as *oratio*. However, we have seen that Melanchthon was also committed (even before meeting Luther) to the idea of biblical inspiration and the Bible's authority as a uniquely divine revelation from God. The normative sense of Scripture was for him sacred in a way that made it *alone* originally and universally binding. It was not one revelation alongside others, nor merely a complement to incomplete ones, but was in a class by itself in the way of

Kierkegaard's "infinite qualitative distinction." Philip often used the adjective "sola" to qualify the word "scriptura."

Nevertheless, we have seen that the very expression and defense of this *discrimen* between Scripture and philosophy betrayed an indestructible bond between them on the deepest levels of Philip's psyche and world view. His cosmos was one in which truth was always a matter of both knowledge and passion. Knowledge without passion was for him barren scholasticism; passion without knowledge, frightening fanaticism. It was precisely this philosophical view of the cosmos that Melanchthon believed was in the very substance of both biblical and classical doctrine. The very language of "difference" and separation between Scripture and philosophy was also the language of identity and correspondence between them. Both had their roots in the same basic beliefs about the ontological structure and value of the world, and also in the truth theory, epistemology and linguistic principles which grew from that metaphysical vision. For the young (and older) Melanchthon, Scripture and the classics were, on one level, radically divided and opposed to each other. He was an enthusiastic proponent of the Protestant principle of *sola scriptura*. On another level, though, they were strangely united with each other as one. Both philosophy and Scripture were, in part, expressions of the same universal truth-norms, or *caussae communes*. We have sought to identify both of these complex movements of his thought that reach back into his early days at Heidelberg and Tübingen, when he walked between the extremists on each side of the *Wegestreit*.

The practice of both separating and uniting revelation and reason emerged in Philip long before he met Martin Luther. We observed something of the same pattern in his formative environment, where Plato and Aristotle played complementary parts. As a young Master at Tübingen he had learned to think and live between the extremes of nominalism and realism. In the essay *De artibus liberalibus*, the divine and the human were properly separated through precise distinction of categories and terms; the methods and theories of Steinbach had sped him in this direction. And yet, how he loved the rich Platonism of Reuchlin and of John Stöffler! The divine and the human were united by the universal order, apprehended by the intellect and heart as intellectual passion, and passionate understanding. In this sense, he could write, "Jupiter rex idem omnibus." Had he not adopted Luther's doctrine of grace, he would most likely have fallen in with a strand of reforming Catholicism that extended back to Geyler, Gerson, Agricola and, through them, to the Fathers. His modified philosophical nominalism would then have caused no trouble for his theology. But adopt Luther's doctrine of grace, and its concomitant view of human depravity, he did, and the result was great difficulty in finding an integrated theological self. The constant debates about his true identity are signs that this search went on after his death, and it goes on still for the "unknown Melanchthon."

Anyone who has written about Melanchthon has been conscious of how difficult it is to say exactly how the philosophical and theological dimensions of his world view fit together. For more than a century, this subject has been the center of intense debate. The issue, of course, is much larger than Melanchthon.

In the balance is the identity of Protestantism and its ability to engage human culture constructively in the arts and sciences and in the extended realms of social, political and economic life. And the issue blends with the problem of ecumenical outreach toward Catholicism. Wiedenhofer has rightly summed up the entire controversy as about how, to use his terms, the "disjunctive" and "conjunctive" elements of Melanchthon's thought were related to each other.[297] In this final section, we shall make our proposals on "natural theology" in the light of Philip's linguistic understanding of meaning in oration. We shall propose a way of viewing his position as a coherent form of Protestant humanism, if not as entirely identical with Luther's view of philosophy. Our larger thesis will be that, for Melanchthon, the *discrimen* of the biblical text was a property of its *sense*. The literal sense of the text was what made it *itself* and established its distinct relation to other texts, particularly classical ones. Thus, when Melanchthon asserted the *discrimen* of Scripture, he asserted that property of its *sense* which gave it, not just authority as a text, but a kind of transcendence or difference from all other literature. That property was the greater whole that emerged from the sum of several parts that we have examined: the perfect topical relevance to the human condition, compelling clarity and logical power of argument, inter-textual coherence and a basic perspicuity as not only factual, but as personal truth, in which one knew oneself to be in "another world" or "seized unto heavenly things," to use two of his expressions from earlier writings. These were the properties of the *sensus* of the biblical text that, together, created its *discrimen*. On the noetic side, he also affirmed the work of the Spirit and the role of living faith. In our view, though, this man who loved texts was a theologian of the text, and for him the transcendent authority of Scripture belonged mainly to the literature and its *sensus literalis*.

But what exactly was that *sensus*? What were the properties of its terms (for its sense was, after all, the sense of words)? As we have seen, he pictured the normative text, or sense of the text, as a system of diverse teachings that were related logically to each other in something like the manner of concentric rings, the position of each decided by its relation to the center of existence, the *quaestiones* in reflection upon the identity of the self. The core of the biblical *sensus* was the clustered doctrine of law, sin and grace; one then looked outward toward the limits or boundaries of the rhetorical sphere. All the parts were authoritative, but the whole had its essential meaning in reference to the center. If the topical dimension of the *sensus* could be pictured as concentric rings, the organizational (dispositional) one looked very like a structured work of didactic oration, with each *locus* positioned in its logically appropriate place. The *sensus* of Scripture was the whole of the canon defined by its *scopus*, and, for him, the *scopus* was equivalent to one's logical *status*. The whole oration, as the Word of God, had its identity and authority in reference to a central proposition, on which the meaning of every part was hermeneutically dependent for its full meaning and power. Thus the *discrimen*, or distinctively superior element of one's oration (in this instance, one's tradition), was essentially in its *scopus* and, for Melanchthon, the *scopus* of Scripture was its *status* on justification by grace through faith.

How one imagined the *scopus* of the oration, or tradition as a whole, thus determined how one pictured its distinctive authority. Therefore, before one can properly assess Melanchthon's stance on the difference between faith and reason, one must have a clear view of how he imagined and defined the "difference" of authoritative oration with respect to its *scopus*. Our proposal is that, if one assesses Melanchthon's view of the *discrimen* in the context of his rhetorical belief that the meaning and authority of a textual tradition was dependent upon its *status dicendi* as the *scopus* of the whole, then one begins to see the general coherence of his position and to sympathize with his pained insistence that, in spite of accusations to the contrary, "rem ipsam semper retinui." He had always retained the essential theme, he believed, and was deeply wounded by the thought that he had betrayed Luther and the gospel of Christ. His development, from pre-Lutheran humanism to the Lutheran Protestantism of his later years, displayed much greater intellectual stability and strength than one finds credited to him in the standard histories. And, in our judgment, his undying concern for the creation and for humanity, in every phase of his life, was neither inconsistent with a distinctively Protestant doctrine of grace and biblical authority, nor clearly inferior to Luther's rather dialectical approach to the mind. Indeed, the case can be made that Melanchthon's manner of relating faith to reason on this level generated a form of Protestantism that was superior to Luther's in holding out any promise of having a powerful influence on the structure and operation of cultural systems.

The Historiography

From a Protestant point of view, Melanchthon's "conjunctive" impulse has caused the most fundamental debate. Few Protestants have accused him of dividing between faith and reason too sharply, or of setting the one too authoritatively above the other.[298] There are really two schools of thought on the nature of such "conjunction" in Melanchthon. The commonest and most popular is that, as a humanist, Philip was an incurable synthesist, intuitively and systematically committed to bringing the two realms of truth together. Bornkamm described Melanchthon's purposes and procedures in this way: "...Melanchthon is not so very interested in the boundaries [*Grenzen*] between reason and faith, but much more in their mutual interpenetration."[299] He compared the relationship between reason and faith in Melanchthon to that between law and gospel, where the law served as the mechanism for synthesis, the gospel as the discriminating element.[300] The works of Hartfelder, Herrlinger, Maier, Seeberg, Hübner, Bauer, Schwarzenau, Sick, Neuser, Bornkamm, Greschat, Hildebrandt and Brüls all represent versions of this interpretation.[301] The view that a first-order aim for Melanchthon as a theologian was finding the "inner relation,"[302] a "complementarity"[303] or a "naive harmony" between faith and reason[304] has usually stemmed from a generic view of his humanism as having been committed to a similar philosophy of truth, and it has not gone deeply into the theological and philosophical frameworks *for* his humanism. This image of Melanchthon's development makes his early Lutheran period (1519-1521) seem a dramatic interruption of his basic intellectual values and makes the later Lutheran years, in which a natural theology unfolded, appear badly inconsistent with the earlier ones. It gives the impression that Melanchthon was more shaped by persons and events than actually shaping them. Very frequently, though not always, this model is combined with what is more an assumption than a conclusion from arguments, that Luther's Lutheranism is the norm and that Melanchthon's short-lived early Lutheranism produced his best theology, while his later Lutheranism was mainly a humanistic *post mortem* on better days.

The second broad hermeneutical approach to Melanchthon holds, on the contrary, that his fundamental aim was to define the boundary lines *between* faith and reason. The view that separation, rather than synthesis, was a first-order aim arose with Troeltsch, who was, to our knowledge, the first to suggest that German nominalism had left an important mark upon Melanchthon's theological method.[305] Others, such as von Waltershausen, Sell, Heim and Geyer, have agreed with this main thesis that an "Occamist" influence accounted in part for the powerful motivation to preserve faith and reason as logically distinct categories, retaining the "purity" and integrity of each in its own rightful realm.[306] Wiedenhofer's position is unique in that he attributed the "disjunctive" moment to Melanchthon's pre-Lutheran past, but connected this with a disposition toward realism in theology, within the framework of "Erasmian humanism."[307] The work of Wilhelm Maurer is also difficult to classify. In his great biography of Melanchthon, he was keenly aware of a more differentiated humanism than that proposed by Wiedenhofer, but it must be said that (as we have observed in his handling of the declamation *De artibus liberalibus*)[308] he did not apply the structures of the early nominalism to his analysis of Philip's beliefs on natural theology and ethics. Maurer seemed to view this development entirely in the context of Reuchlin's and Stöffler's philosophy of nature, and so his (Maurer's) interpretation perhaps fits the first school of thought better than it does this second one. At any rate, this second model of Melanchthon's development has the advantage of disclosing greater continuity of intellectual integrity between the pre-Lutheran and early Lutheran years, but the nearly universal conclusion of its proponents is that the *older* Melanchthon abandoned important first principles in making peace with philosophy in the form of a "natural theology."

Within each of these two large frameworks there is some diversity of opinion on how to assess Melanchthon. Among those who view him as having consciously undertaken the job of conjoining faith with reason, some judge his principles themselves to have been unfaithful to the essence of Protestant theory, his theology a form of treachery or poison, or simply a blight upon biblically pure truth.[309] Where strong forms of fideistic Protestant biblicism have been erected to stem the tide of Kantian Protestant liberalism (in whatever form), Melanchthon is once again caught between the extremes of a great struggle for power. Some recent writers have been sympathetic and generous in their appraisals, seeking to appreciate the pressures for concession that weighed upon this sensitive man. For instance, Bornkamm concluded that there was a "synthesis," but that it is one which "quite obviously stands under the dominance of the gospel and the biblical image of man."[310] In the aftermath of World War II and in the wake of Barthianism, F. Hildebrandt wrote that he was "sick...of dictatorship in both politics and theology, of 'secular despair,' and 'Christian Realism.'" He thus turned gratefully to the Hellenic style of Melanchthon.[311] But even so, the dominant image in Hildebrandt's book was "concession," and the mood was still that of having come, in Melanchthon, "suspiciously near to Thomas Aquinas" in forging an *analogia entis* between God and the creation.[312] The standard of assessment seems, as an almost universal axiom of Melanchthon's own people and of our own age, to penalize any leaning toward rationality as the basic structure for consensus in theology. So it has been, with few interruptions, for a very long time.

To attempt an evaluation of any theologian on the level of "natural theology" makes one aware of a conflict over authority and the biblical canon that arose long before Melanchthon and has continued long after him. One can well imagine why he was so highly esteemed by Elizabeth I, and that his natural audience today, if he were more widely read, would, ironically enough, have its roots partly in Thomism or in Jeffersonian theism. But does this observation mean that he was a perpetrator of a "catholicizing" or "rationalizing" natural theology, or that his system was inferior to those who view their dogmatism and incapacity to work constructively with culture as a virtue? Perhaps there is a way of affirming both Protestant doctrine and a kind of natural religion. Our own proposals about the "disjunctive" moment as a matter of fundamental principle for Melanchthon militate strongly against the widespread opinion that he was *intuitively* committed to a synthesis of faith and reason; we believe that his natural theology (or rather his affirmations of it) arose on a different basis from that of integrative synthesis as a principle of his humanism. Further, his self-awareness as a methodological theologian and his personal stability make it difficult to believe that he was blatantly incoherent in setting forth the essential distinction between reason and faith.

Nevertheless, those who have interpreted Melanchthon in the context of nominalism, or disjunctive principles of another sort, have generally held that synthetic pressures within his environment and world view overwhelmed him on important levels of his work. The presupposition is that there was something disintegrated about Melanchthon from the start; his natural bent toward pious discrimination was never quite at one with the *Naturfrömmigkeit* that arose from his infection with Platonism. Our earlier discussion of Maurer would suggest that he viewed Melanchthon in that way. Others, like Troeltsch and von Waltershausen, implied something similar by concluding that, in spite of the desire for sharp *Trennung*, his conception of nature and natural law defeated him, particularly when pressed by the practical necessities involved in reshaping the institutional orders of church, school and government.[313] Again, his system of thought, in the course of his development, appears as somewhat small, tangled and weak. The picture that emerges is of a man who was less the master of events than he was mastered by them, Alice swimming in a pool of pragmatism to go with her tears. It is difficult for us to believe that Philip operated in such an unprincipled, incoherent manner as that.

There has never been any doubt that the older Melanchthon taught a kind of natural theology. From 1527, when he revised his annotations on Colossians, particularly on Paul's warning against vain philosophy in the second chapter,[314] to the great Romans commentary of 1532,[315] in which he developed his proofs of God's existence, and afterwards, he quite obviously expressed his linguistic values of rational coherence (discussed in the first part of this chapter as an ontological norm for theological propositions) in the form of epistemic mediation between human beings, the cosmic order and the existence of God. The controversy is not about whether he affirmed a natural theology, but about how he did so, that is, about its exact logical structure and how to assess it theologically in the context of his own development and that of normative Lutheranism.

Because the dominant hermeneutic has been disposed, in one way or another, toward the view that Melanchthon suffered from a lack of philosophical will or was simply confused, one is not surprised to find expositions of his actual position on natural theology as equivocal and artificially devised, maintaining that he reduced the uniqueness of Scripture to "the gospel," whereas "the law" was merely a clarification of natural knowledge.[316] It is now generally understood that the Loci communes of 1521 contained seeds of the later development, but, to our knowledge, no one has discussed them in the light of Melanchthon's rhetorical theory with the purpose of illumining the debate on natural theology. In what remains of our discussion, we should like to examine the relevant sections of this work and weigh them in the light of our own interpretive theory about the context of Melanchthon's development. Our purpose is not to answer the question in any final sense, but to establish a hermeneutical framework for stating it in the right way and for suggesting what the answer is likely to be.

Natural Theology in the Loci Communes

In the 1521 edition of the Loci, Melanchthon stressed the importance of relating laws of nature to ethics and to a doctrine of the law. On one level, it is clear that he affirmed both the existence and the natural knowledge of a moral order and of the God who created it. This was a primitive form of an argument from design, even though he professed reticence about constructing such an argument. In his section on the law, he affirmed the category of "natural law," but also judged that nothing had yet been written on the subject that he found satisfactory. As we have observed, what worried him was that a naive correlation of natural to human law had commonly occurred, even among Christian theologians, and that the outcome was confusion between the divine and human realms. In another section, he revealed his epistemic caution by writing of this knowledge as more an external traditio than the product of an intuitive capacity, and, as we have also seen, he proposed that natural law existed in objective reality, that God had insculpted it on the minds of all human beings, but with the epistemic qualification that this law cannot be systematized at all well through reason alone, that, thus approached, "it can scarcely be known." Nevertheless, he affirmed both the existence and qualified knowledge of the moral order and its creator. As we would expect in this time of early Lutheran enthusiasm, the forces of "disjunction" were uppermost, but those of "conjunction" were present in an important way.

The metaphysical and epistemic relation of natural law to natural theology appeared in Melanchthon's list of the three universal laws: worship God, do harm to no one and have things in common to the extent that is possible. Again he stressed the revelatory foundations of these beliefs. The clear view of Paul was that "God must be worshiped" is a natural law. That the existence of God might be proved through reason was another matter, irrelevant to the quest for a living faith. That we ought to do harm to no one was deduced from the social doctrine of Genesis 2, "it is not good that man should be alone"; that we ought to have all things in common was the (common) property of Scripture and the Greeks. An *ius gentium* could be harvested from pagan authors, but was not the fruit of any particular system or school of pagan thought. Indeed, every system tended to err in the direction of evil self-interest, and sometimes such evil was explicitly taught as virtue.

For Melanchthon, then, there was a sense in which the pagans knew both the moral order and, through it, God. There was also a sense in which this knowledge was fragmented, incomplete and even false, and he stressed the inadequacy of reason. There was a sense in which they did not know God. On balance, the young Melanchthon gave room in his world view for a kind of "natural theology," or knowledge of God and morality through intuition, reason and/or tradition. The rudiments of his later position were in place. But the context of this natural theism was that of radical, Lutheran "disjunction."

How could Melanchthon account for this truth about God without compromising his Lutheran principles on human nature and the absolute sufficiency of grace and, thus, the particularity of Scripture? It is interesting that the idea of "common grace" never occurred to him. It is clear that he looked to the creation itself for an ontological explanation; that does not imply, however, that he was not interested in defining the *Grenzen* between Scripture and philosophical reflection. It seems that he thought about the creation and Scripture in the context of a larger, rhetorical vision which encompassed both the world of God and that of human beings. Like all theologians, more or less, his theology needed a philosophical framework of some kind. In his philosophy, human beings and their world necessarily retained a common nature, in spite of the ravages of sin, and that nature also had a common dignity and value. For him, there was nothing distinctively Christian or secular about this truth; it was inherent in human experience and discourse. Deep in Melanchthon's psyche, the intuition persisted that one could, indeed must, affirm this common nature and dignity in order even to assert Lutheran doctrines of sin and grace, or the norm of *sola scriptura*, in meaningful language. The categories of his world view enabled him to think that one could walk between the dangers of language about "merit," no matter how one qualified it, and those of "antinomianism," even when contrived as humility.

The one led to a flood of arrogance, he believed, the other to a dark night of nonsense, obscurantism and fanatical action. Let us try to explain these claims in the light of his *Loci communes* of 1521.

We have seen that Melanchthon made several epistemic qualifications of his judgment that there was a natural law and a natural knowledge of God and the good. These emerged from innate Lutheran suspicion, but also from a prudence that was thoroughly learned from experience. Theologically and empirically, he insisted, one must be critical of the classics, even as one approaches them for wisdom. It is no secret that Melanchthon softened this criticism in the years ahead, though he never dropped it entirely.[317] We believe that this critique, in both the early and later Melanchthon, must be viewed not only in the context of his biblicism, but also in that of a structurally deeper view of reality as shaped through his rhetorical system and its metaphysical foundations. Even in the cautious mood of the early Melanchthon, the deepest level of his critique, and of asserting the *discrimen* between Scripture and philosophy, was not that of comparing propositions of philosophers with those of Scripture and, thus, weighing them either as explicitly true or false. It was rather that of comparative *doctrine*. One should rather say, the critique was that of comparative *rhetoric*, that is, comparison between the *power* of truth-claims in their fullest elocutionary form as *oratio*.

Notice how quickly Melanchthon, in the *Loci communes*, hastened to contrast the living power of biblical doctrine with that of natural knowledge. His style of presentation was constantly to remind the reader of the *scopus*, the *status* of Christian doctrine as a whole, and how that placed individual *loci* in a new oration, which gave them new meaning and power. He informed us that this was why he began with the doctrine of free will and sin, at once affirming the wisdom of the Socratic quest for self-knowledge and negating it through the biblical concept of *peccatum*. The concept of sin had a power, but only when construed in its nexus with law and grace. The same held all around; law had its truth and power in its nexus with sin and grace, grace with law and sin. Earlier documents have clearly shown that he took this constellation of concepts, not piecemeal, but as a whole, to be essential to the logic and sense of the *scopus* and *status* of Scripture. This *was* the discriminating sense of Scripture. And that is why it was so very important to him that *all* Scripture, in one way or another, teach both law and gospel together. Notice, too, how his critique of natural knowledge thus referred to its abstract, displaced position. As doctrines or *loci* in a human system of merit, he argued, no matter how accurate, such knowledge of divine things absorbed a spirit of self-righteousness in moral theory and what he called a frigidity in religious metaphysics.

In the section on the power of the law, he argued that Scripture and human reason gave contradictory views of the law's *purpose*. For Scripture viewed the law as an exactor of wrath and dread; human reason viewed it as the corrector of faults and the teacher of right living.[318] These two contradictory views of the law's purpose, he wrote, emerged from contradictory species of humans, the spiritual and the carnal.[319] The carnal person believed in the possibility of justifying oneself through moral discipline; in stark contrast, the spiritual person beheld in the mirror of law someone horribly sinful and became sick with fear of God's wrath.[320] Thus, knowledge of the self, as sinful, and knowledge of the good, as moral law, were dialectically related. The law was known rightly in relation to oneself as sinful; knowing oneself as sinful depended upon contact with the law.[321] Knowledge of the gospel and its power was possible only in relation to that of sin and law.[322] That certain individual laws, even very many of them, might be cognitively true was not to say that they replicated the biblical *senses* of moral law as an essential part of a rhetorical whole. On this deeper level, he imagined the distinction between philosophy and Scripture as one of nearly complete separation.[323]

Melanchthon applied the same form of teleological reasoning to the issue of knowing God. In his section on justification and faith, he asserted that what nature knows of God is not faith, but is "frigid opinion."[324] One will recall that his argument unfolded from texts in Ezekiel 29:9, Psalm 14:1 and 1 Corinthians 2:14. From these texts, he concluded that "the flesh" does not know that there is a God, that He wields wrath toward sin and that He offers mercy to those who repent.[325] One might conclude from these comments by themselves that Melanchthon flatly denied natural knowledge of true propositions about God; but the section which followed explained the connection between knowing that there *is* a God and knowing that He acts out of this disposition of *wrath* toward sin and *mercy* toward sinners. On the basis of Hebrews 11:3, that we know by faith that the world was made, Melanchthon compared biblical knowledge of a creator with that of ancient philosophy, whose "faith" in God he called "common opinion." He contrasted these belief systems "teleologically" rather than stressing individual points of agreement or disagreement. Biblical faith in a creator was, he wrote, "not frigid opinion, but a very living knowledge of both the power and goodness of God...."[326] The difference between systems was, therefore, not primarily on the level of individual, first-order propositions, right or wrong, but that Christian knowledge of a creator occurred in relation to knowledge of the final point, or *scopus*, of the creation, defined in the *status* of grace, law and sin, together, in their proper function as *oratio*. Again, Melanchthon could assert the nearly absolute *discrimen* of biblical truth in this sense, while at the same time affirming the truth of natural theology in another.

The unaided human mind had discovered individual *loci communes*, but these were unconnected with the greater whole; in fact, they were connected with a *scopus* that was tragically confused and false in its optimism about changing society through moral discipline. But since these individual *loci*, apart from their places in the larger whole, or *scopus*, were not "Scripture" or "revelation" in the logically precise, literal sense, there was nothing inconsistent or compromising about comparing philosophy favorably with the wisdom of biblical tradition. There were variations on the term "truth," which made it quite coherent both to say that "philosophy was lies and darkness" (with respect to the full sense of truth as *oratio*) and that the pagans attained to first-order propositions about God and morality that corresponded to reality as affirmed by Christians. The *oratio* of philosophy was false; the *oratio* of Scripture was sacred and true. The *loci* of philosophy were often true, not just *loci*, but *loci communes*, universal norms as affirmed in the light of revelation.

In the context of the first distinction, Melanchthon felt free to make overtures (rather than "concessions") to philosophy and to his past and, in later years, to develop this model of judicious affirmation in his Christian theology.

Thus we believe that Melanchthon's distinction between Scripture and philosophy (on the level where it is usually assessed) was logically clear, not the expression of two unintegrated strands of thought, and that the developments yet to come were mainly expansions of the same principled logic. Moreover, it is reasonably clear that this philosophical framework enabled him to uphold a very strong doctrine of grace and the principle of *sola scriptura*. The question, put in this context, is whether it was strong enough, since all the underlying structures of his distinction, the structures of *oratio*, were themselves the product of pagan reason. Nowhere did Melanchthon ever think to claim that Cicero had possibly learned his rhetoric from a tradition that eventually had grown from biblical revelation; nor did he qualify the truth-norms of rhetoric as having been mysteriously revealed by God's general or common grace. We have observed many times that he simply took them for granted as "commonplaces," before going to Wittenberg and ever afterwards, and that he was constantly caught off his guard by his failures to elicit a consensus. On the most basic level of *inventio*—the intuition about self-knowledge, the essential connection between virtue and human identity, the normative status of logic in a rational universe and all the various functions of plain human language as *oratio*—there was, for him, no distinction between faith and reflective reason. Human identity simply required the structures of *oratio*, and *oratio* simply expressed the values inherent in these structures, when one reflected upon them. This *was* our humanity, *humanitas*, in action. The power to pause and reflect upon oneself is the assumption of all great teachers, their most basic expectation of students. But is it a violation of Protestant Christian norms? Was it wrong of him to believe that the wisdom of the *quaestiones*, or *organon inveniendi*, was the same for Plato as for Paul, for Aristotle as for the other apostles, for Socrates as for the Master, Christ Himself? Was he wrong to imply that pagan thinkers might actually *welcome* the grace of God as extended to them in the gospel of Christ?

How is one to assess this deepest bond between Christianity and human identity in the system of Melanchthon? That could well become the subject of an entire book by itself. Nevertheless, we offer the simple proposal that Melanchthon's interest and faith in the creation (for that is what this bond was the expression of) helped put together a Protestant framework in which one could remain faithful to the essential insights of that movement, while making it possible to affirm the basic goodness of humanity and human life—an intuition that is simply necessary for the constructive engagement of secular and ecclesiastical culture. Finally, in spite of the protests of "orthodox" Lutherans and later Reformed theologians, intent upon expelling every last vestige of *humanitas* from the Christian gospel, we can see no compelling reason to think that Melanchthon's view of humanity revealed "dangerous tendencies" toward the errors of sixteenth-century Catholicism. On the contrary, his model might have neutralized destructive tendencies toward separation, dogmatism and war within sixteenth-century Protestantism—if only the times had not become so very violent.

This simple conceptual and moral action of making genuine overtures to human beings and their culture has not come easily to any of the successive Protestant communities, whether Lutheran, Reformed, Anglican or something else. Mapping the exact trajectories of Melanchthon's influence on later generations is something that is best left to experts on the subject. However, no one disputes that there was an influence; and, conceptually, his was a strand of Protestantism that was capable of recovering the best insights of Catholicism (as he later demonstrated not merely in his negotiation with Rome, but in his subtle use of Chrysostom to elaborate a humane doctrine of election and grace). In this, he resembled Bucer, Bullinger, Arminius, Hugh Grotius, Cranmer and others outside Lutheranism, and the Lutheran Calixtus was no doubt indebted to the Preceptor.[327] Philip's brand of Protestantism could also function in a climate of civil polity and consensus. It did not require theocracy or the divine right of kings, but only a willing spirit of reasonable discourse. His bitter bouts with the self-designated Gnesio-Lutherans remind us that, right or wrong, defending the universals and the universally absolute dignity of the creation and culture called for as much courage then as it does now. In view of the secularization of the modern state, it seems doubly urgent that Christianity maintain its mechanisms for constructive discourse with non-Christian cultural models.

Melanchthon's kind of Protestantism was, thus, one which stressed the order of the world and the integrity and goodness of the mind and its best moral intuitions; it was thereby strongly motivated to foster learning of the liberal arts in Christian universities, a spirit of ecumenical peaceableness while holding the full set of one's Protestant convictions and the hope that political and social consensus might one day evolve, if only people would persevere in using the best gifts of both nature and grace. Melanchthon no doubt underestimated the power of sin over human processes of thought, and that will be obvious to "post-modern" people, who discard these impulses and adopt one or another form of epistemic relativism. Not everyone, however, believes that this option is necessary or that the life of the mind has come to an end in Western theology. Moreover, our conclusion that he worked out his "conjunctive" projects in the context of his rhetorical philosophy and its special forms of "disjunctive" thought encourages one to take seriously his beleaguered self-defense that, through it all, he redeemed the *res ipsam*.[328]

The question whether or not the deeper level of ontologically common nature—this native passion for the world and for life in the world, this basic affirmation of *oratio humana*—was itself somehow wrong, may never be settled among Protestants. Do the assertions of basic, created goodness and dignity, and, in later years, of a God-given freedom to respond to the grace of God (unlike wood, stone, or the devils),[329] imply a denial of God's grace in the distinctive sense comprised by the *rem ipsam* of biblical Protestantism? Surely the view that man is a kind of "devil" is at least as troublesome as Melanchthon's belief in human dignity. This is not the place to pursue such a complex question about the norms of biblical, ecumenical hermeneutics.

Nevertheless, the case for Melanchthon's approach has a long and distinguished history in the church; one might well judge that the Synod of Orange had established it, centuries before, as the best interpretation of Scripture, supported by the full weight of arguments from men like Chrysostom, Damascus and many others who were no less troubled by Pelagianism than Augustine was, or Luther for that matter.[330] And the works of Protestants like Bullinger, Bolsec, Arminius and Grotius, to name a few, must be considered along with recent scholarship on the textual foundations of classical predestinarianism and its social contexts.[331] It is difficult to see how Melanchthon's position, as we have described it, could be shown beyond serious controversy to have been inconsistent with all distinctively Protestant doctrines of grace, or that his doctrine of grace was itself clearly unbiblical. Indeed, to the extent that his doctrine of creation was more strongly integrated into his theory and practice than Luther's was, one might consider that this was an improvement and that both liberal and orthodox Protestantism might yet learn from the Preceptor of Germany in the arts of ecumenism and cultural engagement.

Notes to Chapter 11

1. W. Maurer, *Der junge Melanchthon*, Bd. 2, Göttingen 1969, p. 152.
2. *Ibid.*
3. *Ibid.*, pp. 170ff.
4. *Ibid.*, pp. 175ff.
5. *Ibid.*, pp. 202ff.
6. *Ibid.*, p. 153.
7. Esp., W. Maurer, *Historischer Kommentar zur Confessio Augustana*, Bd. 1, 2, Gütersloh 1976, 1978. This is a brilliant discussion of the diverse parts played out by individuals in what became, essentially, Melanchthon's finest hour, perhaps his answer to Luther's Worms.
8. W. Maurer, *Der junge Melanchthon*, Bd. 2, pp. 159ff.
9. *Ibid.*, p. 160; cf. *MW* IV, p. 11, on table of Melanchthon's exegetical lectures alone, which included Romans, Colossians, Galatians and 1 and 2 Corinthians. Also K. Hartfelder, *Philipp Melanchthon als Praeceptor Germaniae*, Berlin 1889, pp. 556f., indicating that Philip also held lectures on Pliny in the autumn and on Lucian, dialectic and rhetoric in the winter.
10. K. Hartfelder, *op. cit.*, pp. 581f. In quantity, quality and sheer diversity, the list is monumentally impressive.
11. *MW* II/1, pp. 15f.
12. W. Maurer, "Zur Komposition der Loci Melanchthons von 1521," in *Luther-Jahrbuch*, 25, 1958, pp. 148ff., and "Melanchthons Loci communes von 1521 als wissenschaftliche Programmschrift," in *Luther-Jahrbuch*, 27, 1960, pp. 2ff.
13. *SM* VI/1, pp. 98ff.; *CR* I, pp. 155ff.; date in *MB* I, p. 72.
14. *CR* I, p. 157.
15. W. Maurer, "Zur Komposition der Loci Melanchthons von 1521," pp. 155f.
16. *Ibid.*
17. *Ibid.*; also, W. Maurer, *Der junge Melanchthon*, Bd. 2, p. 15, "...Melanchthon directed the main theological work of his life against Erasmus." This antagonism was most evident in the doctrine of predestination.
18. G. L. Plitt and D. Th. Kolde (hrsg.), *Die Loci Communes Philipp Melanchthons in ihrer Urgestalt*, Erlangen/Leipzig 1890.
19. *MW* II/1, introductory comments, pp. 7ff.; the text, pp. 16ff.
20. W. Pauck (ed.), *Loci communes theologici*, in *Melanchthon and Bucer*, (tr.) L. J. Satre, Library of Christian Classics, XIX, Philadelphia 1969, introduction, pp. 3ff.; text, pp. 18ff.
21. See mainly W. Maurer, *Der junge Melanchthon*, Bd. 2, pp. 230-414 and references, *passim*.
22. *Ibid.*, pp. 152 and 185.
23. *MW* II/1, p. 17.9f., "...indicantur hic christianae disciplinae praecipui loci...."
24. *Ibid.*, p. 17.10ff., "...ut intelligat iuventus, et quae sint in scripturis potissimum requirenda et quam foede hallucinati sunt ubique in re theologica, qui nobis pro Christi doctrina Aristotelicas argutias prodidere."
25. *Ibid.*, p. 17.14ff., "Parce vero ac breviter omnia tractamus, quod indicis magis quam comentarii vice fungimur, dum nomenclaturam tantum facimus locorum, ad quos veluti divertendum est erranti per divina volumina...." Cf. also *ibid.*, p. 55.1ff.
26. *Ibid.*, p. 17.19f., "...e quibus summa christianae doctrinae pendeat."
27. *Ibid.*, pp. 17.25-18.1ff., "Immo nihil perinde optarim, atque si fieri possit, christianos omnes in solis divinis literis liberrime versari et in illarum indolem plane

transformari. Nam cum in illis absolutissimam sui imaginem expresserit divinitas, non poterit aliunde neque certius neque propius cognosci. Fallitur, quisquis aliunde christianismi formam petit quam e scriptura canonica."

28. *Ibid.*, p. 18.3ff., "Quantum enim a huius puritate absunt commentarii? In hac nihil reperias non augustum, in illis quam multa, quae a philosophia, ab humanae rationis aestimatione pendent, quae cum iudicio spiritus prorsus ex diametro pugnant."

29. *Ibid.*, p. 18.7f., "Non sic detriverant *to psychikov* scriptores, ut nihil nisi *pneumatika* spirarent."

30. *Ibid.*, p. 18.12ff.

31. *Ibid.*, p. 18.13ff.; on this opinion, which P. Fraenkel has called "Tertullian's Rule" in Melanchthon, cf. P. Fraenkel, *Testimonia Patrum*, Geneva 1961, pp. 137ff.

32. *MW* II/1, p. 19.3ff., "Requiri solent in singulis artibus loci quidam, quibus artis cuiusque summa comprehenditur...."

33. *Ibid.*, p. 19.4ff., "...qui scopi vice, ad quem omnia studia dirigamus...."

34. *Ibid.*, p. 19.8ff., "Nimium enim philosophatur Damascenus, Longobardus congerere hominum opiniones quam scripturae sententiam referre maluit."

35. *Ibid.*, p. 19.12ff.

36. *Ibid.*, p. 19.16ff.

37. *Ibid.*, p. 19.28ff., "In his, ut quidam prorsus incomprehensibiles sunt, ita rursus sunt quidem, quos universo vulgo christianorum compertissimos esse Christus voluit."

38. *Ibid.*, p. 19.30f., "Mysteria divinitatis rectius adoraverimus quam vestigaverimus."

39. *Ibid.*, "Immo sine magno periculo tentari non possunt, id quod non raro sancti viri etiam sunt experti."

40. *Ibid.*, p. 20.2ff., "Et carne filium deus Optimus Maximus induit, ut nos a contemplatione maiestatis suae ad carnis adeoque fragilitatis nostrae contemplationem invitaret."

41. *Ibid.*, p. 20.9ff.

42. *Ibid.*, p. 20.12ff., "...quid assecuti sunt iam tot seculis scholastici theologistae, cum in his locis solis versarentur?"

43. *Ibid.*, p. 20.14ff.

44. *Ibid.*, p. 20.17ff., "Et dissimulari eorum stultitia posset, nisi evangelium interim et beneficia Christi obscurassent nobis illae...disputationes."

45. *Ibid.*, p. 20.24f.

46. *Ibid.*, p. 20.26ff., "Nam ex his proprie Christus cognoscitur, siquidem hoc est Christum cognoscere beneficia eius cognoscere, non, quod isti docent, eius naturas, modos incarnationis contueri." On the historical influence of this famous statement, cf. pp. 210ff., above.

47. *Ibid.*, pp. 20.29-21.1ff., "Ni scias, in quem usum carnem induerit et cruci affixus sit Christus, quid proderit eius historiam novisse?"

48. *Ibid.*, p. 21.2ff.

49. Paul was the theologian's model, *ibid.*, p. 21.12ff., "Paulus in epistola, quam Romanis dicavit, cum doctrinae christianae compendium conscriberet, num de mysteriis trinitatis, de modo incarnationis, de creatione activa et creatione passiva philosophabatur? At quid agit? Certe de lege, peccato, gratia, e quibus locis solis Christi cognitio pendet."

50. *Ibid.*, p. 21ff.

51. *Ibid.*, pp. 31ff.

52. *Ibid.*, pp. 55ff.

53. *Ibid.*, pp. 82ff.

54. *Ibid.*, pp. 103ff.

55. *Ibid.*, pp. 144ff.

56. *Ibid.*, pp. 161ff.
57. *Ibid.*, pp. 179ff.
58. Cf. *ibid.*, pp. 195ff. and edition of 1559; on this expansion, E. P. Meijering, *Melanchthon and Patristic Thought: The Doctrines of Christ and Grace, the Trinity and the Creation*, Leiden 1983, and pp. 212ff., above.
59. Cf. E. P. Meijering, *op. cit.*, pp. 1ff.
60. A. Ritschl, *The Christian Doctrine of Justification and Reconciliation*, Edinburgh 1902, p. 393.
61. *Ibid.*, pp. 388f.
62. *Ibid.*, pp. 393ff.
63. Q. Breen, "The Two-fold Truth Theory in Melanchthon," in *Review of Religion*, 1945, pp. 115ff. The author views Melanchthon as, in part, responsible for the rise of the Enlightenment and its rejection of Christianity as irrational.
64. E. Brunner, *The Mediator*, London 1959, p. 408.
65. *Ibid.*
66. W. Kasper, *Jesus the Christ*, (tr.) V. Green, London/New York 1976, p. 22.
67. Cf. Barth's diary entry on his Melanchthon seminar, in E. Busch, *Karl Barth*, (tr.) J. Bowden, London/Philadelphia 1976, p. 90. Barth observed in the *Loci* of 1521 "anthropocentric" tendencies which reminded him of the methods of Rudolf Bultmann.
68. H. Thielicke, *Evangelical Faith*, (tr.) G. W. Bromiley, Grand Rapids 1974, pp. 40ff. Thielicke places Melanchthon in line with the later "Cartesian theology," i.e., one in which all theological propositions must be related to human experience. He does, however, acknowledge that humanity is not Melanchthon's sole focus.
69. P. Wernle, *Melanchthon und Schleiermacher: Zwei dogmatische Jubiläen*, (Sammlung gemeinverständlicher Vorträge, 98), Tübingen 1921, esp. pp. 51f.
70. Cf. E. P. Meijering, *op. cit.*, for many references throughout the discussion.
71. *Ibid.*, Meijering also suggests the presence of nominalistic influences through Gerson, but does not develop this point in any significant detail, cf. p. 14.
72. A. Brüls, *Die Entwicklung der Gotteslehre beim jungen Melanchthon, 1518-35*, (Untersuchungen zur Kirchengeschichte, 10), Bielefeld 1975, p. 169.
73. *MW* II/1, pp. 19.28f.
74. *Ibid.*, pp. 19.30f.
75. *Ibid.*, pp. 20.26ff.
76. *Ibid.*, pp. 21.12ff.
77. *Ibid.*, pp. 20.1ff. Meijering, *op. cit.*, has shown that such warnings were pervasive during Melanchthon's entire career, pp. 5ff., not just in the early years, when the focus was intensively on the "benefits of Christ."
78. Cf. pp. 237ff., above.
79. *MW* II/1, p. 20.18ff., "Et dissimulari eorum stultitia posset, nisi evangelium interim et beneficia Christi obscurassent nobis illae stultae disputationes."
80. *MW* I, p. 76.8ff.
81. *Ibid.*
82. This development is the main subject of Meijering's book, *op. cit.*, *passim*.
83. *CR* XIV, p. 1050, "Porro personis verbis melioribus discernere non possemus, quam quibus scriptura docet....pater, sese intuens, concipit sui imaginem, quae verbum dicitur: et qui perfecta imago est, tota substantia patris in eo relucet...." And "...non communicatione nominis sicut Ariani senserunt, sed natura Deus est." p. 1051.
84. Cf. *MW* II/1, pp. 195ff., *passim*, for his use of Plato's concept of God as *mens aeterna, causa boni in natura*, to develop the biblical senses of terms such as "goodness"; and on the incarnation and trinity, pp. 204ff.

85. That Meijering affirmed the proverbial thesis that Melanchthon's development was inconsistent at such fundamental levels seems a major weakness of his otherwise useful monograph. Cf. pp. 114-115, 119 on the inconsistencies in Melanchthon. The author is well aware that there was also a level of consistency, but seems to grope somewhat for a satisfactory way of accounting for it. His explanatory notion that Melanchthon blurred Scripture with the use of it by certain Greek Fathers begs the question of how Melanchthon might have *construed* Scripture and its concepts in such a way that this fusion of patristics and the Bible made sense to him. Cf. esp. pp. 109ff.

86. P. Fraenkel, *op. cit.*, pp. 43ff., held the same general view that Melanchthon's development on this level seems more an expansion than a substantive change of principles. Our rhetorical model of interpretation helps to support this intuition and to put it in Melanchthon's own systematic terms.

87. Paper found after Melanchthon's death, cited by E. G. Rupp, "Philip Melanchthon and Martin Bucer," in *A History of Christian Doctrine*, (ed.) H. Cunliffe-Jones, Philadelphia (1980) 1984, p. 378.

88. *MW* II/1, pp. 21f., "Scripsere de libero arbitrio Augustinus et Bernardus et ille quidem sua posterioribus libris, quos adversus Pelagianos edidit, multipliciter retractavit. Bernardus non est similis sui. Sunt hac de re etiam apud Graecos quaedam, sed sparsim." Cf. p. 21, n. 31. On the development of Melanchthon's appreciation for the Fathers, especially Chrysostom, cf. 1559 edition, p. 271. One is also struck by two facts. First, the edition of 1559 begins with the doctrines of God, creation and original sin, rather than with predestination, and, second, the doctrine of election itself is greatly expanded in both mass and in the extent of logical qualification. Note also Philip's musing that it was rather hard to believe that, through all the centuries, Augustine alone rightly understood this essential doctrine. Also, H. Gerhards, *Die Entwicklung des Problems der Willenfreiheit bei Philipp Melanchthon*, (diss.) Bonn 1955.

89. *MW* II/1, p. 22.4f.

90. *Ibid.*, p. 22.7ff.

91. *Ibid.*, p. 22.9ff.

92. *Ibid.*, p. 22.16f.

93. *Ibid.*, p. 22.17ff. Blame is placed on both Aristotle and Plato.

94. *Ibid.*, p. 22.31ff.

95. *Ibid.*, p. 23.26ff., "Haec oportet monere, quo facilius postea indicari posset legis ac gratiae discrimen...."

96. Cf. pp. 247ff., above.

97. *MW* II/1, pp. 24f. Matt. 10:29-31; Rom. 9; 11:36; and Eph. 1:11 were cited as individual texts which asserted the main proposition of God's control over human affairs. To these texts were added passages from the Old Testament, including Gen. 15:16; a variety of verses from 1 and 2 Kings; Prov. 16:4; 20:24; Jer. 10:23 and others.

98. *Ibid.*, p. 25.7ff., "Neque enim vel timorem dei vel fiduciam in deum certius aliunde disces, quam ubi imbueris animum hac de praedestinatione sententia."

99. *Ibid.*, p. 25.15ff., "Annon hoc uno loco efficacissime consolatur discipulos Christus, cum inquit: 'Omnes capilli capitis vestri numerati sunt'?"

100. *Ibid.*, p. 31.16.

101. *Ibid.*, p. 31.20ff., "Peccatum originale est nativa propensio et quidam genialis impetus et energia, qua ad peccandum trahimur...." The same definition had already emerged in the *Institutio theologica*, cf. pp. 137ff., above.

102. *Ibid.*, p. 32.14ff., "Ita fit, ut anima luce vitaque coelesti carens excaecitur..."; p. 32.18ff., "...et sese ardentissime amet...." Melanchthon viewed the negative element of this definition as in line with that of "the sophists," p. 32.28ff. Cf. his references to

Augustine, Aquinas and Scotus, n. 1. He wondered why they failed to go all the way, logically, to the correct view of human nature as *wholly* sinful.

103. Citation, *ibid.*, p. 33.16f.; biblical references, pp. 33f.

104. *Ibid.*, p. 35.4ff.

105. *Ibid.*, p. 35.5ff., "...negant tamen eam esse vim peccati originalis...."

106. *Ibid.*, p. 35.31ff.

107. *Ibid.*, p. 36.1f.

108. *Ibid.*, p. 36.5ff., "Tolerans fuit Socrates, sed amans gloriae aut certe placens sibi de virtute."

109. *Ibid.*, p. 36.16f.

110. *Ibid.*, p. 36.18ff., "Quantum in Platone tumoris est et fastus!"

111. *Ibid.*, p. 36.22ff.

112. *Ibid.*, p. 36.27ff.

113. *Ibid.*, p. 36.29ff., "Ubi nos legimus, prona est ad malum..., tamen uti malebam germana lectione, quod clarior sit..., hominem pravum esse."

114. *Ibid.*, p. 37.6ff.

115. *Ibid.*, p. 37.19ff., "Et de iis, qui suis viribus ac operibus iustificari volunt...inquit: 'Dabit impios pro sepultura et divites pro morte sua.'"

116. *Ibid.*, p. 37.25ff.

117. *Ibid.*, pp. 38.7-38.15ff.

118. *Ibid.*, p. 38.22ff.

119. *Ibid.*, p. 40.24, "...obliti phraseos ac tropi scripturae."

120. *Ibid.*, p. 40.23.

121. *Ibid.*, p. 40.24ff., "Non enim corpus, partem hominis, sed totum hominem...scriptura voce carnis signat...."

122. *Ibid.*, p. 41.9f.

123. *Ibid.*, p. 41.15ff.

124. *Ibid.*, p. 42.18ff.

125. *Ibid.*, p. 43.4ff., "Neque fieri potest, ut sit in vobis dei sensus aliquis, cum caro sitis."

126. *Ibid.*, p. 45.20ff., "Quodsi scripturae sermonem et phrasin observassent, facile vidissent mendacia et vanas cogitationes intellectus esse, quae confixerunt de actibus elicitis."

127. *Ibid.*, p. 47.29ff. On the concept of *meritum de congruo*, cf. H. Oberman, *The Harvest of Medieval Theology*, Grand Rapids 1962, esp. pp. 471f.

128. *MW* II/1, p. 49.11ff.

129. *Ibid.*, pp. 49.24-50.1ff.

130. *Ibid.*, p. 51.5ff., "Unus est idemque ut simplicissimus, ita certissimus doctor, divinus spiritus, qui sese et proxime et simplicissime in sacris literis expressit, in quas ubi animus tuus velut transformatus fuerit, tum demum absolute, simpliciter, exacte, ut aliarum rerum theologicarum, ita huius loci rationem comprehendes."

131. *Ibid.*, p. 55.1ff.

132. *Ibid.*, p. 55.16ff.; also p. 55.15 on Scripture as a source of pure, sweet water.

133. *Ibid.*, p. 55.24f.; cf. the fuller discussion by G. Kisch, *Melanchthons Rechts- und Soziallehre*, Berlin 1967; also W. Maurer, *Der junge Melanchthon*, Bd. 2, pp. 287ff.

134. *MW* II/1, p. 55.25, "De naturalibus legibus nondum vidi digne scriptum."

135. *Ibid.*, p. 55.31; on Melanchthon's sources, which included Cicero, Plato, Gerson, Reuchlin, Erasmus and also Luther, cf. G. Kisch, *op. cit.*, pp. 44ff.; W. Maurer, *Der junge Melanchthon*, Bd. 2, pp. 287ff. We have been unable to determine the source of Melanchthon's three-fold classification of law. For a useful discussion of Luther on the

Decalogue and natural law, cf. H. Bornkamm, *Luther und das Alte Testament*, Tübingen 1948, pp. 107ff.
136. *MW* II/1, pp. 55.32-56.1f., the reference to Rom. 2:15ff.
137. *Ibid.*, p. 56.6ff.
138. *Ibid.*, p. 56.16ff.
139. *Ibid.*, p. 56.19f.
140. *Ibid.*, p. 56.21ff.
141. *Ibid.*, p. 56.24ff.
142. *Ibid.*, p. 56.26f., "...tamen eae deprehendi vix possint."
143. *Ibid.*, p. 56.30ff.
144. *Ibid.*, p. 57.5ff.
145. *Ibid.*, p. 57.10ff.
146. *Ibid.*, p. 57.15f.
147. *Ibid.*, p. 57.20ff.
148. *Ibid.*, p. 57.22f.
149. *Ibid.*, p. 58.9f.
150. *Ibid.*, p. 58.10f., citing the saying from the *Laws*, 5:10, and the *Ethics*, 8:11; see n. 11.
151. *Ibid.*, p. 58.17-31.
152. *Ibid.*, p. 58.32ff.
153. *Ibid.*, p. 59.18ff.
154. *Ibid.*, p. 59.20ff.
155. *Ibid.*, p. 59.24ff.
156. *Ibid.*, p. 59.28ff.; n. 29 for reference.
157. *Ibid.*, p. 59.32.
158. *Ibid.*, pp. 59.34-60.1ff.
159. *Ibid.*, p. 60.15f.
160. *Ibid.*, p. 60.16ff., "Ordines earum tres fecerunt: sunt enim aliae morales, aliae judicales, aliae ceremoniales." We have been unable to locate a similar classification in other sources known to Melanchthon.
161. *Ibid.*, p. 60.18ff.
162. Worship refers to the affections, *ibid.*, p. 61.3ff.; the first commandment requires faith, p. 62.15; the second, praise which flows from faith, p. 62.15; the third, allowing God to work *in* us rather than trying to work on our own strength, p. 62.16, in contrast to a doctrine of free will, p. 62.16ff.; on his references to Luther, p. 63.2ff., and n. 3.
163. So G. Kisch, *op. cit.*, p. 83, n. 3 and references.
164. *MW* II/1, p. 64.26ff.; also cf. Luther, *LW* 21, *The Sermon on the Mount*, pp. 3ff.
165. *Ibid.*, p. 67.15ff.; cf. esp. W. Maurer, *Der junge Melanchthon*, Bd. 2, pp. 169ff. on Luther's influence here.
166. *MW* II/1, p. 67.23ff.
167. *Ibid.*, p. 69.20ff.
168. *Ibid.*, p. 69.22ff.
169. *Ibid.*, p. 69.29ff.
170. *Ibid.*, p. 69.31ff.
171. *Ibid.*, p. 69.33 and ref. to 1 Cor. 10:4.
172. *Ibid.*, p. 70.3ff.
173. *Ibid.*, p. 70.10f.
174. *Ibid.*, p. 70.13ff.
175. *Ibid.*, p. 70.17ff.
176. *Ibid.*, p. 70.18ff.

177. Cf. H. Bornkamm, *op. cit.*, pp. 70ff. on Luther's strong statements about differences between Testaments. On unifying them through finding "heimlichen Hinweisen auf Christus," pp. 82ff.

178. *Ibid.*, p. 108ff.

179. *Ibid.*, on the commandments against graven images and on the Sabbath.

180. R. Preus, *The Inspiration of Scripture*, Edinburgh/London, 1957, esp., pp. 85ff. on Dannhauer, Calov and others, who believed that the relationship between Old and New Testament theology was a matter of pure induction, unmediated even by literary devices such as those used by Melanchthon to warrant his procedure. This theory of reference grew in part from a "dictation-model" of inspiration that was very different from Melanchthon's rhetorical image of the origin of the biblical writings.

181. On the other hand, cf. the affirmative use of Melanchthon's idea of the covenant as "promise" in R. Thiemann, *Revelation and Theology: The Gospel as Narrated Promise*, Notre Dame 1985.

182. *MW* II/1, p. 70.25f. Melanchthon's final section on human law need not detain us, since in it he repeated the several points of earlier documents, such as the letter to Hess and the *oratio* from Didymus Faventinus. The main element was the formal authority of Scripture to legislate what pertains to faith. The main issues were papal authority, pp. 72ff., and decrees such as transubstantiation, pp. 75f., whereby he applied his principle of exclusivity or Tradition I, as defined above.

183. *Ibid.*, p. 82.18ff., "Duae in universum scripturae partes sunt, lex et evangelium."

184. See the discussion in J. S. Preus, *From Shadow to Promise*, Cambridge, Mass. 1969, pp. 188ff. on the distinction for Luther, particularly in his use of the Old Testament, between the grammatical-literal sense and the theological-literal sense.

185. *Ibid.*, p. 190 and references.

186. *Ibid.*, pp. 226ff. on tropology and theological warrant in Luther.

187. *MW* II/1, pp. 82.24-83.1ff.

188. *Ibid.*, p. 83.1ff.

189. *Ibid.*, p. 83.4ff.; a fuller exposition of Melanchthon's idea of grace as "promise" occurs in W. Maurer, *Der junge Melanchthon*, Bd. 2, pp. 349ff.

190. *MW* II/1, p. 83.18ff.; cf. pp. 237ff., above.

191. *Ibid.*, p. 83.28ff.

192. *Ibid.*, pp. 83.34-84.1ff.

193. *Ibid.*, p. 84.12ff.

194. *Ibid.*, p. 84.21ff.

195. *Ibid.*, p. 85.1f.

196. *Ibid.*, p. 85.18ff.

197. *Ibid.*, p. 85.26ff.

198. *Ibid.*, p. 85.28ff.

199. *Ibid.*, p. 86.8f.

200. *Ibid.*, p. 86.11ff.

201. Cf. J. S. Preus, *op. cit.*, pp. 176ff. on the very difficult subject of interplay in Luther between literal, figurative and prophetic senses of the Old Testament text as *promisio* and *testimonium*.

202. *MW* II/1, p. 86.13ff.

203. *Ibid.*, p. 86.15.

204. *Ibid.*, p. 86.15ff.

205. *Ibid.*, p. 86.20ff.

206. *Ibid.*, p. 86.31ff.

207. *Ibid.*, p. 87.5ff.

208. *Ibid.*, p. 88.1ff.

209. *Ibid.*, p. 88.20ff. Cf. also, p. 85.28ff., in reference to the promises of Deut. and of Exod. 34:6ff., "...vide ex legislatore Mose, quomodo evangelista...."
210. *Ibid.*, p. 89.1ff.
211. *Ibid.*, p. 89.16ff.
212. *Ibid.*, p. 91.4ff.
213. *Ibid.*, p. 91.15ff.
214. *Ibid.*, p. 93.9ff.
215. *Ibid.*, p. 93.19f., on Ps. 97:2ff.; p. 93.23ff., on Ps. 76:9.
216. *Ibid.*, p. 93.25, on Zech. 2:17; p. 93.26ff., on Isa. 11:4; p. 93.28f., on Hab. 3:6, among others; cf. p. 94.1ff.
217. *Ibid.*, p. 94.4, on Exod. 34:7.
218. *Ibid.*, pp. 94.19ff. and 95.19f., "Nusquam vim rationemque legis tam copiose tractavit apostolus Paulus ut hoc loco...."
219. *Ibid.*, p. 93.13ff.
220. *Ibid.*
221. *Ibid.*
222. *Ibid.*
223. *Ibid.*, p. 95.
224. *Ibid.*, p. 96.22ff., "Hanc esse vim legis, etiam *typi* scripturae plerique."
225. *Ibid.*, p. 96.30ff.
226. *Ibid.*, p. 97.15f., "Tantum abest enim, ut ratio humana videat peccatum suum, ut sanctos etiam et plenos spiritu oporteat pro ignorantiis supplicare."
227. *Ibid.*, p. 100.
228. *Ibid.*, p. 100.6f.
229. *Ibid.*, p. 100.16ff.
230. *Ibid.*, p. 100.21ff.
231. *Ibid.*, p. 100.20f.
232. *Ibid.*, p. 100.24ff.
233. Melanchthon's *In obscuriora aliquot capita Geneseas P. M. annotationes*, Tubingae 1523, made his literary construals and theology of the text clear. Contrary to Jerome, he argued, the letter of the text was to shape one's interpretation. Cf. A7, "Nos simplicissime literam sequemur, ut debemus, siquidem ea sola facit ad aedificandam fidem." In the instance of Genesis 2-3, the letter was allegorical with simple theological propositions to teach us. Cf. B7, on the trees in the garden, "Et ex iis facile est allegoriam invenire ut verbum vivificum boni...." And the theology of the text was all about law and gospel. Cf. introductory comments, "...ad hoc ea [the story of Genesis] potissimum utendum est, ut inde discas originem peccati, et primam gratiae promissionem, *ex quibus duobus locis postea universa pendet scriptura.*"
234. *MW* II/1, p. 100.29ff.
235. *Ibid.*, pp. 100.33-101.1.
236. *Ibid.*, p. 101.1ff.
237. *Ibid.*, p. 101.6ff.
238. *Ibid.*, p. 101.3f.
239. *Ibid.*, p. 101.8ff., "Addes his, si voles, acervum historiarum evangelicarum...."
240. *Ibid.*, p. 101.10ff., Luke 7.
241. *Ibid.*, p. 101.12ff., Luke 15.
242. *Ibid.*, p. 101.15ff., Luke 5.
243. *Ibid.*, p. 101.18ff., "Ex his exemplis credo possi intelligi, quid inter legem et evangelium intersit, quae vis sit legis quae evangelii."
244. *Ibid.*, p. 101.27ff.

245. *Ibid.*, p. 102.28ff., on Zech. 9:9; p. 103.6f., on 2 Cor. 3:13ff.; p. 103.17ff., on John 3:14ff.
246. *Ibid.*, p. 105.13f., "...secuti *phrasin* scripturae...."
247. *Ibid.*, p. 105.1.
248. *Ibid.*, p. 105.13ff.
249. *Ibid.*, p. 106.11ff.
250. *Ibid.*, p. 106.28ff.
251. *Ibid.*, p. 106.25.
252. *Ibid.*, p. 107.23f.
253. *Ibid.*, p. 107.25ff. The distinction between knowledge of God as "frigid opinion" and as living faith is important to his outlook on the question of natural theology, cf. pp. 236ff., above.
254. *Ibid.*, p. 117.23f.
255. *Ibid.*, pp. 117.36-118.1ff.
256. *Ibid.*, p. 118.22f.
257. *Ibid.*, p. 110.9f.
258. *Ibid.*, p. 111.34ff. The reader was also directed by Melanchthon to Luther's book *On Christian Freedom*, p. 111.36; here, "...fidei vim opinor e scripturae exemplis clarius cognoscemus," p. 112.2f.
259. *MW* II/1, p. 112.11ff.
260. *Ibid.*, p. 112.28ff.
261. *Ibid.*, pp. 112.34-113.1f., "...ea quidem nobis exempla sunt exhibita, ut discamus credere...."
262. *Ibid.*, p. 113.13ff., on Deut. 1:31ff.
263. *Ibid.*, p. 113.28ff.
264. *Ibid.*, p. 114.1ff.
265. *Ibid.*, p. 114, on 2 Chron. 20.
266. *Ibid.*, p. 114.15ff., "Plenae sunt generis exemplorum sacrae historiae omnes."
267. *Ibid.*, p. 114.16ff.
268. *Ibid.*, p. 116.1ff.
269. *Ibid.*, p. 114.18ff., "Repetemus autem aliquot locos etiam ex literis novi testamenti vel in hoc, ut intelligatur idem spiritus esse historiarum utriusque testamenti."
270. *Ibid.*, p. 114.27ff.
271. *Ibid.*, p. 116.20f.
272. *Ibid.*, p. 116.22ff.
273. *Ibid.*, p. 116.26ff.
274. *Ibid.*, pp. 118.32-119.1ff.
275. *Ibid.*, p. 119.3ff.
276. *Ibid.*, p. 119.12ff.
277. *Ibid.*, p. 120.10ff.
278. *Ibid.*, p. 121.7ff.
279. *Ibid.*, p. 121.13ff.
280. *Ibid.*, p. 119.20ff. and 120.30f.
281. *Ibid.*, p. 122.2ff., "Vides hic praelusum esse peccato et morti et iustificationi et resurrectioni adeoque toti novo testamento."
282. *Ibid.*, p. 124.25ff.
283. *Ibid.*, p. 125.35f.
284. *Ibid.*, p. 128.16ff., "Nam fidei naturam ac vim non videor mihi posse verbis, ut optabam, explicare. Qui norunt peccati vim ..., iis demum voluptati est hanc de fide doctrinam audire."

285. Cf. his handling of problem texts, such as Rom. 2:10 and James 2:24, both of which stated that people were justified by works. His commitment to Luther's doctrine and to an image of the text as a propositional unity pressured him to find ways of harmonizing them with what he took to be the weight of "all Scripture." Esp. pp. 134ff. Our point is not that these texts cannot be viewed as consistent with each other, but that it is more difficult than Melanchthon believed it was to show that they are all consistent with Luther's position that works contribute nothing to our salvation.

286. W. H. Neuser, *Der Ansatz der Theologie Philipp Melanchthons*, Neukirchen 1957, pp. 2ff.

287. H. Heppe, *Die konfessionelle Entwicklung der altprotestantischen Union und die gegenwärtige konfessionelle Lage und Aufgabe des deutschen Protestantismus*, Marburg 1854; also W. H. Neuser, *op. cit.*, p. 2, "Die wenigen Bearbeiter Melanchthons vor Heppes Veröffentlichungen sind unkritisch eingestellt...."

288. F. Hildebrandt, *Melanchthon: Alien or Ally?*, Cambridge 1946, esp. pp. 18-33.

289. R. R. Caemmerer, "The Melanchthon Blight," *Concordia Theological Monthly*, XVIII, 1947.

290. K. Barth, *Protestant Theology in the Nineteenth Century*, (1959), (1972), Valley Forge 1973.

291. P. Fraenkel, *op. cit.*, p. 24, "It is one of the most respectable traditions of Reformation historiography to describe the theology of Melanchthon as subject to a process of development that led him from original, classical Reformation thinking to a position that is generally estimated to bear a greater resemblance to later Lutheran scholasticism."

Among the main scholars who have pictured Melanchthon as the initiator of a steady process by which Luther's original insights became "fossilized" in the works of lesser lights are: O. Ritschl, *Dogmengeschichte des Protestantismus*, Bd. I, II, Leipzig 1908, 1912, esp. p. 227; F. Loofs, *Leitfaden zum Studien der Dogmengeschichte*, Halle 1906, pp. 785ff.; R. Seeberg, *Lehrbuch der Dogmengeschichte*, Bd. IV/2, Basel/Stuttgart (1920), 1960, pp. 429ff. and p. 473; H. E. Weber, *Reformation, Orthodoxie und Rationalismus*, Bd. I, Gütersloh 1937, pp. IXff. In America, J. Pelikan has argued that Melanchthon, in contrast to Luther who was "incapable of carefully defining his faith in an orderly and systematic treatment," viewed man's intellect and reason as the main features of his humanity, and thus "it naturally followed that divine revelation addresses itself to them primarily rather than to the total person." J. Pelikan, *From Luther to Kierkegaard*, St. Louis 1950, p. 25. (Against this view of Luther, cf. W. Maurer, *Historischer Kommentar zur Confessio Augustana*, Bd. 1, pp. 20ff., on Luther's very succinct confession in the work *Vom Abendmahl Christi* of the year 1528.) Revelation, in Melanchthon's conception of it, was lowered to the state of being "needed information about God," a dramatic shift from Luther which was to have "serious consequences in theology...." Pelikan, *op. cit.*, p. 28. For similar assessments, J. K. S. Reid, *The Authority of Scripture: A Study of the Reformation and Post-Reformation Understanding of the Bible*, Westport (1962), 1981; and R. Schäfer, *Christologie und Sittlichkeit in Melanchthons frühen Loci*, Tübingen 1961, who was deeply critical of "intellectualism" in the *Loci communes* of 1521.

292. In recent years, the view of Melanchthon's work as what E. Troeltsch called "a theology of definitions," *Vernunft und Offenbarung bei Johann Gerhard und Melanchthon*, Göttingen 1891, p. 59, has been subjected to criticism. H. Engelland argued that the term *doctrina* served in Melanchthon's system as something like a "verbal noun." H. Engelland, *Melanchthon: Glauben und Handeln*, München 1931, pp. 192ff. Fraenkel supported Engelland on the grounds that Melanchthon considered human speech, especially in Scripture, to be something more than just a rational process. P. Fraenkel, *op. cit.*, pp. 142f. Also, the serious criticisms of E. Bizer, *Theologie der Verheissung: Studien*

zur theologischen Entwicklung des jungen Melanchthons 1519-1524, Neukirchen 1964, pp. 9-34, particularly against Schäfer for having drawn such conclusions apart from a larger developmental and exegetical context of Melanchthon's early works; and K. Haendler, *Wort und Glaube bei Melanchthon: Eine Untersuchung über die Voraussetzungen und Grundlagen des Melanchthonischen Kirchenbegriffes*, Gütersloh 1968, p. 59, n. 23, and p. 103, n. 11, on the importance of the affective dimension arising from the structures of Melanchthon's rhetoric. Haendler was the first, to our knowledge, to propose rhetoric as the appropriate field within which to discuss the alleged "intellectualism." Finally, the works of H.-G. Geyer, *Von der Geburt des wahren Menschen*, Neukirchen 1965; W. H. Neuser, *op. cit.*, and esp. S. Wiedenhofer, *Formalstrukturen humanistischer und reformatorischer Theologie bei Philipp Melanchthon*, Bd. I, II, Bern/Frankfurt/München 1976, have contributed variously to our sense that Melanchthon's rhetoric was a philosophy, and that it is important to our grasp of his terms and methods.

293. Cited in *The Lutheran Quarterly*, April 1916, p. 68, on the edition of 1545.

294. C. Manschreck (tr./ed.), *Melanchthon on Christian Doctrine*, (1965), Grand Rapids 1982, p. xx, on the influence of Melanchthon's *Loci communes*.

295. See *Why Narrative Theology? Readings in Narrative Theology*, (eds.) S. Hauerwas and L. G. Jones, Grand Rapids 1989, esp., S. Hauerwas, "Why the Truth Demands Truthfulness," pp. 308f.

296. Luther, cited in Manschreck, *op. cit.*, p. 68.

297. S. Wiedenhofer, *op. cit.*, Bd. I, pp. 186ff.

298. The position of Q. Breen, *op. cit.*, on Melanchthon's twofold truth theory, is rare.

299. H. Bornkamm, "Melanchthons Menschenbild," in *Philipp Melanchthon: Forschungsbeiträge zur vierhundertsten Wiederkehr seines Todestages dargeboten in Wittenberg, 1960*, (hrsg.) W. Elliger, Göttingen 1960, p. 87.

300. *Ibid.*

301. K. Hartfelder, *op. cit.*, p. 181; G. A. Herrlinger, *Die Theologie Melanchthons in ihrer geschichtlichen Entwicklung und im Zusammenhang mit der Lehrgeschichte und Kulturbewegung der Reformation dargestellt*, Gotha 1879, p. 402; H. Maier, *An der Grenze der Philosophie*, Tübingen 1909, p. 128; R. Seeberg, *op. cit.*, Bd. IV/2, p. 440; F. Hübner, *Natürliche Theologie und theokratische Schwärmerei bei Melanchthon*, Gütersloh 1936, p. 2; C. Bauer, "Melanchthons Naturrechtslehre," in *Archiv für Reformationsgeschichte*, 1951, pp. 64ff., and, *eodem*, "Die Naturrechtsvorstellungen des jungeren Melanchthon," in *Festschrift für Gerhardt Ritter zu seinem 60. Geburtstag*, Tübingen 1950, pp. 224ff.; P. Schwarzenau, "Der Wandel im theologischen Ansatz bei Melanchthon," (diss.) Münster 1954, p. 113; H. Sick, *Melanchthon als Ausleger des Alten Testaments*, Tübingen 1959, pp. 30ff.; W. H. Neuser, *op. cit.*, p. 39; H. Bornkamm, "Melanchthons Menschenbild," pp. 87ff.; M. Greschat, *Melanchthon neben Luther*, Wittenberg 1965, p. 155; F. Hildebrandt, *op. cit., passim*; A. Brüls, *op. cit.*, p. 92.

302. So Herrlinger, *op. cit.*, p. 402.

303. So Hartfelder, *op. cit.*, p. 181.

304. So Maier, *op. cit.*, p. 128.

305. E. Troeltsch, *op. cit.*, esp. p. 70.

306. B. S. von Waltershausen, "Melanchthon und das spekulative Denken," in *Deutsche Vierteljahresschrift für Literatur und Geistesgeschichte*, 5, 1927, p. 649; K. Sell, *Philipp Melanchthon und die deutsche Reformation bis 1531*, (Schriften des Vereins für Reformationsgeschichte, XIV.3), Halle 1897, p. 20; K. Heim, *Das Gewissheitsproblem in der systematischen Theologie bis zu Schleiermacher*, Leipzig 1911, p. 264; H.-G. Geyer, *Welt und Mensch: Zur Frage des Aristotelismus bei Melanchthon*, (diss.) Bonn 1959, p. 45.

307. S. Wiedenhofer, *op. cit., passim*; we have registered our points of disagreement with this massive and often very insightful treatment.

308. Cf. pp. 38ff., above.

309. F. Hübner, on the premise that theologies are either Christian or natural, *op. cit.,* p. 2, and that the historian must force the theologian to play his hand and declare "ja oder nein!" to natural theology. For Hübner, Melanchthon's views on the subject constituted a *Giftstoff, ibid., passim;* C. Bauer, *op. cit.,* viewed Melanchthon's position as a *Fremdkörper* in Lutheran theology; we have already cited the essay by Caemmerer, "The Melanchthon Blight."

310. H. Bornkamm, *op. cit.,* p. 87.

311. F. Hildebrandt, *op. cit.,* p. ix.

312. *Ibid.,* p. 25.

313. E. Troeltsch, *op. cit.,* pp. 70ff.; B. S. von Waltershausen, *op. cit.,* p. 665.

314. Cf. *MW* IV, notes on p. 209; his commentary on Col. 2:8 was a reaction against anti-philosophical groups within Lutheranism and was later expanded to be published by itself as a pamphlet. This work represented a watermark for Melanchthon on the question of free will and natural theology. See references, *ibid.*

315. Cf. text and notes *MW* V, entire volume. In this commentary Melanchthon developed his explicit system of arguments for God's existence, pp. 70ff.

316. H. Sick, *op. cit.,* pp. 30ff., has argued that it was not the law but rather the gospel which was unique in Scripture, over and against pagan wisdom. So also R. Seeberg, *op. cit.,* p. 440; B. S. von Waltershausen, *op. cit.,* p. 665; C. Bauer, *op. cit.,* pp. 64ff., first reference, and pp. 224ff., the second; P. Schwarzenau, *op. cit.,* p. 113; W. H. Neuser, *op. cit.,* p. 39; and F. Hübner, *op. cit.,* pp. 2ff.

317. Cf. his *De philosophia oratio* of 1536, *MW* III, pp. 88ff., for a superb example of "conjunctive" reasoning within a larger context of "disjunctive" values.

318. *MW* II/1, p. 91.4ff., "Scriptura legem vocat virtutem irae, peccati, sceptrum exactoris, fulmen tonitru. Ratio humana emendationem vitiorum et doctrinam vivendi. Sic enim Cicero vocat de legibus."

319. *Ibid.,* p. 91.12ff.

320. *Ibid.,* pp. 91.14ff., 91.16ff. and 93.9ff.

321. *Ibid.,* pp. 97.15ff. and 98.11, "Habes legis opus esse revelationem peccati."

322. *Ibid.,* p. 99.8ff.

323. Thus we are in general support of J. T. McNeill, "Natural Law in the Teachings of the Reformers," *Journal of Religion,* XXVI, July 1946, pp. 175ff., who doubted that natural law became the basis for a natural theology in Melanchthon. We have sought to offer the conceptual mechanism for seeing the sense in which this was so.

324. *MW* II/1, p. 107.25ff.

325. *Ibid.,* p. 107.23ff.

326. *Ibid.,* pp. 117.36-118.1ff.

327. On connections between Melanchthon and Reformed theologians on the subject of human capacity, cf. C. Venema, "Heinrich Bullinger's Correspondence on Calvin's Doctrine of Predestination 1551-1553," *The Sixteenth Century Journal,* XVII, no. 4, 1986, pp. 435ff., esp. pp. 443ff.; on Calixtus, J. Gonzalez, *The Story of Christianity,* vol. 2, San Francisco 1984, pp. 176ff.; on Arminius's "Melanchthonian tendencies," R. Muller, "Arminius and the Scholastic Tradition," *Calvin Theological Journal,* vol. 24, no. 2, November 1989, pp. 263ff.

328. *CR* VII, p. 756.

329. *MW* II/1, p. 273.7f., "Discrimen igitur inter Diablos et genus humanum consideretur."

330. Cf. J. Gonzalez, *op. cit.*, vol. 1, p. 215, for a useful summary and references.

331. Cf. T. Cranfield, *The Epistle to the Romans*, vol. 2, The International Critical Commentary, (eds.) J. A. Emerton and C. E. B. Cranfield, pp. 445-591, on the Pauline doctrine of election. Cranfield has argued forcefully against using this text as the basic foundation for high Calvinism.

Selected Bibliography

Primary Sources (and abbreviations)

(Abbreviations)

Agricola, Rudolf. *De inventione dialectica,* (ed.) W. Risse, Hildesheim/New York, (repr.) 1976.

(CR)   Brettschneider, G. C. and H. E. Bindseil (eds.). *Corpus Reformatorum: Philippi Melanchthonis Opera, quae supersunt omnia,* 28 vols., Halis Saxonum, 1834-1860.

Calvin, John. *Institutes of the Christian Religion,* (ed.) J. T. McNeill, (tr.) F. L. Battles, Philadelphia, 1960.

Camerarius, Joachim. *De vita Philippi Melanchthonis narratio,* Recensuit, notas, documenta, bibliothecam librorum Melanchthonis aliaque addidit. Ge. Theodor. Strobelius, Praefatus est Iohannes Auc. Noessell, Halle, 1777.

(SM)   Clemen, O. (hrsg.). *Supplementa Melanchthoniana, Werke Philipp Melanchthons, die im Corpus Reformatorum vermisst werden,* Bd. 1-6, Leipzig, 1910ff., Frankfurt, 1968.

(LB)   Erasmus, D. *Desiderii Erasmi Roterdami Opera Omnia,* (ed.) J. Clericus, Leiden, 1703-16.

(Holborn) _____. *Desiderius Erasmus Roterodamus ausgewählte Werke,* (eds.) H. and A. Holborn, München, 1933.

(Allen)   _____. *Opus Epistolarum Erasmi,* (eds.) P. and H. M. Allen, Oxford, 1906-47.

Luther, Martin. *D. Martin Luther. Operationes in Psalmos 1519-1521,* (hrsg.) G. Hammer und M. Biersack, (wissent. Leitung) H. A. Oberman, Köln/Wein, 1981.

(LW)   _____. *Luther's Works,* (eds.) J. Pelikan and H. T. Lehmann, Philadelphia/St. Louis 1955ff.

(WA)   _____. *Werke: Kritische Gesamtausgabe,* Weimar 1883ff.

(WABr)   _____. *Werke: Kritische Gesamtausgabe, Reihe Briefwechsel,* Weimar, 1930ff.

Melanchthon, Philip. *In obscuriora aliquot capita Geneseas P. M. annotationes,* Tubingae, 1523.

_____. *Institutiones rhetoricae longe alitertractatae quam antea, Philippi Melanchthon,* Basileae, 1522.

_____. *Philippi Melanchthonis de rhetorica libri tres,* Wittenberg, 1519.

Pauck, W. (ed.). *Loci communes theologici*, in *Melanchthon and Bucer*, (tr.) L. J. Satre, Library of Christian Classics, vol. XIX, Philadelphia, 1969.

Plitt, G. L. and D. Th. Kolde (eds.). *Die Loci Communes Philipp Melanchthons in ihrer Urgestalt*, Erlangen/Leipzig, 1890, 4th ed., 1925.

(*MB*) Scheible, Hans (ed.). *Melanchthons Briefwechsel*, (Kritische und kommentierte Gesamtausgabe), Bd. 1-3, Stuttgart/Bad Cannstatt, 1978ff.

Seitz, Otto. *Der authentische Text der Leipziger Disputation*, Leipzig, 1903.

(*MW*) Stupperich, Robert, (ed.). *Melanchthons Werke in Auswahl: Studienausgabe*, Bd. I, II/1, II/2, III, IV, V, VI, VII/1, VII/2. Gütersloh, 1951ff.

Wimpfeling, Jacob. *Epistola Jacobi Wimpfelingi de inepta et superflua verborum resolucione in cancellis: et de abusu exempcionis in favorem omnium episcoporum et archiepiscoporum*, Basel, 1503.

————. *Jakob Wimpfelings Adolescentia,* (ed.) O. Herding, München, 1965.

————. *Rhetorica Jacobi Wimpfelingi pueris utilissima*, Pforzheim, 1509.

Ziegler, Donald (ed.). *Great Debates of the Reformation*, New York, 1969.

Secondary Sources

Aldridge, John William. *The Hermeneutic of Erasmus*, Richmond/Zurich, 1966.

Barth, Karl. *Protestant Theology in the Nineteenth Century*, (1959), (1972), Valley Forge, 1973.

————. Cf. under Busch, Eberhard.

Barton, Peter. "Die exegetische Arbeit des jungen Melanchthon, 1518/19 bis 1528/29: Probleme und Ansätze," in *Archiv für Reformationsgeschichte*, 54, 1963, pp. 52ff.

Bauer, Clemens. "Melanchthons Naturrechtslehre, in *Archiv für Reformationsgeschichte*, 1951, pp. 64ff.

————. "Die Naturrechtsvorstellungen des jungeren Melanchthon," in *Festschrift für Gerhardt Ritter zu seinem 60. Geburtstag*, Tübingen, 1950.

Bizer, Ernst. *Texte aus der Anfangszeit Melanchthons*, Neukirchen, 1966.

_____. *Theologie der Verheissung: Studien zur theologischen Entwicklung des jungen Melanchthon 1519-1524,* Neukirchen, 1964.

Bornkamm, Heinrich. *Luther und das Alte Testament,* Tübingen, 1948.

_____. "Melanchthons Menschenbild," in *Philipp Melanchthon: Forschungsbeiträge zur vierhundertsten Wiederkehr seines Todestages dargeboten in Wittenberg, 1960,* (hrsg.) Walter Elliger, Göttingen, 1960.

Brake, John Robert. *Classical Conceptions of "Places": Study in Invention,* (diss.) Michigan State University, 1965.

Brecht, Martin (ed.). *Theologen und Theologie an der Universität Tübingen, Beiträge zur Geschichte der Evangelisch-Theologischen Fakultät,* Tübingen, 1977.

Breen, Quirinus. "The Subordination of Philosophy to Rhetoric in Melanchthon," in *Archiv für Reformationsgeschichte,* 1952.

_____. "The Terms Locus and Loci Communes in Melanchthon," in *Christianity and Humanism: Studies in the History of Ideas,* (ed.) N. P. Ross, Grand Rapids, 1968, pp. 93ff.

_____. "The Two-fold Truth Theory in Melanchthon," in *Review of Religion,* 1945, pp. 115ff.

Brüls, Alfons. *Die Entwicklung der Gotteslehre beim jungen Melanchthon, 1518-1535,* (Untersuchungen zur Kirchengeschichte, 10), Bielefeld, 1975.

Brunner, E. *The Mediator,* London, 1959.

Bullemer, K. *Quellenkritische Untersuchungen zum 1. Buche der Rhetorik Melanchthons,* (diss.) Erlangen, 1902.

Busch, Eberhard. *Karl Barth,* (tr.) J. Bowden, London/Philadelphia, 1976.

Caemmerer, R. R. "The Melanchthon Blight," in *Concordia Theological Monthly,* XVIII, 1947.

The Cambridge Modern History, vol. II, New York, 1907.

Cranfield, T. *The Epistle to the Romans,* vol. 2, The International Critical Commentary, (eds.) J. A. Emerton and C. E. B. Cranfield, Edinburgh, 1975.

Ebeling, Gerhard. *Lutherstudien,* Bd. I, Tübingen, 1971.

Ellinger, Georg. *Philipp Melanchthon: Ein Lebensbild,* Berlin, 1902.

Engelland, Hans. "Der Ansatz der Theologie Melanchthons," in *Philipp Melanchthon: Forschungsbeiträge zur vierhundertsten Wiederkehr seines Todestages dargeboten in Wittenberg, 1960,* (hrsg.) Walter Elliger, Göttingen, 1960.

_____. *Die Frage der Gotteserkenntnis bei Melanchthon,* München, 1930.

_____. *Melanchthon: Glauben und Handeln,* München, 1931.

_____. Introduction to *Melanchthon on Christian Doctrine,* (ed./tr.) C. L. Manschreck, (1965), Grand Rapids, 1982, pp. xxvff.

Faust, A. "Die Dialektik R. Agricolas," *Archiv der Geschichte der Philosophie*, 34, 1922, pp. 118ff.

Feld, Helmut. *Martin Luthers und Wendelin Steinbachs Vorlesungen über den Hebräerbrief: Eine Studie zur Geschichte der neutestamentlichen Exegese und Theologie*, 62, Wiesbaden, 1971.

Fraenkel, Peter. "Fünfzehn Jahre Melanchthonforschung: Versuch eines Literaturberichtes," in *Philipp Melanchthon: Forschungsbeiträge zur vierhundertsten Wiederkehr seines Todestages dargeboten in Wittenberg, 1960*, (hrsg.) Walter Elliger, Göttingen, 1960.

_____. *Testimonia Patrum: The Function of the Patristic Argument in the Theology of Philipp Melanchthon*, Geneva, 1961.

_____, and Martin Greschat. *Zwanzig Jahre Melanchthonstudium*, Geneva, 1967.

Froehlich, K. *Biblical Interpretation in the Early Church*, Philadelphia, 1984.

Gerhards, H. *Die Entwicklung des Problems der Willenfreiheit bei Philipp Melanchthon*, (diss.) Bonn, 1955.

Geyer, Hans-Georg. *Von der Geburt des wahren Menschen*, Neukirchen, 1965.

_____. *Welt und Mensch: Zur Frage des Aristotelismus bei Melanchthon*, (diss.) Bonn, 1959.

Ghizzoni, F. (ed./tr.). *Orazione Contro Filippo Melantone*, Brescia, 1973.

Gonzalez, J. *The Story of Christianity*, vol. 2, San Francisco, 1984.

Grassi, Ernesto. *Rhetoric as Philosophy: The Humanist Tradition*, University Park/London, 1980.

Green, Lowell C. "Die exegetischen Vorlesungen des jungen Melanchthons und ihre Chronologie," in *Kerygma und Dogma*, III, 1957, pp. 141ff.

_____. "Formgeschichtliche und inhaltliche Probleme in den Werken des jungen Melanchthon," in *Zeitschrift für Kirchengeschichte*, 1973, pp. 30ff.

_____. *How Melanchthon Helped Luther Discover the Gospel*, Fallbrook, 1980.

Greschat, Martin. *Melanchthon neben Luther: Studien zur Gestalt der Rechtfertigungslehre zwischen 1528 und 1537*, (Untersuchungen zur Kirchengeschichte, I), Wittenberg, 1965.

_____. Cf. under Fraenkel, Peter.

Grossmann, Maria. *Humanism in Wittenberg 1485-1517*, Bibliotheca humanistica et reformatorica II, Nieuwkoop, 1975.

Guelick, Robert. *The Sermon on the Mount: A Foundation for Understanding*, Waco, Texas, 1982.

Haendler, Klaus. *Wort und Glaube bei Melanchthon: Eine Untersuchung über die Voraussetzungen und Grundlagen des Melanchthonischen Kirchenbegriffes*, Gütersloh, 1968.

Haikola, Lauri. "Melanchthons Lehre von der Kirche," in *Philipp Melanchthon: Forschungsbeiträge zur vierhundertsten Wiederkehr seines Todestages dargeboten in Wittenberg, 1960,* (hrsg.) Walter Elliger, Göttingen, 1960.

Haller, Johannes. *Die Anfänge der Universität Tübingen, 1477-1537,* Bd. I and II, Stuttgart, 1927.

Hammer, Wilhelm. *Melanchthonforschung im Wandel der Jahrhunderte,* Bd. I, 1519-1799, Bd. II, 1800-1968, Gütersloh 1967, 1968.

Hannemann, Kurt. "Reuchlin und die Berufung Melanchthons nach Wittenberg," in *Festgabe Reuchlin,* Pforzheim, 1955.

Harnack, Adolf von. *Philipp Melanchthon: Akademische Festrede,* Berlin, 1897.

Hartfelder, K. *Philipp Melanchthon als Praeceptor Germaniae,* Berlin, 1889.

_____. *Philippus Melanchthon: Declamationes,* Lateinische Literaturdenkmäler des XV. und XVI. Jahrhunderts, 4, Berlin, 1891.

Hauerwas, S. and L. G. Jones (eds.). *Why Narrative Theology? Readings in Narrative Theology,* Grand Rapids, 1989.

Heim, Karl. *Das Gewissheitsproblem in der systematischen Theologie bis zu Schleiermacher,* Leipzig, 1911.

Heppe, Heinrich. *Die konfessionelle Entwicklung der altprotestantischen Union und die gegenwärtige konfessionelle Lage und Aufgabe des deutschen Protestantismus,* Marburg, 1854.

Hermelink, Heinrich. *Die theologische Fakultät in Tübingen vor der Reformation 1477-1534,* Tübingen, 1906.

Herrlinger, G. A. *Die Theologie Melanchthons in ihrer geschichtlichen Entwicklung und im Zusammenhang mit der Lehrgeschichte und Kulturbewegung der Reformation dargestellt,* Gotha, 1879.

Heyd, L. F. *Melanchthon und Tübingen 1512-1518: Ein Beitrag zu der Gelehrten- und Reformationsgeschichte des sechszehnten Jahrhunderts,* Tübingen, 1839.

Hildebrandt, Franz. *Melanchthon: Alien or Ally?,* Cambridge, 1946.

Holstein, Hugo. *Johann Reuchlins Komödien,* Halle, 1888.

Hoppe, Th. "Die Ansatz der späteren theologischen Entwicklung Melanchthons in den Loci von 1521," in *Zeitschrift für systematische Theologie,* 6, 1928-9, pp. 607ff.

Hübner, Franz. *Natürliche Theologie und theokratische Schwärmerei bei Melanchthon,* Gütersloh, 1936.

Jens, Walter. *Eine deutsche Universität: 500 Jahre Tübinger Gelehrtenrepublik,* Tübingen, 1977.

Joachimsen, Paul. "Der Humanismus und die Entwicklung des deutschen Geistes," in *Gesammelte Aufsätze, Beiträge zu Renaissance, Humanismus und Reformation; zur Historiographie und zum deutschen Staatsgedanken,* (Ausgewählt und eingeleitet von N. Hammerstein), Aalen, 1970, pp. 325ff.

_____. "Loci communes: Eine Untersuchung zur Geistesgeschichte des Humanismus und der Reformation," in *Gesammelte Aufsätze, Beiträge zu Renaissance, Humanismus und Reformation; zur Historiographie und zum deutschen Staatsgedanken*, (Ausgewählt und eingeleitet von N. Hammerstein), Aalen, 1970, pp. 387ff.

Jüngel, Eberhard. *Paulus und Jesus: Eine Untersuchung zur Präzisierung der Frage nach dem Ursprung der Christologie*, Tübingen, 1972.

Kasper, Walter. *Jesus the Christ*, (tr.) V. Green, London/New York, 1976.

Keen, R. *A Checklist of Melanchthon Imprints*, Sixteenth Century Biography 27, St. Louis, 1988.

Kelsey, D. *The Uses of Scripture in Recent Theology*, Philadelphia, 1975.

Kennedy, George. *Classical Rhetoric and Its Christian and Secular Tradition from Ancient to Modern Times*, Chapel Hill, 1980.

_____. *New Testament Interpretation Through Rhetorical Criticism*, Chapel Hill, 1984.

Kisch, Guido. *Melanchthons Rechts- und Soziallehre*, Berlin, 1967.

Knod, Gustav. "Wimpfeling und die Universität Heidelberg," *Zeitschrift für die Geschichte des Oberrheins*, 40, 1886, pp. 331ff.

Költzsch, Franz. *Melanchthons philosophische Ethik*, Freiburg, 1889.

Kristeller, Paul Oskar. *Renaissance Thought and Its Sources*, New York, 1979.

Küng, Hans. *Justification: The Doctrine of Karl Barth and a Catholic Reflection*, Philadelphia, 1981.

Lang, Albert. "Die Loci theologici des Melchior Cano und die Methode des dogmatischen Beweises: Ein Beitrag zur theologischen Methodologie und ihrer Geschichte," *Münchener Studien zur historischen Theologie*, Heft 6, München, 1925.

Lauchert, F. *Die italienischen literarischen Gegner Luthers*, Freiburg, 1912.

Lindbeck, G. *The Nature of Doctrine*, Philadelphia, 1984.

Loofs, Friedrick. *Leitfaden zum Studien der Dogmengeschichte*, Halle, 1906.

Luthardt, Christian Ernst. *Melanchthons Arbeiten im Gebiete der Moral*, Leipzig, 1884.

Maier, Heinrich. *An der Grenze der Philosophie*, Tübingen, 1909.

Manschreck, Clyde Leonard. *Melanchthon: The Quiet Reformer*, New York/Nashville, 1958.

_____, (tr./ed.). *Melanchthon on Christian Doctrine*, (Oxford, 1965), Grand Rapids, 1982.

Maurer, Wilhelm. *Historischer Kommentar zur Confessio Augustana*, Bd. 1, 2, Gütersloh, 1976, 1978.

_____. *Der junge Melanchthon*, Bd. 1, 2, Göttingen, 1967, 1969.

_____. "Melanchthon als Humanist," in *Philipp Melanchthon: Forschungsbeiträge zur vierhundertsten Wiederkehr seines Todestages dargeboten in Wittenberg, 1960,* (hrsg.) Walter Elliger, Göttingen, 1960.

_____. "Melanchthons Loci communes von 1521 als wissenschaftliche Programmschrift," in *Luther-Jahrbuch,* 27, 1960, pp. 2ff.

_____. "Zur Komposition der Loci Melanchthons von 1521," in *Luther-Jahrbuch,* 25, 1958, pp. 148ff.

McNeill, John T. "Natural Law in the Teachings of the Reformers," in *Journal of Religion,* vol. XXVI, July 1946, pp. 167ff.

Meijering, E. P. *Melanchthon and Patristic Thought: The Doctrines of Christ and Grace, the Trinity and the Creation,* Leiden, 1983.

Meinhold, Peter. *Philipp Melanchthon: Der Lehrer der Kirche,* Berlin, 1960.

Mühlen, K.-H. zur. *Luther: Sol, Ratio, Erudio, Aristoteles,* (Probeartikel zum Sachregister der Weimarer Lutherausgabe, Sonderdrücke aus *Archiv für Begriffsgeschichte,* Bd. XIV, Heft 2, und Bd. XV, Heft 1), Bonn, 1971.

_____. "Luthers deutsche Bibelübersetzung als Gemeinschaftswerk," in *Die Bibel in der Welt,* Bd. 18, (ed.) S. Meurer, Stuttgart, 1978.

Mühlenberg, E. "Humanistisches Bildungsprogramm und reformatorische Lehre beim jungen Melanchthon," *Zeitschrift für Theologie und Kirche,* 65, 1968.

Muller, R. "Arminius and the Scholastic Tradition," *Calvin Theological Journal,* vol. 24, no. 2, November 1989, pp. 263ff.

Needon, K. *Jacob Wimpfelings pädagogische Ansichten,* (diss.) Leipzig, 1898.

Neuser, Wilhelm Heinrich. *Die Abendmahlslehre Melanchthons in ihrer geschichtlichen Entwicklung 1519-1530,* Neukirchen, 1968.

_____. *Der Ansatz der Theologie Philipp Melanchthons,* (Beitrag zu Geschichte und Lehre der Reformierten Kirche, 9. Melanchthonstudien, I), Neukirchen, 1957.

Oberman, Heiko Augustinus. *Forerunners of the Reformation,* Philadelphia, (1965), 1981.

_____. *The Harvest of Medieval Theology,* Grand Rapids, 1962.

_____, (ed.). *Luther: Sol, Ratio, Erudio, Aristoteles,* (Probeartikel zum Sachregister der Weimarer Lutherausgabe, Sonderdrücke aus *Archiv für Begriffsgeschichte,* Bd. XIV, Heft 2, and Bd. XV, Heft 1), Bonn, 1971.

_____. "Via moderna–devotio moderna: Tendenzen in Tübinger Geistesleben 1477-1516," in *Theologen und Theologie an der Universität Tübingen,* (ed.) M. Brecht, Tübingen, 1977, pp. 1ff.

_____. *Werden und Wertung der Reformation,* Tübingen, 1977.

Ochs, J. Donavon. *The Tradition of the Classical Doctrines of Rhetorical Topoi,* (diss.) University of Iowa, 1966.

O'Malley, J. W. "Grammar and Rhetoric in the Pietas of Erasmus," *Journal of Medieval and Renaissance Studies,* Spring 1988, pp. 90ff.

O'Rourke Boyle, M. *Erasmus on Language and Method in Theology*, Toronto/Buffalo, 1977.

_____. *Rhetoric and Reform*, Cambridge, Mass./London, 1983.

Pelikan, Jaroslav. *From Luther to Kierkegaard*, St. Louis, 1950.

Peterson, Peter. *Geschichte der aristotelischen Philosophie im protestantischen Deutschland*, Leipzig, 1921.

Pflüger, J. *Geschichte der Stadt Pforzheim*, Pforzheim, 1862.

Plantinga, A. and N. Wolterstorff (eds.). *Faith and Rationality: Reason and Belief in God*, Notre Dame/London, 1983.

Preus, J. S. *From Shadow to Promise*, Cambridge, Mass., 1969.

Preus, R. *The Inspiration of Scripture*, Edinburgh/London, 1957.

Rau, Rheinhold. "Philipp Melanchthons Tübinger Jahre," in *Tübinger Blätter*, 47, 1960, pp. 16ff.

Reid, J. K. S. *The Authority of Scripture: A Study of the Reformation and Post-Reformation Understanding of the Bible*, Westport, (1962), 1981.

Ritschl, Albrecht. *The Christian Doctrine of Justification and Reconciliation*, Edinburgh, 1902.

_____. "Die Entstehung der lutherischen Kirche," in *Gesammelte Aufsätze*, Freiburg/Leipzig, 1893, pp. 170-217.

Ritschl, Otto. *Dogmengeschichte des Protestantismus*, Bd. I, II, Leipzig, 1908, 1912.

Ritter, Gerhardt. *Die Heidelberger Universität*, I, 1306-1509, Heidelberg, 1939.

Rosin, Wilbert H. "In Response to Bengt Hägglund: The Importance of Epistemology for Luther's and Melanchthon's Theology," in *Concordia Theological Quarterly*, 44, 2-3, July 1980, pp. 134ff.

Rupp, E. Gordon. *Luther's Progress to the Diet of Worms*, New York/Evanston, 1964.

_____. "Philip Melanchthon and Martin Bucer," in *A History of Christian Doctrine*, (ed.) H. Cunliffe-Jones with Benjamin Drewery, Philadelphia, (1980), 1984.

Schäfer, Rolf. *Christologie und Sittlichkeit in Melanchthons frühen Loci*, Tübingen, 1961.

Schirmer, Arno. *Das Paulus Verständnis Melanchthons 1518-1522*, Wiesbaden, 1967.

Schnell, Uwe. *Die homiletische Theorie Philipp Melanchthons*, Berlin/ Hamburg, 1968.

Schwarzenau, Paul. *Der Wandel im theologischen Ansatz bei Melanchthon*, (diss.) Münster, 1954.

Seeberg, Reinhold. *Lehrbuch der Dogmengeschichte*, Bd. IV/2, Basel/ Stuttgart, (1920), 1960.

Sell, Karl. *Philipp Melanchthon und die deutsche Reformation bis 1531*, (Schriften des Vereins für Reformationsgeschichte, XIV. 3), Halle, 1897.

Sick, Hansjörg. *Melanchthon als Ausleger des Alten Testaments,* Tübingen, 1959.

Sperl, Adolf. *Melanchthon zwischen Humanismus und Reformation: Eine Untersuchung über den Wandel des Traditionsverständnisses bei Melanchthon und die damit zusammenhängenden Grundfragen seiner Theologie,* (Forschung zur Geschichte und Lehre des Protestantismus, 10, XV), München, 1959.

Spitz, Lewis. "Reuchlin's Philosophy: Pythagoras and Cabala for Christ," in *Archiv für Reformationsgeschichte,* 47, 1956, pp. 1ff.

Stempel, Hermann-Adolf. *Melanchthons pädagogisches Wirken,* Bielefeld, 1979.

Stern, Leo. *Philipp Melanchthon: Humanist, Reformator, Praeceptor Germaniae,* (Festgabe des Melanchthon-Komitees der Deutschen Demokratischen Republik), Halle, 1960.

Stolz, E. "Die Patrone der Universität Tübingen und ihre Fakultäten," in *Theologische Quarterschrift,* 108, 1927, pp. 1ff.

Stupperich, Robert. "The Development of Melanchthon's Theological-Philosophical World View," *Lutheran World,* 7, 1960, pp. 168ff.

_____. "Der junge Melanchthon als Sachwalter Luthers," in *Jahrbuch des Vereins für Westphälische Kirchengeschichte,* 1949, pp. 47ff.

_____. "Luther und Melanchthon in ihrem gegenseitigen Verhältnis," in *Philipp Melanchthon, 1497-1560: Gedenkenschrift zum 400. Todestag des Reformators,* (hrsg.) G. Urban, Bretten, 1960, pp. 93ff.

_____. *Melanchthon,* (tr.) R. H. Fischer, Philadelphia, 1965.

_____. "Melanchthons Weg zu einer theologisch-philosophischen Gesamtanschauung," in *Lutherische Rundschau,* 10, 1960, pp. 152ff.

_____. *Der unbekannte Melanchthon,* Stuttgart, 1961.

Thielicke, Helmut. *Evangelical Faith,* (tr.) G. W. Bromiley, Grand Rapids, 1974.

Thiemann, R. *Revelation and Theology: The Gospel as Narrated Promise,* Notre Dame, 1985.

Töpke, G. *Die Matrikel der Universität Heidelberg,* Heidelberg, 1884.

Troeltsch, Ernst. *Vernunft und Offenbarung bei Johann Gerhard und Melanchthon,* Göttingen, 1891.

Venema, C. "Heinrich Bullinger's Correspondence on Calvin's Doctrine of Predestination 1551-1553," *The Sixteenth Century Journal,* XVII, no. 4, 1986, pp. 435ff.

Waltershausen, Bodo Sartorius von. "Melanchthon und das spekulative Denken," *Deutsche Vierteljahresschrift für Literatur und Geistesgeschichte,* 5, 1927, pp. 644ff.

Weber, Gottfried. *Grundlagen und Normen politischer Ethik bei Melanchthon,* München, 1962.

Weber, H. E. *Reformation, Orthodoxie und Rationalismus,* Bd. I, Gütersloh, 1937.

Wernle, Paul. *Melanchthon und Schleiermacher: Zwei dogmatische Jubiläen,* (Sammlung gemeinverständlicher Vorträge. 98), Tübingen, 1921.

Wiedenhofer, Siegfried. *Formalstrukturen humanistischer und reformatorischer Theologie bei Philipp Melanchthon,* Bd. I, II, Bern/Frankfurt/München, 1976.

Zika, Charles. "Reuchlin and Erasmus: Humanism and Occult Philosophy," in *Journal of Religious History,* 9, 1977, pp. 233ff.

Index of Names

Index of Subjects

TEXTS AND STUDIES IN RELIGION

1. Elizabeth A. Clark, **Clement's Use of Aristotle: The Aristotelian Contribution to Clement of Alexandria's Refutation of Gnosticism**

2. Richard DeMaria, **Communal Love at Oneida: A Perfectionist Vision of Authority, Property and Sexual Order**

3. David F. Kelly, **The Emergence of Roman Catholic Medical Ethics in North America: An Historical-Methodological-Bibliographical Study**

4. David Rausch, **Zionism Within Early American Fundamentalism, 1878-1918: A Convergence of Two Traditions**

5. Janine Marie Idziak, **Divine Command Morality: Historical and Contemporary Readings**

6. Marcus Braybrooke, **Inter-Faith Organizations, 1893-1979: An Historical Directory**

7. Louis William Countryman, **The Rich Christian in the Church of the Early Empire: Contradictions and Accommodations**

8. Irving Hexham, **The Irony of Apartheid: The Struggle for National Independence of Afrikaner Calvinism Against British Imperialism**

9. Michael Ryan, **Human Responses to the Holocaust: Perpetrators and Victims, Bystanders and Resisters**

10. G. Stanley Kane, **Anselm's Doctrine of Freedom and Will**

11. Bruce Bubacz, **St. Augustine's Theory of Knowledge: A Contemporary Analysis**

12. Anne Barstow, **Married Priests and the Reforming Papacy: The Eleventh-Century Debates**

13. Denis Janz (ed.), **Three Reformation Catechisms: Catholic, Anabaptist, Lutheran**

14. David Rausch, **Messianic Judaism: Its History, Theology, and Polity**

15. Ernest E. Best, **Religion and Society in Transition: The Church and Social Change in England, 1560-1850**

16. Donald V. Stump *et al.*, *HAMARTIA:* **The Concept of Error in the Western Tradition Essays in Honor of John M. Crossett**

35. André Séguenny, **The Christology of Caspar Schwenckfeld: Spirit and Flesh in the Process** of Life Transformation, Peter C. Erb and Simone S. Nieuwolt (trans.)

36. Donald E. Demaray, **The Innovation of John Newton (1725-1807): Synergism of Word and Music in Eighteenth Century Evangelism**

37. Thomas Chase, **The English Religious Lexis**

38. R.G. Moyles, **A Bibliography of Salvation Army Literature in English (1865-1987)**

39. Vincent A. Lapomarda, **The Jesuits and the Third Reich**

40. Susan Drain, **The Anglican Church in the 19th Century Britain: Hymns Ancient and Modern (1860-1875)**

41. Aegidius of Rome, **On Ecclesiastical Power: De Ecclesiastica Potestate**, Arthur P. Monahan (trans.)

42. John R. Eastman, **Papal Abdication in Later Medieval Thought**

43. Paul Badham (ed.), **Religion, State, and Society in Modern Britain**

44. Hans Denck, **Selected Writings of Hans Denck, 1500-1527**, E. J. Furcha (trans.)

45. Dietmar Lage, **Martin Luther on the** *Imitatio Christi* **and** *Conformitas Christi* **and Their Relationship To Good Works**

46. Jean Calvin, *Sermons on Jeremiah by Jean Calvin,* Blair Reynolds (trans.)

47. Jean Calvin, *Sermons on Micah by Jean Calvin*, Blair Reynolds (trans.)

48. Alexander Sándor Unghváry, **The Hungarian Protestant Reformation in the Sixteenth Century Under the Ottoman Impact: Essays and Profiles**

49. Daniel B. Clendenin & W. David Buschart (ed.), **Scholarship, Sacraments and Service: Historical Studies in Protestant Tradition, Essays in Honor of Bard Thompson**

50. Randle Manwaring, **A Study of Hymnwriting and Hymnsinging in the Christian Church**

51. John R. Schneider, **Philip Melanchthon's Rhetorical Construal of Biblical Authority: Oratio Sacra**